Cloud Computing Technology

Huawei Technologies Co., Ltd.

Cloud Computing
Technology

Huawei Technologies Co., Ltd.
Hangzhou, Zhejiang, China

ISBN 978-981-19-3025-6   ISBN 978-981-19-3026-3   (eBook)
https://doi.org/10.1007/978-981-19-3026-3

Jointly published with Posts & Telecom Press, Beijing, China
The print edition is not for sale in China (Mainland). Customers from China (Mainland) please order the
print book from: Posts & Telecom Press.

Preface

The sudden outbreak of novel coronavirus pneumonia (2019-nCoV) in 2020 has greatly affected people's lives. During the severe epidemic, everyone was quarantined at home and in the community, unable to go to work and school as usual. As a university teacher, the editor originally worried that normal teaching could not be carried out. Fortunately, with the help of the Internet and cloud services, even when the campus is closed, teaching and work in the university can still continue, teachers can teach online, and students can learn online. Cloud computing technology plays an important role in the information technology that has made a major contribution to the fight against the epidemic. As far as teaching is concerned, the communication between teachers and students is through the cloud: the teacher uploads the slides and teaching materials into the cloud, and the students obtain the materials from the cloud. The teaching cloud platform provides various functions such as sign-in, study, homework, and test. The communication among teachers and between teachers and students is through instant messaging software such as WeChat and QQ (the backend of these software is the cloud), and the meeting is through cloud conference systems such as Zoom, Tencent Meeting, and Webex. With the help of cloud computing technology, we can still teach and work normally during the epidemic, and this book can be completed.

Cloud computing technology has changed people's lifestyles, helped improve people's convenience and quality of life, and made a better future. Its emergence is a realistic portrayal of "technology changes life and changes the future." However, cloud computing technology itself integrates a variety of information technologies and is relatively complex. It is still difficult for beginners to have a more complete understanding of cloud computing technology. With regard to this reason, East China Normal University cooperated with Huawei to write this book on the basis of Huawei's certified cloud computing series of training materials.

There are eight chapters in this book. Chapter 1 introduces an overview of cloud computing. It includes common cloud computing scenarios in life. The characteristics, definition, origin and development of cloud computing, as well as advantages and classification of cloud computing are discussed in this chapter. It also mentioned various types of supporting technologies for cloud computing and three perspectives on comprehending the business model, computing model and implementation of cloud computing. It also presents the state-of-art open source approach in cloud computing. Chapter 2 introduces the cloud computing system, starting from the four aspects of cloud infrastructure mechanism, cloud management mechanism, cloud security mechanism, and basic cloud architecture, and discusses some of the main technical mechanisms for building cloud technology architecture. Chapter 3 introduces virtualization technology, focusing on server virtualization technology, including its basic knowledge and supporting technologies, and discusses some actual virtualization products or applications based on theoretical knowledge, such as open-source virtual machine software KVM, Huawei FusionCompute cloud operating system, and desktop cloud. Chapter 4 introduces the basic knowledge of network in cloud computing, including an overview of computer networks, basic principles of computer networks, network interconnection equipment, network virtualization and software-defined networks, etc., so that readers can better understand some important concepts of computer networks, principles, equipment, and new network technologies supporting cloud computing. Chapter 5 introduces the basic knowledge of storage in cloud computing and also introduces storage in cloud computing in detail from the basic knowledge of storage, basic storage units, network storage, storage reliability technology, storage virtualization, distributed storage, etc. Chapter 6 starts from practice, introduces the popular open-source cloud operating system framework OpenStack, analyzes various components of OpenStack, discusses its operating mechanism, and enables readers to master the skills of implementing and managing OpenStack. Chapter 7 introduces the container technology that is widely concerned in cloud computing. It introduces the knowledge of container technology and container orchestration from the aspects of platform architecture, basic core functions, network, security, and resource management in a theoretical as well as practical model, which is convenient for readers to have a comprehensive understanding of Docker and Kubernetes ecosystem. Chapter 8 introduces the development status of cloud computing at home and abroad, analyzes and predicts its development trend, and discusses and analyzes the relationship between the Internet of Things, big data, artificial intelligence, 5G and other popular cutting-edge technologies, and cloud computing. It also introduces additional emerging technologies, such as edge computing and fog computing, microservices, and serverless computing.

This book was edited by Huawei Technologies Co., Ltd. The specific authors are as follows: Wang Wei formulated the outline and was responsible for the overall draft of the book, Zheng Kai was responsible for the main review, and Yang Lei provided training handouts. Chapters 1, 2, 4, and 8 are written by Zheng Kai. Chapters 3 and 5 are written by Huang Libo, and Chaps. 6 and 7 are written by Xu Yanjun.

In the process of writing this book, the editors have referred to and cited many works or papers by colleagues at home and abroad (see references for details), and I would like to express my gratitude to them. At the same time, I sincerely thank the training teachers and engineers of Huawei for their help and support.

Shanghai, China   Huawei Technologies Co., Ltd.
December 2021

Contents

About the Author

Huawei Technologies Co., Ltd. Founded in 1987, Huawei is a leading global provider of information and communications technology (ICT) infrastructure and smart devices. We have approximately 197,000 employees and we operate in over 170 countries and regions, serving more than three billion people around the world.

Huawei's mission is to bring digital to every person, home and organization for a fully connected, intelligent world. To this end, we will: drive ubiquitous connectivity and promote equal access to networks to lay the foundation for the intelligent world; provide the ultimate computing power to deliver ubiquitous cloud and intelligence; build powerful digital platforms to help all industries and organizations become more agile, efficient, and dynamic; redefine user experience with AI, offering consumers more personalized and intelligent experiences across all scenarios, including home, travel, office, entertainment, and fitness & health.

Chapter 1
Introduction to Cloud Computing Computing

This chapter is an overview of cloud computing, including common cloud computing scenarios in life, the characteristics, definitions, origins and development of cloud computing, the advantages and classification of cloud computing, various supporting technologies of cloud computing. The business model, computing model, and implementation of cloud computing are three perspectives for understanding, as well as open source methods that are currently very popular in the cloud computing field. Through the study of this chapter, I hope that readers have a clearer understanding of the general picture of cloud computing and lay the foundation for the in-depth study of the following chapters.

1.1 Ubiquitous Cloud Computing

As a representative of a new technology, cloud competing, like internet, has closely penetrated into our daily live. For example, we want to share an electronic material of hundreds of Mb with a friend from distance place, what happens if it exceeds the limitation of email attachment size? In the past, we generally used express delivery of storage media such as CDs, flash drives, or mobile hard drives which is time consuming and cost more work. Now we have a much more convenient way with the help of cloud storage service such as Baidu disk. Just put the data file into your own cloud disk and send the sharing link and access password to the recipient. The recipient can obtain the shared data file anytime and anywhere via the Internet. Another example is that an organizer wants to hold a special meeting while the participants are located all over the country. In an epidemic prevention and control situation, having participants gather by transport from all over the country for an on-site meeting not only takes considerable time and expense to travel back and forth, but also increases the risk of spreading the epidemic. Therefore, people will prioritize ZOOM meeting, Tecent meeting, or Webex as an option to hold online meeting. Participants only need to use the Internet to perform simple operations using a

© The Author(s) 2023
Huawei Technologies Co., Ltd., *Cloud Computing Technology*,
https://doi.org/10.1007/978-981-19-3026-3_1

Fig. 1.1 Huawei cloud website

browser, and they can quickly and efficiently share voice, data files, and videos with participants in different geographical locations. In fact, participants in a cloud conference only need to have a device (computer, mobile phone, tablet, etc.) that can access the Internet that can be used normally to achieve online communication and video conferences without having to care about the complex technologies such as data transmission and data processing, all of which are provided by cloud conference service providers.

Such a way of preparing resources in advance and using these resources to perform specific tasks through specific technologies anytime and anywhere is generally a cloud computing type. The provider is a cloud service provider such as Huawei's public cloud. Let's take a look at the Huawei cloud website as shown in Fig. 1.1.

Under "Product" → "Fundamental services", we can find computing, storage, network, database, container services, etc. These divisions can be divided into different subdivision types. Take a popular service—ECS, an elastic cloud server, as an example, as shown in Figs. 1.2 and 1.3.

The elastic cloud server on the website is actually a virtual server (we will introduce it later). Similar to our own purchase of computer, the website provides different grades and types of cloud server instances to choose from. The configuration includes parameters such as the number of CPU, frequency, memory, and network bandwidth. Users can choose the most effective cloud server according to their needs. In fact, buying a cloud server instance is like buying a physical machine. You can complete most of the work that can be done on a physical machine, such as editing documents, sending emails, or working together. It's just that the cloud server is not in front of you, but on the far end of the network (cloud). In addition, the cloud server also has some advantages that the local physical machine does not have. For example, the access to the cloud server is not restricted by time and place. As long as there is Internet, it can be used anytime and anywhere. And the equipment (terminals) for operating the cloud server can be varied. For example, the user can

Fig. 1.2 Elastic cloud server

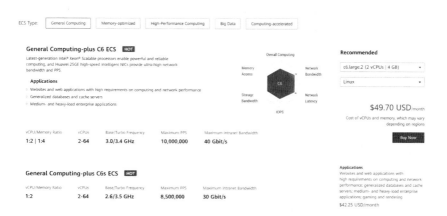

Fig. 1.3 Elastic cloud server specifications

operate the cloud server through a personal computer (PC), mobile phone, etc., and can modify or expand the performance configuration of the cloud server if necessary.

In addition to providing cloud servers to users, cloud service providers generally provide some other cloud services. For example, on Huawei's public cloud, users who need to build a website can purchase the cloud speed website building service, which can help users quickly complete the construction of the website; users who need to store data can purchase object storage services or cloud hard drives. More advanced services also include artificial intelligence (Artificial Intelligence, AI) functions such as face recognition, voice recognition, image recognition, or text recognition.

In short, cloud computing allows us to use IT services like water and electricity as soon as the user turns on the faucet, water rushes out. This is because the water plant has sent water into the pipeline network (water network) that connects thousands of households; electricity is similar. For cloud computing, cloud service providers have prepared all resources and services for users, and users can use them via the Internet. The Internet here is similar to the previous water network, and the tap can be a browser or a mobile application (App).

In fact, cloud services around you can be seen everywhere. In addition to the examples introduced in the previous article, other cloud services such as automatic backup of mobile phones, Youdao Cloud Notes and NetEase Cloud Music are all cloud services around us. At present, mainstream mobile phone manufacturers such as Huawei and Apple provide cloud-based mobile phone backup and recovery services. Users can back up files on the mobile phone to a data center in the cloud. After replacing the phone, you can restore your data to the new phone using your account and password. Youdao Cloud Notes is a product launched by NetEase, which provides online document creation and editing functions. When the user needs to record his inspiration at a certain moment, but unfortunately finds that there is no paper and pen around, the user can use Youdao Cloud Notes to record the inspiration online. Another advantage of this product is that no matter when and where, no matter what terminal the user uses (personal computer, mobile phone, etc.), online data can be edited, shared, and collaborated anytime, anywhere, and every edit can be done immediately Sync to the cloud. Music lovers may like NetEase Cloud Music App, through which songs can be listened to online and played at any time.

With the rapid development of cloud computing technology, similar cloud services will increasingly penetrate our daily lives. The spring weather turns rain, moisturizing things silently. We can truly feel the convenience of cloud computing technology in our lives.

1.2   The Properties of Cloud Computing

Cloud computing, as a new computing model, mainly has the following characteristics.

1.2.1   On-Demand Self-Service

Speaking of on-demand self-service, the first thing comes to your mind is supermarket. Every customer can collect goods according to their requirements. If it is the same type of goods, you can check description, price, and brand information to decide whether to buy or which one to buy. On-demand self-service is one of the mail characteristics of cloud computing. We will later introduce the Infrastructure as a Service (IaaS), platform as a service (PaaS) and Software as a Service (SaaS) model. Users can choose among one of these models based on their necessity. After selecting the mode, there will generally be different configurations to choose from, and users can purchase the services according to their needs. The entire process is generally self-service and does not require third-party intervention unless you have a problem that requires consultation. As shown in Fig. 1.3, Huawei's elastic cloud server specifications for public clouds have many different configurations of cloud server instances to choose from.

On-demand self-service is premised on knowing your needs and which products will address them. This requires the relevant expertise of users using cloud computing. Users who do not have the knowledge and capabilities to use cloud services can consult a cloud service provider or turn to a relevant professional services provider.

1.2.2   Extensive Network Access

Another feature of cloud computing is that all clouds must rely on network connectivity. It can be said that the network is the foundation of cloud computing. Especially the Internet, the cloud is always inseparable from the Internet. The Internet provides remote, anytime, anywhere access to IT resources. Some people even think of cloud computing as "Internet plus computing," and network access is an intrinsic property of cloud computing.

Although most cloud access is over the Internet, cloud users also have the option of using a private channel to access the cloud. The level of service for network connectivity between cloud users and cloud service providers (quality of service, Quality of Service, QoS) depends on the Internet Service Provider (ISP) that provides them with network access.

In today's society, the Internet can cover almost every corner of the world, we can connect to the Internet through a variety of digital terminals, such as personal computers and mobile phones and connect to the cloud through the Internet, using cloud services. Therefore, extensive network access is an important feature of cloud computing. This can either be a wired network or a wireless network such as a Wi-Fi network. In short, without the network, there would be no cloud computing.

1.2.3   Resource Pooling

Resource pooling is one of the prerequisites for on-demand self-service, through resource pooling can not only put similar goods together, but also can refine the units of goods. Slightly large-scale supermarkets will generally be divided into fresh areas, fruit and vegetable areas, daily necessities areas and other areas to facilitate customers to quickly find their own needs of goods, but this form is not a pool of resources, can only be regarded as a classification of resources. So what is pooling resources? In addition to converting similar resources into resource pools, resource pooling requires the decomposition of all resources into smaller units. If we buy our own hard drives, a mechanical drive (Hard Disk, HDD) often has a few terabytes (TB, 1TB, 1012B); solid-state drives (Solid State Drive, SSDs) have a slightly smaller capacity, and an SSD typically has a capacity of 128 to 512GB (Gigabytes, 1GB, 109B). Storage pooling cannot be measured in the number of hard drives because a hard drive has a large capacity, some applications only need a few gigabytes (GB), allocating the capacity of a hard disk is obviously a huge waste. Therefore, the way to use resource pooling need to break the number of physical hard disk unit "one" and combined all the capacity of the hard disk, gathered into a "pool." Then allocation can be assigned in smaller units such as "GB" as a unit. Users can apply for as much as they need.

The computing resources include CPU and memory. If the CPU is pooled, the smallest unit of the CPU that the user sees can be a virtual core, and the CPU manufacturer no longer reflects the physical attributes of AMD or Intel.

Another function of resource pooling is to screen the differences between different resources. After the storage resources containing the mechanical hard drive and the SSD are pooled, if the user requests a certain amount of storage space, which corresponds to the mechanical hard drive or SSD, or both, he cannot tell the difference. In cloud computing, resources that can be pooled include computing, storage, and networking. Computing resources include CPU and memory. If CPU is pooled, the smallest unit of the CPU that the user sees can be a virtual core, and no longer reflect physical attributes such as the CPU's manufacturer being AMD or Intel.

1.2.4   Fast and Elastic Scaling

Fast elastic scaling is one of the characteristics of cloud computing and is often cited as one of the core reasons for attracting users to "embrace" cloud computing. Cloud users can automatically and transparently scale their IT resources according to their needs. For example, in order to deal with the sudden high traffic of hot events, users can temporary self-purchase a large number of virtual resources to expand capacity. When hotspot events "cool down" and access traffic tends decline, users can release these newly added virtual resources, which is typical of fast elastic scaling. Cloud providers with large IT resources can provide a wide range of elastic scaling.

Fast elastic scaling includes several types, and in addition to manual capacity expansion or reduction, cloud computing supports automatic scaling or reduction based on preset policies. Scaling can be an increase or decrease in the number of servers, or an increase or decrease in resources for a single server.

In cloud computing, the biggest benefit of fast elastic scaling for users is cost savings while keeping the business or application running smoothly. Enterprises can purchase small amounts of resources when they are in low initial demand, gradually increase their investment in resources as the size of the enterprise expands, or concentrate all resources on priority business use during special periods, and, if resources are not sufficient, immediately apply for additional resources and, after a special period, release new resources. Either scenario is convenient for the user.

1.2.5 Measurable Services

Measuring is not billing although measuring is the basis of billing. Among the services provided by cloud computing, most services need to be paid for, but there are also services that are free. For example, elastic scaling can be opened as a free service for users.

Metrology is the use of technology and other means to achieve unity and accurate and reliable measurement. It can be said that the services in cloud computing are all measurable, some are based on time, some are based on resource quotas, and some are based on traffic. Measuring service can help users to automatically control and optimize resource allocation accurately according to their own business. In cloud computing systems, there is generally a billing management system that is specifically used to collect and process usage data. It involves the settlement of cloud service providers and the billing of cloud users. The billing management system allows for the development of different pricing rules and can also customize the pricing model for each cloud user or each IT resource.

Billing can choose between prepaid use or pay after use. The latter payment type is divided into predefined limits and unlimited use. If the limit is set, they often appear in the form of quota. When the quota is exceeded, the billing management system can reject the cloud user's further use request. Assuming that a user's memory quota is 500GB, once the user's storage capacity in the cloud computing system reaches 500GB, new storage requests will be rejected.

Users can purchase services according to their needs and can clearly see the usage of their purchased services. For contract users, the type of product used, service quality requirements, cost per unit time, or cost per service request are usually specified in the contract.

Figure 1.4 shows the pricing standards of Huawei Elastic Cloud Server instances, which shows the pricing standards of virtual server instances with different configurations. In this example, they are charged monthly.

1.3 Definition of Cloud Computing

There are several definitions of cloud computing. There are many definitions of what cloud computing is.

Wikipedia: Cloud computing is an Internet-based computing method. In this way, shared hardware and software resources and information can be provided to computers and other devices on demand, just like water and electricity for everyday use, paid for on demand, without caring about their source. National Institute of Standards and Technology, NIST: Cloud computing is a pay-per-use model that provides usable, convenient, on-demand network access to configurable computing resource sharing pools (resources including storage, software, services) that can be delivered quickly with minimal administrative effort or little interaction with service providers.

General Computing-plus C6 ECS `HOT`

vCPU/Memory Ratio	vCPUs	Base/Turbo Frequency	Maximum PPS	Maximum Intranet Bandwidth
1:2 | 1:4	2-64	3.0/3.4 GHz	10,000,000	40 Gbit/s

Applications
Websites and web applications with high requirements on computing and network performance; generalized databases and cache servers; medium- and heavy-load enterprise applications; gaming and rendering

General Computing S6 ECS `HOT`

vCPU/Memory Ratio	vCPUs	Base/Turbo Frequency	Maximum PPS	Maximum Intranet Bandwidth
1:1 | 1:2 | 1:4	1-8	2.6/3.5 GHz	500,000	3 Gbit/s

Applications
Websites and web application with high requirements on PPS; small-scale databases and cache servers; light- and medium-load enterprise applications
$7.70 USD/month

General Computing S3 ECS

vCPU/Memory Ratio	vCPUs	Base/Turbo Frequency	Maximum PPS	Maximum Intranet Bandwidth
1:1 | 1:2 | 1:4	1-16	2.2/3.0 GHz	300,000	4 Gbit/s

Applications
Websites and web applications; small-scale databases and cache servers; light- and medium-load enterprise applications
$7.70 USD/month

General Computing-basic T6 ECS

vCPU/Memory Ratio	vCPUs	Base/Turbo Frequency	Maximum PPS	Maximum Intranet Bandwidth
1:1 | 1:2 | 1:4	1-16	2.2/3.0 GHz	600,000	3 Gbit/s

Applications
Microservices; low-latency interactive applications; small- and medium-scale databases; virtual desktops; generalized-load websites and web applications, including development, build, and stage environments, code repositories, and product prototypes
$6.13 USD/month

Fig. 1.4 Pricing standards for Huawei Elastic Cloud Server Instances

In the past, engineers used to use clouds to abstractly describe telecommunications networks or the Internet and underlying infrastructure when drawing pictures. The name of cloud computing has an inextricable origin. The "cloud" in cloud computing can be seen as a vast pool of IT resources where users can purchase the services they need on demand and pay for what they use.

Cloud computing is a broad concept, not a specific technology or standard, different people from different perspectives will have different understanding, there is no authoritative definition.

1. The definition of cloud computing by analysts

    Early Merrill Lynch argued that cloud computing was the use of the Internet to run personal applications (E-mail, document processing, and presentations) and commercial applications (sales management, customer service, and financial management) on centrally managed servers. By sharing resources from these servers, such as storage and processing power, resources can be used more efficiently and costs can be reduced by 80% to 90%. Information Week, on the other hand, defines cloud computing more broadly: cloud computing is an environment in which any IT resource can be delivered as a service. The media is also interested in cloud computing. The Wall Street Journal, America's best-selling magazine, is also keeping a close eye on the evolution of cloud computing. It argues that cloud computing enables enterprises to gain computing power, storage space, software applications, and data from very large data centers over the Internet. Customers pay only for the resources they use when necessary, avoiding the huge costs of building their own data centers and purchasing servers and storage devices.

2. The definition of cloud computing by enterprises

    IBM believes that cloud computing is a computing style based on the delivery of services, software, and processing power over public or private networks. Cloud computing focuses on the user experience, with the core separating the delivery of computing services from the underlying technology. Cloud computing is also a way to share infrastructure, using pools of resources to connect public or private networks together to provide IT services to users. Eric Schmidt, Google's former CEO, argues that cloud computing distributes computing and data across a large number of distributed computers, making computing and storage capabilities highly scalable and allowing users to easily access applications and services over the network through a variety of access methods, such as computers and mobile phones. Its important feature is open, there will not be an enterprise can control and monopolize it. According to Kaifu Li, a former global vice president at Google, the entire Internet is a beautiful cloud where Internet users need to easily connect to any device, access any information, create content freely, and share it with friends. Cloud computing is based on open standards and services, the Internet as the center, to provide secure, fast, and convenient data storage and network computing services, so that the Internet "cloud" is to become every Netizen's data center and computing center. Cloud computing is actually Google's business model, and Google has been working hard to promote the concept.

Microsoft's approach to cloud computing is much more contradictory than Google's. If future computing power and software are all concentrated in the cloud, then clients don't need a lot of processing power, and Windows loses most of its power. As a result, Microsoft's approach has always been "cloud+end." Microsoft believes that the future of computing model is not just cloud computing. The "end" here refers to the client, which means that cloud computing must have a client to work with. "From an economic point of view, bandwidth, storage, and computing are not going to be free, and consumers need to find a model that fits what they need, so there must be end-of-the-line computing. In terms of communication supply and demand, although bandwidth has increased, content is also growing simultaneously, such as video and images. Bandwidth limitations are always there. From a technical point of view, the end of the computing power is strong, in order to bring users more exciting applications" said Dr. Yaqin Zhang, a former senior global vice president at Microsoft. Microsoft's definition of cloud computing is no different, it just underlines the importance of the "end" in cloud computing. Today, with the rise of Azure Cloud, Microsoft has embraced cloud computing across the scale.

The overview of cloud computing across the business market is shown in Fig. 1.5.

3. The definition of cloud computing by academia

In academia, Ian Foster, the father of grid computing, argues that cloud computing is a model of large-scale distributed computing driven by the economics of scale. In this model, abstract, virtualized, dynamically scalable, and managed computing power, storage, platforms, and services converge into a pool of resources that are delivered to external users on demand over the Internet. He believes that several key points of cloud computing are: high scalability; can be encapsulated as an abstract entity and provide different levels of service for

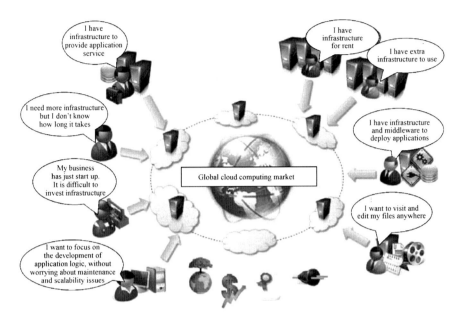

Fig. 1.5 Overview of cloud computing

external users; economics resulting from scale; and services can be dynamically configured (via virtualization or other means) to deliver on demand.

Based on these different definitions, it's not hard to find out that the basic view of cloud computing is the same, but there are differences in the delimitation of certain areas. A more complete definition of cloud computing can be given from a comprehensive perspective: "Cloud computing is a computing model in which dynamically scalable and virtualized resources are delivered as services over the Internet." End-users don't need to know the details of the infrastructure in the cloud, do not need to have the appropriate expertise knowledge, do not need direct control, just pay attention to what resources they really need, and how to get the appropriate services over the network."

Zhu Jinzhi, who once worked at IBM, gave a relatively broad definition in his book *Smart Cloud Computing: The Platform of the Internet of Things* in order to cover cloud computing more comprehensively. The definition is as follows: "Cloud computing is a computing model: IT resources, data and applications are provided as services to users through the network." Its practical definition of "cloud" is a metaphorical method used to express the abstraction of complex infrastructure. Cloud computing is an abstraction of traditional computing infra-structure, so we choose to use "cloud" as a metaphor, as shown in Fig. 1.6.

Cloud computing starts with "software as a service," and then transforms all IT resources into services and provide to users. Think of cloud computing as a model that can easily access a common set of configurable computing resources (such as servers, storage devices, software, and services) through the network. These

Fig. 1.6 Cloud computing
is an abstraction of
traditional computing
infrastructure

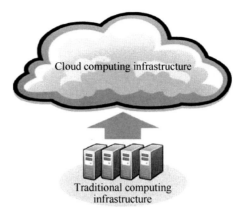

resources can be quickly provided and released, while minimizing management costs and the intervention of service providers.

We can look at cloud computing from two perspectives, the place where computing occurs and the form of resource supply. From the perspective of where computing occurs, cloud computing moves the operation of software from a personal computer (or desktop computer) to the cloud, that is, on a server or server cluster located in a "mysterious" geographic location. These servers or server clusters can be local, remote, or even far away. This seems to be a Client/Server (C/S) model, but cloud computing is not a traditional client/server model, but a huge improvement on this model. From the perspective of resource supply, cloud computing is a computing service, that is, all IT resources, including hardware, software, and architecture, are sold and charged as a service. For cloud computing, there are three main types of services: infrastructure as a service, providing hardware resources, similar to the traditional CPU, memory and I/O; platform as a service, providing an environment for software operation, similar to traditional operating system and programming framework in programming mode; software as a service, providing application software functions, similar to application software in traditional mode. In the cloud computing model, users no longer purchase or buy out certain hardware, system software, or application software to become the owner of these resources, but purchase the usage time of the resource, and consume according to the billing model such as paying for the length of use.

It can be seen that cloud computing treats all resources as services and consumes them in a pay-as-you-go manner, which is the characteristic of the host era. In the host era, all users are connected to the host through a display terminal and a network cable, and billing is based on the consumed CPU time and storage capacity. The difference is that in the host mode, the calculation occurs on one host; in the cloud computing mode, the calculation occurs in a server cluster or data center.

Therefore, cloud computing is both a new computing model and a new business model. It is a new computing model because all computing is organized as a service; it is a new business model because the way users pay is different from the past, and pay according to what you use, which greatly reduces resource users' operating costs. It is not difficult to see that these two aspects of cloud computing rely on each other and are indispensable. Because only using resources as services can support the pay-as-you-go payment model; because the billing is based on what you use as you pay, resources can only be provided as services (not as packaged software or hardware). In fact, it can be said that cloud computing is a computing model, where computing boundary here is not determined by technical limitations, but by economic factors.

In a nutshell, cloud computing is the result of the hybrid evolution and integration of various concepts such as virtualization, utility computing, service computing, grid computing, and automatic computing. It started from mainframe computing and went through minicomputer computing, client/server computing, distributed computing, grid computing, and utility computing. It is not only a technological breakthrough (technical integration), but also a leap in business model (pay as much as you use, no waste). For users, cloud computing shields all the details of IT. Users do not need to have any knowledge or any control over the technical infrastructure of the services provided by the cloud, or even the system configuration and geographic location of the services provided. They only need to "turn on the switch"(Connect to the Internet) to enjoy the service.

It can be seen that cloud computing describes a new mode of supplying, consuming, and delivering IT services. This model is based on the Internet protocol and will inevitably involve the configuration of dynamically scalable and often virtualized resources. To some extent, cloud computing is a by-product of people's pursuit of easy access to remote computing resources.

The huge advantages of cloud computing in both technology and business model determine that it will become the leading technology and operating model of the IT industry in the future.

1.4 The Emergence and Development of Cloud Computing

The origin of cloud computing can be traced back to the concept of utility computing proposed by John McCarthy in 1961. He mentioned: "If the kind of computer I am advocating becomes the computer of the future, then the computer may one day be organized into a public facility like a telephone system...Computer facilities may become the basis of a new and important industry." Contains the initial thoughts of cloud computing. In the late 1990s, Salesforce took the lead in providing remote customized services to enterprises. In 2002, Amazon started operating the Amazon Web Services (AWS) platform, providing enterprises with services such as remotely customized storage, computing resources, and business functions. In 2006, Eric Schmidt, the CEO of Google, proposed the concept of "cloud computing."

In fact, the emergence of cloud computing is not isolated, but the product of the development of computer technology and communication technology to a certain stage. Cloud computing technology is the product of a collection of various technologies.

There is a view that cloud computing is equivalent to the "Internet + computing" model, and the history of cloud computing is the history of the development of the Internet and computing models. So let's briefly review the development history of the two.

1.4.1   The History of the Network and the Internet

In the early days, computers all operated on a stand-alone computer, and the calculation and transmission of data were all done on the local computer. The birth of the Internet connected these computers and ultimately connected the entire world. The following are some very representative milestones in the history of Internet development.

In 1969, ARPANET was born, and it is considered the predecessor of the Internet. There were only four nodes that first joined ARPANET, namely University of California, Los Angeles (UCLA); Stanford Research Institute (SRI); University of California, Santa Barbara (UC Santa Barbara); and University of Utah. The birth of ARPANET marked the beginning of the Internet era. In the following years, more and more nodes joined ARPANET, and more and more users in the non-military field. In 1983, out of security considerations, ARPANET separated 45 of these nodes to form a special military network called MILNET. The remaining nodes were used for civilian purposes.

In 1981, the first complete specification of TCP/IP was established, and the Internet has since had unified communication rules. TCP/IP is actually a collection of protocols, which includes Transmission Control Protocol (TCP), Internet Protocol (IP), and some other protocols. The earliest protocol used on ARPANET is called Network Control Protocol (NCP), but with the growth of ARPANET, NCP cannot meet the needs of large networks, while TCP/IP seems to be tailored for large or even giant network services. Therefore, in 1983, ARPANET replaced NCP with TCP/IP.

In 1983, ARPANET, PRNET, and SATNET were the three original networks that used TCP/IP communication. The first three networks switched to TCP/IP at the same time, marking the beginning of rapid development of the Internet.

In 1984, the Domain Name System (DNS) was born. After TCP/IP was adopted, the development of the Internet became more rapid, and more and more computers joined the network, and each computer used the digital IP address of the TCP/IP standard to identify each other. The common version 4 IP address (IPv4), an address corresponds to four bytes, and each byte is represented by a decimal number from 0 to 255. A typical IP address is in the form of 202.120.80.1. This type of digital IP address is not suitable for people to remember. It is like using an ID number to call the person you meet. I believe that few people can remember the ID number of everyone around them. Therefore, a new mechanism that is easy for people to remember is needed to replace the IP address to identify computers on the Internet.

Thus, DNS came into being. DNS can realize the mutual conversion between digital IP addresses and domain names that are easier for people to remember, which is equivalent to using short, easy-to-remember names instead of ID numbers, which greatly reduces the difficulty of remembering. For example, the previous IP address is 202.120.80.1, and the associated domain name is www.ecnu.edu.cn, which represents the official website of East China Normal University. The domain name is hierarchical. For example, the official website of Huawei www.huawei.com, the com on the far right represents the enterprise or company, the Huawei in the middle represents the enterprise name, and the www on the far left represents the default website server name. For general corporate websites, there will also be a top-level domain name (cn is China) that represents the country (or region) on the far right. Through DNS, we can use the domain name to visit the corresponding homepage worldwide.

In 1986, the modern mail routing system MERS was developed.

In 1989, the first commercial network operator PSINet was established. Prior to the establishment of PSINet, most networks were funded by the government or the military for military, industrial, or scientific research. The establishment of PSINet represents that the Internet has entered the era of commercial operation.

In 1990, the first Internet search engine Archie appeared. In the early days of the Internet, although there was relatively little information on the Internet, there were already many valuable files (data), but these files were scattered on various File Transfer Protocol (FTP) servers, which made it difficult for users turn up. Therefore, a search engine or search website is needed for indexing and searching. So Archie was developed. Using Archie can easily find the location of the FTP server where the file is located by the file name, and then download it to the local with tools such as FTP.

In 1991, the World Wide Web (WWW) was invented by Tim Berners-Lee, a scientist at the European Center for Particle Research. It was a landmark technology in the history of the Internet. Spread and interconnected on the Internet. Hypermedia can be documents, voice or video, and it is a new way of expressing information. After the birth of the World Wide Web, some great and landmark Internet companies were born, and various network applications that really changed people's lives began to emerge.

In 1995, e-commerce companies such as Amazon and eBay were established. In the history of Internet development, many companies have appeared, such as Yahoo! and Google. Amazon is the first Internet company to truly implement cloud computing. Amazon's early products sold were books. In order to process product information and user data, Amazon established a huge data center. In the United States, there is a "Black Friday" similar to "Double Eleven." On this day, Amazon needs to process a large amount of information, and all equipment in the data center will be turned on. But after this day, a lot of equipment will be idle. In order not to cause waste, Amazon will rent out the excess equipment. So in 2006, Amazon launched its first cloud computing product-EC2 (Elastic Compute Cloud).

In the late 1990s, the Internet was surging and experienced an "explosive" development. Domestic Internet companies "BAT" (Alibaba, Tencent, Baidu) were established during this period. The Internet has allowed people to see its magic, leading to rapid development, spawning a large number of "bubbles," and finally around 2000, the Internet bubble burst. However, after experiencing the bubble burst, the Internet has rapidly developed, and 2004 is also known as the "first year of social networking." With the rapid development of domestic Internet applications, from 2000 to 2020, a large number of domestic Internet companies have rapidly developed and become industry "giants." In addition to the BAT mentioned above, there are also JD.com, Ant Financial, ByteDance, Pinduoduo, Meituan, NetEase, Sina, Sohu, Didi, Suning, Xiaomi, etc. These Internet companies have penetrated deeply into people's daily lives. And even changed people's lifestyle to a certain extent.

1.4.2 The History of Computing Models

Cloud computing does not appear suddenly, but a result of the development and evolution of past technologies and computing models. It may not be the ultimate result of computing models, but a model suitable for current business needs and technical feasibility. The following describes the emergence of cloud computing by analyzing the development history of computing models. Figure 1.7 shows the development history of cloud computing from the perspective of computing models.

Cloud computing is a master of multiple computing technologies and computing models. Therefore, it has similarities with many existing computing models. For example, the software runs in the cloud, and the way customers access cloud services through mobile terminals or clients is somewhat similar to the client/server model; the automatic scaling of cloud resources is somewhat similar to automatic computing; cloud computing gathers resources for customers to use, and grid computing,

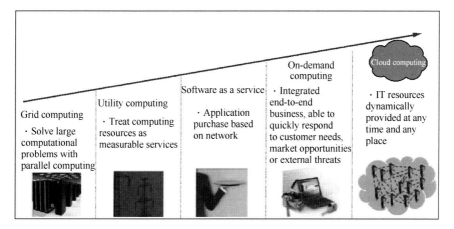

Fig. 1.7 Show the development history of cloud computing from the perspective of computing mode

which was once a smash hit, is somewhat similar; a large number of computing nodes in cloud computing work at the same time, which seems to be somewhat similar to parallel computing; nodes that make up the cloud are distributed in multiple locations and are somewhat similar to distributed computing. Billing based on usage is somewhat similar to utility computing.

Although cloud computing does have similarities with various computing models that we are familiar with, they are not exactly the same. In fact, there are huge differences between cloud computing and certain computing models.

1. Cloud computing and mainframe computing

As early as a few decades ago, shortly after the computer was invented, the computing model at that time had a "shadow" of cloud computing. In 1964, the world's first mainframe System/360 was born, triggering a "revolution" in the computer and business fields.

The market for the mainframe system is mainly enterprise users, and these users generally have a variety of business systems that need to use the mainframe system. So IBM invented the virtualization technology, which divides a physical server into many different partitions, and each partition runs an operating system or a set of business systems. In this way, each enterprise only needs to deploy a mainframe system to meet the needs of all business systems. Since the system has experienced decades of development, its stability is high and it has the reputation of "never shut down." The IBM mainframe is responsible for the most extensive and most important information and data processing tasks in the finance, communications, energy, and transportation industries. Before the emergence of cloud computing, more than 70% of the world's corporate data was running on mainframe platforms, and most of the top companies in the world's wealth rankings were using mainframes.

One characteristic of the mainframe is the concentration of resources, the concentration of computing and storage, which is a typical representative of the centralized computing model. Enterprises using mainframes will concentrate the business to be processed, usually in the form of batch processing and send them to the mainframe for processing. Most of the users of the mainframe use the terminal mode to connect to the mainframe, no data processing and storage are performed locally, and no measures such as patch management, firewall protection, and virus prevention are required. In fact, the mainframe system is the earliest "cloud, but these clouds are for specialized services, private networks, and specific fields.

Cloud computing and mainframe computing actually have many things in common, such as centralized management and billing based on usage. However, there is a big difference between cloud computing and mainframe computing. One of the important differences is the different user groups. The users of mainframe computing are usually large organizations and are prepared for key software, such as census, consumption statistics, enterprise resource planning (ERP), and financial transactions; while cloud computing is for the general public and can run a variety of large, medium, and small software. In addition, the processing unit of mainframe computing is usually a single mainframe, while the processing unit of cloud computing is generally composed of a large number of IT resources in a cluster manner, and the processing capacity is much greater than that of the early single mainframe.

2. Utility calculation

Utility computing emerged with the development of the mainframe. Considering the high purchase cost of the host, some users can only rent it instead of buying it. So some people put forward the concept of utility computing, whose goal is to package the server and storage system for users to use, and to charge users according to the amount of resources actually used by the users. This model is similar to the provision of water, electricity, gas, and telephone services, enabling users to use computer resources as if plugging a light bulb into a lamp holder. This model eliminates the need for users to own resources in order to use services and can also achieve the goal by leasing resources. Utility computing can be regarded as the predecessor of cloud computing.

The actual application of utility computing is mainly represented by IBM. IBM leases its own host resources to different users according to time. The host is still stored in IBM's data center, and users use IBM's resources remotely or on site in IBM's data center. The key technology in utility calculation is resource usage measurement, which guarantees the accuracy of pay-per-use.

From the perspective of the billing model, cloud computing is exactly the same as utility computing. Utility computing packages IT resources into measurable services for users to use, that is, CPU, memory, network bandwidth, and storage capacity are all treated as traditional utility usage (such as telephone networks) for packaging. The biggest advantage of this computing model is that users do not need to pay in advance, nor do they need to buy out IT resources. For most of the small- and medium-sized enterprises, there is not enough capital and technology to construct an IT infrastructure comparable to the Fortune 500 companies. They welcome the concept of utility computing because utility computing enables them to access and use advanced information technology and resources like the Fortune 500 like companies.

Compared with cloud computing, utility computing only specifies the billing model of IT assets and does not limit other aspects of IT assets, such as technology, management, configuration, and security. There are many more factors to consider in cloud computing, and the billing model is only one of the factors.

3. Client/server model

From the perspective of service access mode, cloud computing does have the shadow of a client/server model: customers connect with the remote cloud through a certain device and use the services provided by the application software running in the cloud. However, behind this similarity, the "remote server" provided by cloud computing has unlimited computing power, unlimited storage capacity, and never crashes, and all software can run on it. Users can also publish their own software to the "remote server," and the "remote server" can automatically configure the required resources for the software and change it as needed. In addition, cloud computing has its own set of models and rules (explained later), while the client/server model, on the other hand, refers to all Distributed Systems that can distinguish between a service provider (server) and a service requester (client).

4. Cluster computing

Since the cloud of cloud computing contains a large number of server clusters, it is very similar to cluster computing. However, cluster computing based on server clusters uses a tightly coupled group of computers to achieve a single purpose, while cloud computing can provide different supports according to the needs of users to achieve different purposes. In addition, cluster computing is limited distributed computing, which is not as complicated as the distributed computing faced by cloud computing. In addition, cluster computing does not consider interactive end-users, while cloud computing does. Obviously, cloud computing includes elements of server cluster computing.

5. Service computing

The service provided by cloud computing is called cloud service, which is naturally reminiscent of service computing. Service computing is also called service-oriented computing and has the same concept as SaaS described later. This computing model provides all applications as services, and users or other applications use these services instead of buying out or owning software. In the service computing mode, different services are relatively independent, loosely coupled, and freely combined. For service computing, discovery of service is the key point.

Cloud computing has largely adopted the technology and way of thinking of service computing, but there are still important differences between service computing and cloud computing. First, although service computing is generally implemented on the Internet, service computing does not necessarily have to be provided in the cloud. A single server, small-scale server clusters, and a limited range of network platforms can provide service computing. Secondly, service computing is generally limited to providing services at the software level, while cloud computing extends the concept of services to hardware and operating environments, including the concepts of IaaS and PaaS. In other words, the concept of cloud computing is more extensive than the concept of traditional service computing.

6. Personal computer and desktop computing

In the 1980s, with the development of computer technology, the volume and cost of computer hardware were greatly reduced, making it possible for individuals to own their personal computers. The appearance of personal computers has greatly promoted the development of the software industry, and various end-consumer-oriented software has emerged. Software running on personal computers requires a simple and easy-to-use operating system. The Windows operating system just meets the needs of the public, and it has occupied the market with the popularity of personal computers. Personal computers have their own independent storage space and processing capabilities. Although their performance is limited, they are sufficient for individual users within a period of time. Personal computers can complete most of the personal computing needs; this model is also called desktop computing.

Before the advent of the Internet, the sales model of software and operating systems was an authorization model, that is, the software code was copied to a computer through a floppy disk or CD-ROM, and each copy required a payment to the software developer. After several years of development of this model, some problems appeared, such as high cost and cumbersome software upgrades. The purpose of the upgrade is to solve some of the previous problems or to use new features, but the upgrade process can sometimes be cumbersome. For a large enterprise, its IT department may need to manage hundreds of software, thousands of versions, and tens of thousands of computers. Each version of the software needs to be maintained, including problem tracking, patch management, version upgrades, and data backup. This is by no means a simple job.

7. Distributed computing

The personal computer did not solve the problem of data sharing and information exchange, so the network-Local Area Network (LAN) and later the Internet appeared. The network connects a large number of computers distributed in different geographical locations, including personal computers and servers (large mainframes and later medium and small mainframes). With so much computing power, can an application run on multiple computers to complete a computing task together? The answer is of course yes, this is distributed computing.

Distributed computing relies on distributed systems. A distributed system consists of multiple computers connected through a network. Each computer has its own processor and memory. These computers cooperate with each other to complete a goal or computing task together. Distributed computing is a large category, which includes many familiar computing modes and technologies, such as grid computing, P2P computing, client/server computing, and Browser/Server (B/S) computing. Of course, cloud computing is also included. In today's network age, there are very few non-distributed computing applications, and only some stand-alone applications fall into this category, such as word processing and stand-alone games.

8. Grid computing

One of the main functions of computers is to perform complex scientific calculations, and a "master" in this field is supercomputers, such as China's "Galaxy" series, "Dawn" series, "Tianhe" series, and "Shenwei·Light of Taihu Lake." In foreign countries, there are Japan's Fugaku, which ranks first in the global supercomputing rankings in 2020, and the US's Summit, which is the second. The computing model centered on supercomputers has obvious shortcomings: Although it is a "big Mac" with powerful processing capabilities, it is extremely expensive, and is usually only used by some state-level departments (such as aerospace, meteorology, and military industries) who have the ability to configure such equipment. As people increasingly need computers with more powerful data processing capabilities, people began to look for a low-cost computing model with superior data processing capabilities. Finally, scientists found the answer, that is, grid computing.

Grid computing appeared in the 1990s. It is a new type of computing model that has been developed rapidly with the development of the Internet, specifically for complex scientific computing. This computing model uses the Internet to organize computers distributed in different geographical locations into a "virtual supercomputer." Each computer participating in the calculation is a "node," and the entire calculation is composed of thousands of "nodes," so this calculation mode is called grid computing. In order to perform a calculation, grid computing first divides the data to be calculated into a number of "small pieces," and then distributes these small pieces to each computer. Each computer executes its assigned task segment and returns the calculation result to the master control node of the calculation task after the task calculation is completed.

It can be said that grid computing is an extension of supercomputers and cluster computers. Its core is still trying to solve a huge single computing problem, which limits its application scenarios. In fact, in non-scientific fields, only a limited number of users need to use huge computing resources. Grid computing once became "hot" after entering the twenty-first century. Major IT companies have made many investments and attempts, but they have not found a suitable use scenario. In the end, grid computing has made a lot of progress in the academic field, including some standards and software platforms have been developed, but it has not been popularized in the commercial field.

To some extent, many things that grid computing must do are also things that cloud computing must do, but grid computing cannot be regarded as cloud computing. First of all, grid computing is mainly for scientific computing and simulation, while cloud computing is made for general public. Secondly, grid computing does not consider interactive end-users, while cloud computing must consider.

9. SaaS

SaaS is a computing model that uses software as a service. It is a mode of providing software through the Internet. Service providers uniformly deploy the software on their own servers. Users can order the required software services from the service provider through the Internet according to their actual needs and pay the service provider according to the number of services ordered and the length of time and obtain the services provided by the service provider through the Internet. Users no longer need to purchase software, but instead rent Web-based software from service providers to manage business activities, and there is no need to maintain the software. The service provider will have full authority to manage and maintain the software. While providing Internet software to users, service providers also provide offline operation of the software and local data storage, so that users can use the software and services they have ordered anytime, anywhere.

SaaS first appeared in 2000. At that time, with the vigorous development of the Internet, various new business models based on the Internet continued to emerge. For traditional software companies, SaaS is the most significant change.

This model turns the one-time software purchase income into continuous service income. Software providers no longer calculate how much software they sell but need to always pay attention to how many paying users there are. Therefore, software providers will pay close attention to their own service quality, and continuously improve their own service functions to enhance their own competitiveness. This model can reduce piracy and protect intellectual property rights, because all the code is at the service provider, users cannot obtain it, nor can it be cracked or decompiled.

In summary, in addition to utility computing, the computing models discussed above are all technical aspects, and the cloud computing model covers both technical and commercial aspects. This may be the biggest difference between cloud computing and the above-mentioned computing models.

10. The emergence of cloud computing

Looking back at the history of the development of computing models, it can be summarized as: Concentration-Decentralization-Concentration. In the early days, limited by technical conditions and cost factors, only a few companies could have computing power. Obviously, the computing model at that time could only be centralized. Later, with the miniaturization and low cost of computers, computing also became decentralized. Up to now, there is a trend toward centralization in computing, and this is cloud computing.

Users can use cloud computing to do many things. As we can see from the previous article, there are three basic services provided by cloud computing: the first one is hardware resource services; the second is operating environment services; and the third is software services. Then users can also use the cloud computing platform (also called cloud platform) in at least three ways: the first one is to use the cloud platform to save data (using the hardware resources provided by the cloud environment); the second is to run software on the cloud platform (using the cloud the operating environment of the environment); the third is to use software services on the cloud platform (using software services arranged on the cloud, such as maps, search, and mail).

The service provided by cloud computing is not only the IT resource itself, if it is nothing more than that, there is no need to develop cloud computing. Storage of data, running programs, and using software can be implemented on many platforms, and cloud computing is not required. The reason for using cloud computing is a result of the way and the ability to provide resources. Cloud computing has great advantages in resource provision methods and capabilities.

In addition to the scale advantages of the cloud platform mentioned above, another important advantage of cloud computing is elastic resource allocation. The resources provided by cloud services are more when need is high, and less when need is low. If we deploy an application software on the cloud, the cloud controller will dynamically adjust the resources allocated to the application according to the changes in customer needs of the software, so as to ensure that it can meet any sudden increase in customer demand at any time and at the same time avoid waste of resources when customer demand is low.

In addition, cloud platform also provides another advantage that most people may not know. Some operations can only have a powerful effect if they are placed in the cloud, while direct deployment on the business location or the user's client has limited or no effect. This is because technically, the desktop or server operation mode is no longer adequate for many challenges faced by IT systems, and these challenges can be solved in the cloud. For example, in terms of virus checking and killing, the antivirus software on the desktop has a lackluster checking and killing effect, and the highest antivirus efficiency can only reach 49% to 88% (according to the data of Arbor Networks in the United States). In addition, scanning and killing also occupies a large amount of computing resources of the personal computer, resulting in extremely low efficiency of the entire system. But moving the antivirus operation to the cloud can solve this problem. Note that moving antivirus operations to the cloud mentioned here is very different from the "cloud antivirus" promoted by some antivirus software companies. The cloud antivirus technology on the market refers to deploying antivirus software in the cloud and checking and killing remote clients through the network. The only advantage of this kind of cloud antivirus is that it is easier to update and maintain antivirus software, but the antivirus capability has not improved. However, if a variety of different antivirus software is deployed in the cloud and the network data is cross-checked and killed in the cloud, the antivirus efficiency can be increased to more than 96%, and it will not occupy the computing resources of the client.

Another example is, in the market, the operating modes of personal computers, servers, or clusters face difficulties in updating and maintaining. Only changing the functional role of a server (replacement of the system and software) requires a lot of effort and is prone to errors. The installation, configuration, upgrade, and other management operations of software distributed on various computers in the organization are a headache for many companies. Moving these services to the cloud can solve these problems.

In general, cloud computing mainly has the following four advantages:

- On demand, unlimited computing resources.
- Instantly available software/hardware resources and IT architecture.
- Charge by usage model.
- Processing environment that is difficult to provide by a single machine.

Although various service concepts with the title "cloud computing"emerge in an endless stream, not every service can be classified as a cloud computing service. How to judge whether a service is a true cloud computing service? Generally speaking, you should see whether the following three conditions are satisfied at the same time.

1. The service should be accessible anytime, anywhere. Users can use the services at anytime, anywhere, and through any device that can connect to the Internet, without having to consider the installation of applications or the implementation details of these services.

2. The service should always be online. Occasional problems may occur, but a true cloud computing service should always ensure its availability and reliability. That is, ensure that it can be accessed through the network at any time and provide services normally.
3. The service has a large enough user base. This is the so-called "multi-leasing," a "leasing" in which a basic platform provides services to multiple users. Although there is no clear number to divide, it is only for a small number of users, that is, using cloud computing-related technologies to support its basic system architecture, it should not be classified as a cloud computing service. Because only a large user base will generate pressure to access massive amounts of data. This is the most fundamental reason for the emergence of cloud computing, and it is also one of the signs that cloud computing services are different from other Internet services.

1.4.3   The Driving Force of Cloud Computing

Cloud computing does not appear from nowhere. Its emergence is promoted by a variety of factors, which has a certain inevitability.

1. The improvement of internet broadband
    Bandwidth is a necessary condition for the popularization of cloud computing. Since computing and storage are placed on the other side of the network, it is necessary to allow users to easily access these data. In recent years, with the popularization of the Internet, major network operators have also continued to improve their Internet infrastructure. On the one hand, the bandwidth of the core network is rapidly expanding; on the other hand, the network access of home and business users has also undergone essential changes. Take home users as an example. From the very beginning dial-up Internet access (speeds in the range of tens to hundreds of kilobits per second), to the later Asymmetric Digital Subscriber Line (ADSL) (speeds in the hundreds of thousands). Bits per second to several megabits per second), and then to the current fiber to the home (network speeds are tens to hundreds of megabits per second or even higher). The increase in bandwidth has changed the mode of use of the network and the types of network application. With the development of 4G/5G technology, network bandwidth will further increase until users do not perceive the limitation of bandwidth.
2. Technology maturity
    There are many similarities between cloud computing and utility computing, but utility computing is not really popular because of the lack of sufficient operability. Any idea, if there is no practical way to realize it, will become a fantasy. The recognition of cloud computing by the public is also closely related to its technological maturity. Cloud computing corresponds to not one technology, but a combination of multiple technologies, which turns the concept of IT as a service into reality. At different levels, different technologies may be used.

These technologies are hidden in the background and are invisible to users. This is also the hidden part of the cloud. We can imagine a data center that provides cloud computing services as a huge factory filled with hundreds of servers and connected by intricate cables. Many intelligent applications are running on these servers. They can manage these servers efficiently, ensure that the system can automatically recover when server fails, and also ensure that the entire center is running at a very low cost.

3. The Development of Mobile Internet

The rapid development of the mobile Internet has led to a rapid increase in the number of digital mobile terminal devices represented by mobile phones and tablet computers. On average, everyone in the country has multiple digital mobile terminal devices that can access the Internet. How to manage the data in these devices has become a big problem. One is that these devices cannot all have strong computing power; the other is that data is scattered on each device, with duplication and redundancy, and the same data may also exist in both new and old versions. So the cloud computing model has become an ideal solution to this problem. For example, users may need to uniformly manage photos on computers, mobile phones, and digital cameras. Although they can be copied or transferred between devices, it is very troublesome. If these devices are connected to the Internet, the photos are synchronized to the cloud via the Internet, and the cloud-based photo management is performed, and the classification, update, synchronization, and access of the photos become very convenient.

4. The evolution of data center

For users, a data center is a "factory" that provides computing and storage capabilities on the other end of the Internet and is a "power plant" for the IT industry. Data centers are unfamiliar to ordinary Internet users, just as everyone who uses electricity does not care about how power plants operate. In fact, data centers are constantly evolving. Data centers can be divided into two types: one is to provide services to the Internet; the other is private to the enterprise and only open to the inside. Regardless of the type, the data center needs someone to operate it to ensure that it can provide services uninterrupted. According to a survey, more than 90% of 1000 organizations worldwide believe that they need to make major changes to their data centers in recent years. For them, the current challenges include expensive management costs, rapidly increasing energy consumption, rapidly increasing user demand, and inefficient use of IT resources. In view of these problems, data centers urgently need a new architecture and management concept, and cloud computing is a solution from the perspective of service providers.

5. Economic factor

When a product is technically feasible and has a wide range of needs, the only factor that determines its success or failure is the price, or user cost. The most fundamental factor in changing the computing mode is cost, and technology is the triggering condition. In the era of mainframes, the main reason for the use of centralized computing is that the cost of the mainframe is too high, and the appearance of personal computers has greatly reduced the user's cost of use, so that each enterprise can afford its own data center at a price. Today, the emergence of the Internet and cloud computing has made it possible to further reduce costs. If costs can be reduced, companies will of course consider adopting new technologies.

What is the trick to saving costs in cloud computing? In fact, it is the scale effect. For example, for power generation, each household uses its own generator to generate electricity. Obviously, the total cost is higher than that of centralized power supply through power plants. Another example is transportation. It is obviously more economical to use a bus to transport the same number of people than a car. Through scale, cloud computing can not only reduce fixed asset investment, but also reduce operating costs. When resources are concentrated, time-sharing or partition sharing of resources can make the same resources play a greater role. Coupled with intelligent resource allocation, the maximum use of resources can be realized. As far as energy usage efficiency is concerned, the value of Power Usage Effectiveness (PUE) has become an internationally accepted measure of data center power usage efficiency. The PUE value refers to the ratio of all energy consumed by the data center to the energy consumed by the IT load. The benchmark is 2, and the closer to 1, the better the energy efficiency level or the higher the power usage efficiency. The average PUE value of the data center is 1.21, so the use of the data center can greatly save energy.

6. Big data

Big data is another major driving force for cloud computing. Because processing massive amounts of data requires massive storage capacity and massive computing power. The general IT architecture is already incompetent, so standard equipment clusters were born, which evolved into cloud computing platforms. In fact, the two well-known commercial cloud platforms-Amazon's AWS and Google's App Engine are both spawned by processing big data.

In addition, some other driving forces that promote the development of cloud computing include the following.

- Improve resource utilization, save energy, and reduce consumption: Cloud computing (strictly speaking, virtualization) can increase server utilization from 15% to 60% or even higher, thereby reducing the energy consumption of unit computing tasks.
- Reduce the maintenance cost of the information system: The maintenance is all in one place and completed by specialized personnel.
- Improve the security posture of IT assets: All security issues are solved in one place, which is much easier than scattered in the business location of many users.
- Improve the disaster recovery capability of the information system: Cloud computing providers can conduct centralized investment and management for disaster recovery.

All in all, the driving force that promotes the emergence and development of cloud computing is economic, flexibility, convenience, elasticity, unlimited, and charge by usage.

1.4.4 The Development of Cloud Computing

Since the initial appearance of the concept of cloud computing, enterprise IT architecture has evolved from a traditional non-cloud architecture to a target cloud-based architecture. In summary, it has experienced the following three major milestone development stages.

1. Could computing 1.0
   IT infrastructure resource virtualization stage for data center administrators. The key feature of this stage is that through the introduction of computing virtualization technology, enterprise IT applications are completely separated and decoupled from the underlying infrastructure, and multiple enterprise IT application instances and operating environments (guest operating systems) are reused in on the same physical server. And through virtualized cluster scheduling software, more IT applications are reused on fewer server nodes, thereby achieving an improvement in resource utilization efficiency.

2. Cloud computing 2.0
   Resource servicing and management automation stage for infrastructure cloud tenants and cloud users. The key features of this stage are reflected in the introduction of standardized services and resource scheduling automation software on the management plane, as well as software-defined storage and software-defined network technologies on the data plane, for internal and external tenants, This would transform the complex and inefficient application, release, and configuration process of infrastructure resources that originally required manual intervention by data center administrators into one-click, fully automated resource distribution service process under necessary restricted conditions (such as resource quotas and permission approval). This change has greatly improved the rapid and agile distribution of infrastructure resources required for enterprise IT applications, shortened the preparation cycle of infrastructure resources required for enterprise IT applications to go online, and transformed the static rolling plan of enterprise infrastructure into the elastic on-demand supply of dynamic resources. This change also laid the foundation for enterprise IT to support its core business to move toward agility and better respond to the ever-changing business competition and development environment of the enterprise. In the cloud computing 2.0 stage, the provision of infrastructure resource services for cloud tenants can be in the form of a Virtual Machine (VN), a container (lightweight virtual machine), or a physical machine. The evolution of enterprise IT cloudification at this stage does not involve changes in enterprise

IT applications, middleware, and database software architectures above the infrastructure layer.

3. Cloud computing 3.0

Distributed microservices of enterprise application architecture for enterprise IT application developers and management and maintainers, Internet reconstruction of enterprise data architecture, and big data intelligence stage. The key feature of this stage is reflected in the fact that the enterprise IT's own application architecture has gradually shifted from (relying on traditional business databases and middleware business suites, specifically designed for each business application field, chimney-like, high-complexity, stateful, large-scale) vertical scale application layered architecture to (relying on open source enhanced, highly shared across different business application domains) database, middleware platform service layer and (more lightweight and decoupling functions, complete separation of data and application logic) distributed stateless architecture. This enables enterprise IT to reach a new level in supporting enterprise business agility, intelligence, and resource utilization efficiency and pave the way for the rapid iterative development of enterprise innovative business.

Regarding the above three development milestones, cloud computing 1.0 is already the past, and some industries and enterprise customers have completed the initial scale of cloud computing 2.0 construction and commercial use and are considering further expansion at this stage and the evolution toward cloud computing 3.0. Another part of the customers is moving from cloud computing 1.0 to cloud computing 2.0, and even start the evaluation and implementation of the evolution of cloud computing 2.0 and cloud computing 3.0 simultaneously.

1.5   The Advantage of Cloud Computing

The implementation and innovation of any technology is to meet the application needs of a certain group of people. Cloud computing is not an exception. It gradually penetrates into all areas of people's life and production, bringing convenience and benefits to people. The advantages of cloud computing are as follows:

1. Cut costs

Through cloud computing, companies can minimize or completely cut initial investment because they do not need to build data centers or build software/hardware platforms on their own, nor do they need to hire professionals for development, operation, and maintenance. It is usually much cheaper to use cloud computing services than to purchase software/hardware to build the required system.

2. Data can be accessed instantly anytime, anywhere

"Cloud" brings greater flexibility and mobility. Using the cloud, companies can instantly access their accounts through any device anytime, anywhere; data can be stored, downloaded, restored, or processed easily, saving a lot of time and effort.

3. Improve adaptability and flexibly expand it needs

   In most cases, the capacity of the IT system does not match the needs of the enterprise. If an enterprise configures IT equipment according to the peak demand, it will be idle at ordinary times, resulting in a waste of investment. If an enterprise configures IT equipment according to average demand, it will not be enough during peak demand. However, with cloud services, companies can have more flexible choices and can increase, decrease, or release the resources they apply for at any time.

4. Unified platform

   Companies may be running different types of platforms and devices at the same time. In the cloud service platform, the application and the hardware platform are not directly related, thereby eliminating the need for multiple versions of the same application.

1.6 Classification of Cloud Computing

The layering of clouds focuses on the construction and structure of the cloud, but not all clouds of the same construction are used for the same purpose. Traditional operating systems can be divided into desktop operating systems, host operating systems, server operating systems, and mobile operating systems. Cloud platforms can also be divided into many different types. Cloud classification is mainly based on the cloud's operating mode and service mode. The former category is concerned with who owns the cloud platform, who is operating the cloud platform, and who can use the cloud platform. From this perspective, clouds can be divided into public clouds, private clouds (or dedicated clouds), community clouds, hybrid clouds, and industry clouds. The latter classification is based on the service model of cloud computing, and the cloud can be divided into three layers: IaaS, PaaS, and SaaS.

1.6.1 Classification by Operating Model

1. Public cloud

   Public cloud is a type of cloud environment that can be publicly accessed, usually owned by a third-party cloud service provider. It is called public cloud because it can be accessed by the unrestricted public. Public cloud service providers can provide the installation, management, deployment, and maintenance of IT resources in all aspects, from applications and software operating environments to physical infrastructure. End-users achieve their goals through shared IT resources, and only pay for the resources they use, and obtain the IT resource services they need in this relatively economical way.

   In the public cloud, users do not know with whom to share resources, and how the underlying resources are implemented, and they cannot control the physical infrastructure. Therefore, the cloud service provider must guarantee the security and reliability of the provided resources and other non-functional requirements. The level of these non-functional services also determines the service level of the cloud service provider. For those cloud services that need to strictly comply with security and regulatory compliance, higher level and more mature service levels are required. Examples of public clouds include foreign Google App Engine, Amazon EC2, IBM Developer, etc. domestic Tencent Cloud, Alibaba Cloud, Huawei Cloud, Ucloud, etc.

2. Private cloud

   Enterprises and other social organizations are not open to the public. Data centers that provide cloud services (IT resources) for the enterprises or organizations are called private clouds. Compared with public clouds, users of private clouds own the entire cloud center facility, can control where program run and can decide which users are allowed to use cloud services. Since private cloud services are provided for enterprises or organizations, private cloud services can be less subject to many restrictions that must be considered in public clouds, such as bandwidth, security, and regulatory compliance. Moreover, private clouds can provide more guarantees of security and privacy through means such as user range control and network restrictions.

   The types of services provided by private clouds can also be diversified. Private cloud can not only provide IT infrastructure services, but also support cloud services such as application and middleware operating environment, such as internal management information system (IMS) cloud services.

3. Community cloud

   Both public and private clouds have disadvantages. A compromised cloud is the community cloud. As the name suggests, it is a cloud platform owned by a community, not an enterprise. Community cloud generally belongs to a certain enterprise group, institution alliance or industry association, and generally also serves the same group, alliance, or association. If some organizations are closely connected or have common (or similar) IT needs and trust each other, they can jointly construct and operate a community cloud in order to share infrastructure and enjoy the benefits of cloud computing. All members of the group can use the community cloud. In order to facilitate management, community cloud is generally operated and maintained by one organization, but it can also be managed by a cloud platform operation and maintenance team formed by multiple organizations.

   Public cloud, private cloud, and community cloud are shown in Fig. 1.8.

4. Hybrid cloud

   Hybrid cloud combines "public cloud" and "private cloud" together. Users can partly own and share partly with others in a controlled way. Enterprises can take advantage of the cost advantages of public clouds to run non-critical applications on the public cloud, and at the same time provide services through the internal

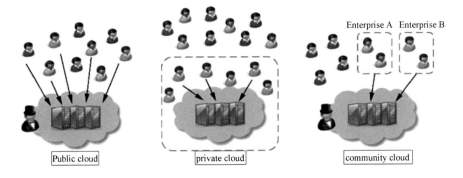

Fig. 1.8 Public cloud, private cloud, and community cloud

private cloud for major applications with higher security requirements and more criticality.

There are many reasons for using hybrid cloud. There are two main reasons: the compromise of various considerations; the transition from private cloud to public cloud. For the first reason, although some organizations are eager to use the public cloud, because of various regulations, confidentiality requirements or security restrictions, they cannot put all their resources on the public cloud, so some IT resources will be deployed in the public cloud. In the above situation, part of the IT resources is deployed in the business location, which will form a hybrid cloud.

In the long run, public cloud is the mainstream of cloud computing development due to its higher resource utilization efficiency, but private cloud and public cloud will coexist for a long time in the form of common development. Just like the emergence of banking services, the transfer of currency from individuals to bank custody is a safer and more convenient process, but some people may choose to keep them on their own.

5. Industry cloud

The industry cloud is for the purpose of the cloud, not for the owner or user of the cloud. If the cloud platform is customized for a certain industry (e.g., for the automotive industry), it is called an industry cloud. The components used in the industry cloud ecological environment should be more suitable for related industries, and the software deployed on it is also industry software or its supporting software. For example, for the cloud platform established by the hospital, the data storage mechanism deployed above should be particularly suitable for the storage, indexing, and query of medical data.

There is no doubt that the industry cloud is suitable for the specified industry, but it may be of little value to the average user. Generally speaking, the structure of the industry cloud will be simpler, and its management is usually taken care of by the industry's "leading" or a computing center (supercomputer center) designated by the government.

The relationship between the industry cloud and the four types of clouds mentioned above is not exclusive, and there may be an overlapping or overlapping relationship between them. For example, industry clouds can be built on public clouds, private clouds, and more likely community clouds.

6. Other cloud types

In addition to the cloud types above, there are other cloud types. For example, according to whether the cloud is aimed at individuals or enterprises, it can be divided into consumer cloud and enterprise cloud. The consumer cloud audience is the general public or individuals, so it is also called the public cloud. This kind of cloud promotes personal storage and document management needs; the enterprise cloud is for enterprises and promotes comprehensive IT services for enterprises. The classification of these clouds is still a certain segmentation or combination of the above cloud types in essence.

1.6.2 Classification by Service Model

According to the service model of cloud computing, the cloud can also be divided into three layers: IaaS, PaaS, and SaaS. Different cloud layers provide different cloud services. Figure 1.9 shows the composition of a typical cloud computing.

1. IaaS

IaaS is at the bottom of the three-layer service of cloud computing, and it is also the scope covered by the narrow definition of cloud computing. IaaS provides IT infrastructure to users in the form of services like water and electricity and provides highly scalable and on-demand IT capabilities based on hardware resources such as servers and storage in the form of services. It is usually charged according to the cost of the resources consumed.

This layer provides basic computing and storage capabilities. Taking the provision of computing capabilities as an example, the basic unit it provides is a virtual server, including CPU, memory, operating system, and some software, as shown in Fig. 1.10. Specific instance is Amazon EC2.

2. PaaS

PaaS is located in the middle of the three-layer service of cloud computing and is often referred to as a "cloud operating system," as shown in Fig. 1.11. It provides end-users with an Internet-based application development environment, including application programming interfaces and operating platforms and supports various software/hardware resources and tools required for the entire life cycle of applications from creation to operation. The billing is usually based on user or login status. At the PaaS layer, service providers provide encapsulated IT capabilities, or some logical resources, such as databases, file systems, and application operating environments. Examples of PaaS products include Huawei's software development cloud DevCloud, Salesforce's Force.com, and Google's Google App Engine.

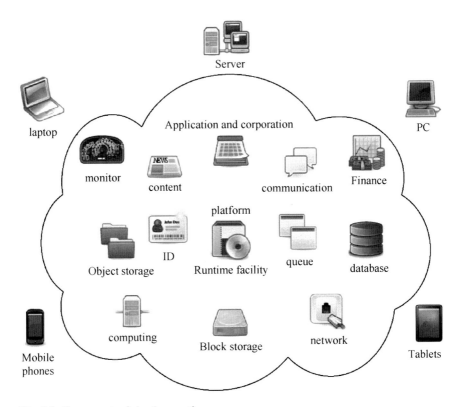

Fig. 1.9 Components of cloud computing

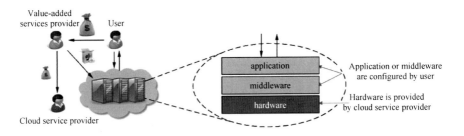

Fig. 1.10 IaaS structure

PaaS is mainly for software developers. It used to be a difficult problem for developers to write and run programs in a cloud computing environment through the network. Under the premise of gradual increase in network bandwidth, the emergence of two technologies has solved this problem. One is online development tools. Developers can use browsers, remote consoles (running development tools in the console), and other technologies to directly develop applications remotely, without the need to install development tools locally; the other is

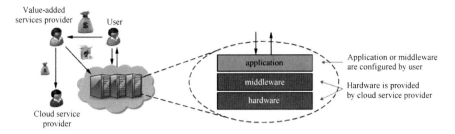

Fig. 1.11 PaaS structure

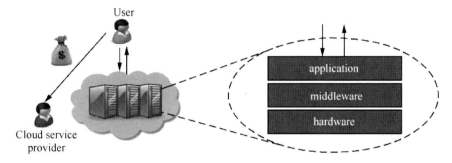

Fig. 1.12 SaaS structure

local development tools and cloud computing integrated technology, that is, deploying the developed application to the cloud computing environment through local development tools, while enabling remote debugging.

3. SaaS

SaaS is the most common cloud computing service, located at the top of the three-tier cloud computing service, as shown in Fig. 1.12. The user uses the software on the Internet through a standard Web browser. Cloud service providers are responsible for maintaining and managing software and hardware facilities and provide services to end-users for free or on-demand rental.

These services are both for general users, such as Google Calendar and Gmail, and for enterprise groups to help with payroll processes, human resource management, collaboration, customer relationship management and business partner relationship management, such as Salesforce.com and Sugar CRM. These SaaS-provided applications reduce the time for users to install and maintain software and their skills requirements and can reduce software license fees through pay-per-use.

The above three layers, each has corresponding technical support to provide the services of this layer, with the characteristics of cloud computing, such as elastic scaling and automatic deployment. Each layer of cloud services can be independent into a cloud or based on the services provided by the clouds below. Each kind of

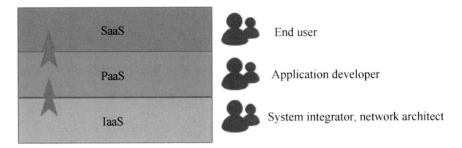

Fig. 1.13 Types of user groups of the three types of service models

cloud can be directly provided to end-users for use, or it can only be used to support upper-layer services. The three types of service models usually have different user groups (see Fig. 1.13).

1.7   Cloud Enabling Technology

This section introduces some basic key technologies included in the current cloud computing technology, which called cloud enabling technology. This includes broadband network and internet architecture, data center technology, virtualization technology, Web technology, multi-tenant technology, and service technology.

From a technical point of view, cloud computing is inextricably linked with various technologies such as distributed systems, virtualization technology, and load balancing. Like the "Je Kune Do" in information technology although it combines the essence of various types, it still forms its own types.

In terms of specific technical realization, the cloud platform innovatively integrates a variety of technical ideas, through different combinations, to solve different problems encountered in specific applications. Therefore, people will find a variety of technologies in the cloud platform, and some people will also judge that cloud computing is nothing but an old tune. However, if we only focus on the existence of a certain technology and ignore the integration and innovation of cloud computing itself in technical applications, there will be a situation of "seeing the trees, not the forest," which is not only biased, but also leads to perception errors.

As far as technology is concerned, cloud computing is essentially derived from ultra-large-scale distributed computing and is an evolved distributed computing technology. Cloud computing also extends the Service-Oriented Architecture (SOA) concept and integrates virtualization, load balancing, and other technologies to form a new set of technical concepts and implementation mechanisms. Specifically, the core significance of cloud computing lies not only in the development of technology, but also in the organization of various technologies to change people's thinking about building IT systems and at the same time make fundamental changes in the structure.

1.7.1 Broadband Network and Internet Architecture

All clouds must be connected to the network, and this inevitable requirement forms an inherent dependence on network interconnection. The Internet allows remote provision of IT resources and directly supports ubiquitous network access. Although most clouds rely on the Internet for access, cloud users can also choose to access the cloud only through private or proprietary network connections. The attractiveness of the cloud platform is closely related to the quality of the service provided by the access network.

The Internet's largest backbone network is established and deployed by ISPs, and they rely on core routers for strategic interconnection. These routers are in turn connected to transnational networks in the world. Figure 1.14 shows the interconnection between a backbone ISP network and other ISP networks and various organizations.

The concept of the Internet is based on a non-centralized supply and management model. ISPs can freely deploy, operate, and manage their networks, and they can also freely choose other ISPs that need to be interconnected. Although there are companies such as The Internet Corporation for Assigned Names and Numbers (ICANN) that supervise and coordinate important Internet affairs, there is actually no central entity to fully control the Internet. For specific countries, government regulations and regulatory laws supervise the services provided by domestic institutions and ISPs.

The topology of the Internet has become a dynamic and complex collection of ISPs. These ISPs are highly interconnected through their core protocols. Smaller branches are expanded from the main node, and these branches can be extended outward to new branches, until finally reaching every digital device or terminal connected to the Internet.

The communication path connecting cloud users and their service providers may include multiple ISP networks. The net structure of the Internet connects the digital terminals that are connected through a number of selectable network routes. In actual operation, it is determined which route to choose according to the current network conditions. Therefore, when using cloud services, even if a certain network or even multiple networks fails, the communication is generally guaranteed to be uninterrupted, but it may cause routing fluctuations or delays.

Some more detailed network knowledge, we will specifically introduce in Chap. 4.

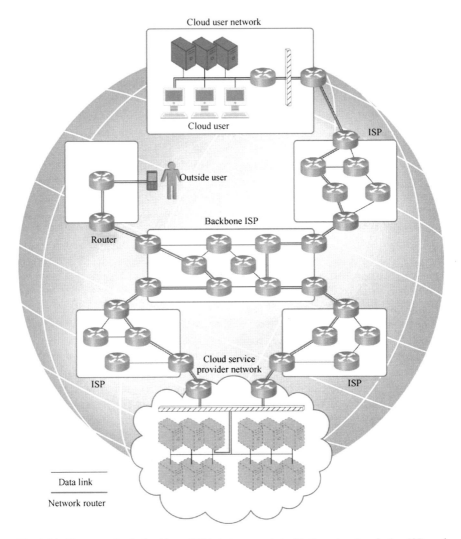

Fig. 1.14 The network of a backbone ISP is interconnected with the networks of other ISPs and various organizations

1.7.2 Data Center Technology

Compared with geographically dispersed IT resources, effectively organizing many IT resources adjacent to each other to form a data center is more conducive to energy sharing, increasing the utilization rate of shared IT resources, and improving IT personnel's efficiency. These advantages make data centers bloom all over the world. A modern data center refers to a particular type of IT infrastructure used to centrally place IT resources, including servers, databases, network and communication equipment, and software systems.

The data center contains physical and virtual IT resources. The physical layer refers to the infrastructure where computing/networking systems and equipment, hardware systems, and operating systems are placed. The virtualization layer abstracts and controls resources and is usually composed of operation and management tools on the virtualization platform. The virtualization platform outlines physical computing and network IT resources into virtualized components, which makes it easier to allocate, operate, release, monitor, and control resources.

The data center is based on standardized commercial hardware, designed with a modular architecture, and integrates multiple identical infrastructure modules and equipment, with features such as scalability, substitutability, and the ability to quickly replace hardware. Modularity and standardization are critical conditions for reducing investment and operating costs because they can achieve economies of scale in procurement, deployment, operation, and maintenance.

Common virtualization strategies and the ever-improving capacity and performance of physical devices have promoted IT resources because fewer physical components can support more complex configurations. Integrated IT resources can serve different systems and can also be shared by other cloud users.

Data centers usually have the following characteristics.

1. Automation

    The data center has a unique platform that can automate tasks such as provisioning, configuration, patching, and monitoring without manual operations.
2. Remote operation and management

    In the data center, most of the IT resources' operation and management tasks are completed through the network remote console and management system. Technicians generally do not need to enter the dedicated room where the server is placed unless they perform equipment handling, wiring, or hardware-level installation and maintenance tasks.
3. High availability

    For data center users, any form of downtime in the data center will significantly impact the continuity of their tasks. Therefore, to maintain high availability, data centers have adopted increasingly high redundancy designs; to cope with system failures, data centers usually have redundant uninterruptible power supplies, integrated wiring, and environmental control subsystems; for load balancing, then there are redundant communication links and cluster hardware.

1.7.3 Virtualization Technology

Among the many existing definitions of cloud computing, there is a definition that describes cloud computing as "accessible through the network, accessible on-demand, subscription-paid, shared by others, packaged outside of your own data center, simple Easy-to-use, virtualized IT resources." Although this definition is not comprehensive, it at least points out that virtualization technology is essential for cloud computing.

Virtualization is a virtual (rather than real) version created for certain things, such as hardware platforms, computer systems, storage devices, and network resources. Its purpose is to get rid of the various limitations of physical resources in reality, that is, "virtualization is a logical representation of resources, and physical limitations do not restrict it."

Although many people are interested in virtualization technology because of cloud computing, virtualization technology is not a new technology. From the virtualization of IBM's mainframe computers to the current VMware series of desktops by EMC (Ian Xin company, acquired VMware in 2003), stand-alone virtualization technology has experienced more than half a century of development. In the early days, virtualization technology was implemented to make a single computer look like multiple computers or completely different computers, thereby improving resource utilization and reducing IT costs. With the development of virtualization technology, the scope of the concept of virtualization is also increasing.

Computer systems are usually divided into several levels, from bottom to top, including the underlying hardware resources, operating systems, user software, etc. The emergence and development of virtualization technology enable people to abstract various underlying resources to form different "virtual layers" and provide upward with the same or similar functions as the real "layers," thereby shielding the differences in equipment and making the underlying equipment Transparent to upper-level applications. Virtualization technology reduces the degree of coupling between resource users and resource entities so that users no longer depend on specific types of certain types of resources.

The virtualization involved in cloud computing is a higher level of virtualization after development. It means that all resources-computing, storage, applications, and network equipment are connected and managed, and scheduled by the cloud platform. With the help of virtualization technology, the cloud platform can uniformly manage the diverse resources at the bottom. It can also conveniently manage resource scheduling at any time and realize the on-demand allocation of resources so that a large number of physically distributed computing resources can be logically controlled. It is presented in an overall form and supports various application requirements. Therefore, the development of virtualization technology is a crucial driving force for cloud platforms.

Although virtualization is a crucial component of cloud computing, cloud computing is not limited to virtualization. Cloud computing also expresses the service model of on-demand supply and billing and technical characteristics such as flexibility, transparency, and building blocks. Chapter 3 of this book will describe in detail the related technologies of virtualization.

1.7.4 Web Technology

Cloud computing has a deep-rooted dependence on the Internet and Web technologies. Web technology is often used as the realization medium and management interface of cloud services.

1. Basic web technology

The World Wide Web is a system of interconnected IT resources accessed through the Internet. Its two fundamental components are the Web browser client and the Web server. Other components, such as proxies, caching services, gateways, and load balancing, are used to improve Web application features such as scalability and security. These additional components are located in the hierarchy between the client and the server.

Web technology architecture consists of three basic elements.

- Uniform Resource Locator (URL): A standard syntax used to point to Web resources' identifier. URLs usually consist of logical network locations. If you want to locate Huawei's official website, enter the URL in the browser, and you can see the homepage of the official website.
- HyperText Transfer Protocol (HTTP): The basic communication protocol for exchanging content and data through the World Wide Web. Usually, the URL is transmitted via HTTP. When a user visits a webpage, the browser will send a webpage request to the website corresponding to the URL, using HTTP, and the website will return the requested webpage to the browser after receiving the request.
- Markup Language-Markup Language: It provides a lightweight method to represent Web-centric data and Metadata. At present, Hyper Text Markup Language (HTML) is commonly used in webpages, and the meaning of its tags is fixed. For example, the tag <p > means segmentation in the page; while the user defines Extensible Markup Language (XML) tags, the user can freely assign meaning to the Web data through the metadata. Metadata refers to data describing other data, or structural data used to provide information about a certain resource. If "<author>Lu Xun</author>"is defined in the XML file, the custom tag <author> here belongs to metadata. HTML and XML are the two main markup languages that are currently widely used.

Web resources are also called hypermedia to distinguish them from hypertext. This also means that all kinds of media, such as images, audio, video, and plain text, can be referenced in a single file. However, some types of hypermedia require additional software or Web browser plug-ins to play or watch. The Web browser can request to perform read, write, update, or delete operations on Web resources on the Internet, and identify and locate them through the URL of the resource. A request for a webpage is sent to a resource host identified by a URL through HTTP, and then the Web server locates the resource and processes the requested operation, and sends the processing

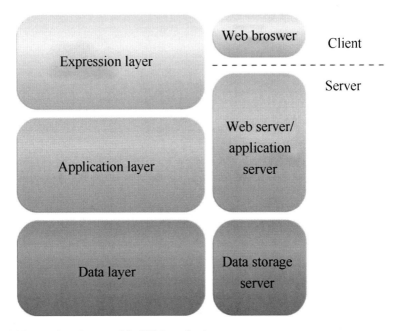

Fig. 1.15 The three-layer model of Web applications

result back to the browser client. Processing results generally consist of HTML or XML statements.

2. Web application

Distributed applications based on Web technology (usually displaying the user interface through a Web browser) are generally considered Web applications. Due to their high accessibility, these applications appear in all types of cloud-based environments.

A typical Web application may have a three-tier model, as shown in Fig. 1.15. The first layer is the Presentation Layer, which is used to represent the user interface. The second layer is the Application Layer, which is used to implement application logic. The third layer is the Data Layer, which consists of persistent data storage. This pattern is also commonly referred to as the Model-View-Controller (MVC) pattern.

The MVC pattern model is the part of the application used to process the data logic of the application. Usually, model objects are responsible for accessing data in the database. This is corresponding to the data layer. The core device is a Data Storage Server or a Database Server. The view is the part of the application that handles the display of data. Usually, views are created based on model data. This corresponds to the presentation layer. The browser on the client-side is used for requesting and displaying Web data; the Web server on the server-side is used to process the browser's request and return the requested webpage (corresponding to a static website) or corresponding to the results of program execution (corresponding to dynamic webpages). The controller is the part of the application that handles user interaction. Usually, the controller is responsible for reading data from the view, controlling user input, and sending data to the model. Corresponding to the application layer here, it mainly deals with transaction logic, and the core device is the Application Server.

The MVC model helps manage complex applications, simplifies group development, and makes application testing easier.

1.7.5   Multi-Tenant Technology

- The purpose of designing multi-tenant applications is to make it possible for multiple users (tenants) to logically access the same application simultaneously. Each user has his view of the application that he uses, manages, and customizes, corresponding to a specific instance of the application. At the same time, each tenant will not realize that other tenants are using the application.

Multi-tenant applications ensure that each tenant will not access data and configuration information that is not their own. Moreover, each tenant can independently customize its application features.

- User Interface: Tenants can define application interfaces with special interface appearances.
- Business Process: When implementing applications, tenants can customize the rules, logic, and workflow of business processing.
- Data Model: Tenants can extend the application data model to include, exclude or rename the fields of the application data structure.
- Access Control: Tenants can independently control the access rights of users or groups.

Multi-tenant application architecture is usually much more complicated than single-tenant application architecture. It needs to support multi-user sharing of various components (including entrance, data model, middleware, and database), and it also needs to maintain a security level to isolate different tenants' operating environments.

The general characteristics of multi-tenant applications are as follows:

- Usage Isolation: The usage behavior of a tenant will not affect the availability and performance of the application to other tenants.
- Data Security: Tenants cannot visit data of other tenants.
- Recovery: Data backup and recovery processes are operated separately for each tenant.

- Application Upgrade: The upgrade of shared software will not have negative influence on tenants.
- Scalability: The application can be expanded according to the increase in the use demand of existing tenants or the increase in the number of tenants.
- Metered Usage: Charge based on the application processing and functions actually used by the tenant.
- Data Tier Isolation: Tenants have independent databases, tables, and schemas that are isolated from other tenants. Or, it can also be specially designed for multi-tenant shared databases, tables, and schemas.

1.7.6   Service Technology

Service technology is the foundation of cloud computing. It laid the foundation of "as a service" cloud delivery model. The typical realization and construction of service technology of cloud computing are as follows:

1. Web service

    The technical standard of Web service are as follows:

    - Web Service Description Language, WSDL: This markup language is used to create WSDL definitions, which define the application programming interface (API) of Web services, including its independent operations (functions) and input/output messages for each operation.
    - XML Schema Definition Language, XML: The messages exchanged by Web services are generally expressed in XML. This language is used to describe the XML schema. The XML schema defines the data structure of XML-based input/output messages, which are exchanged by Web services. The XML schema can be directly linked to the WSDL definition or embedded in the WSDL definition.
    - Simple Object Access Protocol, SOAP: This protocol defines the general message format of the request and response messages exchanged by Web services. A SOAP message consists of a body and a header. The body is the content of the message. The header generally contains metadata that can be processed at runtime.
    - Universal Description, Discovery, and Integration, UDDI protocol: The protocol stipulates that the server must register and publish the WSDL definition to the service catalog so that users can discover the service.

        The above four technologies form a classic Web service technology, and the relationship is shown in Fig. 1.16.

2. REST service

    Compared with complex technologies such as SOAP and WSDL, REST (Representational State Transfer translated as representational state transfer) is a

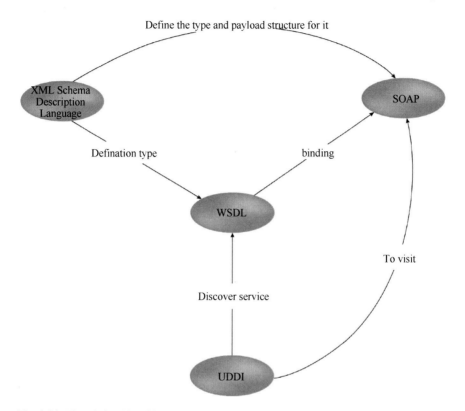

Fig. 1.16   The relationship of four Web service technologies

lightweight and concise software architecture style that can reduce the complexity of development and improve the scalability of the system. Mainstream cloud service providers are increasingly adopting REST-style design and implementation to provide Web services. For example, Amazon offers REST-style Web services for book searches; Yahoo! provides REST-style Web services.

REST services do not have an independent technical interface. Instead, they share a common technical interface called a uniform contract, which corresponds to a set of architectural constraints and principles. An application or design that meets these constraints and regulations is called REST. REST is usually based on existing widely popular protocols and standards such as HTTP, Uniform Resource Identifier (URI), XML, and HTML.

3. Service agent

Cloud-based environments rely heavily on service agents to perform most tasks such as monitoring and metering. These service agents are usually customized to accomplish specific tasks such as elastic expansion and pay-per-use. The service agent is an event-driven program, which intercepts messages and performs related processing at runtime.

Service agents are divided into active service agents and passive service agents. Both service agents are common in cloud-based environments. After the active service agent intercepts and reads the message, it may take certain measures, such as modifying the message content or message path. The passive service agent does not modify the content of the message, but after reading the message, it captures the specific content for monitoring, recording, or reporting.

1.8 Understand Cloud Computing

We can understand cloud computing from multiple perspectives: cloud computing is a business model and a computing model or an implementation method. At the same time, open source technology has also been widely used in cloud computing. Open source technology and software have promoted the development of cloud computing technology, and the research on cloud computing technology has further boosted the development of open source technology. The two complement each other.

1.8.1 The Ternary Epistemology of Cloud Computing

With the development of cloud computing ecosystem, today's cloud computing should include three aspects: business model, computing model, and implementation method.

1. Cloud computing as a business model

Cloud computing services represent a new business model. SaaS, PaaS, and IaaS are the three manifestations of this business model. For any business model and being feasible in theory, it is also necessary to ensure that it is feasible in practice. Therefore, along with the development of cloud computing service concepts, cloud computing has also formed a set of software architecture and technical implementation mechanisms, and the cloud platform we often hear is a concrete manifestation of this mechanism.

Amazon sells all "commodities" suitable for e-commerce, including books, DVDs, computers, software, video games, electronic products, clothes, furniture, computing resources, and so on. When launching EC2, Amazon also faced many questions about "why does this retailer want to do this," but the company's CEO Bezos had a much broader understanding of business concepts at the time. Bezos believes that whether it is "personal computer + software" or this way of obtaining services from the "cloud," it is not only a technical issue, but also a "business model."

To enable the website to support large-scale business, Amazon has made excellent infrastructure construction efforts and has naturally accumulated much experience. In order to sell a large number of idle computing resources as commodities, Amazon has successively launched storage and computing rental services such as S3 (Simple Storage Service) and EC2. Bezos said, "We think this will be an exciting business someday, so our purpose of doing this is straightforward: we think this is a good business." Although the media thinks this is a safe time for Bezos. A risky bet after the dot-com bubble, "The CEO of Amazon wants to use the technology behind his website to run your business, but Wall Street only wants him to be optimistic about his storefront." But EC2 did affect the entire industry, and it also affected many people, the industry was obviously shaken at the time.

Before Amazon, although many services have the characteristics of cloud computing services, even the services provided by Google can still be regarded as a business model within the meaning of Internet services. After Amazon launched IaaS, it seems to have opened a window to the Internet world, telling people that computing resources can also be operated in this way, and there is a new business model called cloud computing. And those service models that are similar to traditional Internet services can finally be independent and find their own position-cloud computing services.

The University of California, Berkeley pointed out in a report on cloud computing that cloud computing refers to applications provided in the form of services on the Internet and the hardware and software that provide these services in data centers. The hardware and software are called "clouds."

The National Institute of Standards and Technology issued Cloud Computing Synopsis Recommendations in 2011, in which PaaS, SaaS, and IaaS were explained in detail. Many people think that SaaS must run on PaaS, PaaS must run on IaaS, but in fact, there is no absolute hierarchical relationship between the three. They are all a kind of service, which can have a hierarchical stacking relationship or not.

2. Cloud computing as a computing model

From the perspective of computing mode, the earliest origin of cloud computing should be ultra-large-scale distributed computing. For example, Yahoo!'s ultra-large-scale distributed system designed to solve system support for large-scale applications is to decompose large problems and solve them together by a large number of computers distributed in different physical locations. However, with the continuous development and improvement of technology, cloud computing draws on many other technologies and ideas, including virtualization technology and SOA concepts, when solving specific problems. Cloud computing is fundamentally different from these technologies, not only in commercial applications but also in implementation details.

As a computing model, cloud computing has its computing boundary determined by upper-level economic and lower level technical factors. Economic factors determine the business form of this computing model from top to bottom, and technical factors determine the technical form of this computing model from bottom to top.

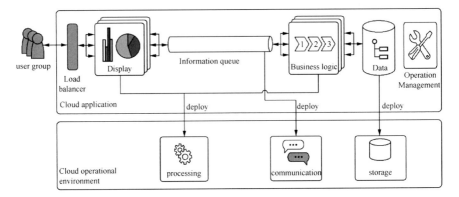

Fig. 1.17 Cloud computing's logical structure of horizontal cloud body

The computing model as a cloud computing service can be further understood from two perspectives: the horizontal cloud body's logical structure and the logical structure of the vertical cloud stack.

(a) Logical structure of horizontal cloud

The logical structure of the horizontal cloud body of cloud computing is shown in Fig. 1.17. From the perspective of the horizontal cloud, cloud computing is divided into two parts: Cloud Runtime Environment and Cloud Application.

The cloud runtime environment includes Processing, Communication, and Storage, which together support all aspects of upper cloud applications.

From this perspective, we can see that the structure of cloud computing is very similar to the structure of the personal computer we usually use. And Chaps. 3 to 5 of the book cover the 3 dimensions of processing (virtualization technology), communication (networking) and storage (distributed storage) respectively.

(b) Logical structure of vertical cloud stack

The logical structure of the vertical cloud stack is similar to the previous business model, and it is also composed of three parts: SaaS, PaaS, and IaaS, except that it will be viewed from a technical point of view.

SaaS, PaaS, and IaaS have become the "recognition cards" for people to perceive cloud computing. Many people will view the relationship between these three technical layers in a hierarchical manner. For example, SaaS runs on PaaS, and PaaS runs on Above IaaS. It can be further seen that the IaaS layer includes Physical Hardware and Virtual Hardware; the PaaS layer includes operating systems and middleware; and there are business processes on top of the application software of the SaaS layer. The logical structure of the vertical cloud stack of cloud computing is shown in Fig. 1.18.

From a technical point of view, there is no obvious difference between SaaS users and the users of ordinary stand-alone software. PaaS provides

Fig. 1.18 Logical structure of vertical cloud stack for cloud computing

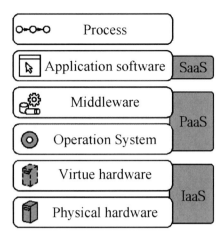

platform services, so users are developers and need to understand the development and deployment of applications in the platform's environment. And IaaS delivers the lowest level of infrastructure services, so the users it faces are IT managers, that is, IT managers will configure and manage them first, and then perform software deployment and other tasks on it.

Although people are accustomed to dividing services according to the content provided by service providers, there is no absolute clear boundary between these three service models. Some more powerful cloud computing service providers may provide products with both SaaS and PaaS features, and some cloud computing service providers try to provide a complete set of cloud computing services, further blurring the differences in the three service models at levels.

People are slowly realizing that there are infinite possibilities of services provided through the Internet, and many companies have discovered new directions for Internet services. Therefore, in addition to SaaS, PaaS, and IaaS, some new service form names have appeared, such as Business Process as a Service, Database as a Service, and Security as a Service.

It is undeniable that these emerging cloud computing services extend the concept of Internet services and provide information services that are more in line with the laws of commercial development. If the emergence of the Internet has greatly satisfied people's needs for rapid acquisition and sharing of knowledge, then cloud computing services have met people's needs for convenient acquisition, sharing, and innovation of knowledge to a greater extent based on traditional Internet services.

After this "business model" concept of "simpler, more convenient, and lower cost" through the Internet has been widely used to meet various needs, service providers are gradually trying all services that can be provided to users through the Internet. "Cloud," so now there is a term XaaS. Where X refers to Anything or Everything, which stands for "everything can be a service." It now appears that the commercial practice of various new possibilities has continued to develop and enrich the possible meaning of cloud computing services.

(c) Cloud computing as a realization model

The ultimate realization of cloud computing requires a new generation of software/hardware technology to promote, that is, the current popular data center, and evolve toward a software-defined data center (SDDC). The data center is the ultimate home of cloud computing, including a full range of computing, storage, and communication requirements. With the data center's operation, everyone began to encounter a series of common problems, including hardware resource utilization, scalability, and automated management. Hardware upgrades take years and months, and it is usually difficult to meet the needs of a fast-developing business. Software definition is a realistic and feasible way out. Therefore, the software-defined data center has quickly become a hot keyword in the IT industry.

The software-defined data center is a relatively new concept that extends virtualization concepts (such as abstraction, centralization, and automation) to all data center resources and services to achieve IT as a Service (ITaaS). In a software-defined data center, all infrastructure elements (network, storage, CPU, and security) are virtualized and delivered as services.

The core resources of a software-defined data center are computing, storage, and networking. These three are undoubtedly the basic functional modules. Unlike traditional concepts, the software-defined data center emphasizes the capabilities abstracted from the hardware rather than the hardware itself.

For computing, computing capabilities need to be abstracted from the hardware platform, so that computing resources can break away from the hardware constraints and form a resource pool. Computing resources also need to be able to migrate within the software-defined data center's scope to adjust the load dynamically. Although virtualization is not a necessary condition, it is non-virtualization that can meet these requirements. The requirement for storage and network is the separation of the control plane and data plane. This is the first step to break away from hardware control, and it is also the initial stage of being able to define the behavior of these devices with software. After that, it is possible to consider connecting the control layer and the data layer to the software-defined data center. Security has increasingly become a factor that needs to be considered separately in data centers. Security hazards may appear between basic computing, storage, and the network or hidden in the data center's management system or the user's software. Therefore, it is necessary to regard safety as a basic functional module alone, parallel with the above three basic available modules.

Having these basic functional modules is not enough. A centralized management platform is needed to link them together, as shown in Fig. 1.19.

Automated management is the key to organizing the basic functional modules of the software-defined data center. Here it must emphasize

Fig. 1.19 Software-defined
data center function division

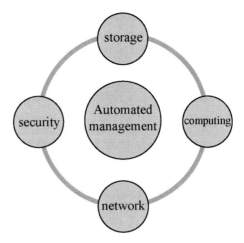

"automated" management, not just a set of exquisite interfaces. An important
driving force of the software-defined data center is the user's management of
ultra-large-scale data centers, and "automation" is undoubtedly a must.

In summary, there is no inevitable relationship between cloud computing
services, cloud computing models, and cloud computing implementation. If a
service implemented with traditional underlying architecture or similar to
supercomputing has the three characteristics of cloud computing services: a
large user base, always online, and accessibility anytime, anywhere, it can
also be called cloud computing. The architecture and specific implementation
itself are designed to put forward various solutions to the problems of "big
users," "big data," and "big systems," which are also typical problems
encountered when providing cloud computing services. Therefore, cloud
computing services supported by cloud computing architecture and implementation can improve service efficiency and give full play to the capabilities
and advantages of cloud computing.

Just like the evolution of species, society itself will continue to advance
and develop, and as a result, different progressive service models and technical needs will be generated. People's demand for computing has promoted
the popularization and development of computers, and the demand for communication and sharing has promoted the birth of the Internet. Cloud computing is also a result of social demand. With the desire for knowledge,
continuous innovation and sharing, people continue to put forward new
information services and products. The emergence of cloud computing, on
the one hand, solves the increasingly prominent pressure problem at the
system level; on the other hand, it broadens the scope of network applications
and the possibility of innovation and further satisfies the premise of significantly reducing the cost of people creating and sharing knowledge. The needs
of human society to acquire, innovate, and share knowledge. Therefore, cloud
computing is an inevitable product of the development of the information

society. With the development of the application environment, cloud computing will become more and more popular, which will bring a new experience of information society to humanity.

One of the significances of the "industrial revolution" is to free people from the shackles of production conditions and greatly liberate the productivity of material products and tangible services. The emergence of cloud computing is also gradually freeing people from the constraints of using computing resources and information services, reducing the cost of knowledge acquisition, making knowledge generation easier and sharing more convenient. It revolutionized the productivity of information products and knowledge services. Therefore, cloud computing is as important as steam engines, internal combustion engines, and electricity and will bring about an industrial revolution in the information society.

Nowadays, cloud computing is still developing, and the extent to which it will develop in the future is still unknown. We are still exploring and deepening our understanding of cloud computing. After all, we have a process of "hearing and knowing" for new things. For cloud computing at this stage, what is most needed is support, and what is most feared is to belittle, or to be contemptuous of conclusions. But in any case, cloud computing has already had a positive impact on some areas of human society's production and life. I believe that with the development of technology and service innovation, the "cloud computing era" will come soon, and ultimately affect each of us.

1.8.2 Open Source Methodology of Cloud Computing

Open source technology has been widely used in the field of cloud computing. In the era of cloud computing, open source is not only an open source software product, but also a methodology and a collaborative way to construct large-scale and complex software.

1. The definition of open source and relative concepts

    Open source refers to the opening of the source code, source data, source assets of a type of technology or a product, which can be technologies or products of various industries, and its scope covers multiple social dimensions such as culture, industry, law, and technology. If it is software code that is open, it is generally called open source software, or open source software for short. Open source's essence is to share assets or resources (technology), expand social value, improve economic efficiency, and reduce transaction barriers and social gaps. Open source is closely related to open standards and open platforms.

    Open source software is a kind of computer software that the copyright holder provides anyone with the right to study, modify, and distribute, and publish the source code. The Open Source Initiative (OSI) has a clear definition of open source software, and it is recognized in the industry that only software that meets this definition can be called open source software. This name stems from the proposal of Eric Raymond. OSI defines the characteristics of open source software as follows:

- The license of open source software should not restrict any individual or group from selling or gifting broad-based works containing the open source software.
- The program of open source software must contain source code, and the release of source code and subsequent programs must be allowed.
- Open source software licenses must allow modification and derivative works and be published using the original software's license terms.

An open source license is a license for computer software and other products that allows source code, blueprints, or designs to be used, modified, or shared under defined terms and conditions. At present, there are 74 kinds of OSI-certified open source licenses, and the most important are only 6–10 kinds (the most important two are GPL and Apache). Under the wave of open source commercialization, moderately loose Apache and other licenses are more popular.

Free software is software that users can freely run, copy, distribute, learn, modify, and improve. Free software needs to have the following characteristics: no matter what purpose the user is in, he can freely run the software according to his own wishes; the user can freely learn and modify the software to help users complete their calculations as a prerequisite. The user must have access to the source code of the software; the user can freely distribute the software and its modified copies, and the user can share the improved software with the entire community for the benefit of others.

Free software is a kind of free computer software that the developer owns the copyright and reserves the right to control the distribution, modification, and sale. The source code is usually not released to prevent users from modifying the source code.

In a broad sense, free software is a subset of open source software, and the definition of free software is stricter than that of open source software. At the same time, open source software requires the source code to be attached when the software is released, and it is not necessarily free; similarly, free software is just the software provided to users for free, not necessarily open source. The relationship between open source software, free software, and free software is shown in Fig. 1.20.

The open source software market is widely used. According to a Gartner survey, 99% of organizations use open source software in their IT systems. At the same time, open source software is widely used in server operating systems, cloud computing, and the Web.

The scale of the open source software market ranks first among server operating systems. According to statistics, more than 90% of the operating systems running on global public cloud vendors' servers are open source

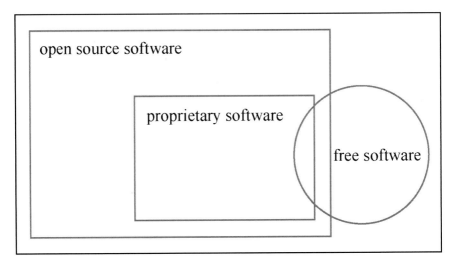

Fig. 1.20 The relationship between open source software, proprietary software and free software

Linux operating systems. Its market share in the embedded market is 62%, and its market share in the field of supercomputing is even higher. Reached 99%. The Android system based on the Linux kernel runs on more than 80% of smart phones in the world.

The 2019 annual report released by GitHub, the world's largest developer community, revealed a data: GitHub currently has more than 40 million developer users worldwide, 80% of which are from outside the United States, and the use of open source in China is proliferating. In 2018 alone, nearly 10 million new developer users joined the GitHub community and contributed to 44 million open source projects worldwide.

Open source software is also widely used in the field of cloud computing. Open source in the cloud computing field is currently mainly based on two levels: IaaS and PaaS. The IaaS level includes OpenStack, CloudStack, oVirt, ZStack, etc., and the PaaS level includes OpenShift, Rancher, Cloud Foundry, and the scheduling platform Kubernetes, Mesos, etc. For example, OpenStack software is widely used in IT, telecommunications, research, finance, and other fields. Another example is the open source application container engine Docker. Since its release in 2013, its technology has become increasingly mature. At present, the number of container image downloads has exceeded eight billion times.

The wide application of open source software in other fields also includes big data, Software Defined Network (SDN), Network Function Virtualization (NFV), artificial intelligence, and other areas. For example, big data basic analysis platforms include Hadoop, Spark, etc., NFV has OPNFV, and artificial intelligence has TensorFlow.

1.8.2.1 The Significance of Open Source

1. The open source ecology promotes national information technology innovation and drives economic development.

   Open source effectively promotes technological innovation. The open source model can effectively achieve information exchange, obtain newer source codes of key technologies, use global technical resources to promote technological development iterations rapidly, break technical barriers, and promote new technologies' popularization.

   Open source can realize software autonomous and controllable. Open source is more transparent and open. The establishment of my country's open source software industry can effectively guarantee information security, achieve autonomy and control, and ensure that information security is easier to manage. Products and services generally do not have malicious backdoors, and vulnerabilities can be continuously improved or patched.

   Open source promotes the development of education and scientific research. Open source provides more independent learning resources for teachers and students in colleges and universities. Students can join open source projects directly and quickly, with continuous technical level improvement and continuous enrichment of experience.

   Open source promotes the development of industry informatization. The open source model can effectively reduce application costs and technical thresholds, accelerate enterprise informatization, and promote the vigorous development of my country's economy.

2. Software vendors rely on open source technology to enhance R&D capabilities.

   Software vendors use open source technology to reduce research and development costs, communicate through open source communities, and are familiar with the use of open source technology, which facilitates tracking of open source technology updates and adapts them according to business needs.

   Well-known open source projects have the participation of high-level R&D personnel in the industry, and their source code has many references for technical personnel in terms of coding style and algorithm ideas. In using open source projects or conducting secondary development based on open source projects, software manufacturer R&D personnel can learn innovative methods to solve problems by reading source code and other methods.

   After software vendors open the project, the project has a wider range of users and more complex application scenarios. R&D personnel should consider the company's business needs and personnel usage when developing but need to pay more attention to code compatibility and standardization.

3. Users use open source technology to change the route of informatization.

   Enterprise users can carry out customized development based on open source technology. The functions that end-user information systems need to achieve are different. Compared with closed-source software, open source software is more flexible and has a higher degree of customization. End enterprise users can do secondary development based on open source code to achieve the requirements of specific scenarios and specific functions and avoid binding risks.

Use open source technology to allow companies to focus on innovation. As more business resources get rid of developing software shackles, the focus of enterprises will shift to innovation. Creativity flourishes in small- and medium-sized enterprises because they are better able to create competitive alternative technologies and proprietary software to obtain more unique and forward-looking thinking than their competitors.

4. Enterprises independently open source and lead the technological development path.

Enterprises' independent open source can effectively improve R&D efficiency and enhance the quality of code. The project's open source process can attract outstanding developers and users to participate in it, inject more "fresh blood," and allow the project to continue to develop. At the same time, open source projects are deployed in different application scenarios, exposing more problems in the project and saving test costs.

Enterprises' independent open source can lead the development of technology and establish an ecosystem with open source enterprises as the core. During the operation of open source projects, potential users can be attracted to use open source software, so that more companies and developers in the industry can understand the technological development of the companies that belong to the open source project, and establish an upstream and downstream ecosystem of providers and users through open source technology, and keep abreast of users. Demand, seize the business territory, and drive the healthy development of the enterprise.

1.8.2.2 Open Source Is a Methodology

The vital impact of open source is that it makes learning programming easier. Any novice can access countless mature products for free as a reference, and the novice will one day become an experienced developer and feedback the open source community. Therefore, the open source community can develop continuously and sustainably, and the open source culture has become the programmer community's representative culture.

Open source has two aspects: one is open source software technology and related aspects, including open source software history, open source software agreements, technical products, open source communities, related hardware, technical personnel, open source software-related industries and enterprises. The second is open source values and methodology. Relevant content includes open source value system, open source methodology system, non-technical projects carried out with open source methodology, related non-technical organizations, communities, and people. Open source values' connotation mainly includes six aspects: dedication, sense of gratitude, open spirit, courage, pursuit of continuous progress, and the spirit of obtaining fair value returns based on labor. The connotation of open source methodology mainly includes promoting progress and innovation through open sharing, solving complex and systemic problems through gathering and accumulating the labor and wisdom of many references, completing open source projects through community platforms, and through effective organization and organization of well-known companies and individuals to develop and complete the project. Open source values and open source methodology are valuable spiritual wealth contributed by open source technology to mankind.

1.8.2.3   Open Source Brings Challenges to Cloud Computing

The open source development model provides a new way for the revolution and transformation of the industry model, and the open source software resources provide directly usable software technologies, tools, and products for the development of the IT industry. The open source development model's openness and transparency help to quickly gather public wisdom and effectively promote the formation and development of technology and application ecology.

Since the development of open source, the types of software products have become more and more diverse, their functions have become more and more powerful, and the scale of the community has become larger and larger. Accordingly, the tools and technical systems supporting open source development have become more difficult to master. The new situation has brought challenges to the further prosperity and development of open source software and put forward higher requirements for open source participants. In terms of participation in open source software development, studies have pointed out that the number and proportion of long-term contributors in well-known open source communities has declined in recent years. The survey found that in the application of open source products and technologies, quite a few IT companies lack talents who master open source technologies. Only by effectively cultivating open source talents can the team of open source contributors be expanded.

Compared with the traditional software development field, open source has different or even broader requirements for software talents, so that the conventional talent training system may need to adapt to the needs and pay attention to specific aspects of open source talent education.

1.9   Exercise

(1) Multiple Choice

   1. The "cloud" in "cloud computing" is more credible about its origins ().

     A. Some aspects of cloud computing are as elusive as the cloud.
     B. The supporting technology of cloud computing is often represented by a cloud-like pattern on the Internet, so the network that provides resources is often called "cloud."
     C. The scale of cloud computing is generally as broad as the cloud.
     D. Users cannot see the resources contained in cloud computing, as if hidden behind the cloud.

   2. () is not a major feature of cloud computing.

     A. On-demand self-service.
     B. Extensive network access.
     C. Complementary resources.
     D. Fast elastic scaling.

   3. Systems or services that do not rely on cloud computing are ().

     A. Baidu net disk.
     B. Attention to the conference system.
     C. There are Cloud Notes.
     D. The remote login system for the supercomputer.

   4. The misconception about resource pooling is ()

     A. Resource pooling is one of the prerequisites for on-demand self-service.
     B. Resource pooling is equivalent to resource classification.
     C. Resource pooling requires that all resources are decomposed to a minimum unit.
     D. Resource pooling masks the differences between different resources.

   5. The misconception about the rapid elastic scaling of cloud computing is () .

     A. Elastic expansion is considered one of the core reasons to engage users in cloud computing.
     B. Rapid elastic scaling means that cloud users can automatically and transparently scale their IT resources according to their needs.
     C. Rapid elastic scaling must be manually expanded or reduced.
     D. Rapid elastic scaling enables users to save money while keeping their business or applications running smoothly.

   6. The misconception about the metering service for cloud computing is ().

     A. Metering is the basis of billing.
     B. Services in cloud computing are measured based on the time of use.

   C. Billing management systems are commonly available in cloud computing systems and are designed to collect and process usage data.

   D. Using a quota billing system prevents further usage requests from cloud users when the quota is exceeded.

7. () is not a service provided by cloud computing.

   A. IaaS.

   B. PaaS.

   C. SaaS.

   D. RaaS.

8. () is not a key driver of the birth and development of cloud computing technology.

   A. Increase in network bandwidth B. The emergence of deep learning techniques.

   B. The emergence of virtualization technology D. The development of the mobile Internet.

   C. Enter the era of big data.

9. The benefits of cloud computing do not include:

   A. Cost savings.

   B. Data is instantly accessible from anywhere.

   C. Improve adaptability and scale IT needs flexibly. D. Enhance the security and confidentiality of user data.

10. Multi-tenant technology is an important support technology for cloud computing. () is not a general feature of multi-tenant applications.

   A. Use isolation.

   B. B. Data security.

   C. C. Recoverability.

   D. Scalability E. Synergy.

(2) Fill in the Blanks

1. Cloud computing technology provides computing resources, _____, and other various resources to resource users in the form of services through the network.

2. _____technology is the basic support of cloud computing. The cloud is inseparable from the _____network.

3. The English abbreviation of the Internet service provider that provides network access services for cloud services is _____.

4. According to the classification of cloud computing operation mode, cloud can be divided into _____, _____, community cloud, hybrid cloud, and industry cloud.

5. _____provides highly scalable and on-demand IT capabilities based on hardware resources such as servers and storage in the form of services. Usually charged according to the cost of the resources consumed.

6. _____is located in the middle of the three-tier service of cloud computing, usually also called "cloud operating system," which provides end-users with an Internet-based application development environment, including application programming interfaces and operating platforms, etc.

(3) Answer the Following Questions

1. What is the definition of cloud computing?
2. What are the features of cloud computing? What are the benefits of using cloud computing?
3. What are the types of cloud computing that can be divided into operational models? What kind of security and privacy guarantees?
4. What do cloud computing have in common with traditional host computing?
5. What are the key technologies included in cloud computing technology, called cloud enabling technology?
6. What are three service models for cloud computing? Which one does Amazon's AWS and Microsoft's Windows Azure belong to?
7. How to understand cloud computing from the perspective of triadic epistemology?
8. What are the differences and connections between open source software, free software, and free software?

Chapter 2
Cloud Computing System

Cloud computing is based on a variety of existing technologies and is a master of existing information technologies. Cloud computing has the characteristics of being technology-centric, and its architecture includes a variety of technical mechanisms. This chapter will start with four aspects: cloud infrastructure mechanism, cloud management mechanism, cloud security mechanism, and basic cloud architecture, and discuss some of the main technical mechanisms for building the foundation of cloud technology architecture.

2.1 Cloud Infrastructure Mechanism

Just as a house has foundations, walls or columns, slabs and floors, stairs, roofs, doors, windows, and other main building components, the cloud computing environment, as a complex IT resource integrated system, also has some basic building blocks, called cloud infrastructure. These facilities are the basis for building a basic cloud environment. This section will introduce five main cloud infrastructures, namely Logical Network boundary, Virtual Server, Cloud Storage Device, Cloud Usage Monitoring, and Resource Replication.

2.1.1 Logical Network Boundary

The logical network boundary can be regarded as a relatively independent area. This area uses firewalls and other network devices to isolate a certain network environment from other network parts, forming a virtual network boundary.

The logical network boundary isolates a group of related cloud-based IT resources from other entities in the cloud (such as unauthorized users). The resources in the logical network boundary may also be physically distributed in different areas.

© The Author(s) 2023
Huawei Technologies Co., Ltd., *Cloud Computing Technology*,
https://doi.org/10.1007/978-981-19-3026-3_2

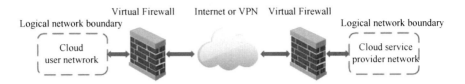

Fig. 2.1 Two logical network boundaries including cloud users and cloud service provider network environments

To provide a virtualized isolation mechanism, there must be corresponding network equipment. These network equipment usually include the following.

- Virtual Firewall:Can actively filter the network traffic of the isolated network and control its interaction with the Internet.
- Virtual Network:Generally formed by virtual local area network (VLAN), used to isolate the network environment in the data center infrastructure.

Logical network boundaries are generally deployed as virtualized IT environments.

Figure 2.1 shows two logical network boundaries, one is the internal enterprise environment containing cloud users, and the other is the cloud environment belonging to the cloud service provider. The two logical network boundaries are connected through the Internet or a virtual private network (VPN). The advantage of using VPN is that the data between the two parties can be encrypted and the communication content can be protected.

The logical network boundary's main function is network segmentation and isolation to ensure the relative independence of the IT facilities in the area. Usually, the network infrastructure needs to be virtualized before the logical network boundary forms a logical network layout. A virtual firewall based on a physical firewall is used for network isolation. For example, an enterprise may divide its entire network into an internal network and an external network. The enterprise's internal network is a virtual network isolated by the internal firewall and can only access resources within the internal network. For example, the data in the internal data center cannot access the external network and the Internet; the external network located outside the external firewall is directly connected to the Internet; the area located between the external firewall and the internal firewall is called the control zone (Demilitarized Zone) (DMZ). The DMZ is abstracted as a virtual network, which generally includes a proxy server and a Web server. The proxy server is responsible for coordinating access to common network services (DNS, E-mail, and Web), while the Web server provides webpage access functions. The company's network is divided into three logical network boundaries: extranet, intranet, and DMZ.

2.1.2   *Virtual Server*

A virtual server is a server that is virtualized on a physical server with virtualization software. Through virtualization, applications' monopoly of physical resources is avoided, and the same physical server can generate multiple virtual server instances. By providing independent virtual server instances to cloud users, cloud service providers can use limited physical servers and other IT resources and improve resource utilization efficiency.

A virtual server is the most basic building block of a cloud environment. Each virtual server can store a large amount of IT resources, such as CPU, memory, external storage, and network. To facilitate users to create virtual server instances, cloud service providers or users usually prepare some customized virtual server images in advance. As mentioned earlier, the several products listed in the Huawei Elastic Cloud Server ECS can actually be regarded as customized virtual server images. Each product generally specifies the number of virtual CPUs contained in its corresponding virtual server instance. Specific performance indicators such as clock speed, memory, and network bandwidth. Creating a virtual server instance from an image file is a resource allocation process that can be completed quickly and on-demand.

By installing or releasing virtual servers, cloud users can customize their own environment, which is independent of other cloud users based on virtual servers based on the same underlying physical server.

The two virtual servers in Fig. 2.2 are based on the same physical server, and they can provide services for different users.

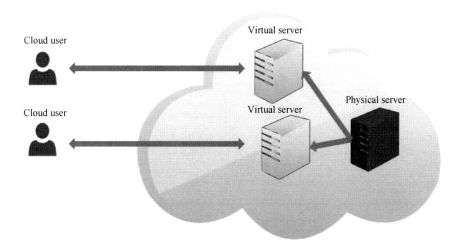

Fig. 2.2   Two virtual servers based on the same physical server can provide services to different users

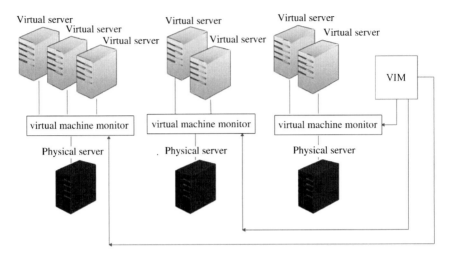

Fig. 2.3 The virtual machine monitor controls and manages virtual servers running on physical servers

Virtual Machine Monitor software is usually run on the physical server to control and manage the virtual server. A Virtual Infrastructure Manager (VIM), also known as a virtual device manager, is used to coordinate work related to the creation of virtual server instances. Figure 2.3 shows several virtual servers running on physical servers. They are created by the central VIM and controlled and managed by a virtual machine monitor.

The virtual server and virtual machine used in this book are synonymous. To quickly create a virtual machine, you can usually use a pre-customized virtual machine image (VM image).

Virtual machine images are usually stored in common cloud storage devices as files. Cloud service providers or cloud users can prepare virtual machine images with different hardware and performance specifications for users to choose according to business needs. For example, on Huawei Cloud's website, the elastic cloud server ECS provides many types of virtual machine images for different user needs, such as general computing scenarios, memory-intensive scenarios, high-performance computing scenarios, big data, and computing acceleration scenarios. The category also contains a large number of sub-categories, giving different CPU/memory ratios, virtual CPU quantity ranges, base frequency/turbo frequency, network speed, applicable scenarios, and other performance or product parameters. Cloud users can choose the most suitable product according to their needs.

2.1.3 Cloud Storage Devices

Cloud storage devices refer to storage devices that are used to provide cloud services. These physical storage devices are usually virtualized to offer services to cloud users in the form of virtual storage devices, just as physical servers are virtualized into virtual servers (virtual machines). Generally, cloud storage devices support remote access by cloud users.

Since cloud services are usually billed according to usage, cloud storage devices need to support a pay-per-use mechanism. When a cloud user and a cloud service provider negotiate a Service-Level Agreement (SLA), the user's initial and highest cloud storage capacity is usually determined. When capacity needs to be expanded, cloud storage devices can generally provide a fixed increase in capacity allocation, such as increasing 1GB each time. If the maximum capacity limit is reached, new expansion requests can be rejected, and cloud users can apply for new and larger storage capacity.

The main issues related to cloud storage are data security, integrity, and confidentiality. If the user is using a public cloud service, its data will be stored in the cloud service provider's cloud storage device. These cloud storage devices are managed and operated by cloud service providers. Cloud users have only access rights to these data, but no control rights. There is no guarantee that these data will not be peeped, tampered with, or deleted. There must be some corresponding mechanisms to ensure this data. Security. For example, the data to be saved to the cloud storage device is encrypted before storage. Or the data is divided into blocks and the order is shuffled and then stored. Or special redundant coding mechanisms such as erasure codes, regeneration codes are used to realize data storage and restore; or verify the integrity and validity of the data stored in the cloud through some special mechanisms such as data ownership verification schemes. Research in this area is also a hot spot in the field of cloud computing. If the security, integrity, and confidentiality of the data stored in the cloud cannot be guaranteed, cloud computing will lose its appeal. Especially when data is entrusted to external cloud providers and other third parties, more attention should be paid to data protection. Besides, due to the emergence of cross-regional and cross-border cloud services, legal and regulatory issues may arise when data is migrated across regions or national borders.

Cloud storage devices can be divided into four categories according to data storage levels: files (File), blocks (Block), data sets (Dataset), and objects (Object). There are three types of corresponding storage interfaces: network storage interface, object storage interface, and database storage interface.

1. Cloud storage level

   The cloud storage device mechanism provides the following standard data storage levels.

   (a) File

   A file refers to a collection of data stored on a permanent storage device such as a hard disk. The file can be a text document, picture, program, etc.

Files usually have a file extension to indicate the file type. File storage provides external services at the file system level, and the main operation objects are files and folders. Access to data in file operations is usually sequential.

(b) Block

Block storage divides data into fixed-length data blocks, which are directly stored on permanent storage devices such as hard disks in units of data blocks. Compared with file storage, block storage does not have the concept of files and directory trees. A data block is the smallest unit of data that can be accessed independently, and its size is generally fixed. For example, the Hadoop Distributed File System (HDFS) data block length is 64 MB by default. Block storage can be regarded as the lowest storage level closest to hardware and has higher storage efficiency.

(c) Data set

Data sets generally refer to table-based data in a relational database. These data are composed of records, and each record contains fields separated by separators. These data are usually stored in a relational database, and the Structured Query Language (SQL) statement can be used to query, insert, modify, and delete the data. After entering the big data era, to improve the storage efficiency of big data, a non-relational database (NoSQL) data set storage type appeared.

(d) Object

Object storage manages data in the form of objects. The biggest difference between objects and files is that metadata (i.e., data describing data) is added to the file. In general, an object is divided into three parts: data, metadata, and object ID (object identification). Object data is usually unstructured data, such as pictures, videos, or documents. The metadata of an object refers to the related description of the object, such as the picture's size and document owner. Object ID is a globally unique identifier used to distinguish objects. Object storage generally corresponds to Web-based resources. We can use HTTP CRUD operations, that is, add (Create), read (Retrieve), update (Update), and delete (Delete) to manage stored data. Each data storage level is typically associated with some type of storage interface that corresponds not only to a specific type of cloud storage device, but also to the access protocol it uses (see Fig. 2.4).

2. Network storage interface

File storage or block storage is mainly affected by the network storage interface category, which includes storage devices that comply with industry-standard protocols, such as the Small Computer System Interface (SCSI) used for storage blocks and server message blocks. Common Internet File System (CIFS) and Network File System (NFS) for file and network storage.

The main operation objects of file storage are files and folders, and the protocols used are NFS and CIFS that comply with POSIX (Portable Operating System Interface) standards. POSIX is a set of standards developed by IEEE and ISO/IEC. Based on the existing UNIX practice and experience, the standard

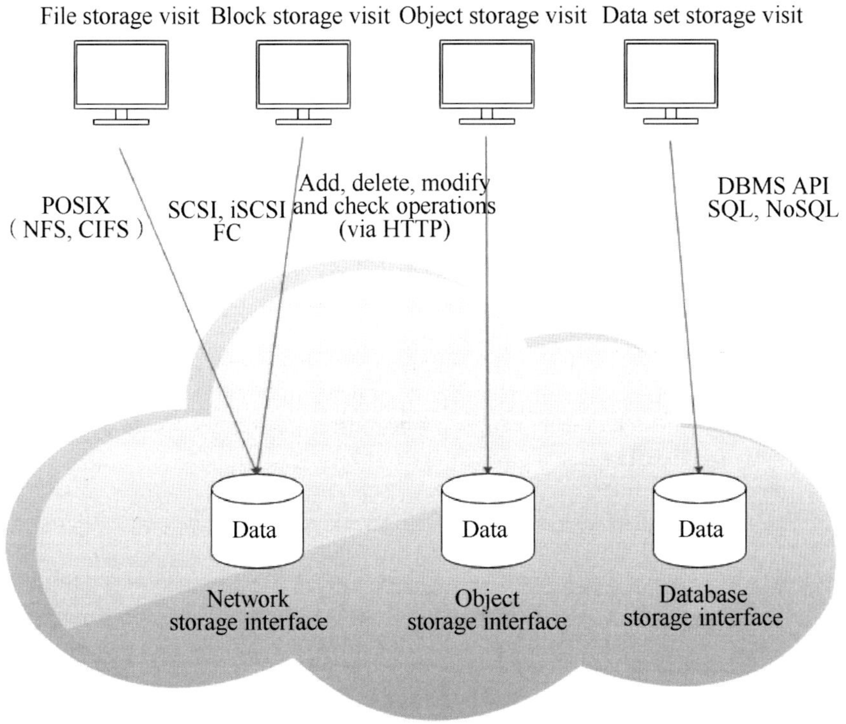

File storage visit Block storage visit Object storage visit Data set storage visit

Fig. 2.4 Use different access interface technologies to operate virtualized cloud storage devices

describes the operating system's calling service interface, which ensures that the compiled application program can be transplanted and run on multiple operating systems at the source code level. Take NFS as an example. File-related interfaces include lookup (LOOKUP)/access (ACCESS)/read (READ)/write (WRITE)/create (CREATE)/delete (REMOVE)/rename (RENAME), etc. Folder-related interfaces include creating a folder (MKDIR)/deleting a folder (RMDIR)/reading a folder (READDIR), etc. Simultaneously, there are interfaces such as FSSTAT/FSINFO to provide file system-level information.

SCSI represents the protocol used by block storage. SCSI is an independent processor standard for system-level interfaces between computers and their peripheral devices (such as hard disks, optical drives, printers, scanners). The SCSI standard defines commands, communication protocols, and electrical characteristics of entities and is mainly used in storage devices (such as hard disks and tape drives). The main interfaces of SCSI are READ/WRITE/READ CAPACITY/INQUIRY, etc. FC (Fibre Channel) and iSCSI (Internet Small Computer System Interface) also block storage protocols. Compared with file storage, block storage does not have the concept of files and directory trees and usually does not define disk creation and deletion operations but pays more attention to transmission control efficiency.

The data search and extraction performance of file storage are usually not optimal. Block storage requires data to have a fixed format (called data block). This format is closest to hardware and is the smallest unit of storage and access. Compared with file storage, block storage usually has better performance.

3. Object storage interface

Various types of data can be referenced and stored as Web resources, which is object storage. It is based on technologies that support multiple data and media types. The cloud storage device mechanism that implements this interface can usually be accessed through REST with HTTP as the main protocol or cloud services based on Web services.

The main operation object of object storage is the object. Take Amazon's S3 storage as an example. The main interfaces are upload (PUT)/download (GET)/ delete (DELETE), etc. Object storage does not have a random read/write interface, and there is no concept of a directory tree. The protocols it uses such as HTTP is more focused on simplicity and efficiency.

4. Database storage interface

In addition to basic storage operations, cloud storage device mechanisms based on database storage interfaces usually support query languages and implement storage management through standard APIs or management user interfaces.

According to the storage structure, there are two types of this storage interface.

(a) Relational database

Relational databases use tables to organize related data into rows and columns. Usually, it uses industry-standard SQL to operate the database. Most commercial database products use relational database management systems. Therefore, the cloud storage device mechanism implemented by using relational data storage can be based on many existing commercial database products.

The challenges of cloud-based relational databases mainly come from expansion and performance. It is difficult to scale a relational cloud storage device horizontally, and vertical expansion is more complicated than horizontal expansion. When remotely accessed by cloud services, complex relational databases and databases containing a large amount of data will have higher processing costs and longer delays.

For large databases, its performance is also closely related to the location of data storage. Local data storage is better than storage on a Wide Area Network (WAN) in terms of network reliability and latency.

(b) Non-relational database

Traditionally, data set storage corresponds to relational databases. After entering the era of big data, because relational databases are not easy to expand horizontally and their storage efficiency is low, non-relational databases are also widely used. These non-relational databases are often referred to as NoSQL. One of the main features of NoSQL databases is the removal of the relational characteristics of relational databases. Compared with traditional relational databases, a "more loose" structure is used to store data, and no emphasis is placed on defining relationships and realizing data standardization. The database has a simple structure and is very easy to expand. Generally, NoSQL databases have very high read/write performance, especially under large amounts of data.

The main motivation for using non-relational storage is to avoid the possible complexity and processing costs of relational databases. At the same time, compared with relational storage, non-relational storage can be scaled more horizontally.

Non-relational storage generally does not support the functions of relational databases, such as transactions and connections. The storage is usually non-standard data, which limits the portability of the data.

2.1.4 Cloud Usage Monitoring

According to usage, the feature of cloud service billing makes the cloud computing system have a mechanism for monitoring and measuring cloud users' resource usage. Cloud usage monitoring is a lightweight autonomous software program used to collect and process cloud users' usage data of IT resources.

Depending on the type of usage indicators that need to be collected and the method of collecting usage data, cloud usage monitoring can exist in different forms. The following are three common agent-based forms, each sending the collected usage data to the log database for subsequent processing and reporting.

1. Monitoring agent

   The monitoring agent is an intermediate event-driven program, which resides on the existing communication path as a service agent, and transparently monitors and analyzes the data flow. This type of cloud usage monitoring is usually used to measure network traffic and message metrics (see Fig. 2.5).

   In this example, the cloud user sends a request message to the cloud service and the monitoring agent intercepts this message. On the one hand, the user's request message is sent to the cloud service, on the other hand, the relevant usage data is collected and stored in the log database. After the cloud service receives the request message, it will return a response message, which the monitoring agent will not intercept.

2. Resource agent

   Resource agent is a processing module that collects usage data by interacting with specialized resource software in an event-driven manner. It works based on resource software, monitoring the usage indicators of predefined and observable events, such as the start, pause, resume, and vertical expansion of each entity. An example of a resource agent is shown in Fig. 2.6.

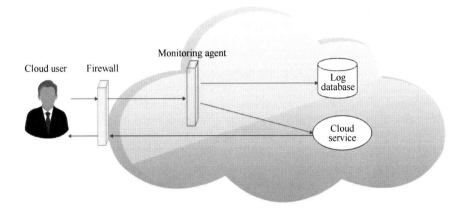

Fig. 2.5 Example of monitoring agent

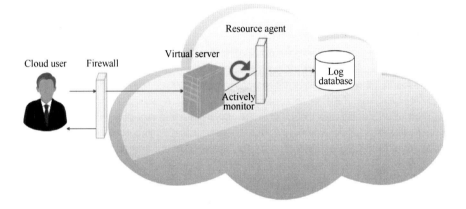

Fig. 2.6 Example of resource agent

   In this example, the resource agent actively monitors the virtual server and detects increased resource usage. Specifically, the resource agent receives notifications from the underlying resource management program, and as the amount of user requests increases, the virtual server expands. The resource agent will store the collected usage data in the log database according to its monitoring indicators.
3. Polling agent
   A polling agent is a processing module that collects cloud server usage data by polling IT resources. It is usually used to periodically monitor the status of IT resources, such as uptime and downtime.
   The polling agent in Fig. 2.7 monitors the status of cloud services on the virtual server and sends polling messages periodically. When the received polling response changes (e.g., when the usage status changes from A to B), record the new usage status to the log database.

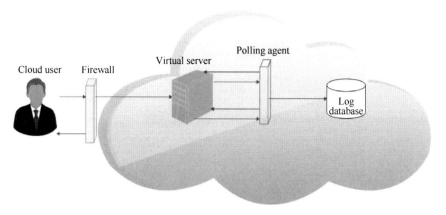

Fig. 2.7 Example of polling agent

2.1.5 Resource Replication

The resource replication mentioned here refers to using customized resource templates (such as virtual machine images) to create multiple virtual server instances. This is usually performed when the availability and performance of IT resources need to be enhanced.

The resource replication mechanism uses virtualization technology to realize the replication of cloud-based IT resources. In Fig. 2.8, the virtual machine monitor uses the stored virtual server image to replicate multiple virtual server instances.

2.2 Cloud Management Mechanism

Cloud-based IT resources need to be established, configured, maintained, and monitored. This section mainly introduces the system that contains these mechanisms and can accomplish these management tasks. They promote the control and evolution of IT resources that form cloud platforms and solutions, thus forming a key part of cloud technology architecture.

The management mechanisms or systems introduced in this section mainly fall into four categories: Remote Administration, Resource Management System, SLA Management System, and Billing Management System. These systems usually provide integrated APIs and can be provided to users in the form of individual products, customized applications, various combined product packages, or multi-functional applications.

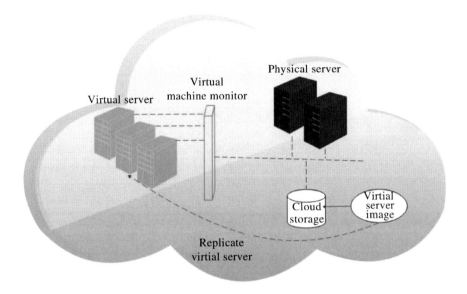

Fig. 2.8 The virtual machine monitor uses the stored virtual server image to replicate multiple virtual server instances

2.2.1 *Remote Management System*

The remote management system provides external cloud resource managers with tools and user interfaces to configure and manage cloud-based IT resources.

The remote management system will establish an entrance to access the control and management functions of various underlying systems, including resource management systems, SLA management systems, and billing management systems (see Fig. 2.9).

Cloud providers generally use the tools and APIs provided by the remote management system to develop and customize online portals, which provide cloud users with various management and control.

The remote management system mainly creates the following two types of entrances.

1. Usage and administration portal
   A universal portal that centrally manages different cloud-based IT resources and provides IT resource usage reports. This portal is an integral part of many cloud technology architectures.
2. Self-service portal
   It is a portal that allows cloud users to search for the latest cloud services and IT resources (usually available for cloud users to rent) lists provided by cloud service providers. Then, cloud users submit their options to cloud service providers for resource allocation.

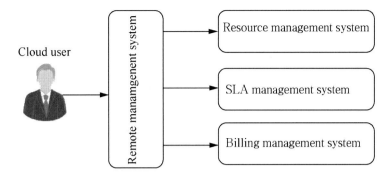

Fig. 2.9 Centralized management and control of external cloud resource managers through the remote management system

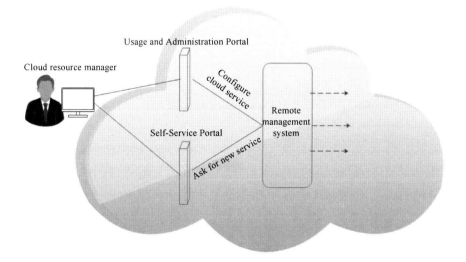

Fig. 2.10 Cloud resource managers use two types of portals

Figure 2.10 shows an example of a cloud resource manager using two portals to access a remote management system. Among them, the cloud resource manager requests the cloud service provider to provide a new cloud service through the self-service portal; after the cloud service provider provides the service, the cloud resource manager completes the configuration of the newly provided cloud service through the use and management portal.

Through the remote management console, cloud users (cloud resource managers) can perform the following tasks.

- Configure and establish cloud services.
- Provide and release IT resources for on-demand cloud services.

- Monitor the status, usage, and performance of cloud services.
- Monitor the implementation of QoS and SLA.
- Manage rental costs and usage expenses.
- Manage user accounts, security credentials, authorization, and access control.
- Track internal and external access to rental services.
- Plan and evaluate the supply of IT resources.
- Capacity planning.

2.2.2 Resource Management System

The resource management system helps coordinate IT resources in order to respond to management operations performed by cloud users and cloud service providers. Its core is VIM, which is used to coordinate server hardware so that virtual server instances can be created based on the most suitable underlying physical server. VIM is a commercial product used to manage a series of IT resources across multiple physical servers.

The tasks that are usually automated and realized by the resource management system are as follows:

- Manage virtual IT resource templates, such as virtual server images.
- Allocate, release, and coordinate virtual IT resources in the available physical infrastructure.
- Monitor the operating conditions of IT resources and enforce usage policies and security regulations.

Figure 2.11 shows two different access methods for resource management. Among them, the cloud resource manager of the cloud user accesses the use and management portal from the outside (① in the figure), and the cloud resource manager of the cloud service provider uses the local user interface provided by VIM to perform internal resource management tasks (② in the figure).

2.2.3 SLA Management System

SLA is a contract between a network service provider and a customer, which defines service type, service quality, and customer payment.

The SLA management system represents a series of commercially available cloud management products, and its functions include the management, collection, storage, reporting, and runtime notification of SLA data.

When deploying an SLA management system, it often includes a library (QoS measurement library) for storing and retrieving collected SLA data based on predefined indicators and report parameters. Collecting SLA data also requires one or more SLA monitoring agents. Through the monitoring agents, cloud resource

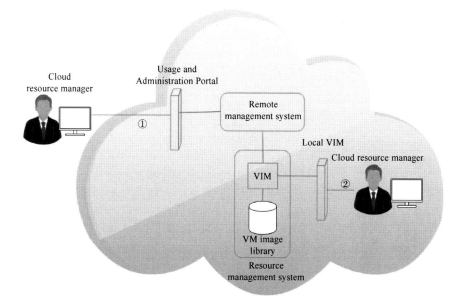

Fig. 2.11 Two different access methods for resource management

managers can query and obtain these data in approximately real-time through the use and management portal.

Figure 2.12 shows the SLA interaction between cloud users and cloud services. First, the cloud user sends an interaction message to the cloud service, the SLA monitoring agent intercepts the interaction message, evaluates the interaction and collects relevant runtime data, which is related to the service quality assurance defined in the cloud service SLA; then, the SLA monitoring agent will The collected data is stored in the QoS measurement library, which is also part of the SLA management system; finally, external cloud resource managers can issue queries and generate reports through the use and management portal, and internal cloud resource managers can directly query SLA management system.

2.2.4   Billing Management System

The billing management system is specifically used to collect and process the usage data of cloud users. It involves the settlement of cloud service providers and the billing of cloud users. Specifically, the billing management system relies on pay-per-use monitors to collect user usage data during operation. These data are stored in a library (pay-per-use measuring library) inside the system.

Figure 2.13 shows the interaction between cloud users and cloud services related to billing. Among them, when a cloud user accesses a cloud service, a pay-per-use

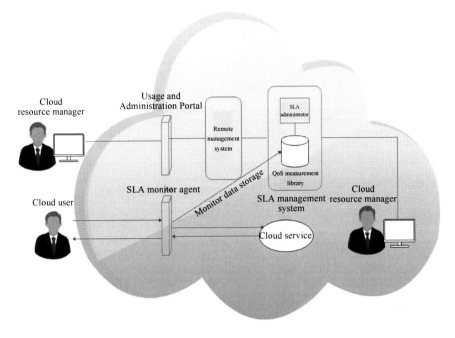

Fig. 2.12 SLA-related interaction between cloud users and cloud services

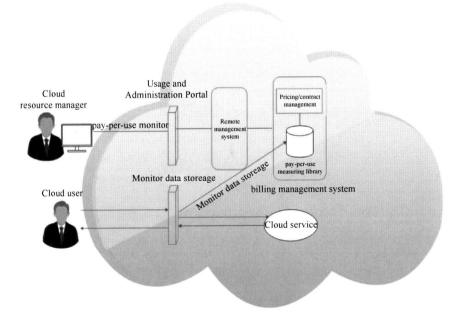

Fig. 2.13 Billing interaction between cloud users and cloud services

monitor tracks usage, collects billing-related data, and sends it to the library in the billing management system. The system regularly calculates usage fees and generates invoices for users. Invoices can be provided to cloud users or cloud resource managers through the use and management portal.

2.3 Cloud Security Mechanism

Users move their business data into the cloud, which means that cloud service providers have to bear the responsibility for this part of data security. The remote use of IT resources requires the cloud user to extend the trust boundary to the external cloud used by the user. It is very difficult to establish a security architecture that includes such a trust boundary without introducing security vulnerabilities. This section will introduce a set of basic cloud security mechanisms to counter the security threats that may be encountered in cloud services.

2.3.1 Encryption

An encryption mechanism is a digital coding system used to protect data to ensure its confidentiality and integrity. It is used to convert Plaintext into a protected, unreadable format. The Plaintext here refers to data encoded in a readable format.

Encryption technology usually relies on a standardized algorithm called an encryption component (Cipher) to convert the original Plaintext into ciphertext, encrypted data. If you don't know the secret key, even if you get the ciphertext, unless you master superb deciphering techniques, you generally cannot analyze the original Plaintext from it, except metadata such as the length of the message and the creation date.

When encrypting the Plaintext, a key is needed. The key is a secret message established and shared by authorized parties. The key is also needed to decrypt the ciphertext.

Encryption mechanisms can help combat security threats such as traffic eavesdropping, malicious media, insufficient credit, and overlapping trust boundaries.

There are two common encryption keys: Symmetric Encryption and Asymmetric Encryption.

Figure 2.14 shows an example of using encryption mechanisms to defend against malicious service agent attacks. After the document is encrypted, the malicious service agent cannot obtain data from the encrypted message.

1. Symmetric encryption

    Symmetric encryption uses the same key for encryption and decryption. The encryption and decryption processes are all done by authorized parties using a

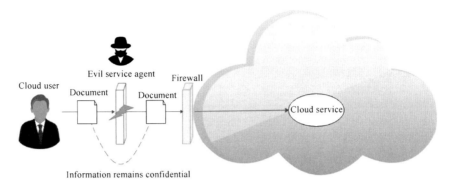

Fig. 2.14 After encryption, the content of the document remains confidential through the untrusted transmission channel

shared key, that is, a message encrypted with a specific key can only be decrypted with the same key.

Symmetric encryption has no Non-Repudiation. If more than one party owns the key, it is impossible to determine which party performed the message encryption or decryption.

2. Asymmetric encryption

Asymmetric encryption uses two keys, Public Key and Private Key. In asymmetric encryption, only the owner has the private key, and the public key is generally publicly available. A document encrypted with a certain private key can only be decrypted correctly with the corresponding public key. Similarly, a document encrypted with a certain public key can only be decrypted with the corresponding private key.

Because two different keys are used, asymmetric encryption is generally slow to calculate, but encryption with a private key can provide authenticity, non-repudiation, and integrity protection. The private key is only owned by the user. If a document is encrypted with the user's private key, he cannot deny that the document was not sent by himself. The document can only be decrypted with the user's public key, and a third party cannot tamper with its content. Similarly, the message encrypted with the public key can only be decrypted by the legal owner of the private key, and the third party cannot snoop on its content, which provides confidentiality protection for the data.

2.3.2 *Hashing*

When a one-way, irreversible form of data protection is needed, a hashing mechanism is used. Hashing is a commonly used technique in mathematics. It can also be translated as "hash" or transliterated as "hash." It transforms an input of any length

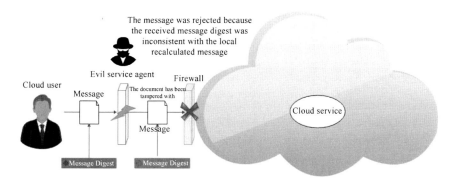

Fig. 2.15 Hashing mechanism's protection of message integrity

into a fixed-length output through a hashing algorithm. The output is the hash value. This conversion is a compression mapping, that is, the space of the hash value is usually much smaller than the space of the input, and different inputs may be hashed into the same output, so the unique input cannot be determined based on the hash value.

But conversely, if the hash values are different, it can be concluded that the inputs are also different. So hashing is simply a function that compresses messages of any length into a fixed-length Message Digest. If you compare a message to a person, and hash the message, it's like taking a low-pixel photo of the person, which can roughly depict the person's appearance and outline, as long as the compared photos are exactly the same If the photos are taken under different conditions, it can be concluded that the people being photographed are also different.

A common application of the hashing mechanism is the storage of passwords.

Hashing techniques can be used to obtain the message digest of the message. The message digest is usually fixed in length and smaller than the original message size. The message sender can append the message digest to the message, and the receiver uses the same hash function to regenerate the message digest on the received message and compare it with the original message digest attached to the message. Determine whether the original message has been tampered with by observing whether they are consistent. Using a suitable hash algorithm, under the same computing conditions, the probability of two different messages generating the same message digest is very small. So in general, as long as the original message is modified, a completely different message digest will be generated. Therefore, as long as the newly generated message digest is the same as the original message digest sent with the message, it can be concluded that the message has not been tampered with during transmission. This method can ensure the integrity and consistency of the message.

Figure 2.15 shows the protection of message integrity by the hashing mechanism. In the figure, a cloud user wants to transmit a document to the cloud service, and the document is summarized by a hash function in advance and attached to the trans-mitted document. If the document is intercepted and tampered with by a malicious service agent, the firewall will recalculate the summary of the received document and compare it with the original summary before the document enters the cloud service. If it is inconsistent, it proves that the document has been tampered with and the document is rejected.

2.3.3   Digital Signature

A digital signature is a string of information that can only be generated by the sender of the information that others cannot forge. This string of information is also an effective proof of the authenticity of the information sent by the sender. It is a kind of ordinary physical signature similar to that written on paper, but it is realized by the technology in the field of public key encryption. A set of digital signatures usually defines two complementary operations, one for signing and the other for verification. Digital signature is the application of asymmetric key encryption technology and digital digest technology.

The digital signature mechanism is a means to provide data authenticity and integrity through identity verification and non-repudiation. Before sending the message, give the message a digital signature. If the message is subsequently modified without authorization, the digital signature will become illegal. The digital signature provides a proof that the received message is consistent with the one created by the legitimate sender.

The creation of digital signatures involves hashing and asymmetric encryption. It is actually a message digest encrypted by the private key and appended to the original message. The receiver needs to verify the legality of the digital signature, decrypt the digital signature with the corresponding public key, and get the message digest. At the same time, a hash mechanism is applied to the original message to get the message digest. Two different treatments give the same result, which indicates that the message maintains its integrity.

Digital signature mechanisms can help counter security threats such as malicious media, insufficient authorization, and overlapping trust boundaries.

The malicious service agent in Fig. 2.16 intercepted and tampered with a legitimate cloud user's data-signed document and pretended to be the cloud user to request cloud services, but the digital signature of the document was verified as invalid when the document passed through the firewall, so the service request was rejected.

2.3.4   Public Key Infrastructure

Public Key Infrastructure (PKI) is a system composed of protocols, data formats, rules, and implementations. It is used to manage asymmetric key issuance so that large-scale systems can safely use public-key cryptography. This system links the

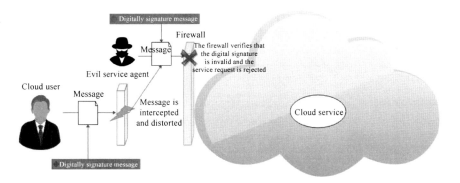

Fig. 2.16 Verify the legitimacy of the document through data signature

public key with the corresponding key owner, and at the same time, verifies the validity of the key.

PKI relies on digital certificates, which are data structures with digital signatures, which are generally issued by a third-party certificate authority (CA). The difference between digital certificates and ordinary digital signatures is that digital certificates usually carry these pieces of information: the identity information of the certificate owner, which the CA has verified; the public key of the certificate owner; the certificate issued by the CA and the digital signature of the CA. The digital signature uses the CA's private key to encrypt the digest of the certificate; there are other related information such as the validity period. A CA is generally an authority trusted by the outside world, and its public key is usually public. The outside world can use the CA's public key to verify the CA's digital signature's authenticity. If it is true, it means that the CA has verified the authenticity of the certificate owner's identity. Indirectly verified the authenticity and validity of the certificate. The typical steps for CA to generate a certificate are shown in Fig. 2.17.

Although most digital certificates are issued by a few trusted CAs such as VeriSign (manufacturers in the domain and Internet security field), digital certificates can also be generated by other methods. Larger companies such as Microsoft can act as their own CA, issuing digital certificates to other customers and the public, and even individual users can generate digital certificates as long as they have the appropriate software tools.

PKI is a reliable method for realizing asymmetric encryption, managing the identity information of cloud users and cloud service providers, and defending against malicious intermediaries and insufficient authorization threats.

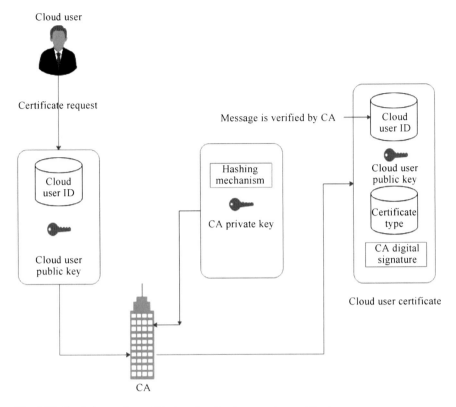

Fig. 2.17 Typical steps for certificate authorities to generate a certificate

2.3.5   Identity and Access Management

The identity and access management (IAM) mechanism includes authentication and the necessary components and strategies for managing user identities, as well as related IT resources, environment, and system access privileges.

     The IAM mechanism has the following four main components.

1. Certification

     In addition to supporting the most common username and password combination authentication methods, it also supports digital signatures, digital certificates, biometric hardware (such as fingerprint readers), special software (such as voice analysis programs), and the combination of user accounts and registered IP or The MAC address is bound.

2. Authorization

     The authorization component is used to define the correct access control granularity and manage the relationship between user identity, access control authority, and IT resource availability.

3. User management

   User management is responsible for creating new user identities and access groups, resetting passwords, defining password policies and managing privileges.

4. Certificate management

   The Credential Management system has established a set of rules to manage the defined user accounts, including user identity management and corresponding access control and policies.

In addition to assigning specific user privilege levels, the IAM mechanism also includes formulating corresponding access control and management strategies. This mechanism is mainly used to combat security threats such as insufficient authorization, denial of service attacks, and overlapping trust boundaries.

2.3.6   Single Sign On

Cloud users sometimes need to use multiple cloud services simultaneously or continuously. If every cloud service has to re-authenticate the user, the user will be annoying. However, it is not easy to provide cloud users with authentication and authorization information across multiple cloud services. The Single Sign On (SSO) mechanism enables a cloud user to be authenticated by a security agent. This security agent establishes a security context. When the cloud user accesses other cloud services or cloud-based IT resources, the security context will be persisted. Otherwise, the cloud user has to re-authenticate himself when sending each subsequent request.

The SSO mechanism allows independent cloud services and IT resources to generate and circulate runtime authentication and authorization certificates. The certificate is first provided by the cloud user and remains valid during the session, while its security context information is shared. The concept of security context mentioned here has a wide range. It generally refers to a collection of permissions and permissions that define what an entity is allowed to do. Permissions, privileges, access tokens, integrity levels, etc. are all included in it. When cloud users want to access cloud services located in different clouds, the SSO mechanism's security agent is particularly useful.

Figure 2.18 shows an example of achieving access across multiple cloud services through single sign-on. First, the cloud user provides the security certificate for login to the security agent on the firewall. After successful authentication, the security agent responds with a security token representing the completion of the authentication. The token contains the user's identity information and can be authenticated by multiple cloud services.

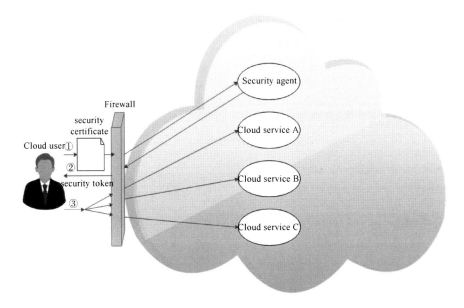

Fig. 2.18 Achieving access across multiple cloud services through single sign-on

2.3.7 Cloud-Based Security Group

Setting up isolation between IT resources can increase data protection. The separation of cloud resources creates separate physical and virtual IT environments for different users and groups, forming independent logical network boundaries. For example, according to different network security requirements, an enterprise's network can be divided into extranets and intranets. The external network deploys a flexible firewall for external Internet access; while the internal network can only access the internal data center's resources but cannot access the Internet.

The cloud-based resource segmentation process creates a Cloud-Based Security Group mechanism, and security policies determine the division of security groups. According to the established security strategy, the entire cloud environment is divided into several logical cloud-based security groups, and each security group forms an independent logical network boundary. Every cloud-based IT resource belongs to at least one logical cloud-based security group. The communication between these security groups is carried out through some special rules.

Multiple virtual servers running on the same physical server can belong to different cloud-based security groups.

Figure 2.19 shows an example of enhancing data protection by dividing cloud-based security groups. Among them, the cloud-based security group A includes virtual servers A and D, which are assigned to cloud user A; the cloud-based security group B includes virtual servers B, C, and E, and is assigned to cloud user B. Even if cloud user A's certificate is compromised, the attacker can only attack the virtual

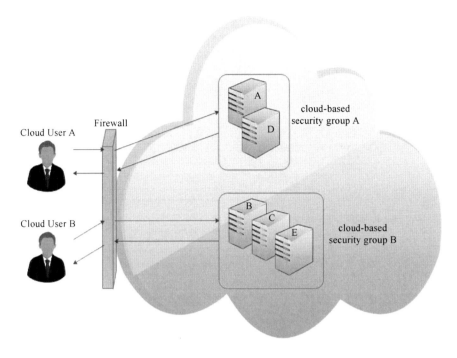

Fig. 2.19 Enhance data protection by dividing cloud-based security groups

servers A and D in the cloud-based security group A. The virtual servers B, C, and E
in the cloud-based security group B cannot be affected.

2.3.8   Hardened Virtual Server Image

A virtual server is created from a template called a virtual server image (or virtual
machine image). Hardening is the process of stripping unnecessary software from
the system and limiting potential vulnerabilities that attackers may exploit. Remov-
ing redundant programs, closing unnecessary server ports, closing unused services,
internal root accounts, and guest access permissions are all examples of
enhancements.

Hardened Virtual Server Image is a hardened template used to create virtual
server instances, which is usually safer than the original standard image.

Enhanced virtual server images can help combat security threats such as denial of
service, insufficient authorization, and overlapping trust boundaries.

Figure 2.20 shows an example of an enhanced virtual server image. Among them,
the cloud service provider applies its security strategy to the enhanced virtual server
image. As part of the resource management system, the enhanced virtual server
image template is stored in the VM image library.

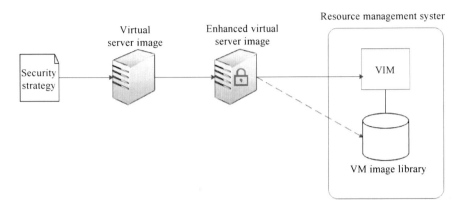

Fig. 2.20 Enhanced virtual server image

2.4 Basic Cloud Architecture

This section will describe some common basic cloud architectures. These architectures are common in modern cloud environments and are usually an important part of cloud environments.

2.4.1 Load Distribution Architecture

The level of IT resources can be expanded by adding one or more IT resources of the same kind, and the load balancer that provides runtime logic can evenly distribute the workload on the available IT resources. The resulting Workload Distribution Architecture relies to a certain extent on complex load balancing algorithms and runtime logic to reduce overuse or underuse of IT resources.

The load distribution architecture can be used to support distributed virtual servers, cloud storage devices, and cloud services. In fact, this basic architecture can be applied to any IT resource.

Figure 2.21 shows an example of a load distribution architecture. Among them, cloud service A has a redundant copy on virtual server B. If the load on cloud service A is too large, the load balancer will intercept cloud user requests and locate them on virtual servers A and B, respectively, to ensure uniform load distribution.

In addition to the basic load balancing mechanism and the virtual server and cloud storage device mechanism that can be used for load balancing, the following mechanisms are also part of the cloud architecture:

- Audit monitor.
- Cloud usage monitor.
- Virtual machine monitor.
- Logical network boundary.

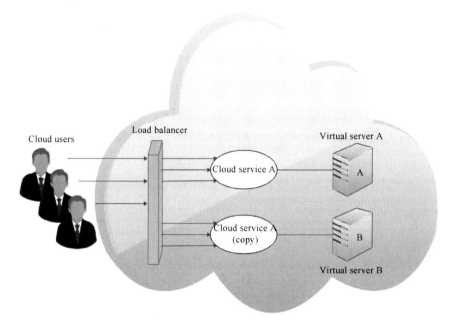

Fig. 2.21 Example of load distribution architecture

- Resource cluster.
- Resource replication.

2.4.2   Resource Pooling Architecture

Resource Pooling Architecture is based on the use of one or more resource pools, where the same IT resources are grouped and maintained by the same system to automatically ensure that they are kept in sync.

Common resource pools are as follows:

1. Physical server pool

    The physical server pool consists of networked servers. These servers have already installed the operating system and other necessary programs and application software and can be put into use immediately.

2. Virtual server pool

    The virtual server pool is generally configured through a customized available template, which is selected by cloud users from a variety of available templates during preparation. A cloud user can configure a low-end server pool, each virtual server is equipped with 2 vCPUs and 4GB of memory; it can also configure a high-end server pool, each virtual server is equipped with 16 vCPUs and 32GB of memory.

3. Storage pool

Storage pools or cloud storage device pools generally consist of file-based or block-based storage structures.

4. Network pool

The network pool is composed of different pre-configured network interconnection devices. For example, for redundant connections, load balancing, or link aggregation, you can create a virtual firewall device pool or a physical network switch pool.

5. CPU pool

The CPU pool can be allocated to virtual servers, usually with a single virtual processing core (vCPU) as the basic unit.

6. Memory pool

The memory pool can be used as a new supply or vertical expansion of the physical server.

A dedicated pool can be created for each type of IT resource, or multiple pools of different types can be aggregated into a larger mixed pool. In this mixed pool, each individual pool is called a sub-resource pool.

2.4.3   Dynamic Scalability Architecture

Dynamic Scalability Architecture has some predefined expansion conditions model. Triggering these conditions will cause the system to allocate IT resources from the resource pool automatically dynamically. The dynamic allocation mechanism allows the number of resources available to users to change in accordance with changes in user needs.

Common types of dynamic expansion are as follows:

1. Dynamic horizontal scaling

Expand IT resources by adding or subtracting instances of the same type of IT resources to handle changes in workload. If resources need to be added, the automatic extension listener will request resource replication according to requirements and permissions and send a signal to start IT resource replication.

2. Dynamic vertical scaling

When it is necessary to adjust the processing capacity of a single IT resource, expand the IT resource instance up (enhance the configuration) or down (down the configuration). For example, when a virtual server is overloaded, its memory capacity can be dynamically increased, or a processing core can be added.

3. Dynamic relocation

Relocate service requirements to other IT resources that can provide similar services at runtime. For example, the virtual server corresponding to the cloud service is migrated to a more powerful physical host.

The dynamic expansion architecture can be applied to a range of IT resources, including virtual servers and cloud storage devices. In addition to the core automatic extension listener and resource replication mechanism, the following mechanisms are also used in this form of cloud architecture.

1. Cloud usage monitor
    In response to the dynamic changes caused by this architecture, a special cloud usage monitor can be used to track runtime usage.
2. Virtual machine monitor
    The dynamically scalable system calls the virtual machine monitor to create or remove virtual machine server instances or extend itself.
3. Pay-per-use monitor
    The pay-per-use monitor collects usage cost information in response to the expansion of IT resources.

2.4.4 Elastic Resource Capacity Architecture

The Elastic Resource Capacity Architecture is mainly related to the dynamic supply of virtual servers. The architecture allocates and recycles related IT resources based on real-time changes in user needs, relying on the resource pool containing IT resources such as CPU and memory in the system, so as to respond to changes in user needs instantly.

The flexible resource capacity architecture monitors the needs of cloud users through the automatic extension of the monitor. Once the requirements change, it will execute the pre-deployed intelligent automation engine script, interact with the virtual machine monitor and VIM, and automatically process user requests and notify the resource pool to allocate or reclaim corresponding resources on the processing results. The elastic resource capacity architecture monitors the runtime processing of the virtual server. Before the cloud service capacity reaches the capacity threshold, it can obtain additional processing power from the resource pool through dynamic allocation. Under this architecture, virtual servers and their hosted applications and IT resources can be seen as vertically expanding.

Figure 2.22 shows an example of a flexible resource capacity architecture. The cloud user actively sends a request to the cloud service, and the automatic extension listener monitors this. The intelligent automation engine script is deployed together with the workflow logic to automatically process changes in user requests and send the processing results to the virtual machine monitor. The virtual machine monitor controls the resource pool to allocate or reclaim the corresponding IT resources. When cloud users increase requests, the automatic extension listener will send a signal to the intelligent automation engine to execute the script. After the script runs, the virtual machine monitor will allocate more IT resources from the resource pool to the virtual machine so that the increased workload can be processed.

This type of cloud architecture can also include the following additional mechanisms.

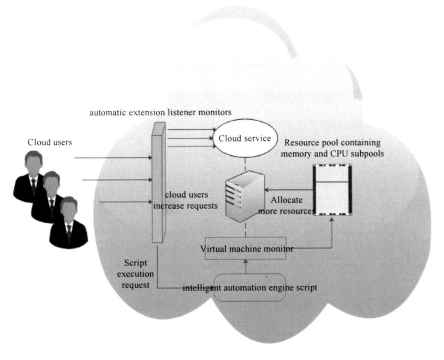

Fig. 2.22 Example of flexible resource capacity architecture

1. Cloud usage monitor

   Before, during, and after the expansion, the cloud usage monitor collects IT resources' usage information to help define the future processing capacity threshold of the virtual server.

2. Pay-per-use monitor

   The pay-per-use monitor is responsible for collecting resource usage cost information, which changes with elastic supply.

3. Resource replication

   Resource replication is used in this architecture to generate new instances of extended IT resources.

2.4.5   Service Load Balancing Architecture

The Service Load Balancing Architecture can be considered a special variant of the load distribution architecture, which is specifically used to implement the expansion of cloud services. By adding a load balancing system to dynamically distributed workloads, redundant deployments of cloud services can be created. The load balancer can intercept cloud users' service requests and distribute them to multiple

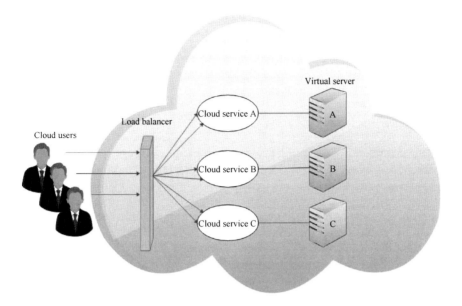

Fig. 2.23 Example of service load balancing architecture

IT resources that can provide similar services according to the principle of load balancing so that the workload of the cloud service system is balanced. The load balancer can either become a built-in component of an IT device in the cloud environment or exist independently of the cloud device and its host server.

Sometimes, a copy of a cloud service instance (such as a redundant virtual server) is organized as a resource pool, and a load balancer acts as an external or built-in component, allowing the hosting server to balance the workload by itself.

Figure 2.23 shows an example of a service load balancing architecture. The load balancer intercepts the messages sent by cloud users and forward them to multiple virtual servers, so that the workload processing can be scaled horizontally.

In addition to the load balancer, the service load balancing architecture can also include the following mechanisms.

1. Cloud usage monitor

    The cloud usage monitor can monitor cloud service instances and their respective IT resource consumption levels and involve various runtime monitoring and usage data collection tasks.
2. Resource cluster

    The architecture includes active-active cluster groups, which can help load balance among different members of the cluster.
3. Resource replication

    Resource replication is used to support the implementation of cloud services to support load balancing requests.

2.4.6 *Cloud Bursting Architecture*

The Cloud Bursting Architecture establishes a form of dynamic expansion. As long as the preset capacity threshold is reached, the IT resources within the enterprise will be expanded or "burst" to the cloud.

Some cloud-based IT resources in the cloud burst architecture are redundantly pre-deployed, and they will remain inactive until the cloud bursts. When these resources are no longer needed, cloud-based IT resources are released, and the architecture returns to the internal environment of the enterprise.

The cloud burst architecture is an elastic expansion architecture that provides cloud users with an option to use cloud-based IT resources, but this option is only used to cope with higher usage requirements. The basis of this architecture is the automatic extension of the listener and the resource replication mechanism.

The automatic extension listener decides when to redirect requests to cloud-based IT resources, and the resource replication mechanism maintains the synchronization of state information between the enterprise's internal and cloud-based IT resources.

Figure 2.24 shows an example of cloud burst architecture. The automatic extension listener monitors the use of service A within the enterprise. When the usage threshold of service A is broken, the request of cloud user C is redirected to the redundant implementation of service A in the cloud (cloud service A).

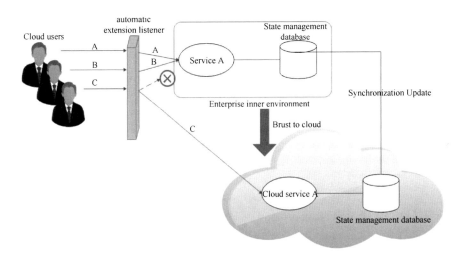

Fig. 2.24 Example of cloud burst architecture

2.4.7 Elastic Disk Provisioning Architecture

Generally, users who use cloud-based storage space are charged according to the fixed allocated disk storage capacity. This means that the cost has been determined based on the pre-allocated storage capacity and has nothing to do with the actual amount of data stored. For example, cloud service provides users with a virtual machine configured with 200GB of storage capacity. Even if the user has not stored any data, they still need to pay for the 200GB of storage space.

The Elastic Disk Provisioning Architecture establishes a dynamic storage provisioning system, which ensures accurate billing based on the amount of storage actually used by cloud users. The system uses automatic streamlined supply technology to automatically realize automatic allocation of storage space and further supports runtime usage monitoring to collect usage data for billing purposes accurately.

The thin provisioning software is installed on the virtual server, and the dynamic storage allocation is handled through the virtual machine monitor. At the same time, the pay-per-use monitor tracks and reports accurate billing related to disk usage data.

In addition to cloud storage devices, virtual servers, and pay-per-use monitors, the architecture may also include cloud usage monitors and resource replication mechanisms.

Figure 2.25 shows an example of an elastic disk supply architecture. The cloud user requests a virtual server with three hard disks, each with a capacity of 120GB. According to the flexible disk supply architecture, the virtual server is allocated a

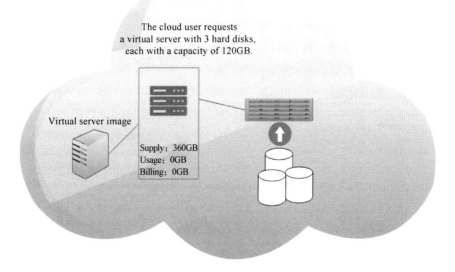

Fig. 2.25 Example of an elastic disk supply architecture

total capacity of 360GB, which is the maximum disk usage. The current cloud user has not installed any software and uses 0GB, so the cloud user does not have to pay any disk space usage fees.

2.4.8   Redundant Storage Architecture

Cloud storage devices sometimes encounter some failures or damages. The reasons for this situation include network connection problems, controller or general hardware failures, and security vulnerabilities. The reliability of cloud storage devices in a combination will have a ripple effect, which will cause all services, applications, and infrastructure components in the cloud that depend on their availability to be affected by failures.

The Redundant Storage Architecture introduces the replicated secondary cloud storage device as part of the failure response system, which must be synchronized with the primary cloud storage device's data. When the primary cloud storage device fails, the storage device gateway transfers the cloud user's request to the secondary cloud storage device.

Figure 2.26 shows an example of redundant storage architecture. The primary cloud storage device regularly copies data to the secondary cloud storage device to achieve data synchronization. When the primary cloud storage device is unavailable, the storage device gateway automatically redirects the cloud user's request to the secondary cloud storage device.

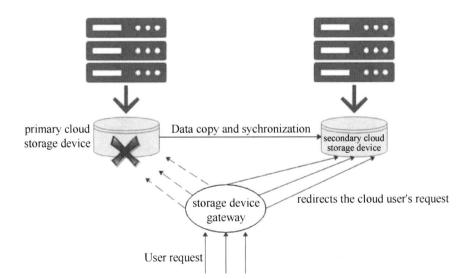

Fig. 2.26 Example of redundant storage architecture

The cloud architecture mainly relies on a storage replication system, which keeps the primary cloud storage device synchronized with its replicated secondary cloud storage device. The storage replication mechanism is a variant of the resource replication mechanism, which is used to synchronously or asynchronously copy data from the primary cloud storage device to the secondary cloud storage device.

Cloud service providers sometimes place the secondary cloud storage device in a different geographic area from the main cloud storage device. On the one hand, it may be because of the economy, and on the other hand, it may be convenient for load balancing and disaster recovery. At this time, to achieve replication between the devices in the two places, the cloud service provider may need to rent a third-party network connection.

2.5   Exercise

(1) Multiple choice.

1. Virtual servers typically do not contain () class IT resources.

   A. CPU.
   B. Memory.
   C. External.
   D. Peripheral.

2. The false statement about the virtual machine monitor is ().

   A. Virtual machine monitors are used to control and manage virtual servers.
   B. A virtual machine monitor is software that runs on a physical server.
   C. Virtual machine monitors are primarily used to create virtual server instances.
   D. Virtual machine monitors can work with VIMs to replicate virtual server instances using stored virtual server images.

3. The network storage interface protocol independent of block storage is ().

   A. SCSI.
   B. NFS.
   C. iSCSI.
   D. FC.

4. The false claim about the NoSQL database is ().

   A. NoSQL refers to a non-relationship database.
   B. The NoSQL database is easier to scale than the relationship database.
   C. The NoSQL database emphasizes data normalization and supports transaction and connection operations.
   D. NoSQL databases have better storage and read/write performance than relationship databases in large data environments.

5. () is not the main work of the resource management system.

   A. Manage virtual IT resource templates, such as virtual server images.
   B. Manage user accounts, security credentials, authorization, and access control.
   C. Allocate, free up, and coordinate virtual IT resources among available physical infrastructure.
   D. Monitor the operational conditions of IT resources and enforce usage policies and security regulations.

6. The misconception about encryption is ().

   A. Symmetric encryption is not undeniable.
   B. Non-symmetric encryption provides authenticity, non-denial, and integrity protection.
   C. Documents encrypted with the private key can only be decrypted correctly with the appropriate public key.
   D. Symmetric encryption is generally slower to calculate than non-symmetric encryption.

7. Under the premise of applying the same hash algorithm to the message, the correct statement about the message summary is ().

   A. Different messages must not produce the same message summary.
   B. The same message must produce the same message summary.
   C. The length of the message summary is generally the same as the message.
   D. Message summaries for different messages generally have different lengths.

8. The digital certificate requested by the cloud user generally does not contain ().

   A. CA-certified identity data for cloud users.
   B. The public key of the cloud user.
   C. Cloud user private key.
   D. CA digital signature.

9. Elastic resource capacity architectures typically do not include ().

   A. SLA Monitoring Agent.
   B. Intelligent automation engine scripts.
   C. Resource Pool.
   D. The listener is automatically extended.

10. By establishing a dynamic storage provisioning system, the basic cloud architecture that ensures accurate billing based on the amount of storage actually used by cloud users is ().

   A. Service load balancing architecture.
   B. Elastic resource capacity architecture.

      C. Dynamic extensible architecture.

      D. Elastic disk provisioning architecture.

(2) Fill in the blanks.

1. _____isolate a related set of cloud-based IT resources from other entities in the cloud, such as unauthorized users, whose primary function is network segmentation and isolation to ensure the relative independence of IT facilities within the region.

2. The main issues associated with cloud storage are data security,_____ and confidentiality。 .

3. Cloud storage devices can be divided into four categories by data storage level: files, blocks, data sets, and _____.

4. _____is a contract between a network service provider and a customer that defines terms such as service type, quality of service, and customer payment.

5. _____mechanism helps cloud users provide them with authentication and authorization information services across multiple cloud services, i.e., point authentication and multiple accesses.

6. _____establish a form of dynamic scaling that extends or "explodes" from IT resources within the enterprise to the cloud as long as a pre-set capacity threshold is reached.

(3) Answer the following questions.

1. What mechanisms are necessary for a cloud computing system to function properly?

2. What are the main principles of digital certificates? What are the uses?

3. From a functional point of view, what are the main categories of basic cloud architecture? Which features match?

Chapter 3
Virtualization Technology

Virtualization technology emerged with the emergence of computer technology and has always played an essential role in computer technology development. From the introduction of the concept of virtualization in the 1950s to the commercialization of virtualization on mainframes by IBM in the 1960s, from the virtual memory of the operating system to the Java virtual machine, to the server virtualization technology based on the x86 architecture The vigorous development of virtualization has added extremely rich connotations to the seemingly abstract concept of virtualization. In recent years, with the popularization of server virtualization technology, new data center deployment and management methods have emerged, bringing efficient and convenient management experience to data center administrators. This technology can also improve the resource utilization rate of the data center and reduce energy consumption. All of this makes virtualization technology the focus of the entire information industry.

This chapter will explain virtualization technology, focusing on the most important current server virtualization technology, analyze and explain its basic knowledge, supporting technology, main functions, etc. and discuss the application of FusionCompute and desktop cloud.

3.1 Introduction to Virtualization Technology

3.1.1 Definition of Virtualization

Virtualization is a broad and changing concept, so it is not easy to give a clear and accurate definition of virtualization. Currently, the industry has given the following multiple definitions of virtualization.

- Virtualization is an abstract method of expressing computer resources. Through virtualization, the abstracted resources can be accessed in the same way as the

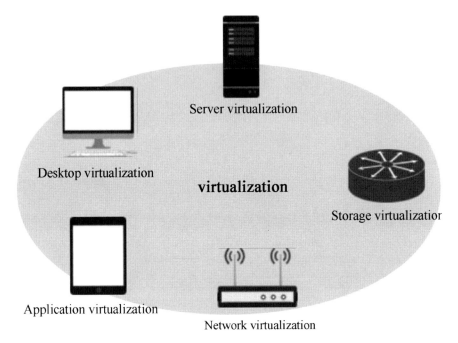

Fig. 3.1 Various virtualization

resources before the abstraction. This abstract method of resources is not limited by implementation, geographic location, or physical configuration of underlying resources. (From Wikipedia).

- Virtualization is a virtual (relative to the real) version created for certain things, such as operating systems, computer systems, storage devices, and network resources. (From What Is Information Technology Terminology Database).
- Although the above definitions are not all the same, after careful analysis, it is not difficult to find that they all illustrate three meanings:
- The objects of virtualization are various resources.
- The virtualized logical resources hide unnecessary details from users.
- Users can realize part or all of their functions in the real environment in the virtual environment.

Virtualization is a logical representation of resources, and physical limitations do not constrain it. In this definition, resources cover a wide range, as shown in Fig. 3.1. Resources can be various hardware resources, such as CPU, memory, storage, network; it can also be a variety of software environments, such as operating systems, file systems, and applications. According to this definition, we can better understand the memory virtualization in the operating system mentioned in Sect. 2.1.2. Memory is a real resource, and virtualized memory is a substitute for this resource. The two have the same logical representation. The virtualization layer hides the details of how to achieve unified addressing and swap in/out between the memory and the hard disk to the upper layer. For software that uses virtual memory, they can still operate on virtual memory with consistent allocation, access, and release instructions, just like accessing real physical memory. Figure 3.1 shows that multiple resources can be virtualized.

The main goal of virtualization is to simplify the representation, access, and management of IT resources, including infrastructure, systems, and software, and provide standard interfaces for these resources to receive input and provide output. The users of virtualization can be end-users, programs, or services. Through standard interfaces, virtualization can minimize the impact on users when IT infrastructure changes. End-users can reuse the original interface because the way they interact with virtual resources has not changed. Even if the implementation of the underlying resources has changed, they will not be affected.

Virtualization technology reduces the degree of coupling between the resource user and the specific realization of the resource, so that the user no longer depends on a particular realization of the resource. Using this loose coupling relationship, system administrators can reduce the impact on users when maintaining and upgrading IT resources.

3.1.2 Development of Virtualization Technology

With the rapid development of information technology today, enterprises and individual users favor virtualization technology mainly since virtualization technology is conducive to solving problems from resource allocation and business management. First of all, the main function of a virtual computer is to give full play to the capacity of idle resources of high-performance computers to achieve the purpose of increasing server utilization even without purchasing hardware; at the same time, it can also complete the rapid delivery and rapid recovery of customer system applications. This is the most basic and intuitive understanding of the public on virtual computers. Secondly, virtualization technology is gradually playing a vital role in enterprise management and business operations. It enables rapid deployment and migration of servers and data centers and reflects its characteristics of transparent behavior management.

The important position of virtualization technology makes its development become the focus of attention in the industry. At the technological development level, virtualization technology is facing four major trends: platform openness, connection protocol standardization, client hardwareization, and public cloud privatization. Platform openness refers to the closed architecture of the basic platform, through virtualization management to enable virtual machines of multiple vendors to coexist under the open platform, and different vendors can implement rich applications on the platform; the standardization of connection protocols aims to solve the current multiple connections Protocols (VMware's PCoIP, Citrix's ICA, etc.) in the case of public desktop cloud complex terminal compatibility issues, so as to solve the wide compatibility issues between terminals and cloud platforms, optimize the industrial chain structure; client hardware in view of the lack of hardware support for desktop virtualization and customer multimedia experience using virtualization technology, the terminal chip technology is gradually improved, and virtualization technology is implemented on mobile terminals; the development trend of public cloud privatization is through technology similar to VPN. Turn the enterprise's IT architecture into a "private cloud" superimposed on the public cloud and ensure that the private cloud supports the security of enterprise data without sacrificing the convenience of the public cloud.

3.1.3 Advantages of Virtualization Technology

Virtualization technology abstracts and transforms various physical resources of a computer (CPU, memory, disk space, network adapter, etc.), divided and combined into one or more computer configuration environments. Allows users to run multiple operating systems on a server simultaneously, and programs can run in mutually independent spaces without affecting each other, thereby significantly improving the efficiency of the computer.

The virtualization layer simulates a set of independent hardware devices for each virtual machine, including hardware resources such as CPU, memory, motherboard, graphics card, and network card, and installs a guest operating system on it. The end-user's program runs in the guest operating system.

Virtual machines can support the dynamic sharing of physical resources and resource pools and improve resource utilization, especially for those different loads whose average demand is far lower than the need to provide dedicated resources for them. This way of virtual machine operation has the following advantages.

1. Reduce the number of terminal equipment

    Reduce the number of terminal equipment and reduce maintenance and management costs. Using virtualization technology can effectively reduce the number of managed physical resources such as servers, workstations, and other equipment, curb the growth of such equipment, and hide part of physical resources' complexity. Simplify public management tasks through automation, access to better information, and central management. Realize load management automation, support the use of common tools on multiple platforms, and improve staff efficiency.

    Integrating multiple systems into one host through virtualization technology can still guarantee one server for one system. Thus, on the basis of not affecting the use of the business, the number of hardware devices can be effectively reduced, and the energy consumption of power resources can be reduced. Simultaneously, it can also reduce the rack location space required by the equipment and avoid the transformation of the computer room environment caused by the increase in the number of equipment.

2. Higher security

Virtualization technology can achieve isolation and division that simpler sharing mechanisms cannot achieve. These features can achieve controllable and secure access to data and services. By dividing the host and the internal virtual machine, you can prevent one program from affecting other programs' performance or causing the system to crash. Even if the original program or system is unstable, it can run safely and isolated. If a comprehensive virtualization strategy is implemented in the future, system administrators can make available fault tolerance planning to ensure business continuity in the event of an accident. By converting operating systems and process instances into data files, it can help realize automated and streamlined backup, replicate, provide more robust business continuity, and speed up recovery after failures or natural disasters. Further development of virtual cluster technology can realize the uninterrupted business function and realize multi-machine hot backup.

3. Higher availability

Virtualize the entire computing infrastructure, and then use specialized software to centrally manage the system and virtual hosts, which can manage physical resources without affecting users. Reduce the management of resources and processes, thereby reducing the complexity of the network management system's hardware architecture. Through centralized, policy-based management, the advantages of end-to-end virtualization technology can be used for both virtual and physical resources, allowing maintenance personnel to handle enterprise-level installation configuration and change management from a central location. Significantly reduce the resources and time required to manage system hardware.

3.1.4 Common Types of Virtualization Technology

In virtualization technology, the virtual entities are various IT resources. According to the classification of these resources, we can sort out different types of virtualization. Here are some common types of virtualization technology.

1. Infrastructure virtualization

Since the network, storage, and file system are all critical infrastructures that support the data center's operation, network virtualization, and storage virtualization are classified as infrastructure virtualization.

Network virtualization refers to the virtualization technology that integrates network hardware and software resources to provide users with virtual network connections. Network virtualization can be divided into two forms: local area network virtualization and wide area network virtualization. In local area network virtualization, multiple local networks are combined into one logical network, or one local network is divided into multiple logical networks, and this method is used to improve the efficiency of large-scale enterprise self-use networks or internal networks of data centers. The typical representative of this technology is virtual local area network (Virtual LAN, VLAN). For wide-area network virtualization, the most common application is Virtual Private Network (VPN). VPN abstracts the network connection, allowing remote users to access the company's internal network anytime, anywhere, without feeling the difference between physical and virtual connections. At the same time, VPN can ensure the security and privacy of this external network connection.

Storage virtualization refers to providing an abstract logical view for physical storage devices. Users can access integrated storage resources through the unified logical interface in this view. Storage virtualization mainly has two forms: storage virtualization based on storage devices and network-based storage virtualization. Disk array technology (Redundant Array of Inexpensive Disks, RAID) is a typical storage virtualization based on storage devices. This technology combines multiple physical disks into a disk array and uses inexpensive disk devices to achieve a unified, high-performance of fault-tolerant storage space. Network Attached Storage (NAS) and Storage Area Network (SAN) are typical representatives of network-based storage virtualization.

2. Software virtualization

In addition to virtualization technology for infrastructure and systems, there is another virtualization technology for software. For example, the programs and programming languages used by users have corresponding virtualization concepts. Currently, this type of virtualization technology recognized in the industry mainly includes application virtualization and high-level language virtualization.

Application virtualization decouples the application program from the operating system and provides a virtual operating environment for the application program. In this environment, application virtualization includes the executable file of the application and the runtime environment it needs. When a user needs to run a program, the application virtualization server can push the user's program components to the application virtualization operating environment of the client in real time. When the user completes the operation and closes the application, his changes and data will be uploaded to the centralized management server. In this way, users will no longer be limited to a single client and can use their applications on different terminals.

High-level language virtualization solves the problem of migration of executable programs between computers with different architectures. In high-level language virtualization, programs written in high-level languages are compiled into standard intermediate instructions. These intermediate instructions are executed in an interpreted execution or dynamic translation environment to run on different architectures. For example, the widely used Java virtual machine technology removes the coupling between the lower level system platform (including hardware and operating system) and the upper-level executable code to achieve cross-platform execution of code. The user's Java source program is compiled into platform-neutral bytecode through the compiler provided by the JDK, which is used as the input of the Java virtual machine. The Java virtual machine converts bytecode into binary machine code executable on a specific platform, so as to achieve the effect of "compile once, execute everywhere."

3.2 Basic Knowledge of Server Virtualization

3.2.1 System Virtualization

System virtualization is the most widely recognized and accepted virtualization technology. System virtualization realizes the separation of operating system and the physical machine, so that one or more virtual operating systems can be installed and run on a physical machine at the same time, as shown in Fig. 3.2. From the perspective of the applications inside the operating system, there is no significant difference between the virtual operating system and the operating system directly installed on the physical machine.

The core idea of system virtualization is to use virtualization software to virtualize one or more virtual machines on a physical machine. A virtual machine refers to a logical computer system that uses system virtualization technology to run in an isolated environment and has complete hardware functions, including a guest operating system and its application programs. In system virtualization, multiple operating systems can run simultaneously on the same physical machine without affecting each other, reusing physical machine resources. There are various system virtualization technologies, such as system virtualization applied to IBM z-series mainframes, system virtualization applied to IBM p-series servers based on Power Architecture, and system virtualization applied to x86 architecture personal computers. For these different types of system virtualization, the virtual machine operating environment's design and implementation are not the same. However, the

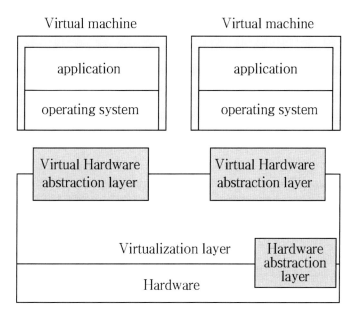

Fig. 3.2 System virtualization

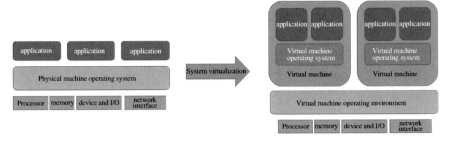

Fig. 3.3 System virtualization

virtual operating environment of system virtualization needs to provide a virtual hardware environment for the virtual machine running on it, including virtual processors, memory, devices and I/O, network interfaces, etc., as shown in Fig. 3.3. At the same time, the virtual operating environment also provides many features for these operating systems, such as hardware sharing, system management, and system isolation.

The more excellent value of system virtualization lies in server virtualization. At present, a large number of x86 servers are used in data centers, and a large data center often hosts tens of thousands of x86 servers. For safety, reliability, and performance considerations, these servers only run one application service, leading to low server utilization. Since servers usually have strong hardware capabilities, if multiple virtual servers are virtualized on the same physical server, each virtual server runs a different service, increasing server utilization, reducing the number of machines, and reducing operating costs. Save physical storage space and electrical energy so as to achieve both economic and environmentally friendly purposes.

In addition to using virtual machines for system virtualization on personal computers and servers, desktop virtualization can also achieve the purpose of running multiple different systems in the same terminal environment. Desktop virtualization removes the coupling relationship between the desktop environment (including applications and files) of the personal computer and the physical machine. The virtualized desktop environment is stored on a remote server instead of on the personal computer's local hard disk. This means that when the user is working on his desktop environment, all applications and data are running and ultimately saved on this remote server. The user can use any compatible device with sufficient display capabilities to access and use his desktop environment, such as personal computers and smart phones.

3.2.2   Server Virtualization

Server virtualization applies system virtualization technology to servers, virtualizing one server into several servers. As shown in Fig. 3.4, before server virtualization was

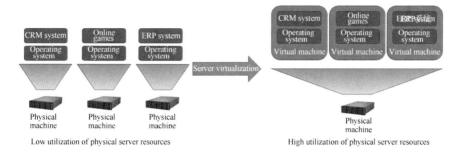

Fig. 3.4   Server virtualization

adopted, three applications were running on three independent physical servers; after server virtualization was adopted, these three applications were running on three separate virtual servers. On the server, the same physical server can host these three virtual servers. Simply put, server virtualization makes it possible to run multiple virtual servers on a single physical server. Server virtualization provides the virtual server with hardware resource abstraction that can support its operation, including virtual BIOS, virtual processor, virtual memory, virtual device I/O, and provides sound isolation and security for virtual machines.

Server virtualization technology was first used in mainframes manufactured by IBM. It was introduced to the x86 platform by VMware in the 1990s, and it was quickly accepted by the industry after 2000, becoming a more popular technology. Seeing the huge advantages of server virtualization, major IT vendors have increased their investments in server virtualization-related technologies. Microsoft's server operating system Windows Server 2008 optional components include server virtualization software Hyper-V and promises that Windows Server 2008 supports other existing mainstream virtualization platforms. At the end of 2007, Cisco announced a strategic investment in VMware through the purchase of shares. Many mainstream Linux operating system distributions, such as Novell's SUSE Enterprise Linux and Red Hat's Red Hat Enterprise Linux, have added Xen or KVM virtualization software, and users are encouraged to install and use it. Virtualization technology is a key direction in technology and strategic business planning by many mainstream technology companies, including Huawei, Cisco, Google, IBM, Microsoft, etc.

3.2.3   Typical Implementation

Server virtualization provides an abstraction of hardware devices and management of virtual servers through virtualization software. At present, the industry usually uses two special terms when describing such software. They are as follows:

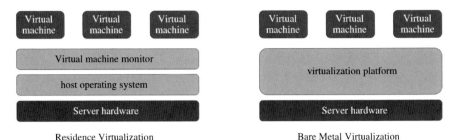

Fig. 3.5 Implementation of server virtualization

Table 3.1 Comparison of implementation methods of server virtualization

Indicators	Residence virtualization	Bare metal virtualization
Does it depend on the host operating system	Fully	Partial
Performance	Low	High
Difficulty of realization	Easy	Difficult

- Virtual Machine Monitor (VMM): responsible for providing hardware resource abstraction for virtual machines and providing a running environment for guest operating systems.
- Virtualization platform (Hypervisor): responsible for hosting and management of virtual machines. It runs directly on the hardware, so the underlying architecture directly constrains its implementation.

These two terms are usually not strictly distinguished, and Hypervisor can also be translated as a virtual machine monitor. In server virtualization, virtualization software needs to implement functions such as hardware abstraction, resource allocation, scheduling, management, isolation between virtual machines and host operating systems, and multiple virtual machines. The virtualization layer provided by this software is above the hardware platform and below the guest operating system. According to the virtualization layer's different implementation methods, server virtualization mainly has two implementation methods, as shown in Fig. 3.5. Table 3.1 shows the comparison of these two implementations.

- Residence Virtualization. VMM is an application program running on the host operating system, which uses the functions of the host operating system to implement the abstraction of hardware resources and the management of virtual machines. Virtualization in this way is easier to implement, but because the virtual machine's resource operations need to be completed by the host operating system, its performance is usually low. Typical implementations of this approach are VMware Workstation and Microsoft Virtual PC.
- Bare Metal Virtualization. In bare metal virtualization, it is not the host operating system that runs directly on the hardware, but the virtualization platform, and the virtual machine runs on the virtualization platform. The virtualization platform

provides instruction sets and device interfaces to provide support for virtual machines. This method usually has higher performance, but it is more difficult to implement. Typical implementations of this approach are Xen Server and Microsoft Hyper-V.

3.2.4 Full Virtualization

From the perspective of the guest operating system, the fully virtualized virtual platform is the same as the real platform, and the guest operating system can run without any modification. This means that the guest operating system will operate the virtual processor, virtual memory, and virtual I/O device just like a normal processor, memory, and I/O device. From an implementation point of view, VMM needs to handle all possible behaviors of the client correctly. Furthermore, the client's behavior is reflected through instructions, so the VMM needs to process all possible instructions correctly. For full virtualization, all possible instructions refer to all instructions defined in the virtual processor's manual specification. In terms of implementation, taking the x86 architecture as an example, full virtualization has gone through two stages: software-assisted full virtualization and hardware-assisted full virtualization.

1. Software-assisted full virtualization

    In the early days of x86 virtualization technology, the x86 system did not support virtualization at the hardware level, so full virtualization can only be achieved through software. A typical approach is a combination of priority compression (Ring Compression) and binary code translation (Binary Translation).

    The principle of priority compression is: because VMM and the client run at different privilege levels, corresponding to the x86 architecture, usually VMM runs at Ring0 level, guest operating system kernel runs at Ring1 level, and guest operating system applications run at Ring3 level. When the guest operating system kernel executes related privileged instructions because it is at the non-privileged Ring1 level, an exception is usually triggered, and the VMM intercepts the privileged instruction and virtualizes it. Priority compression can correctly handle most of the privileged instructions, but because the x86 instruction system did not consider virtualization at the beginning of its design, some instructions still cannot be processed normally through priority compression, that is, when performing privileged operations in the Ring1 level, there is no an exception is triggered, so that the VMM cannot intercept the privileged instruction and deal with it accordingly.

    Binary code translation is therefore introduced to handle these virtualization-unfriendly instructions. The principle of binary code translation is also very simple, that is, by scanning and modifying the client's binary code, instructions that are difficult to virtualize are converted into instructions that support virtualization. VMM usually scans the binary code of the operating system, and once it finds an instruction that needs to be processed, it translates it into an instruction block (Cache Block) that supports virtualization. These instruction blocks can cooperate with VMM to access restricted virtual resources, or explicitly trigger exceptions for further processing by VMM. In addition, because the technology can modify the binary code of the client, it is also widely used in performance optimization, that is, replacing some instructions that cause performance bottlenecks with more efficient instructions to improve performance.

Although priority compression and binary code translation technology can achieve full virtualization, this patching method is difficult to ensure its integrity in the architecture. Therefore, x86 vendors have added support for virtualization to the hardware, thus realizing virtualization on the hardware architecture.

2. Hardware-assisted full virtualization

If many problems are difficult to solve at their level, the next level will become easier to solve by adding one level. Hardware-assisted full virtualization is one such way. Since the operating system is the last layer of system software on top of the hardware, if the hardware itself adds sufficient virtualization functions, it can intercept the execution of sensitive instructions or sensitive to the operating system's sensitive instructions. The resource access is reported to the VMM in an abnormal manner, which solves the virtualization problem. Intel's VT-x technology is representative of this approach. VT-x technology introduces a new execution mode on the processor for running virtual machines. When the virtual machine executes in this particular mode, it still faces a complete set of processor registers and execution environment, but any privileged operation will be intercepted by the processor and reported to the VMM. The VMM itself runs in the normal mode. After receiving the processor report, it finds the corresponding virtualization module for simulation by decoding the target instruction and reflecting the final effect in the environment in the special mode.

Hardware-assisted full virtualization is a complete virtualization method because instructions also carry access to memory and peripherals themselves. The interception of the processor instruction level means that VMM can simulate a virtual host the same as the real host. In this environment, as long as any operating system can run on an equivalent host in reality, it can run seamlessly in this virtual machine environment.

3.2.5 Paravirtualization

Paravirtualization is also called quasi-virtualization. Paravirtualization enables VMM to virtualize physical resources by modifying instructions at the source code level to avoid virtualization vulnerabilities. As mentioned above, x86 has some instructions that are difficult to virtualize. Full virtualization uses binary code translation to avoid virtualization vulnerabilities at the binary code level. Paravirtualization takes another approach: to modify the code of the operating system kernel (i.e., the API level) so that the operating system kernel completely avoids these instructions that are difficult to virtualize.

The operating system usually uses all the processor functions, such as privilege levels, address space, and control registers. The first problem that paravirtualization needs to solve is how to insert the VMM. The typical approach is to modify the processor-related code of the operating system to allow the operating system to actively surrender the privilege level and run on the next level of privilege. In this way, when the operating system tries to execute a privileged instruction, the protection exception is triggered, thereby providing an interception point for the VMM to simulate. Now that the kernel code needs to be modified, paravirtualization can be further used to optimize I/O. In other words, paravirtualization does not simulate real-world devices because too many register simulations will reduce performance. On the contrary, paravirtualization can customize highly optimized I/O protocols. This I/O protocol is wholly based on transactions and can reach the speed of a physical machine.

3.2.6 Mainstream Server Virtualization Technology

Many mainstream virtualization technologies are generally divided into two types: open source and closed source. Open source virtualization technologies include KVM and Xen, and closed source virtualization technologies include Microsoft's Hyper-V, VMware's vSphere, and Huawei's FusionSphere.

Open source virtualization technology is free and can be used at any time. Their source code is public, and users can customize some special functions according to their needs. Open source virtualization technology has high technical requirements for users. Once the system has problems, you need to rely on your own technology and experience to complete the repair of the system. With closed-source virtualization technology, users cannot see the source code, nor can they perform personalized customization. Closed-source virtualization products are generally charged and provide users with "out-of-the-box" services. During use, if there is a problem with the system, the manufacturer will provide full support.

There is no difference between open source and closed source for users, only which one is more suitable.

In the open source virtualization technology, KVM and Xen are equally divided, KVM is full virtualization, and Xen supports both paravirtualization and full virtualization. KVM is a module in the Linux kernel, which is used to realize the virtualization of CPU and memory. It is a process of Linux, and other I/O devices (network cards, disks, etc.) need QEMU to realize. Xen is different from KVM in that it runs directly on the hardware and then runs a virtual machine on it. Virtual machines in Xen are divided into two categories: Domain0 and DomainU. Domain0 is a privileged virtual machine that can directly access hardware resources and manage the DomainU of other ordinary virtual machines. Domain0 needs to be started before other virtual machines are started. DomainU is an ordinary virtual machine and cannot directly access hardware resources. All operations need to be forwarded to Domain0 through the front/back-end driver, and then Domain0 completes the specific operations and returns the results to DomainU.

3.3   Supporting Technology of Server Virtualization

3.3.1   CPU Virtualization

The CPU virtualization technology abstracts the physical CPU into a virtual CPU, and a physical CPU thread can only run the instructions of one virtual CPU at any time. Each guest operating system can use one or more virtual CPUs. Between these guest operating systems, the virtual CPUs are isolated from each other and do not affect each other.

Operating systems based on the x86 architecture are designed to run directly on the physical machine. At the beginning of the design, these operating systems are designed assuming that they completely own the underlying physical machine hardware, especially the CPU. In the x86 architecture, the processor has four operating levels, namely Ring0, Ring1, Ring2, and Ring3. Among them, the Ring0 level has the highest authority and can execute any instructions without restrictions. The run level decreases sequentially from Ring0 to Ring3. Applications generally run at the Ring3 level. The kernel mode code of the operating system runs at the Ring0 level because it needs to control and modify the state of the CPU directly, and operations like this require privileged instructions running at the Ring0 level to complete.

To realize virtualization in the x86 architecture, a virtualization layer needs to be added below the guest operating system layer to realize the sharing of physical resources. It can be seen that this virtualization layer runs at the Ring0 level, and the guest operating system can only run at the level above Ring0, as shown in Fig. 3.6.

However, the privileged instructions in the guest operating system, such as interrupt processing and memory management instructions, will have different

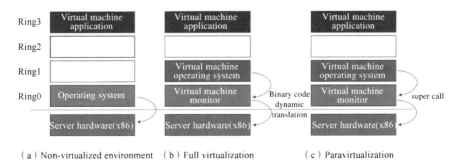

(a) Non-virtualized environment   (b) Full virtualization   (c) Paravirtualization

Fig. 3.6   Software CPU virtualization under the x86 architecture semantics and produce other effects if they are not run at the Ring0 level, or they may not work at all. Due to the existence of these instructions, it is not easy to virtualize the x86 architecture. The key to the problem is that these sensitive instructions executed in the virtual machine cannot directly act on the real hardware but need to be taken over and simulated by the virtual machine monitor.

Full virtualization uses dynamic binary translation technology to solve the guest operating system's privileged instruction problem. The so-called dynamic translation of binary code means that when the virtual machine is running, the trapping instruction is inserted before the sensitive instruction, and the execution is trapped in the virtual machine monitor. The virtual machine monitor dynamically converts these instructions into a sequence of instructions that can perform the same function before executing them. In this way, full virtualization converts sensitive instructions executed in the kernel state of the guest operating system into a sequence of instructions with the same effect that can be executed through the virtual machine monitor, while non-sensitive instructions can be run directly on the physical processor.

Different from full virtualization, paravirtualization solves the problem of virtual machines executing privileged instructions by modifying the guest operating system. In paravirtualization, the guest operating system hosted by the virtualization platform needs to modify its operating system and replace all sensitive instructions with super calls to the underlying virtualization platform. The virtualization platform also provides a calling interface for these sensitive privileged commands.

Whether it is full virtualization or paravirtualization, they are pure software CPU virtualization and do not require any changes to the processor itself under the x86 architecture. However, pure software virtualization solutions have many limitations. Whether it is the fully virtualized binary code dynamic translation technology or the paravirtualized super call technology, these intermediate links will inevitably increase the complexity and performance overhead of the system. In addition, in paravirtualization, support for guest operating systems is limited by the capabilities of the virtualization platform.

As a result, hardware-assisted virtualization came into being. This technology is a hardware solution. The CPU that supports virtualization technology adds a new instruction set and processor operating mode to complete CPU virtualization functions. At present, Intel and AMD have introduced hardware-assisted virtualization technologies Intel VT and AMD-V, respectively, and gradually integrated them into newly launched microprocessor products. Taking Intel VT technology as an example, processors that support hardware-assisted virtualization have added a set of virtual machine extensions (VMX), which adds about 10 instructions to support virtual related operations. In addition, Intel VT technology defines two operating modes for the processor, namely root mode and non-root mode. The virtualization platform runs in root mode, and the guest operating system runs in non-root mode. Since hardware-assisted virtualization supports the guest operating system to run directly on it, there is no need for dynamic translation or hyper-calling of binary codes, thus reducing the related performance overhead and simplifying the design of the virtualization platform.

3.3.2 Memory Virtualization

Memory virtualization technology manages the real physical memory of a physical machine in a unified manner and packs it into multiple virtual physical memories for use by several virtual machines, so that each virtual machine has its own independent memory space. Since memory is the most frequently accessed device by virtual machines in server virtualization, memory virtualization, and CPU virtualization have an equally important position.

In memory virtualization, the virtual machine monitor must manage the memory on the physical machine and divide the machine memory according to the memory requirements of each virtual machine, while keeping the memory access of each virtual machine isolated from each other. Essentially, a physical machine's memory is a contiguous address space, and access to the memory by upper-level applications is mostly random. Therefore, the virtual machine monitor needs to maintain the mapping relationship between the memory address block in the physical machine and the continuous memory block seen inside the virtual machine to ensure that the virtual machine's memory access is continuous. Modern operating systems use segment, page, segment page, multi-level page tables, cache, virtual memory, and other complex technologies for memory management. The virtual machine monitor must be able to support these technologies so that they remain valid in a virtual machine environment and guarantee a high level of performance.

Before discussing memory virtualization, let's review classic memory management techniques. Memory as a storage device is indispensable for applications' operation because all applications must submit codes and data to the CPU for processing and execution through memory. If there are too many applications running on the computer, it will exhaust the memory in the system and become a bottleneck in improving computer performance. People usually use extended memory and optimization procedures to solve this problem, but this method is very costly. Therefore, virtual memory technology was born. For virtual memory, all CPUs based on the x86 architecture are now equipped with Memory Management Unit (MMU) and Translation Lookaside Buffer (TLB) to optimize virtual memory performance. In short, classic memory management maintains the mapping relationship between virtual memory and physical memory as seen by the application.

To run multiple virtual machines on a physical server, the virtual machine monitor must have a mechanism for managing virtual machine memory, that is, a memory virtual management unit. Because a new memory management layer is added, virtual machine memory management is different from classic memory management. The "physical" memory seen by the operating system is no longer the real physical memory, but the "pseudo" physical memory managed by the virtual machine monitor. Corresponding to this "physical" memory is a newly introduced concept-machine memory. Machine memory refers to the real memory on the physical server hardware. In memory virtualization, there are three types of memory: process logical memory, virtual machine physical memory, and server machine

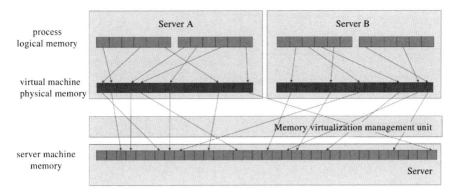

process
logical memory

virtual machine
physical memory

server machine
memory

Server A   Server B

Memory virtualization management unit

Server

Fig. 3.7 Memory virtualization

memory, as shown in Fig. 3.7. The address spaces of these three types of memory are called logical addresses, "physical" addresses, and machine addresses.

In memory virtualization, the mapping relationship between process logic memory and server machine memory is taken care of by the virtual machine memory management unit. There are two main methods for the realization of the virtual machine memory management unit.

The first is the shadow page table method, as shown in Fig. 3.8a. The guest operating system maintains its page table, and the memory address in the page table is the "physical" address seen by the guest operating system. Simultaneously, the virtual machine monitor also maintains a corresponding page table for each virtual machine, but this page table records the real machine address. The page table in the virtual machine monitor is established based on the page table maintained by the guest operating system and will be updated of the guest operating system page table, just like its "shadow,, so it is called a "shadow page" table. VMware Workstation, VMware ESX Server, and KVM all use the shadow page table method.

The second is the page table writing method, as shown in Fig. 3.8b. When the guest operating system creates a new page table, it needs to register the page table with the virtual machine monitor. At this time, the virtual machine monitor will deprive the guest operating system of the write permission of the page table and write the machine address maintained by the virtual machine monitor to the page table. When the guest operating system accesses the memory, it can obtain the real machine address in its page table. Each modification of the page table by the guest operating system will fall into the virtual machine monitor, and the virtual machine monitor will update the page table to ensure that its page table entries always record the real machine address. The page table writing method needs to modify the guest operating system. Xen is a typical representative of this method.

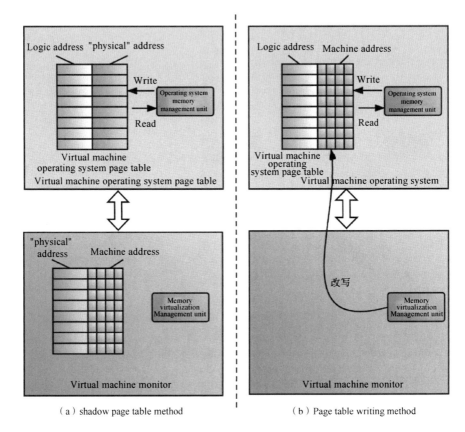

(a) shadow page table method   (b) Page table writing method

Fig. 3.8 Two main methods for implementing the memory management unit of a virtual machine

3.3.3 Device and I/O Virtualization

In addition to CPU and memory, other vital components in the server that need to be virtualized include equipment and I/O. Device and I/O virtualization technology unified management of the real devices of physical machines, packaged them into multiple virtual devices for use by several virtual machines, and responded to the device access requests and I/O requests of each virtual machine.

At present, mainstream equipment and I/O virtualization are all realized through software. As a platform between shared hardware and virtual machines, the virtualization platform provides convenience for device and I/O management and provides rich virtual device functions for virtual machines.

Take VMware's virtualization platform as an example. The virtualization platform virtualizes the devices of physical machines, standardizes these devices into a series of virtual devices, and provides a set of virtual devices that can be used for virtual machines, as shown in Fig. 3.9. It is worth noting that the virtualized device may not completely match the model, configuration, and parameters of the physical

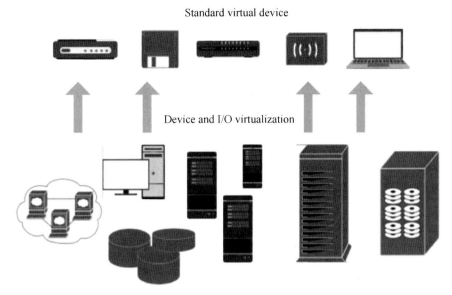

Standard virtual device

Device and I/O virtualization

Different types of server and storage devices

Fig. 3.9 Device and I/O virtualization

device. However, these virtual devices can effectively simulate the actions of the physical device and translate the device operations of the virtual machine to the physical device. And return the running result of the physical device to the virtual machine. Another benefit of this unified and standardized approach to virtual devices is that virtual machines do not depend on the implementation of underlying physical devices. Because for the virtual machine, it always sees these standard equipment provided by the virtualization platform. In this way, as long as the virtualization platform is always consistent, virtual machines can be migrated on different physical platforms.

In server virtualization, the network interface is a unique device that plays an important role. Virtual servers provide services to the outside world through the network. In server virtualization, each virtual machine becomes an independent logical server, and the communication between them is carried out through a network interface. Each virtual machine is assigned a virtual network interface, which is a virtual network card from the inside of the virtual machine. Server virtualization requires modification of the network interface driver of the host operating system. After modification, the network interface of the physical machine must be virtualized with a switch through software, as shown in Fig. 3.10. The virtual switch works at the data link layer and is responsible for forwarding data packets delivered from the physical machine's external network to the virtual machine network interface and maintains the connection between multiple virtual machine network interfaces. When a virtual machine communicates with other virtual machines on the same physical machine, its data packets will be sent out

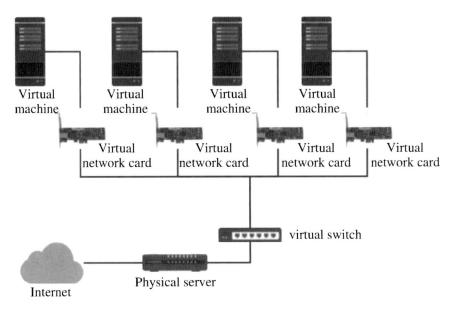

Fig. 3.10 Network interface virtualization

through its virtual network interface, and the virtual switch will forward the data packet to the virtual network interface of the target virtual machine after receiving the data packet. This forwarding process does not need to occupy physical bandwidth because a virtualization platform manages the network in software.

3.3.4 Storage Virtualization

With the continuous development of information services, network storage systems have become the core platform of enterprises. Many high-value data have accumulated, and applications surrounding these data have increasingly higher requirements for the platform. Not only in storage capacity, but also in data access performance, data transmission performance, data management capabilities, storage expansion capabilities, and many other aspects.

RAID technology is the embryonic form of storage virtualization technology. It provides a unified storage space for the upper layer by combining multiple physical disks in an array. For the operating system and upper-level users, they don't know how many disks there are in the server, they can only see a large "virtual" disk, that is, a logical storage unit. NAS and SAN appeared after RAID technology. NAS decouples file storage from the local computer system and centralizes file storage in NAS storage units connected to the network, such as NAS file servers. Heterogeneous devices on other networks can use standard network file access protocols, such as NFS under the UNIX operating system and the Server Message Block (SMB) protocol under the Windows operating system, to follow the permissions of the files on it Restrict access and updates. Unlike NAS, although it also separates storage from the local system and concentrates it on the local area network for users to share and use, SAN is generally composed of disk arrays connected to Fibre Channel. Servers and clients use SCSI protocol for high-speed data communication. SAN users feel these storage resources are the same as the devices directly connected to the local system. The share stored in the SAN is at the disk block-level, while the share stored in the NAS is at the file-level.

At present, not limited to RAID, NAS and SAN, storage virtualization has been given more meaning. Storage virtualization allows logical storage units to be integrated within a wide area network and can be moved from one disk array to another without downtime. In addition, storage virtualization can also allocate storage resources based on users' actual usage. For example, the operating system disk manager allocates 300GB of space to the user, but the user's current usage is only 2GB, and it remains stable for a while, the actual allocated space may only be 10GB, which is less than the nominal capacity provided to the user. When the user's actual usage increases, the appropriate allocation of new storage space will improve resource utilization.

3.3.5 Network Virtualization

Network virtualization usually includes virtual local area networks and virtual private network. A virtual local area network can divide a physical local area network into multiple virtual local area networks, and even divide the nodes in multiple physical local area networks into one virtual local area network. Therefore, the communication in the virtual local area network is similar to the way of physical local area networks and is transparent to users. The virtual private network abstracts network connections, allowing remote users to access the internal network of the organization as if they were physically connected to the network. Virtual private networks help administrators protect the network environment, prevent threats from unrelated network segments on the Internet or Intranet, and enable users to quickly and securely access applications and data. At present, virtual private networks are used in a large number of office environments and become an important supporting technology for mobile office.

Recently, various vendors have added new content to network virtualization technology. For network equipment providers, network virtualization is the virtualization of network equipment, that is, traditional routers, switches and other equipment are enhanced to support a large number of scalable applications. The same network equipment can run multiple virtual network equipment, such as firewalls, VoIP, and mobile services.

The specific content of network virtualization will be introduced in detail in Chap. 4.

3.3.6 Desktop Virtualization

Before introducing desktop virtualization in detail, we must first clarify the difference between server virtualization and desktop virtualization.

Server virtualization is the division of a physical server into multiple small virtual servers. With server virtualization, numerous servers rely on one physical machine to survive. The most common server virtualization method is to use a virtual machine, which can make a virtual server look like an independent computer. IT departments usually use server virtualization to support various tasks, such as supporting databases, file-sharing, graphics virtualization, and media delivery. By consolidating servers into less hardware, server virtualization reduces business costs and increases efficiency. But this kind of merger is not often used in desktop virtualization, and the scope of desktop virtualization is wider.

Desktop virtualization is to replace the physical computer with a virtual computer environment and deliver it to the client. The virtual computer is stored in a remote server and can be delivered to the user's device. Its operation mode is the same as that of a physical machine. One server can deliver multiple personalized virtual desktop images. There are many ways to achieve desktop virtualization, including terminal server virtualization, operating system streaming, virtual desktop infrastructure (VDI), and desktop as a service (DaaS).

Servers are easier to know what to do next than virtual desktops because servers perform the same tasks almost every day. Users need to specify software and tools for server virtualization or use the same management tools for server virtualization and desktop virtualization.

Desktop virtualization usually requires a server to host the virtual image, and sometimes the situation is more complicated. End-users want a good desktop experience, but desktop virtualization cannot accurately predict virtual desktop users' behavior. This means that desktop virtualization needs to support actual computer applications plus all the infrastructure required for virtual desktops. On a regular working day, the machine hosting the virtual desktop may have more workload than other virtual servers.

Desktop virtualization decouples the user's desktop environment from the terminal device it uses. What is stored on the server is the complete desktop environment of each user. Users can use different terminal devices with sufficient processing and display functions, such as personal computers or smartphones, to access the desktop environment through the network, as shown in Fig. 3.11. The most significant benefit of desktop virtualization is using software to configure personal computers and other client devices from a centralized location. The system maintenance department can manage numerous enterprise clients in the data center instead of on the desktop of each user, which reduces on-site support work and strengthens the control of application software and patch management.

Whether it is desktop virtualization or server virtualization, security is an issue that cannot be ignored. In the internal information security of enterprises, the most dangerous element is the desktop device. Many companies have even introduced

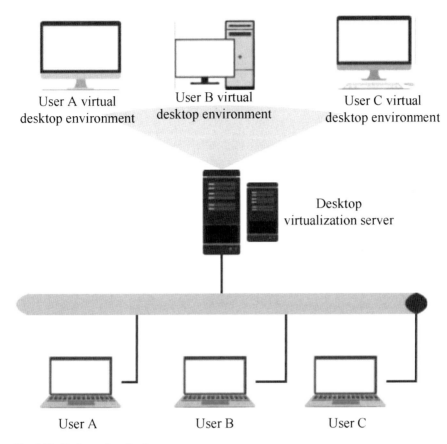

Fig. 3.11 Desktop virtualization

desktop terminal security management software to prevent the hidden dangers of the terminal from affecting the safe operation of other devices in the LAN and the theft of important background data. Through desktop virtualization, all data authentication can achieve consistent policy and unified management, which effectively improves the information security level of the enterprise. Furthermore, through the implementation of desktop virtualization, users can transfer the original terminal data resources and even the operating system to the server in the back-end data center. In contrast, the front-end terminal is transformed into a lightweight display-oriented and computing-assisted client.

Desktop virtualization can help companies further simplify the lightweight client architecture. Compared with the existing traditional distributed personal computer desktop system deployment, the lightweight client architecture deployment service using desktop virtualization can reduce the purchase cost of hardware and software for the enterprise and further reduce the enterprise's internal management cost and risk. With the rapid upgrading of hardware, the increase and distribution of software, and the decentralization of working environments, the work of managing and maintaining terminal equipment has become more and more difficult. Desktop virtualization can reduce the cost of electricity, management, personal computer purchase, operation, and maintenance for enterprises.

Another advantage of desktop virtualization is that because the user's desktop environment is saved as a virtual machine, the user's desktop environment can be snapshot and backed up by taking a snapshot and backup of the virtual machine. When the user's desktop environment is attacked or a major operation error occurs, the user can restore the saved backup, which significantly reduces the maintenance burden of the user and the system administrator.

3.4   Main Functions of Virtual Machine

3.4.1   Virtual Machine Snapshot

In daily life, we will record the beautiful moments in life by taking photos. In virtualization, the "snapshot"of a virtual machine is very similar to taking pictures in our lives. It can record the state of the virtual machine at a certain moment. Through photos, we can retrieve our memories; through snapshots, we can also restore the virtual machine to its state at a certain moment. Virtual machine snapshots are generally used before destructive tests such as upgrading, patching, and testing of the virtual machine. Once the virtual machine fails, the snapshot can be used to restore the virtual machine quickly. The storage system completes the virtual machine snapshot function. The Storage Networking Industry Association (SNIA) defines a snapshot as: an entirely usable copy of a specified data set, which includes the corresponding data at a certain point in time (the point in time when the copy started). A snapshot can be a copy of the data it represents or a copy of the data. Figure 3.12 shows the snapshot.

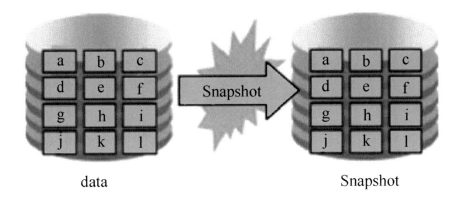

Fig. 3.12   Snapshot

The snapshot has the following characteristics.

Snapshots can be generated quickly and used as a data source for traditional backup and archiving, reducing, or even eliminating the window for data backup. Snapshots are stored on the disk and can be accessed quickly, which improves the speed of data recovery. Disk-based snapshots enable storage devices to have flexible and frequent recovery points. By using snapshots at different time points, accidentally erased or damaged data can be quickly and conveniently restored, and online data recovery can be performed on it.

The snapshot establishes a pointer list to indicate the address where the data is read in terms of specific technical details. When the data changes, the pointer list can provide a real-time data in a very short time and copy it. There are two common snapshot modes: Copy-On-Write (COW) snapshots and Redirect-On-Write (ROW) snapshots. Both COW and ROW belong to the knowledge in the storage field, and most vendors use ROW when creating virtual machine snapshots. No matter it is COW or ROW, there will be no real physical copy action, just make changes on the mapping.

3.4.2   Rapid Deployment and Cloning of Virtual Machines

When we buy a virtual machine on the public cloud, the background will quickly generate a virtual machine with an operating system for us, and it will take much less time than installing the operating system on a computer by ourselves. This is how the use virtual machines can quickly be deployed in virtualization.

The rapid deployment of virtual machines can be achieved in two ways: deployment by template and virtual machine cloning.

The essence of the template is also a virtual machine, which can be understood as a copy of the virtual machine, which also contains the virtual machine disk and the configuration file of the virtual machine. Using templates to create virtual machines can greatly save time for configuring new virtual machines and installing operating systems. After the virtual machine template is created, users are not allowed to start and start at will. This design is to ensure that the template will not be changed due to random editing, and it will never occupy the computing resources of the cluster. The virtual machine deployed using the template and the template are independent of each other. If you want to update or re-edit the template, you need to convert the template to a virtual machine first, and then remake the virtual machine into a template after editing.

Virtual machine templates are very useful for deploying a large number of similar virtual machines because they can maintain the consistency of the virtual machines, and at the same time can automatically modify the parameters (such as host names and security identifiers) that require different parameter values. For example, if an existing group of testers needs to test the company's newly developed software, the administrator can use the virtual mechanism of the software as a template, and then quickly deploy a batch of virtual machines with the same configuration to different

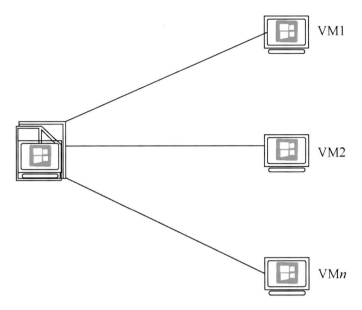

Fig. 3.13 Virtual machine clone

testers. For tests with different scenarios and different requirements, once any problems occur during the testing process, the administrator can delete the faulty virtual machine and then redeploy the same virtual machine to the tester. In addition, different virtual machine templates can contain different software. For example, the template used by financial staff can be pre-installed with the financial system, and the template used by sales staff can be pre-installed with the ERP system. These different templates can be used for the corresponding staff at any time. Create a virtual machine that meets their needs.

In addition to deploying a virtual machine using a template, a virtual machine can also be quickly deployed using the virtual machine itself. This function is called virtual machine cloning (see Fig. 3.13). Different from using template deployment, virtual machine cloning is a complete copy of the source virtual machine at a certain point in time. All cloned virtual machine settings, including personalized data such as hostname and IP address, are identical to the source. The virtual machine is the same. We all know that if two identical IP addresses appear in the LAN, the system will automatically report an error. Therefore, it is best not to start the cloned virtual machine at the same time.

3.4.3   *Virtual Machine Backup*

In the past few years, data protection technology under the virtual server environment has made significant progress. Virtual server backup has evolved from simply backing up virtual machines (just like backing up physical systems) to backing up operating system clients and even dedicated backup programs with all the advantages of virtualization technology.

Anyone who manages a virtual server environment expects backup software for a virtual server environment to have a set of core functions. Of course, not all of them are included, but some mature technologies are needed to bring user experience throughout the backup process.

When evaluating suppliers and their products, it is important to ensure that these functions and features are included, and it is equally important to understand how to implement these technologies when changing from one supplier to another. The following are common backup techniques used in virtual server environments.

1. Changed block tracking

Each backup management software is designed to back up virtual machines and supports Changed Block Tracking (CBT) technology. There is no need to back up the entire virtual machine with CBT technology, only the changed files. When each backup task starts, only the changed blocks of the virtual machine will be backed up. CBT technology effectively reduces the total amount of data backed up to the backup server or backup target through the network.

Usually, when the virtual machine backup software starts to back up, it will take a snapshot of the backup device, so that the state before the backup will be preserved. When performing a CBT backup, the previously backed up virtual machine on the backup device is updated with the changed block. Once the CBT transfer process is completed, the most recent backup data will be retained on the backup device, and the previous backup will be used as a point-in-time recovery in the form of a snapshot.

2. Granular recovery

In the past, CBT backup had a flaw: if you want to restore a file from a backup instance, you must first restore the entire instance. In this respect, CBT is similar to mirror-based backup. However, unlike mirror-based backup, current virtual server backup software can restore part of it, for example, files and mail messages can be restored separately from the mirror.

Generally, granular recovery can be achieved by copying data from the backup device and directly mounting the virtual machine or using the recovery wizard to enter the virtual machine to extract independent components directly. The recovery wizard method is the preferred recovery method because it can be recovered in a few steps on one interface.

3.4.4 Virtualization Cluster

Clustering is a way to combine a group of computers as a whole to provide resources to users. Computing, storage, and network resources can be provided in a virtualized cluster, and the cluster is complete only if they are included.

1. High availability

   The basic principle of high availability: Use cluster technology to overcome the limitations of a single physical host, and ultimately achieve uninterrupted business or reduced interruption time. High availability in virtualization only guarantees the computing level. Specifically, high availability at the virtualization level is the high availability of the entire virtual machine system. That is, when one computing node fails, the other node in the cluster can start it quickly and automatically and replace it.

   Virtualized clusters generally use shared storage. Virtual machines are composed of configuration files and data disks. Data disks are stored on shared storage, and configuration files are stored on computing nodes. When a computing node fails, the virtualization management system (such as vCenter and VRM) will rebuild the failed virtual machine on other nodes according to the recorded virtual machine configuration information.

2. Load balancing technology

   Load balancing is a cluster technology that shares specific services (network services, network traffic, etc.) to multiple network devices (including servers, firewalls, etc.) or multiple links, thereby improving business processing capabilities and ensuring business high reliability. Load balancing has the following advantages.

   - High performance: Load balancing technology distributes services to multiple devices more evenly, improving the performance of the entire system.
   - Scalability: Load balancing technology can easily increase the number of devices or links in the cluster and meet the growing business needs without reducing the quality of the business.
   - High reliability: The failure of a single or even multiple devices or links will not cause business interruption, which improves the reliability of the entire system.
   - Manageability: A large amount of management work is concentrated on the equipment applying load balancing technology, and the equipment group or link group only needs regular configuration and maintenance.
   - Transparency: For users, a cluster is equivalent to a device or link with high reliability and good performance, and users cannot perceive and do not need to care about the specific network structure. Increase and decrease of equipment or links will not affect normal business.

3. High scalability

   In a traditional non-virtualized environment, all services are deployed on physical machines. It is possible that in the early stage of system construction, the business volume is not very large, so the hardware resources configured for the physical machine are relatively low. With the increase in business volume, the original hardware cannot meet the demand, and the hardware can only be upgraded continuously. For example, upgrading the original one-channel CPU to two-channels, and upgrading the 256GB of memory to 512GB, this expansion method is called Scale-Up. However, there is an upper limit on the hardware that a physical machine can bear. If the business volume continues to increase, the server can only be replaced in the end, and it is inevitable to stop and expand the capacity.

In virtualization, all resources are pooled, and all resources that carry service virtual machines come from this resource pool. When the above business volume continues to increase, we do not need to upgrade a single server's hardware resources, but only need to increase the resources in the resource pool. In the implementation, you only need to increase the number of servers. This expansion method is called Scale-Out. The cluster supports horizontal expansion, so it is easier to expand than traditional non-virtualization.

3.4.5 Hot Addition Virtual Machine Resources

Hot additions here refer to adding compute, storage, and network resources to a virtual machine while it is powered on.

From the administrator's point of view, the CPU, memory, and other parameters of the virtual machine are all parameters in the configuration file, the user can modify the hardware configuration of the virtual machine by modifying the corresponding parameters in the configuration file. As shown in Fig. 3.14, CPU and memory usage has reached 75% during the user's use of virtual machines, and the user-side experience can be very poor and may even affect normal usage. At this point, using the functionality added by the virtual machine resource hot, you can add CPU and memory resources to the virtual machine online, so that the user side of the resource utilization quickly down to normal levels.

In addition to CPU and memory, storage and network resources also support hot addition. For example, expanding the capacity of a virtual machine disk, adding a network card to a virtual machine, and so on. In addition to requiring the virtual machine itself to support the hot-added functionality, the virtual machine's operating system must also be supported for the hot-added resources to take effect

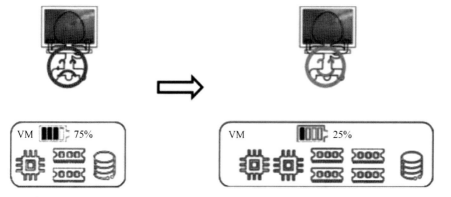

Fig. 3.14 Hot addition of virtual machine resources

immediately. Otherwise, the virtual machine needs to be restarted and only used after the operating system recognizes the hardware resources. In most cases, resources only support heat addition, not reduction. For example, an administrator can scale a virtual machine's disk from 10GB to 20GB, but a reduction from 20GB to 10GB may not necessarily be executable. The addition of storage resources supports the addition of different disks to virtual machines in addition to the expansion of existing disks.

3.4.6 NUMA

Non-Uniform Memory Access Architecture (NUMA) is a technology that improves data read/write speed. In modern times, the computer's single CPU's computing speed has reached the bottleneck, so the designer adopts the multi-core CPU method to improve the computer's computing speed. CPU and memory are connected via Northbridge, and as the number of CPUs increases and memory increases accordingly, the response speed on Northbridge becomes slower and more obvious. As a result, the designers bound memory evenly to each CPU, thus avoiding congestion from sharing the North Bridge. Figure 3.15 shows a multi-way CPU arrangement comparison.

After modification, memory and CPU are bound, the CPU has a shorter response time to read data from the bound memory (local access), and a longer response time to read data across CPU access memory (remote access). Since local access is fast, let the program run with a CPU and its bound memory, which increases productivity, which is NUMA. When NUMA is used, it treats the CPU and the memory bound to it as a NUMA node, each with its own internal CPU, bus, and memory. If you access across nodes, you need to correspond to the virtual machine through the interconnection between CPUs. Using NUMA technology allows virtual machines to use

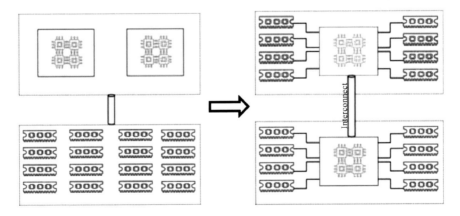

Fig. 3.15 Multi-channel CPU arrangement comparison

hardware resources on the same NUMA node to improve the responsiveness of virtual machines.

3.5   KVM

3.5.1   Introduction to KVM

KVM is an open source virtual machine software based on GPL licensing. KVM was first developed by Qumranet and appeared on the Mailing List of the Linux kernel in October 2006 and was integrated into the Linux 2.6.20 kernel in February 2007 as part of the kernel. The architecture of the KVM is shown in Fig. 3.16. KVM uses a hardware virtualization approach based on Intel VT or AMD-V technology, as well as a combination of QEMU to provide device virtualization. Architecturally, it is argued that KVM is the host model because Linux was not designed with virtualization support in place, and KVM exists as a kernel module. However, as more and more virtualization features are added to the Linux kernel, there is also talk that Linux is already a Hypervisor, so KVM is the Hypervisor model. The promoter and maintainer of the KVM project also considers the KVM to be a Hypervisor model.

KVM supports a variety of hardware platforms, including IA32, IA64, S390, and PowerPC. KVM can also be ported to other operating systems, and there are currently projects to port KVM to Free BSD. KVM is still in its infancy. Today, KVM is proliferating with the addition of many Linux kernel developers. KVM is characterized by a very good combination with the Linux kernel, so KVM inherits

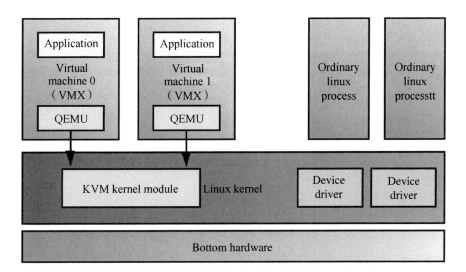

Fig. 3.16 KVM architecture

most of Linux's functionality. Of course, like Xen, KVM is very portable as open source software.

3.5.2   KVM Virtualization Technology

KVM is an x86 hardware based on virtualization extensions (Intel VT or AMD-V) and is a fully native, full virtualization solution for Linux. Some of the virtualization support is mainly used in Linux and Windows client operating systems in quasi-virtual network drivers. KVM is currently designed to support a wide range of customer operating systems, such as Linux, BSD, Solaris, Windows, Haiku, ReactOS, and AROS Research Operating System, through loadable kernel modules.

In the KVM architecture, the virtual machine is implemented as a regular Linux process, scheduled by a standard Linux scheduler. In fact, each virtual CPU appears as a regular Linux process. This enables KVM to enjoy all the features of the Linux kernel. It is important to note that the KVM itself does not perform any simulations and requires the user space program to set the address space of each virtual client server through the /dev/kvm interface, provide it with simulated I/O, and map its video display back to the host's display. At present, this app is the "big name" QEMU.

The functional features of KVM are described below.

1. Memory management

   KVM inherits powerful memory management capabilities from Linux. The memory of a virtual machine is stored like the memory of any other Linux process and can be exchanged in the form of large pages for higher performance or shared as disk files. NUMA allows virtual machines to effectively access large amounts of memory.

   KVM supports the latest hardware-based memory virtualization capabilities, as well as Intel's Extended Page Table (EPT) and AMD's Nested Page Table (NPT) (also known as Fast Virtualization Index-RVI) for lower CPU utilization and higher throughput.

   Memory page sharing is supported by a kernel feature called Kernel Same-Page Merging (KSM). KSM scans each virtual machine's memory, and if the virtual machine has the same memory pages, KSM merges those pages into a page shared between virtual machines, storing only one copy. If a client tries to change this shared page, it gets its own private copy.

2. Storage

   KVM can use any storage supported by Linux to store virtual machine images, including storage devices with IDE, SCSI, SATA interfaces (including mechanical and SSDs), NAS (including NFS and SAMBA/CIFS), or SAN that supports iSCSI and Fibre Channel. Multipath I/O can be used to improve storage throughput and provide redundancy. Because KVM is part of the Linux kernel, it can leverage a mature and reliable storage infrastructure supported by all leading storage vendors, with a well-documented storage stack for production deployments.

KVM also supports virtual machine mirroring on shared file systems such as global file systems (GFS2) to allow virtual machine mirrors to be shared across multiple hosts or using logical volume sharing. Disk mirroring supports on-demand allocation, allocating storage space only when virtual machines need it, rather than allocating the entire storage space in advance, improving storage utilization. KVM's native disk format is QCOW2, which supports snapshots and allows for multiple levels of snapshots, compression, and encryption.

3. Device driver

KVM supports hybrid virtualization, where quasi-virtualized drivers are installed in the customer's operating system, allowing virtual machines to use optimized I/O interfaces instead of analog devices, providing high-performance I/O for networks and block devices. KVM quasi-virtualized drivers use the Virtio standard developed by IBM and Red Hat in the Linux community, which is a stand-alone, build-on device driver interface that allows for better virtual machine interactivity by using the same set of device drivers for multiple hypervisors.

3.6 FusionCompute

3.6.1 Introduction to FusionCompute

FusionCompute is a core component of Huawei's virtualization solutions. By deploying virtualization software on the server, it manages virtualization of computing, storage and network hardware resources and centralizes the management of virtual resources, business resources, and user resources of multiple servers through virtual resource management (VRM) software, forming a clustered virtual resource site and realizing flexible distribution, high reliability, and efficient virtualization resource management system. At the same time, FusionCompute Pro component packages can be deployed to enable unified management of multiple resource sites in different geographies and the ability to enable resource domain management for different users through virtual data centers (VDC).

FusionCompute, eBackup, UltraVR, and other components make up Huawei FusionSphere virtualization suite.

FusionCompute's location in the FusionSphere (version 8.0.0) virtualization suite is shown in Fig. 3.17.

1. Other components in FusionSphere

  (a) Hardware infrastructure layer

   Hardware resources include server, storage, network, security, and other cloud computing basic physical equipment, which supports users from small- to large-scale construction or expansion, and can run various enterprise

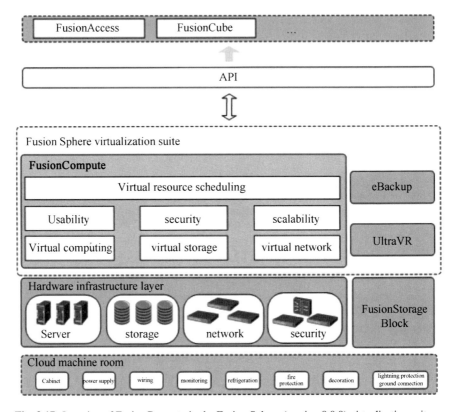

Fig. 3.17 Location of FusionCompute in the Fusion Sphere (version 8.0.0) virtualization suite

applications from entry level to enterprise level. There are many types of equipment, which can provide users with flexible deployment options.

(b) FusionStorage block

FusionStorage Block is a distributed storage software that highly integrates storage and computing. After the software is deployed on a general x86 server, all servers' local hard disks can be organized into a virtual storage resource pool to provide block storage functions.

(c) eBackup

eBackup is a virtualized backup software that cooperates with FusionCompute's snapshot function and CBT backup function to implement FusionSphere virtual machine data backup.

(d) UltraVR

UltraVR is a disaster-tolerant business management software that uses the asynchronous remote replication feature provided by the underlying SAN storage system to provide Huawei FusionSphere with data protection and disaster-tolerant recovery of key virtual machine data.

2. Technical characteristics of FusionCompute
   FusionCompute mainly has the following technical features.

   (a) Unified virtualization platform
       FusionCompute uses virtualization management software to divide com-
       puting resources into multiple virtual machine resources to provide users with
       high-performance, operable, and manageable virtual machines.

       • Support the allocation of virtual machine resources on demand.
       • Support multiple operating systems.
       • QoS guarantees resource allocation and isolates the influence between
         users.

   (b) Support multiple hardware devices
       FusionCompute supports various servers based on x86 or ARM hardware
       platforms and is compatible with a variety of storage devices, allowing
       operators and enterprises to choose flexibly.
   (c) Large cluster
       A single cluster (version 8.0.0) can support up to 128 hosts and 8000
       virtual machines.
   (d) Automated scheduling
       FusionCompute supports customized resource management SLA policies,
       failure judgment standards, and recovery policies.

       • Reduce maintenance costs through unified coordination of IT resource
         scheduling, thermal management, and energy consumption management.
       • Automatically detect the load of servers or services, intelligently schedule
         resources, balance loads of servers and service systems, and ensure a good
         user experience of the system and the service system's best response.

   (e) Perfect authority management
       FusionCompute can provide complete permissions management functions
       based on different roles and permissions and authorize users to manage the
       system's resources.
   (f) Rich operation and maintenance management
       FusionCompute provides a variety of operating tools to achieve control-
       lable and manageable services and improve the entire system's operating
       efficiency. At the same time, it supports "black box" rapid fault location as
       follows:

       • By obtaining the exception log and program stack, the system shortens the
         problem location time and quickly solves the exception problem. Support
         automated health checks.
       • Through automated health checks, the system can promptly detect faults
         and give early warnings to ensure that the virtual machine can be operated
         and managed. Support full Web interface.

- Monitor and manage all hardware resources, virtual resources, user service provisioning, etc. through a Web browser.

(g) Cloud security

FusionCompute adopts various security measures and strategies and complies with information security laws and regulations to provide end-to-end business protection for user access, management and maintenance, data, network, virtualization, etc.

3.6.2 FusionCompute Computing Virtualization

This section will introduce FusionCompute's computing virtualization from five aspects: server virtualization, virtual machine resource management, dynamic adjustment of virtual machine resources, distributed resource scheduling and power management, and virtual machine hot migration.

1. Server virtualization

Server virtualization is the abstraction of server physical resources into logical resources, turning a server into several or even hundreds of isolated virtual servers. Therefore, it is no longer limited by physical boundaries, but makes CPU, memory, disk, I/O, and other hardware into a resource pool that can be dynamically managed, thereby improving resource utilization and simplifying system management. At the same time, hardware-assisted virtualization technology improves virtualization efficiency and increases the security of virtual machines.

(a) Bare metal architecture

The Hypervisor of FusionCompute uses a bare metal architecture to install virtualization software on the hardware to virtualize hardware resources. Due to the use of bare metal architecture, FusionCompute can bring users close to server performance, highly reliable and scalable virtual machines.

(b) CPU virtualization

FusionCompute virtualizes the CPU of a physical server into a virtual CPU (vCPU) for use when the virtual machine is running. When multiple vCPUs are running, FusionCompute will dynamically schedule the physical CPU capabilities among the vCPUs. In FusionCompute 8.0.0, each virtual machine supports a maximum of 255 vCPUs.

(c) Memory virtualization

FusionCompute supports memory hardware-assisted virtualization technology to reduce memory virtualization overhead and improve memory access performance by about 30%. At the same time, FusionCompute supports smart memory reuse strategies, automatically optimizes and combines various memory reuse strategies to achieve a high memory reuse rate. In FusionCompute 8.0.0, each virtual machine supports up to 6 TB of virtual memory.

FusionCompute supports the following memory reuse technologies.

- Memory bubble: The system actively reclaims the physical memory that the virtual machine does not use temporarily and allocates it to the virtual machine that needs to reuse memory. The reclamation and allocation of memory are dynamic, and applications on the virtual machine are unaware. The total amount of allocated memory used by all virtual machines on the entire physical server cannot exceed the server's total amount of physical memory.
- Memory swap: Virtualize external storage into memory for virtual machine use, and store temporarily unused data on the virtual machine on external storage. When the system needs to use these data, it exchanges with the data reserved in the memory.
- Memory sharing: Multiple virtual machines share memory pages with zero data content.

(d) GPU pass-through

FusionCompute supports directly associating the Graphic Processing Unit (GPU) on a physical server to a specific virtual machine to improve the graphics and video processing capabilities of the virtual machine to meet customer demand for high-performance graphics processing capabilities such as graphics and video.

(e) iNIC network card

FusionCompute supports virtualizing the iNIC network card on a physical server and then associates it with multiple virtual machines to meet users' high requirements for network bandwidth. Virtual machines associated with iNIC network cards only support manual migration on hosts that use iNIC network cards in the same cluster.

(f) USB Device Pass-Through

FusionCompute supports directly associating USB devices on physical servers to specific virtual machines to meet users' demand for USB devices in virtualization scenarios.

2. Virtual machine resource management

Customers can create virtual machines through custom methods or based on templates and manage cluster resources. This includes dynamic resource scheduling (including load balancing and dynamic energy saving), virtual machine management (including creating, deleting, starting, shutting down, restarting, hibernation, waking up virtual machines, etc.), storage resource management (including common disks and shared disks), and virtual machine security management (including custom VLANs, etc.). In addition, the QoS of virtual machines (including CPU QoS and memory QoS) can be flexibly adjusted according to the business load.

(a) Virtual machine life cycle management

The virtual machine supports multiple operation modes, and users can flexibly adjust the state of the virtual machine according to the business load. The virtual machine operation method is as follows.

- Create/delete/start/close/restart/query virtual machine

    FusionCompute accepts a request for creating a virtual machine from the business management system and selects appropriate physical resources to create a virtual machine based on the virtual machine specifications (vCPU, memory size, disk size), mirroring requirements, network requirements, etc. defined in the request. After the creation is complete, query the running status and attributes of the virtual machine. In the process of using virtual machines, users can shut down, restart, or even delete their virtual machines. This function provides users with basic virtual machine operation and management functions, which is convenient for users to use virtual machines.

- Sleep/wake up the virtual machine

    When the business is running at a low load, only part of the virtual machines can be reserved to meet business needs, and other idle virtual machines can be hibernated to reduce the energy consumption of the physical server. When a high-load business operation is required, the virtual machine is then awakened to meet the high-load business's normal operation requirements. This function meets the business system's flexibility requirements for resource requirements and can improve the resource utilization of the system.

(b) Virtual machine template

By using the virtual machine template function, the user can define a normalized template for the virtual machine and use the template to complete the creation of the virtual machine.

(c) CPU QoS

The CPU QoS of virtual machines is used to ensure the allocation of computing resources of virtual machines, isolate the mutual influence of computing capabilities between virtual machines due to different services, meet the requirements of different services on virtual machine computing performance, and reuse resources to the greatest extent and reduce costs. When creating a virtual machine, you can specify the corresponding CPU QoS based on the virtual machine's expected deployment service's CPU performance requirements. Different CPU QoS represents different computing capabilities of virtual machines. For a virtual machine with a specified CPU QoS, the system's QoS guarantee for its CPU is mainly reflected in the minimum guarantee of computing power and resource allocation priority.

(d) Memory QoS

Provide virtual machine memory intelligent multiplexing function, relying on memory reservation ratio. Through memory multiplexing technologies such as memory bubbles, the physical memory is virtualized into more virtual memory for use by virtual machines, and each virtual machine can fully use the allocated virtual memory. This function can reuse memory resources to the greatest extent, improve resource utilization, and ensure that at least the reserved size of memory can be obtained when the virtual machine is running, ensuring reliable business operation. The system administrator can set the virtual machine memory reservation according to the actual needs of the user.

(e) Dynamic reuse of virtual resources

When a virtual machine is idle, it can automatically release some of its memory, CPU, and other resources according to the conditions that can be set and return it to the virtual resource pool for the system to allocate to other virtual machines. Users can monitor dynamic resources on the Web interface.

3. Dynamic adjustment of virtual machine resources

FusionCompute supports the dynamic adjustment of virtual machine resources, and users can dynamically adjust resource usage according to business load. The dynamic adjustment of virtual machine resources includes the following aspects.

(a) Adjust the number of vcpus offline/online

Regardless of whether the virtual machine is offline (shutdown) or online, users can increase the virtual machine's number of vCPUs as needed. If you want to reduce the number of vCPUs, the virtual machine needs to be offline. By adjusting the number of vCPUs offline/online, you can meet the demand for flexible computing power adjustment when the business load on the virtual machine changes.

(b) Offline/online adjustment of memory capacity

Regardless of whether the virtual machine is offline or online, users can increase the virtual machine's memory capacity as needed. Like adjusting the number of vCPUs, the virtual machine needs to be offline if the memory capacity is to be reduced. By adjusting the memory capacity offline/online, you can meet the demand for flexible memory adjustment when the business load on the virtual machine changes.

(c) Offline/online mount or unmount virtual network card

When the virtual machine is online or offline, the user can mount or uninstall the virtual network card to meet the business demand for the number of network cards.

(d) Offline/online mount virtual disk

Regardless of whether the virtual machine is offline or online, the user can mount the virtual disk, without interrupting the user's business, increase the storage capacity of the virtual machine, and realize the flexible use of storage resources.

4. Distributed resource scheduling and power management

FusionCompute provides various virtualized resource pools, including computing resource pools, storage resource pools, and virtual networks. Resource scheduling refers to the intelligent scheduling of these virtualized resources according to different loads to balance various resources in the system. While ensuring the high reliability, high availability, and good user experience of the entire system, it effectively improves data center resource utilization.

FusionCompute supports the following two types of scheduling.

(a) Load balancing scheduling

In a cluster, in the process of monitoring the running status of computing servers and virtual machines, if it is found that the business load of each computing server in the cluster is different and exceeds the set threshold, the virtual machine can be implemented according to the load balancing strategy formulated by the administrator in advance. Migration makes the utilization of resources such as CPU and memory of each computing server relatively balanced.

(b) Dynamic energy-saving scheduling

When dynamic energy-saving scheduling is used in conjunction with load scheduling balancing, dynamic energy-saving scheduling can be used only after the load balancing scheduling is turned on. In a cluster, in the process of monitoring the running status of computing servers and virtual machines, if the business volume in the cluster is found to be reduced, the system will concentrate the business on a few computing servers and automatically shut down the remaining computing servers; if it is found in the cluster as the business volume increases, the system will automatically wake up the computing server and share the business.

5. Virtual machine live migration

FusionCompute supports the free migration of virtual machines between hosts on the same shared storage. During the virtual machine migration, there will be no interruption in user business. This function can avoid business interruption caused by server maintenance and reduce the power consumption of the data center at the same time.

3.6.3   FusionCompute Storage Virtualization

This section will introduce FusionCompute's storage virtualization from two aspects: virtual storage management and virtual storage thin provisioning. The specific content of storage virtualization will be introduced in detail in Sect. 5.5.

1. Virtual storage management

Storage virtualization abstracts storage devices as data storage, and virtual machines are stored in their own directories as a set of files in the data storage. Data storage is a logical container, similar to a file system, which hides each storage device's characteristics and provides a unified model to store virtual machine files. Storage virtualization technology can better manage the storage resources of the virtual infrastructure, so that the system can greatly improve the utilization and flexibility of storage resources and improve the uptime of applications.

The storage units that can be packaged as data storage are as follows:

- Logical Unit Number (LUN) divided on SAN storage (including iSCSI or Fibre Channel SAN storage).
- File system divided on NAS storage.
- Storage pool on FusionStorage.
- The local hard disk of the host.
- The local memory disk of the host.
- Data storage can support the following file system formats.
- Virtual Image Management System (VIMS): A high-performance file system optimized for storing virtual machines. The host can deploy the virtual image management system data storage on any SCSI-based local or networked storage devices, including Fibre Channel, Ethernet Fibre Channel, and iSCSI SAN equipment.
- NFS: The file system on the NAS device. FusionSphere supports the NFS V3 protocol and can access the NFS disk designated on the NFS server, mount the disk, and meet storage requirements.
- EXT4: FusionSphere supports server local disk virtualization.

2. Thin provisioning of virtual storage

Virtual storage thin provisioning is a method of optimizing storage utilization by flexibly allocating storage space on demand. Thin provisioning can virtualize a larger virtual storage space for users than the actual physical storage space. Only the virtual storage space that writes data will allocate physical storage space for it, and the virtual storage space that has not written data does not occupy physical storage resources, thereby improving storage utilization.

Thin provisioning of virtual storage is based on disk provision, and administrators can allocate virtual disk files in "normal" format or "compact" format.

- Storage-independent: Thin provisioning of virtual storage has nothing to do with operating system and hardware. Therefore, as long as the virtual image management system is used, thin provisioning of virtual storage can be provided.
- Capacity monitoring: Provide data storage capacity early warning, you can set a threshold, and generate an alarm when the storage capacity exceeds the threshold.
- Space reclamation: Provides virtual disk space monitoring and reclamation functions. When the storage space allocated to the user is large but the actual use is small, the allocated but unused space can be reclaimed through the disk space reclamation function. Currently supports new technology file system (New Technology File System, NTFS) format virtual machine disk recovery.

3.6.4   FusionCompute Network Virtualization

This section will introduce FusionCompute's network virtualization from four aspects: virtual network card, network I/O control, distributed virtual switch (DVS), and virtualized network support IPv6. The specific content of network virtualization will be introduced in detail in Sect. 4.4.

1. Virtual network card

   The virtual network card has its own IP address and MAC address. From a network perspective, the virtual network card is the same as the physical network card. FusionCompute supports smart network cards, which can implement multi-queue, virtual switching, QoS, and uplink aggregation functions to improve the I/O performance of virtual network cards.

2. Network I/O control

   The network QoS strategy provides bandwidth configuration control capabilities, including the following aspects.

   - Bandwidth control based on the sending direction of the network plane: Provides bandwidth control functions based on the network plane. The management plane, storage plane, and service plane are based on physical bandwidth capabilities, and a certain quota of bandwidth is allocated to ensure that traffic congestion on each plane does not affect other planes.
   - Bandwidth control based on the sending direction and receiving direction of port group member interfaces: each member interface of the Port Group provides traffic shaping and bandwidth priority control capabilities.
   - QoS function does not support traffic restriction between virtual machines on the same host.

3. Distributed virtual switch

   The distributed virtual switch's function is similar to that of an ordinary physical switch, and each host is connected to the distributed virtual switch. One end of the distributed virtual switch is a virtual port connected to the virtual machine, and the other end is an uplink connected to the physical Ethernet adapter on the host where the virtual machine is located. Through it, the host and virtual machine can be connected to realize system network intercommunication. Besides, the distributed virtual switch is used as a single virtual switch among all associated hosts. This feature enables virtual machines to ensure that their network configuration remains consistent when migrating across hosts.

4. Virtualized network supports IPv6

   The system supports business plane virtual machine configuration and communication using IPv6 addresses. The virtual machine can support IPv6 single stack, IPv4 single stack or IPv4, and IPv6 dual-stack. The dual-stack is defined in the RFC4213 standard, which refers to the installation of IPv4 and IPv6 protocol stacks on terminal devices and network nodes to achieve information intercommunication with IPv4 IPv6 nodes, respectively. Nodes with IPv4/IPv6 dual protocol stacks are referred to as "dual-stack nodes." These nodes can send and receive IPv4 packets as well as IPv6 packets. They can use IPv4 to communicate with IPv4 nodes, and they can also use IPv6 to communicate with IPv6 nodes.

A device interface configured as a dual-stack can be configured with an IPv4 address or an IPv6 address, or both. The IPv6 address allocation method of virtual machines supports the use of a third-party DHCPv6 server to allocate IPv6 addresses, the use of hardware gateways for stateless address automatic configuration or static IP address injection.

3.7 Desktop Cloud

3.7.1 Introduction to Desktop Cloud

The desktop cloud uses cloud computing and server virtualization technologies to run the computer's desktop in the form of a virtual machine on the virtual background server and provides the desktop virtual machine to the end-user in the form of a cloud computing service. Users can access virtualized desktops in the desktop cloud through remote desktop protocols on dedicated thin clients and ordinary personal computers.

The desktop cloud experience is basically the same as that of a personal computer. It performs the same functions as a personal computer, realizing daily office work, graphics/image processing, and other tasks. Desktop cloud brings the benefits of cost reduction, simple management, easy maintenance, safety and reliability to enterprises, and has been recognized and applied by some industries. Desktop cloud technology has large-scale applications in government offices, bank securities, call centers, school computer rooms, R&D and design units, etc.

3.7.2 Desktop Cloud Architecture and Key Technologies

The desktop cloud architecture is shown in Fig. 3.18.

The desktop cloud architecture is mainly composed of thin clients, network access, consoles, identity authentication, applications, servers, etc.

1. Thin clients

   A thin client is a device that we use on the desktop cloud. It is generally a device embedded with an independent embedded operating system that can connect to the server's desktop through various protocols. In order to make full use of existing resources and maximize the application of IT resources, the architecture also supports some transformations to traditional desktops and installs some plug-ins to make them have the ability to connect to desktops running on the server.

2. Network access

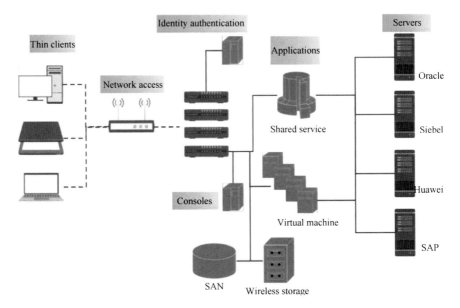

Fig. 3.18 Desktop cloud architecture

The desktop cloud provides various access methods for users to connect. Users can connect through wired or wireless networks. These networks can be local area networks or wide area networks. When connecting, they can use ordinary connection methods or secure connection methods.

3. Consoles

The console can configure the server running the virtual desktop, such as configuring network connections and configuring storage devices. The console can also monitor some basic performance indicators of the runtime server, such as memory usage and CPU usage. If you need to monitor more resources, we can use IBM's Tivoli-related products.

4. Identity authentication

An enterprise-level application solution must have a security control solution. The more important thing in a security solution is user authentication and authorization. In the desktop cloud, users are generally authenticated and authorized through products such as Active Directory or LDAP. These products can easily add, delete, configure passwords, set their roles, and assign different permissions to different roles. Modify user permissions and other operations.

5. Applications

There are some specific application scenarios. For example, the users used are call center operators. They generally use the same standard desktop and standard applications and basically do not need to be modified. In this scenario, the desktop cloud architecture provides a way of sharing services to provide desktops and applications, so that more services can be provided on a specific server.

6. Servers

In desktop cloud solutions, more applications are to distribute various applications to virtual desktops, so that users only need to connect to a desktop to use all applications, as if these applications are installed on the desktop. The experience provided to users under this architecture is the same as using a traditional desktop.

Of course, the architecture shown in Fig. 3.18 is just a rough description of our reference implementation. In a specific application, we should make various decisions in the architecture according to the user's specific situation. These considerations mainly include the type of user, the scale of the user, the user's workload, the user's usage habits, and the user's requirements for service quality. This is a relatively complicated process.

3.7.3 Typical Application Cases of Desktop Cloud

Compared with traditional personal computers for office work, desktop clouds use thin terminals with low hardware configuration as the leading office equipment, which has low cost, information security, easy management, support for mobile office, energy-saving, and environmental protection.

As a concrete embodiment of cloud computing technology, traditional server virtualization technology service providers VMware, Citrix, Microsoft, and other companies have launched desktop cloud solutions. Companies such as IBM and HP also have a lot of investment in desktop clouds, such as IBM's cloud computing smart business desktop solution, Sun's SunRay solution, and Huawei's FusionAccess desktop cloud. Desktop cloud has become a hot spot in the technical field, and major manufacturers will continue to introduce mature overall technical solutions.

Let's take Huawei's desktop cloud application as an example to introduce.

Starting in 2009, Huawei began to deploy desktop clouds at the Shanghai Research Institute (Huawei Shanghai Research Institute for short). About 8000 of the 10,000 employees in the Shanghai Research Institute are R&D personnel. They are mainly engaged in developing technologies and products such as wireless and core networks. These employees no longer need a computer host and can work through thin terminals, LCD monitors, and keyboards. Employees only need to enter the account number and password to connect to the virtual server in the data center and handle daily work anytime, anywhere.

By adopting the desktop cloud system, Huawei Shanghai Research Institute has achieved many resource savings.

In addition, there are many successful application cases of Huawei's desktop cloud. For example, the Dutch National Television (NPO) adopted Huawei's desktop cloud solution FusionAccess to meet the digital new media era's challenges. Huawei helps NPOs build new cloud platforms to improve work efficiency and reduce operation and maintenance costs. Huawei's VDI platform allows NPOs to perform audio and video processing anytime, anywhere.

3.7.4 Introduction to FusionAccess

FusionAccess, a Huawei desktop cloud product, is a virtual desktop application that provides virtual desktop applications by deploying a cloud platform on hardware, allowing end-users to access cross-platform applications and the entire virtual desktop through thin terminals or other devices connected to the network. As of March 2020, Huawei Desktop Cloud has more than 1.1 million users worldwide, while maintaining the No. 1 market in China.

The Huawei FusionAccess solution covers cloud terminals, cloud hardware, cloud software, network and security, consulting and integrated design services, and provides customers with end-to-end cloud office solutions. An example of its solution architecture is shown in Fig. 3.19.

The technologies or components involved in FusionAccess are as follows:

1. HDP

    HDP is called Huawei Desktop Protocol, which is a new generation of virtual desktop transmission protocol developed by Huawei. Through HDP, the thin client can remotely access the virtual desktop. It can achieve clearer and more

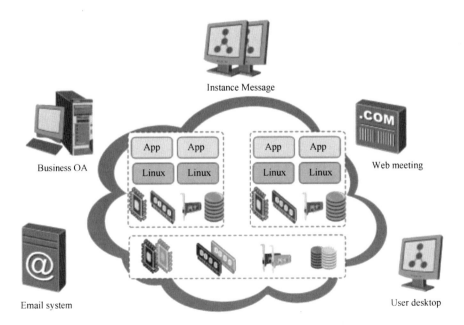

Fig. 3.19 Huawei FusionAccess solution architecture example

detailed text and image display, clearer and smoother video playback, more realistic and full sound quality, better compatibility, and lower bandwidth.

2. Application virtualization

Application virtualization is a set of solutions for delivering applications on demand. It is used to centrally manage applications in the data center and instantly deliver applications to users anywhere and using any device. Application virtualization is based on HDP and is mainly used in four scenarios: simple office, secure Internet access, branch offices, and mobile office.

3. Linux desktop

Huawei FusionAccess supports enterprise users to use Linux or Windows virtual desktops for office work. Users can log in and access virtual desktops using thin terminals, portable computers, smart phones, and other methods.

4. Terminal

The terminal is the terminal device, which is the main device on the terminal user side in the desktop cloud solution. End-users connect to access various virtual desktops on the data center side through this device and connect various peripherals for office use. Currently supported terminals include thin clients, portable computers, tablets, smartphones, etc.

Although it has not been a long time to enter the market, and software and products are constantly being developed and improved, with the continuous deepening of cloud computing applications, Huawei's FusionAccess desktop cloud solution will solve the traditional personal computer office model for customers. Many challenges such as security, investment, and office efficiency bring more ideal solutions and new user experience.

3.8 Exercise

(1) Multiple choices.

1. The following is a compute virtualization of ().

   A. CPU virtualization.
   B. Network virtualization.
   C. Memory virtualization.
   D. I/O virtualization E. Disk virtualization.

2. In Huawei's FusionCompute architecture, the host role is ().

   A. CNA.
   B. UVP.
   C. KVM.
   D. VRM.

3. The following description shows the benefits of virtualization by ().

   A. With virtualization, multiple virtual machines can be run simultaneously on a physical host.

   B. With virtualization, the CPU utilization of a physical host can be stabilized at about 65%.

   C. With virtualization, virtual machines can be migrated between multiple hosts.

   D. With virtualization, multiple applications can run simultaneously on the operating system of a physical host.

(2) Answer the following questions.

1. What is virtualization? What are the characteristics of virtualization?
2. Briefly describe the relationship and difference between virtualization and semi-virtualization.
3. Based on what you have learned, a brief introduction to the supporting technologies for server virtualization and a description of the application scenarios for these technologies.
4. How is memory virtualization different from storage virtualization?
5. What is NUMA? How NUMA works in virtualization?

Chapter 4
Network Basics in Cloud Computing

As mentioned earlier, all clouds must be connected to the network, which provides remote, anytime, anywhere access to IT resources. It can be said that network technology is the essential support of cloud computing. This chapter will introduce the basic network knowledge involved in cloud computing, including an overview of computer networks, the basic principles of computer networks, network interconnection equipment, network virtualization, and software-defined networks, so that readers can better understand some of the important aspects of computer networks, concepts, principles, equipment, and newer network technologies supporting cloud computing.

4.1 Computer Network Overview

Computer network (referred to as network) was born in the 1960s and is a product of the combination of communication technology and computer technology. With the development of network technology, computer networks, a new thing that originally belonged to the field of high-end technology, has gradually penetrated and integrated into people's daily life and profoundly changed people's lifestyles, becoming an indispensable part of people's lives. This section will give an overview of computer networks in terms of basic concepts, formation and development, definitions and functions, composition, classification, and topological structure.

4.1.1 Basic Concepts of Computer Networks

The word "net" in Chinese characters originally refers to a fishing and bird catching device made of ropes such as fishing nets, rope weaving, with small holes in the middle, which can be continuously expanded or connected to several nets according

© The Author(s) 2023
Huawei Technologies Co., Ltd., *Cloud Computing Technology*,
https://doi.org/10.1007/978-981-19-3026-3_4

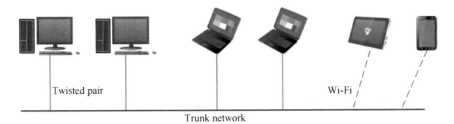

Twisted pair

Wi-Fi

Trunk network

Fig. 4.1 A simple computer network

to needs to cover a larger area. The word "network" has a wide range of meanings. It usually refers to connecting all related things for a certain purpose, such as urban networks, transportation networks, interpersonal networks, and cable TV networks.

In the computer field, a network refers to the connection of multiple computers with independent functions and their peripheral devices in different geographical locations through communication lines. Under the management and coordination of network operating systems, network management software, and network communication protocols, a computer system realizes resource sharing and information transmission. We give this kind of network a proper name: computer network. The network mentioned in the following, unless otherwise specified, refers to a computer network.

Simply put, a computer network is a system that interconnects two or more computers through a connecting medium. The connection medium can be cable, twisted pair, optical fiber, microwave, carrier wave, and communication satellite.

Computer network has the function of sharing hardware, software, and data resources and can centrally process, manage, and maintain shared data. Figure 4.1 shows a simple computer network.

In the era of big data, information has become an essential resource for human survival. The socialization, networking, and integration of the global economy of information have all been greatly affected by computer network technology. The Internet has caused profound changes in people's working methods, learning methods, and even thinking methods. In cloud computing, network technology is one of the core technologies that support cloud computing. All cloud services need to rely on the network, which provides remote access to IT resources anytime, anywhere. In fact, the idea of cloud computing has been around for a long time, but cloud computing has only significantly been developed and widely used in the past 10 years, which is largely due to the popularization of broadband networks. In the 1990s, when dial-up Internet access was used and the network bandwidth was only tens of kilobits per second, cloud services could not be used at all. Therefore, the network is the foundation of cloud computing.

4.1.2 The Formation and Development of Computer Networks

Before creating computer networks, communication mainly relied on the public telephone network, that is, the traditional telecommunications network. The technology used in traditional telecommunications networks is called circuit switching. Before making a call, you must dial the number first. If the dialing call is successful, a physical path is established from the calling end to the called end, and then the two parties can talk to each other. This physical channel is automatically released after the call is finished and hangs up. The traditional telecommunications network is very fragile. Once a switch or a line fails in the communication circuit, the entire communication line will be interrupted. In war situations, this defect can be catastrophic. Therefore, in the early 1960s, the United States proposed to develop a brand-new network that is highly survivable in a war environment. Later, a flexible packet-switched network was born. This type of network is the predecessor of modern computer networks.

Unlike traditional telecommunications networks that use circuit-switching technology, packet-switching networks use packet-switching technology, and its core technology is store-and-forward technology. Assuming that the sender wants to transmit a batch of data (called a message) to the receiver, he will first divide the message to be sent into data segments of equal length and add a header before each data segment. The header usually contains important information such as source address and destination address, also called "header." This information can help packets independently select routes in the network. The data segment with the header added is called a packet, and the packet is the basic data unit transmitted in the computer network. Figure 4.2 shows the structure of the group.

The packet switching network comprises several computer equipment called node switches and the links connecting these node switches. Each node switch has a set of input ports and a set of output ports, which are, respectively, connected to different node switches. When the node switch receives a packet from an input port, it will temporarily store it in the memory of the node switch, and then look up the routing table pre-stored in the node switch (the routing table has information about

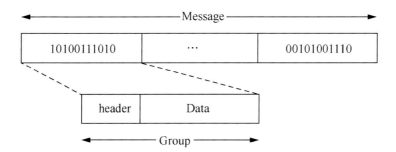

Fig. 4.2 Group structure

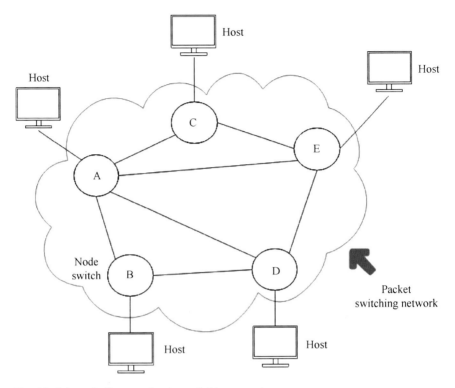

Fig. 4.3 Schematic diagram of packet switching network

which destination address should be forwarded from and which port), and then the packet is forwarded to the found port. The node switch here can be regarded as the predecessor of the modern router.

After the packet switching network divides the data into multiple packets, each packet is independently transmitted in the network according to the destination address stored in the header. The transmission path (i.e., route) of different packets may be different, and then the receiver sorts the received packets after reorganization into a complete message. There is no need to establish a link in advance in the communication process, and each group is independently routed. This is similar to sending a letter through the post office. Each letter contains the recipient's address, and the post office will send it independently according to this address. Even if it is the same destination address, the route of delivery may be different.

A to E shown in Fig. 4.3 are node switches, which receive packets from the host, temporarily store them in the memory, and then look up the local routing table to find a suitable output link to send the packets. Different packets, even if the destination address is the same, may have different transmission paths. Because the routing table will be updated according to the current network conditions, the original route will be replaced with a new route if it fails or is congested.

The advantage of packet switching is that in the process of data communication, the communication line is occupied section by section, that is, only the section of the entire communication line that is currently transmitting packets is occupied, and the other sections are idle and can be used for the transmission of other packets. This is equivalent to dynamically allocating bandwidth in the packet transmission process, which is very suitable for transmitting computer data with bursty characteristics and can greatly increase communication lines' utilization rate. Packet switching also improves the reliability of the network. Since packet switching networks often use mesh topology, there are generally multiple paths to the same destination address. Therefore, when network congestion occurs or a small number of nodes or links fail, the route can be flexibly changed without causing communication interruption. Or the paralysis of the entire network. The disadvantage of packet switching is that each node will always cause a certain delay due to queuing during storage and forwarding. When the network traffic is large, the delay may also be large. At the same time, the control information carried by each packet will also cause a certain amount of overhead. The entire packet-switched network also needs a special management and control mechanism.

In the 1960s, computer networks using packet switching technology appeared. In December 1969, an experimental network with four nodes was put into operation. This was the original form of ARPANET. With the development of technology, ARPANET has proliferated. By the 1980s, there were more than a thousand hosts. At the same time, the National Science Foundation (NSF) built the National Science Foundation Network (NSFnet) and merged with ARPANET, renamed the Internet, which is now called as the Internet. The Internet was mainly used for scientific research in the early days, and the users were mainly a small group of scientific researchers. However, the emergence of the World Wide Web technology in the 1990s caused the Internet to explode. The World Wide Web was developed by the European Organization for Nuclear Research (CERN) and is a combination of information discovery technology based on the client/server model and hypertext technology. The World Wide Web server organizes information into hypertext with both pictures and texts through HTML and uses links to jump from one site to another, which completely simplifies the way of information query and makes the Internet almost no barrier to use. A large number of users began to "embrace" the Internet, with more than 200 million Internet users in the late 1990s. In the twenty-first century, the Internet has developed into an ocean of information resources covering the world. Online content services cover all aspects of social life, and the Internet has become an indispensable part of people's lives. According to statistics, by the end of 2018, the number of Internet users worldwide has reached 3.9 billion.

The success of the Internet has continuously "evolved" computer networks. The early terminal-oriented computer network was a star-shaped network centered on a single host. A large host connects to many terminal devices without processing capabilities. These terminal devices shared the hardware and software resources of the expensive central host through communication lines. The packet switching network is centered on the network. The node switches in the network are used to forward packets for data transmission. The host and terminal devices are located on the periphery of the network, forming a user's resource subnet. Users can share many software/hardware resources of the user resource subnet through the packet-switched network. In order to compare with the user resource subnet, some documents refer to the packet switching network as the communication subnet.

4.1.3 Definition and Function of Computer Network

The previous article has defined computer networks when introducing the basic concepts. In brief, a computer network is a whole system in which multiple computer systems with independent functions are interconnected through communication lines, and network resource sharing and communication are realized under the management of network software. It can be said that a computer network is a product of the combination of computer technology and communication technology. The network mainly uses packet switching technology to realize data transmission, which is essentially a packet switching network.

There are two main purposes for building a computer network: sharing resources and realizing data communication. Perhaps the earliest purpose of establishing a computer network was to share expensive computer hardware equipment, but people soon discovered that communication and data transmission between networked computers can be very convenient. Therefore, data exchange and communication have also become essential functions of the network. Resource sharing can share not only hardware equipment but also software, data, etc. The Internet's attractiveness to people is mainly due to the vast amount of information that can be shared on the Internet, which we call "content services." These content services are provided by hundreds of millions of Websites worldwide, covering all aspects of social life.

In addition to the two major functions of resource sharing and data communication, computer networks also bring some additional benefits. If a network interconnects multiple independent computer systems to form a cluster system, its reliability will also significantly increase. If a computer fails and cannot provide services to the outside world, other computers in the network can replace it and continue to provide services to the outside world. In a cloud computing system, cloud services' reliability relies on multiple connected devices of the same type. At the same time, through networking, it is also convenient to balance the load among the computers to prevent certain computers from failing due to overload.

4.1.4 The Composition of a Computer Network

A typical computer network can be logically divided into two parts: resource subnet and communication subnet. The resource subnet is composed of hosts, terminals and peripherals, various software resources and information resources, and is mainly responsible for the entire network's information processing, providing network services and resource sharing functions for network users. The communication subnet is the packet switching network mentioned above, which is composed of node switches, communication lines, and other communication equipment. It is mainly responsible for the data communication of the whole network, providing the network users with data transmission, transfer, processing and transformation and other communication processing work.

In the modern wide area network structure, as the number of users using mainframe systems decreases, resource subnets have also changed. The resource subnet can be regarded as composed of all the computers or devices connected to the Internet to provide resource services or resource sharing. The node switches in the communication subnet are replaced by network devices such as routers and switches.

From the perspective of the physical composition of a computer network and computers and communication lines, the network also contains a large number of network software/hardware. Computer network software mainly includes network protocol software, network communication software, network operating system, network management software, and network application software.

- Network protocol software: to realize network protocol functions, such as TCP/IP, HTTP, and other protocol software.
- Network communication software: software used to realize communication between various devices in the network, such as QQ, WeChat, and Douyin.
- Network operating system: to realize the sharing of system resources and manage the access to different resources by user processes. Typical network operating systems include Windows, UNIX, Linux, NetWare, etc.
- Network management software and network application software: network management software is used to manage network resources and maintain the network; network application software provides various services for network users, such as Internet cafe charging system and stock trading software.

4.1.5 Classification of Computer Networks

Based on the characteristics of computer networks, there are also many forms of division. For example, it can be classified according to geographic scope, scope of use, and transmission medium, and it can also be classified according to information exchange methods and topological structures.

1. Classification by geographic region

    Classified by geographic area, the network can be divided into three types: local area network, metropolitan area network (MAN), and wide area network.

    (1) Local area network

    The local area network is usually installed in a building or campus (park), covering a geographic range of tens to thousands of meters. For example, a laboratory, a building, a campus, or a unit.

A local area network comprises computers connected by high-speed lines, with a high transmission rate, up to 10 Mbit/s to 1000 Mbit/s. Through the local area network, various computers can share resources, such as sharing printers and databases.

(2) Metropolitan area network

The metropolitan area network is confined to a city, covering a geographic range of tens of kilometers to hundreds of kilometers. The metropolitan area network is an extension of the local area network, used to connect the local area network, covering a wide range in terms of transmission media and wiring structure.

(3) Wide area network

The WAN's geographic range is hundreds of kilometers to thousands of kilometers, or even tens of thousands of kilometers. This range can be a region or a country, or even the whole world, so it is called a wide area network.

The wide area network is different from the local area network and the metropolitan area network in terms of technology, application scope, and protocol standards. In the wide area network, the backbone network or various public switching networks provided by the telecommunications department are usually used to interconnect computer systems distributed in different regions to achieve resource sharing. The Internet is a typical wide area network.

The main technology used in WAN is store and forward technology.

2. Classification by scope of use

Classified by the scope of use, the network can be divided into public and private networks.

(1) Public network

The public network is usually set up, managed, and controlled by the telecommunications department. The transmission and switching devices in the network can be provided (such as leased) for use by any department and unit, such as the Public Switched Telephone Network (PSTN), Digital Data Network (DDN), and Integrated Services Digital Network (ISDN).

(2) Private network

A specific unit or department establishes the private network, and other units or departments are not allowed to use it. For example, industries such as finance, petroleum, and railways have their own private networks. When setting up a private network, you can lease the transmission lines of the telecommunications department, or you can lay the lines yourself, but the cost of the latter is very high.

3. Classified by Transmission Medium

According to the classification of transmission media, the network can be divided into the following two categories:

(1) Wired network

Wired network refers to a network that uses wired physical media such as coaxial cables, twisted pairs, and optical fibers to transmit data.

(2) Wireless network

Wireless network refers to a network that uses wireless forms such as radio waves, satellites, microwaves, and lasers to transmit data.

4. Classified by Application Type

Classified by application type, the network can be divided into Intranet, Extranet, and Internet.

(1) Intranet

Intranet refers to the intranet of an enterprise, which is composed of internal computers and equipment, network environment, software platform, etc., for security reasons, usually only allows access to the internal data center or internal shared resources of the enterprise and does not allow access to extranets and the Internet. It is generally isolated from the extranet by a firewall.

The intranet uses the same technology as the Internet, uses TCP/IP as the communication protocol, Web services as the core, and uses a firewall to isolate the internal network from the external network. Intranet is usually established within an enterprise or organization and provides its members with services such as information sharing and exchange, such as the World Wide Web, which provides file transfer and e-mail.

Since the intranet adopts the mature Internet protocol represented by TCP/IP, it retains compatibility with the Internet. A large number of readymade software/hardware are available, and the construction cost is greatly reduced, which enables the rapid development of the intranet. Compared with the Internet, enterprises have more autonomy in the construction, organization, and management of the intranet, which effectively avoids the inherent short-comings of the Internet such as poor reliability, no overall design, unclear network structure, lack of unified management and maintenance. The security of the network firewall also protects the secret or sensitive information inside. Therefore, the intranet is vividly referred to as the Internet built within the corporate firewall.

What the intranet provides is a relatively closed network environment. This network is hierarchical and open within the enterprise, and internal personnel can generally access it directly, but access by external personnel requires strict authorization. Therefore, the network can be planned and entirely controlled according to the needs of the enterprise, and the security

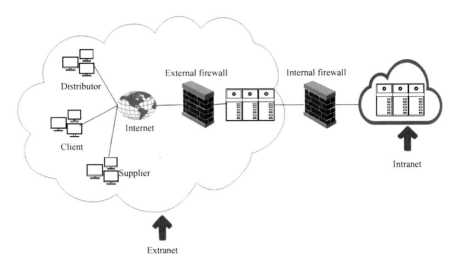

Fig. 4.4 Intranet and Extranet

of the network and data can be ensured by implementing classified management of all information and personnel and setting access control permissions.

(2) Extranet

Extranet is a cooperative network that uses information technology to
interconnect the networks of companies with their customers or assist companies to accomplish their common goals. Users can access it through
different technologies, such as using IP tunnels, VPNs, or dedicated dial-up
networks.

The openness of the extranet lies between the public Internet and the
private intranet. It is neither like the Internet providing public communication
services for the public nor is it like an intranet only serving the enterprise's
internal services and not open to the public, but it is open to selected partners
or provides selective services to the public. Access to the Internet is semi-
private, users are groups formed by affiliated companies and customers, and
information is shared within trusted groups. Extranet is very suitable for time-
sensitive information sharing and activities between enterprises to accomplish common goals.

Figure 4.4 shows the intranet and extranet.

(3) Internet

This part has been included in Sect. 4.1.2

4.1.6 Topology Structure of Computer Network

Topological structure refers to the geometric arrangement between the network's communication lines and each site (computer or network communication equipment, hereinafter referred to as nodes). Classified by topology, the network can be divided into bus network, star network, tree network, ring network, mesh network, hybrid network, etc.

1. Bus-type structure and bus-type network
   A bus-type structure is formed by connecting several nodes by a bus, and its network is called a bus-type network. The bus network uses broadcast communication, that is, multiple nodes can receive the information sent by one node on the network. The bus network's communication lines can be twisted pairs, coaxial cables, fiber-optic cables, etc.
   Bus-type structure is widely used, and its characteristics are as follows:

   (1) Simple structure, expandable, good performance.
   (2) The reliability of the network is high, the response speed between nodes is fast, and the ability to share resources is strong.
   (3) The cost of the network is low, the amount of equipment input is small, the installation is convenient.
   (4) The performance and reliability of the bus have a great impact on the network.

2. Star structure and star network
   The structure that takes the central node as the center and connects several peripheral nodes is called a star structure, and its network is called a star network. The central node centrally controls and manages the communication and information exchange between peripheral nodes in the star structure.
   The features of the star structure are as follows:

   (1) It is easy to build a network, with good scalability and convenient management.
   (2) The central node is the bottleneck of the entire system. If the central node fails, the entire network will be paralyzed.
       The star structure is widely used in local area networks. The central node of the star structure is usually a hub, switch, or router. Take a hub as an example. It connects multiple computer devices through twisted pair cables, presenting a star-shaped topology on the physical structure (although the logical structure is not necessarily a star).

3. Tree structure and tree network
   In a tree network composed of a tree structure, each node (usually a computer) forms a tree-shaped hierarchical structure.

The functions of the low-level computers in the tree are related to the application and generally have well-defined and highly specialized tasks, such as data collection and transformation; while the high-level computers have management functions to coordinate the work of the system, such as data processing, command execution, and comprehensive processing.

Generally speaking, the level of the tree structure should not be too many to avoid the management load of the high-level nodes is too heavy.

4. Ring structure and ring network

In a ring network composed of a ring structure, nodes are connected into a closed loop through point-to-point communication lines. Data will be transmitted station by station along one direction in the ring.

The structure of the ring network is simple, and the transmission delay is determined. However, the communication line between each node in the ring and the connecting node will become a risk point of network reliability. Once a failure occurs, it will affect the normal operation of the entire network. For a ring network, the joining and exiting of network nodes, the maintenance and management of the ring are more complicated.

5. The Mesh Structure and Mesh Network

In a mesh structure, nodes are connected to each other through transmission lines, and any node is connected to at least two other nodes. Therefore, the mesh network made up of mesh structure has high reliability, but its realization is expensive, complex structure, not easy to manage and maintain.

The wide area network basically uses a mesh structure.

6. Hybrid Topology and Hybrid Networks

As you can see from the introduction above, each topology has its own advantages and disadvantages. Some large networks are usually not a single topology, but are a mixture of multiple topology structures, giving full play to various topology strengths, which is called a hybrid topology. The corresponding network is a hybrid network. The Internet is actually a hybrid network.

Figure 4.5 shows the topology of the computer network.

4.2 Network Layering and Encapsulation

Computer network is a very complex system. Take, for example, the simplest two computers that transmit data over the network: first, there must be a path for data transfer between the two computers; if it is not consistent, the format conversion needs to be completed, and if the sender sends the data too quickly and the receiver is too late to receive it, the sender must also be notified to slow it down. In addition, errors or accidents may occur during data transmission, and both parties should have reliable measures in place to deal with anomalies and ensure that the recipient

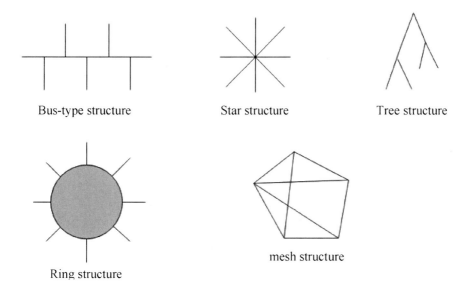

Bus-type structure   Star structure   Tree structure

Ring structure

mesh structure

Fig. 4.5 Topological structure of computer network

receives the data correctly. All this requires a high degree of coordination between the two parties to the communication, strict compliance with the pre-agreed rules, which are network protocols.

4.2.1 Network Layering and Encapsulation

A network protocol is a rule, standard, or convention established for data exchange in a network. General network protocols are complex. To simplify the design of a network, the practice of "layering" the network is often adopted. "Layering" transforms large and complex global problems into smaller, relatively simple local problems that are easy to study and deal with.

Once the network is layered, the layers are independent, and each layer does not need to know how its next layer is implemented, only what services the next layer can provide for the layer, which is provided through an interface between the layers. Since each layer implements only one relatively independent function, the complexity is greatly reduced. Layering also brings benefits such as flexibility, ease of implementation, and maintenance.

When a network is layered, the layers of a computer network and a collection of its protocols, called the network architecture, can be seen as an accurate definition of the functionality that the computer network and its components should accomplish. There are currently two main computer network architectures: the Open System Interconnection (OSI) model developed by the International Organization for Standardization (ISO) in the 1980s, and the TCP/IP model adopted by the Internet. OSI

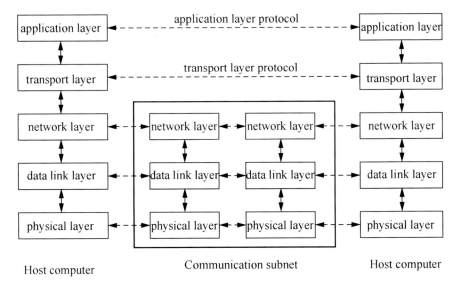

Fig. 4.6 Hierarchical structure of computer network

model has seven levels, the concept is clear, but because it is complex and not practical, did not get echo in the industry, and no corresponding physical products appear, and TCP/IP model although simple structure, but from practice, easy to use, the successful application on the Internet has also made it widely used in the market, become a de facto industrial standard. At present, the vast majority of network devices are compatible with the TCP/IP model.

There are many protocols in the TCP/IP model, and TCP and IP are typical of them, so all protocols in the model are collectively referred to as TCP/IP protocol sets, or TCP/IP for short. The protocol set has the following characteristics: protocol standards are open (independent of hardware, operating system), independent of specific network hardware, unified network addressing (network address uniqueness), and standardized high-level protocols provide a variety of services. These characteristics have also contributed to the wide application of the protocol set in industry.

The TCP/IP model actually has only three layers: the application layer, the transport layer, and the network interface layer, which is almost empty. For the sake of the integrity and systematization of the knowledge system, we moved the bottom two layers of the OSI model (physical layer and data link layer) into the network interface layer, forming a five-tier model (see Fig. 4.6).

In this hierarchy, application data is passed between the layers: assuming that the application AP1 of computer 1 transmits data to the application AP2 of computer 2, AP1 first hands over its data to the application layer (Layer 5), the application layer adds the necessary control information H5 and then passes it to the transport layer (Layer 4), and the transport layer adds its own control information H4 and then hands over to the network layer (Layer 3), and the network layer adds its own control

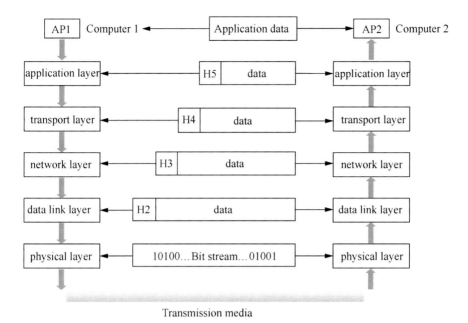

Fig. 4.7 Data transfer process between various layers of the network

information H3 and then transmits it down in turn. The physical layer (Layer 1) is bitstream transmission, so do not add control information. The transfer of data between layers of the network is shown in Fig. 4.7.

4.2.2 Physical Layer

The physical layer specifications are characteristic standards for transport media, and they often refer to standards developed by other organizations. The physical layer's task is to transparently transmit the bit stream, i.e., the unit of data passed on the physical layer is the bit of the binary. Some of the physical media used to transmit information, such as twisted pairs, coaxial cables, and fiber-optic cables, do not belong to the physical layer, but are below the physical layer and are not included in the network architecture.

The physical layer considers how much voltage is used to represent "1" or "0" and how the receiving end can tell whether this level is high or low when the sending end emits a high or low voltage. The physical layer also needs to determine how many pins the plugs connecting the cables should have and how they are defined and connected. The physical layer often uses multiple specifications to complete the definition of all details.

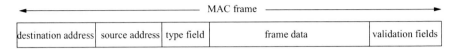

Fig. 4.8 Structure of MAC frame

4.2.3 Data Link Layer

The data link layer first divides the bitstream transmitted by the physical layer into frames, each containing data and the necessary control information. The primary task of the data link layer is to transfer frame-based data without error between two adjacent computer nodes. When transferring data, if the receiving node detects an error in the received data, notify the sender to resend the frame until it is received correctly by the receiver. Also avoid situations in which the sender sends too fast to receive the receiver. In this way, the data link layer transforms an actual link that can go wrong into an error-free data link for use by the network layer above. In order to do this, the frame needs to contain the corresponding control information, including synchronization information, address information, error control information, traffic control information, and so on.

A local area network is a network that contains two levels of data link layer and physical layer. There are several protocol standards for local area networks, such as the IEEE 802 series. There is more content in the LAN data link layer, which is usually divided into two sub-layers: the Logical Link Control (LOGIC Link Control, LLC) sub-layer and the Media Access Control (MAC) sub-layer. The MAC sub-layer's well-known protocol is the IEEE 802.3 standard, commonly known as the Ethernet standard. Ethernet is a broadcast link in which all computer nodes are connected to a shared transmission channel called a "bus" and messages are sent using carrier Sense Multiple Access with Collision Detection (CSMA/CD) protocol. The CSMA/CD protocol principle is that each connected computer site detects whether there are other computers on the bus that are sending data before sending it, and if so, temporarily does not send it to avoid collisions. As soon as the channel is detected to be idle, data frames are sent. However, it is still possible that multiple sites are sending data at the same time, causing a conflict. So the sending station needs to continue listening to the channel after sending the data frame, and if a listening conflict occurs, discard the sending of the data frame immediately, and then the parties to the conflict wait a random period of time to send it again. The computer site's behavior in this protocol can be summed up as: "listen first, then send, conflict stop, listen while sending, random reseeding."

Frames transmitted on MAC sub-layers, we call MAC frames. Mac frames for Ethernet, which typically contain fields such as destination address, source address, type field, frame data, and validation fields. The destination address and the source address each account for 6B, called MAC address, also known as physical address. This address usually corresponds to the address of the network card; network equipment manufacturers in the production of network cards will give this network card a unique MAC address. The structure of the MAC frame is shown in Fig. 4.8.

4.2.4   Network Layer

The network layer in the TCP/IP model is often referred to as the Internet Layer or IP layer. The network layer is responsible for providing communication services to different computers on the Internet. These computers may not be directly connected, and communication between the two computers may pass through multiple inter-mediate nodes and links or pass through multiple communication subnets connected through a router.

At the network layer, the transmission units of data are grouped. Grouping is the addition of a network layer control information, called the first grouping (or header), before a frame at the data link layer. The network layer's primary task is to select the appropriate route so that the packet sent by the sender is transmitted along the appropriate path to the receiver. At the same time, it is also the network layer's task to determine a unique address for both parties to the communication in the network. For example, TCP/IP identifies the host's address throughout the Internet through an IP address. In addition, sometimes limited by the maximum transmission unit length of the lower transmission medium (e.g., the maximum transmission unit of Ethernet (Maximum Transmission Unit, MTU) is limited to 1500B), the grouping of the network layer needs to be subdivided into smaller packets, and the segmentation method is also defined at this layer.

4.2.5   Transmission Layer

The primary job of the transport layer is to be responsible for end-to-end commu-nication. The "end" here refers to the computer process on which the communication is made. A process, which means a running application. Today's computers are generally multitasking operating systems, a computer may run multiple applications simultaneously, such as making PPT to report to the leadership, while using QQ chat listening to music. We can think of an application as a process (some applications correspond to multiple processes), such as QQ chat, the sender's process is an "end," the receiver's process is another "end," and the transport layer is responsible for the data transfer between the two "ends." There are two main ways to transfer data. A connection needs to be established before transmission is made and then transmitted over the connection, and error recovery is required if errors are found and mecha-nisms such as traffic control. This approach is a connection-oriented service that provides reliable data delivery at an inflexible and inefficient price. This approach corresponds to TCP. The other way is similar to the postal system express delivery, each group brings its destination address, before transmission does not need to establish a connection in advance, and according to the network conditions at that time to choose their own transmission path. Data in this way is transmitted on the principle of "best-effort delivery" and does not guarantee reliable data delivery but is flexible and efficient. This corresponds to the User Datagram Protocol, UDP.

The transmission layer exists only in the computer host outside the communication subnet, and there is no transmission layer for switching nodes and network devices such as routers within the communication subnet. The transmission layer solves the problem of information transmission, and the above level, such as the application layer, no longer has to consider the matter related to data transmission.

4.2.6 Application Layer

The application layer is the highest level in the network architecture, which provides communication services directly to the user's processes, such as support for the user's Web access (HTTP), e-mail transmission (SMTP, POP, etc.), file transfer (FTP), and remote login (Telnet protocol). Application-layer protocols typically use services provided by lower level protocols, such as TCP of the transport layer to establish data paths when accessing webpages with HTTP.

4.3 Network Interconnection Equipment

Different computer networks can be connected by internet-connected devices to form a larger network and realize data communication and resource sharing between networks. There are many kinds of Internet-connected devices that work at different levels of network protocols. Common network-connected devices include repeaters, hubs, bridges, switches, and routers.

4.3.1 Repeaters and Hubs

Network-connected devices that work at the physical layer are primarily repeaters and hubs.

1. Repeater

    Repeaters are used to connect the same two types of networks, and their primary function is to extend the network transmission distance of the signal by resending or forwarding the data signal.

    Computer data is generally modulation and transmission using electrical signals, such as high, low, or flat jumps commonly used in computers to represent the "0" or "1" of the binary number. General electrical signals are transmitted on the communication medium, and the greater the distance loss. If the signal is transmitted on a normal twisted pair line, the maximum distance that can be transmitted directly generally does not exceed 100 m, and the signal attenuation is obvious if the distance is further away, and the receiver may not be able to distinguish the contents of the original signal after receiving the signal. Assuming a high level of "1" and a low level of "0", if the signal is attenuated by transmission, the original "1" electrical signal, once the amplitude attenuation is lowered below the set threshold level, it is impossible to determine whether the signal represents "1" or "0". Repeaters are designed to solve this problem. It completes the physical line's connection, amplifies and shapes the attenuated signal, makes the waveform and strength of the signal reach the required indicator, and then forwards it. Therefore, the use of repeaters can extend the length of the network, often used to connect the same LAN segment.

2. Hubs

Hubs are highly reliable internet-connected devices commonly used in star networks. Using the IEEE 802.3 (Ethernet) standard, local area networks are heavily built using twisted pairs and hubs.

Each hub has multiple ports, each connected to the network card of the computer connecting to the network through transmission media such as twisted pairs or fiber-optic cables, forming a star-shaped physical topology. Each port can send and receive data, i.e., when the hub receives data from a port, it regenerates it, shapes it, and forwards it to all other ports. If both ports have data input simultaneously, a conflict occurs and all ports do not receive the correct data.

The hub functions very much like a repeater, so the device also works on the physical layer. For Ethernet, which is widely used today, although it is physically a star structure, the hub uses electronic devices to simulate the actual cable work. It receives data from a port and forwards it to all ports, similar to the Ethernet protocol in which the computer sending data is broadcast on the bus as a public transmission channel, so it is still a bus structure, and the computer nodes connected to the network use Ethernet protocol sharing or competing logic bus.

Multiple hubs can be stacked together to form a stacked group of hubs. Modular smart hubs have a high degree of reliability, all of their network functions are implemented in the form of modules, each module can be hot-swappable, in the event of a failure can be replaced or added new modules. Modern hubs generally have a small amount of fault tolerance and network management capabilities, the panel indicators can also show and locate the network failure situation, to network management brings great convenience, is one of the most commonly used network interconnection devices in lanyons.

4.3.2   Bridges and Switches

Network-connected devices that work at the data link layer are primarily bridges and switches.

1. Bridges

A bridge, also known as a bridge, was an early storage/forwarding device that connected several LAN segments, usually with two or more ports, each connected to a segment. The main function of the bridge is to forward the frames of the received data link layer by destination address, so the bridge has the function of filtering frames. When a frame is received, the bridge does not forward to all ports like a hub, but instead checks the destination address contained in the frame and decides which port the frame is forwarded from based on the destination address.

Bridges do this through internal port management software and bridge protocol entities. It works at the data link layer, allowing LAN segments to connect and isolate conflicts (i.e., computers on both segments send information at the same time without causing conflicts), thereby reducing the load on the extended LAN, which is equivalent to filtering traffic for each segment. Simultaneously, the use of bridges can connect different types and different rates of local area networks, expand the physical scope of the network, and improve the reliability of the network. If one segment fails, other segments will not be affected due to the filtering of the bridge. However, because the bridge needs to store and forward the received frames, the transmission delay of the frames is increased.

2. Switches

There are many types of switches, such as traditional telephone networks, which also use switches, but this is mainly an Ethernet switch that can be seen as an upgrade to a bridge.

The switch is also a network-connected device that works at the data link layer and is characterized by an exclusive electrical signal path for any two network nodes connected to the switch, which is also a significant difference from the hub. The hub forwards the information it receives to all ports, and the switch views the destination address of the information frame and forwards it only to the segment where the destination address is located.

The switch has multiple ports, each with a bridle function that acts as a multi-port bridge. The switch decides which port to forward to based on the destination address contained in each frame, a forwarding decision that generally does not take into account other information hidden deeper in the frame. The forwarding latency of the switch is small and the forwarding performance is better than that of the bridge. Modern switches often also have physical addressing, error checking, traffic control, and other functions. Some of today's premium switches also have VLAN and link aggregation capabilities, and even routing and firewall capabilities.

All ports of the switch are logically exclusive to bandwidth, i.e., enjoy the same theoretical bandwidth as the switch, with efficient data transfer and no waste of network resources. On the one hand, the switch only forwards data frames to the network segment where the destination address of the data frame is located, which is generally not easy to generate network congestion, on the other hand, the switch provides a separate channel for each networked computer, and it is difficult for computers other than the destination address to listen to the sent messages when sending data, which also improves the security of data transmission.

Switches are popular in the industry because they are cost-effective, highly flexible, relatively simple, and easy to implement.

4.3.3 Router

Network-connected devices that work at the network layer mainly have routers.

A router is a network-connected device, also known as a gateway, that connects multiple networks or segments. It works on a network layer that transmits data units that are grouped. The primary function of a router is to choose a suitable route for the grouping to be transmitted. It reads the destination address in each received packet, then looks up the routing table stored inside the router, and decides which path to choose based on the routing table to transmit the packet out. Routers can understand different protocols, which can analyze and interpret the destination addresses of groupings from different types of networks, and then transmit the groupings to the destination computer in the best path according to the selected routing protocol.

Because the primary function of a router is to find the best transport path for the grouping that passes through the router and pass that packet to the destination node error-free, the strategy for choosing the best route, the routing protocol, is the key to the router. Common routing protocols used on the Internet include Routing Information Protocol (RIP), Open Shortest Path First (OSPF), and Border Gateway Protocol (BGP).

To implement the routing capabilities of a router, the router typically holds a data structure called a routing table. How is this routing table formed? This depends on what routing protocol is used.

For example, in the case of the OSPF protocol, all routers in the network maintain a link-state database that can be seen as a topology diagram of the entire Internet. The router's link state is which networks or routers the router is adjacent to and the "cost" of sending these groups to those networks or routers. The "cost" here is not necessarily the money spent, but also distance, delay, bandwidth. According to certain rules, each router calculates its routing table based on the link-state database data, such as Dijkstra's shortest path routing algorithm. Each routing table contains many entries, each of which typically contains the network number of the destination node, the next router, and the current router's cost to the next router. After the router receives a grouping, by looking up the routing table, you can know which routers the next station will group to, and then find the least expensive one from the entries corresponding to those routers, which is the "next router" that the group will transmit. An entry called "default routing" is often added to the routing table, and once the network where the grouping destination node is located is not found in the routing table, the grouping is sent along the default route. The OSPF protocol relies on frequent exchanges of information between routers to establish a link-state database and maintain database-wide consistency. Whenever there is any change in the network topology, the link state database can be updated quickly, enabling individual routers to recalculate the new routing tables. Table 4.1 gives an example of a routing table structure.

The subnet mask in Table 4.1 is used to extract the IP address's network address. Each of the 4 bytes in the subnet mask is converted into a binary number (e.g., 255 corresponds to 8 number of 1), corresponding to the "1" bit, that is, the network

Table 4.1 Example of routing table structure

Destination network	Subnet mask	Next stop router	Cost (hop count)
192.168.27.0	255.255.255.0	193.176.27.1	3
202.120.87.224	255.255.255.224	202.120.87.1	1
202.120.87.224	255.255.255.224	202.120.87.128	2
202.176.50.128	255.255.255.248	222.90.78.1	3

address, corresponding to the "0" bit, is the host address. If the IP address of a destination node is 202.120.87.236, the corresponding subnet mask is 255.255.255.224 because the binary number of the last byte 224 is 1110 00000, the first 3 bits of the binary number in the bytes are 1, plus the first 3 bytes are 255 to indicate that the first 24 bits of binary numbers are 1, so this subnet mask indicates that the IP address of the first 27 bits is the network address, the last 5 bits are the host address. So the IP address 202.120.87.236 network address is the first 27 bits of the address binary number (the IP address and subnet mask can be bit by bit), to get the network address 202.120.87.224. When the router wants to forward a grouping with the destination address of 202.120.87.236, it looks up the destination network with address 202.120.87.224 from the routing table, which finds two items. However, the first item costs the least (the least jump). So the next router selects 202.120.87.1.

If the network size is large, then there will be many entries in the routing table, each packet transmission needs to be routed to find, there will be a large delay, affecting the efficiency of network communication. The default gateway is used. The default gateway is a computer or network node in the computer network that is responsible for forwarding packets to other networks, and it functions like the default route and is the last choice when the route is forwarded, using the default gateway if there are no other appropriate routing entries.

Routers are more powerful than bridges and switches. It can connect different types of networks, resolve the control information corresponding to the grouping network layer (including the source and destination addresses), and select the optimal route for the grouping. Some routers also have administrative capabilities to monitor data transfers, report statistics to the management repository, diagnose internal or other connectivity issues, and trigger alarm signals. Modern routers also provide support for features such as VPNs, firewalls, virtual servers, dynamic DNS, and more. However, the router's data processing speed is much slower than the switch, in order to meet some high-speed networking requirements, some high-end switches fuse some routing functions, can work in the third layer of the network high-speed switching equipment.

Although some high-end switches also have some routing capabilities, they still have many differences.

First, switches and routers do different things. The switch is responsible for high-speed data exchange via a dedicated integrated circuit (Application Specific Integrated Circuit, ASIC) chip, while the router maintains routing between segments of the router, which is inherently isolated from the broadcast domain. But even if routers have switching capabilities, or switches have routing capabilities, their primary functionality remains unchanged, and the new additions are just an add-on that cannot be used as a primary feature.

Secondly, the switch is mainly applicable to LAN, routers are generally applicable to wide area network. Lannet is characterized by frequent data exchange, a single network interface, a large number of switches can provide fast data forwarding, generally provide network cable interface (RJ45) and fiber-optic interface two, and each switch generally has more interfaces, can fully meet the needs of lanyard network. There are many types of networks and interfaces for wide area networks, and router routing is often very powerful, not only between lanyons with the same protocol, but also between local area networks and wide area networks with different protocols. The advantage of routers is that they have the functions of optimal routing, load balancing, link backup, routing information exchange, etc.

Finally, routers and three-tier switches perform differently. Technically, there is a clear difference between routers and three-tier switches in packet switching. Routers typically perform packet exchange by microprocessor-based software routing engines, while three-tier switches perform packet switching through hardware. After routing the first traffic, the three-tier switch produces a map of MAC address and IP address, according to which the same data stream passes directly from the second layer without rerouting, thus avoiding the network delay caused by router routing selection and improving the efficiency of packet forwarding.

At the same time, the three-tier switch routing is for the data flow, it uses ASIC technology caching mechanism, can easily achieve fast forwarding, greatly save costs, while router forwarding using the longest matching method, usually using software to achieve, the implementation of complex, low forwarding efficiency. Therefore, from the overall performance comparison, the performance of the three-tier switch is much better than the router, very suitable for the local area network with frequent data exchange, and the router although the routing function is very powerful, but its packet forwarding efficiency is much lower than the three-tier switch, more suitable for different network types, but the data exchange is not very frequent interconnection, such as the local area network and the Internet interconnection. If the router, especially the high-end router used in the LAN, can be said to be a waste (in terms of its powerful routing function), but also cannot meet the needs of LAN communication performance, affecting the normal communication between subnets.

4.4 Network Virtualization

Network virtualization is one of the basic core technologies supporting cloud computing and plays a vital role in the cloud computing system. Starting from the concept of network virtualization, this section introduces traditional network virtualization and virtual switch-based virtual networks and also the network characteristics of virtualization products using Huawei's virtualized network devices as an example.

4.4.1 Overview of Network Virtualization

Cloud computing is a new computing model based on the principle of distributed computing. Although cloud computing has more flexible service capabilities for multiple users than previous grid computing and service computing, distributed computing is still the foundation of cloud computing. Therefore, computer networks play an important role in all aspects of cloud computing: cloud service providers need to coordinate the management and scheduling of resources through the network and integrate different types of resources for users to access in the form of services. In contrast, users of cloud computing need to access cloud services over the network. These requirements present significant challenges to the network architecture of cloud computing systems. In order to meet these challenges, modern cloud computing network architecture explores a series of effective solutions from infrastructure construction, network behavior control, virtualization of network resources, and management of network functions.

Traditional network equipment is a real visible physical equipment, such as a switch has a specific physical, can touch, can manually plug in the port network cable. In addition to traditional physical network devices, there are many network devices are virtualized in cloud computing. These virtualized network devices may be applications running inside the server and connecting these virtual network devices is often no longer a real network cable but may be a routing message in the routing table, and this new way of virtualizing devices also brings new challenges to network management.

4.4.2 Traditional Network Virtualization

Network virtualization simulates multiple logical networks on a physical network.

Traditional network virtualization content generally refers to VPN, VLAN, and virtual network devices. VPNs abstract the concept of network connectivity, allowing remote users to access an enterprise or organization's internal network as if they were physically connected to that network. VLANs are a logical set of devices and users based on physical local area networks that are not limited by physical location and can be organized according to factors such as functionality, department, and application, communicating with each other as if they were in the same network segment, hinge VLAN.

Network virtualization can help protect IT environments from threats from external networks such as the Internet, while enabling users to access applications and data quickly and securely. Let's cover VPN and VLAN, respectively.

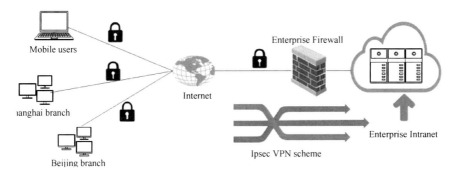

Fig. 4.9 An example of IPsec VPN

1. VPN

A VPN is a temporary, secure connection over a public network, usually the Internet, a secure, stable tunnel through a chaotic public network. The tunnel allows data to be encrypted to use the Internet safely. Simply put, VPNs are private networks that take advantage of public networks, including authentication, encryption, tunneling, and firewall capabilities.

VPN is a remote access technology that is an extension of the enterprise intranet. VPNs can help remote users, corporate affiliates, business partners, and suppliers establish trusted secure connections to the company's Intranet, enabling them to access the resources of the company's Intranet using a VPN, whether they are traveling abroad or working from home, as long as they have Internet access. VPN can be realized by server, hardware, software, and many other ways, mainly using tunneling technology, addition/decryption technology, key management technology, user, and device authentication technology.

There are three main types of tunneling protocols commonly used for VPNs: IP Security (IPSec), Point to Point Tunneling Protocol (PPTP), and layer 2 Tunneling Protocol (L2TP). Among them, IPsec protocol is the standard to protect IP secure communication, it mainly encrypts and authenticates IP packets and is the tunnel protocol that works on the third layer of the network. PPTP is a protocol for establishing IP VPN tunnels on the Internet and a tunneling protocol that works on the second layer of the network. L2TP is a virtual tunneling protocol that works on the second layer of the network and is typically used for VPNs. L2TP itself does not provide encryption and reliability verification capabilities and can be used in combination with security protocols such as IPsec to enable encrypted data transfer. Figure 4.9 gives an example of an IPsec VPN.

2. VLAN

VLAN is a virtual LAN that network administrators can logically divide into different broadcast areas according to the actual application needs of different users in the same physical LAN. Each VLAN is equivalent to a separate local area network. The same VLAN computer users can be interconnected. The computer users between different VLANs cannot communicate directly, the need for

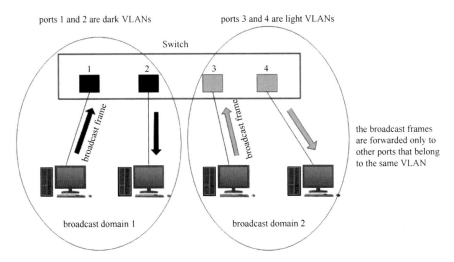

Fig. 4.10   VLAN plays a role in separating broadcast domains

routing configuration to achieve the interconnection of computers between different VLANs.

In a computer network, a two-tier network (a network that contains only the data link layer and the physical layer, such as a local area network) can be divided into several different broadcast domains, one for a specific group of users, which by default are isolated from each other. To communicate between different broadcast domains, you need to forward it over a router.

The concept of broadcast domains is involved here. A broadcast domain, usually corresponding to a local area network with Ethernet technology. Ethernet is characterized by all computers connected to a common bus, data is sent using CSMA/CD protocol, networked computers if there is data to be sent, the data will be broadcast directly on the public bus, but only the destination computer will receive data. There is a problem with this type of broadcasting, which can create conflicts when two networked computers send data at the same time. The solution to Ethernet is to have both parties to the conflict wait a random period of time before resending. But if the broadcast domain is large and there are many computers in it, conflicts can easily occur. So how do you make the broadcast domain small? The technology you use frequently is VLAN.

VLAN is a communication technology that logically divides a physical LAN into broadcast domains. Hosts within the same VLAN can communicate directly with each other, while hosts within different VLANs cannot communicate directly, limiting broadcast frames to one VLAN, as shown in Fig. 4.10.

In Fig. 4.10, if you have a two-tier switch with no VLAN set, any broadcast frame is forwarded to all ports except the send port, but if you have two VLANs in dark and light colors on the switch, ports 1 and 2 are dark VLANs, and ports 3 and 4 are light VLANs, the broadcast frames are forwarded only to other ports that belong to the same VLAN. This isolates the broadcast domain.

Ethernet_II frame

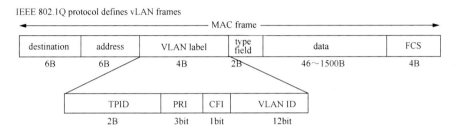

Fig. 4.11 VLAN tag structure of Ethernet frame

With VLAN, you can benefit from the following.

- limit broadcast domains: Broadcast domains are limited to one VLAN, saving bandwidth and increasing network processing power.
- enhances the security of local area networks: messages within different VLANs are isolated from each other at the time of transmission, i.e., users within a VLAN cannot communicate directly with users within other VLANs.
- improves the robustness of the network: failures are limited to one VLAN, and failures within one VLAN do not affect the normal operation of other VLANs.
- Build virtual workgroups flexibly: VLAN allows you to divide different users into different teams. Users in the same team don't have to be limited to a fixed physical scope. Networks are easier and more flexible to build and maintain.

So how does VLAN work? In fact, VLAN is a 4B VLAN-specific identity that is added to a traditional Ethernet data frame, called the 802.1Q Tag. This name is taken because the implementation of VLAN is defined by a protocol standard called IEEE 802.1Q. The 802.1Q label contains a 12-bit VLAN identifier (VLAN ID), which distinguishes between different VLANs. Figure 4.11 shows the VLAN label structure of the Ethernet frame. Among them, the TP ID is called Label Protocol Identifier, which represents the type of data frame. PRI is Priority, which represents the 802.1Q priority of the data frame. CFI, which means that the MAC address is encapsulated in a standard format in different transmission media for compatibility with Ethernet and token ring networks. VLAN ID field represents the number of the VLAN to which the data frame belongs.

Packets sent by each switch that supports the IEEE 802.1Q protocol contain a VLAN ID to indicate which VLAN the switch belongs to. Therefore, in a VLAN switching network, Ethernet frames come in two forms.

- Tagged frame: A frame with a 4B 802.1Q label added.
- Untagged frame: The original frame that is not labeled with a 4B 802.1Q.
- The ports of the operating system or switch can label data frames, and in general, the addition and removal of this label is done by the switch, so there are two link types in the VLAN.
- Access link: A link used to connect a user host to a switch. Typically, hosts don't need to know which VLAN they belong to, and host hardware often doesn't recognize frames with VLAN tags. Therefore, the frames sent and received by the host are unmarked frames.
- Trunk link: Used for connections between switches or between switches and routers. The trunk link can carry data from multiple different VLANs, and when the data frame is transmitted over the trunk link, the devices at both ends of the trunk link need to recognize which VLAN the data frame belongs to, so the frames transmitted on the trunk link are marked frames.

When the IEEE 802.1Q protocol defines vLAN frames, some device interfaces recognize VLAN frames, while others do not. According to the interface's recognition of VLAN frames, the interface can be divided into the following two categories:

- Access interface: The access interface is the interface on the switch that connects to the user's host and can only access the link. Only a unique VLAN ID is allowed to pass through this interface, which is the same as the interface's default VLAN ID. Ethernet frames sent by the access interface to the receiving device are always unmarked frames.
- Trunk interface: The trunk interface is an interface on the switch that is used to connect to other switches and can only connect trunk links, allowing data frames (marked) from multiple VLANs to pass through.

Each type of interface can be configured with a default VLAN and a port with a default VLAN ID, typically 1.

In summary, VLAN increases the flexibility, security, and reliability of a network by logically dividing a physical LAN into broadcast domains. VLAN works on layer 2 and layer 3 of the network hierarchy, a VLAN is a broadcast domain, and communication between VLANs is done through layer 3 routers.

Technologies such as VLAN can also be used to build so-2 networks. A computer network like Ethernet that contains only the physical and data link layers is called a Layer 2 (L2) network. Multiple L2 networks can be connected over bridges or switches to form larger L2 networks, called the so-called so-2 networks. The Layer 3 (L3) network also contains a network layer, and multiple L3 networks form the Internet over a router connection. A data center may have multiple L2/L3 networks, and multiple data centers can be interconnected through L2/L3 switches. Another reason for introducing a so-2 network is the scale scalability requirement. Because support for the number of devices of individual data center is capped in the design of modern data center network architectures. As a result, even without the need for geographical distribution, equipment management and service provision have to be made available by building new data centers as the enterprise's equipment grows. In other words, enterprises have an ever-expanding need for the size of their internal networks.

The so-2 network is common in the infrastructure construction of modern cloud computing network. Because a single data center has limited resources and it is difficult to provide the same quality network services to users in different geographic locations, multiple data centers need to be connected over the Internet over a so-2 network. Virtual network technologies such as VLAN are often used to build so-2 layer coverage networks.

In a cloud computing environment, it is primarily virtual machines that are hosted as a business. In the TCP/IP of the Internet, the IP address identifies a host on the Internet and determines its location. That is, the IP address is both a system identifier and a locator. When a virtual machine moves from one subnet to another, its IP address must change, complicating the route. Despite mobile IP support, moving a system within a subnet (within an L2 domain) is much simpler than moving a system between subnets. This is because the LAN address used in the L2 network, such as the MAC address of Ethernet, is only a system identifier and not a locator and does not change as it moves through the L2 network. Therefore, it is easier to manage and control if multiple L2 networks from different data centers are connected through switches (or virtual switches) to form a large virtual L2 network.

Large IT companies (such as Microsoft, Google, Amazon, Baidu, Alibaba, Tencent) need to set up data centers in different geographic locations worldwide to manage their computing devices. To facilitate the management and scheduling of traffic across the enterprise network, these geographically distributed data centers often need to be under the same two-tier network to ensure that their traffic can be routed over multiple paths below the network layer, as well as controls such as load balancing. This has also contributed to the popularity of so-2 networks.

4.4.3 Virtual Network Based on Virtual Switch

1. From a Physical Switch to a Virtual Switch
   The VLAN technology described above is mainly used in switches and routers. The mainstream application is still in the switch, but only for those VLAN protocol-supporting Layer 2 switches. These switches are physical switches.

   In recent years, with the development of computer technology, especially cloud computing technology, more and more scholars began to study network virtualization, virtual switch has become the trend of communication development. At present, many network servers already have the function of supporting virtual machines, and the virtualization of servers promotes the virtualization of the network. Virtualization technology uses real physical network devices to form virtualized network devices such as virtual switches through the corresponding software to provide virtual machines' corresponding network services. Compared with traditional physical switches, virtual switches have many advantages in providing network services, and virtual switches are likely to be the core of building virtual network platforms in the future.

The principle of virtual switch technology is simpler, in essence, the technology is logically integrated with multiple physically connected switches. Compared with traditional physical switches, virtual switches improve the reliability and productivity of communication by consolidating multiple physical switch resources, reducing the number of network devices and simplifying the network structure.

2. North–south traffic and east–west traffic

In a data center service architecture similar to a cloud computing environment, we often hear north–south traffic and east–west traffic. North–south traffic and east–west traffic are network traffic patterns in data center environments. Let's illustrate this with an example.

Suppose we try to access a Web application through a browser, and the Web application is deployed in an application server located in a data center. In a multi-tiered architecture, a typical data center includes application servers and other servers, such as load balancers, databases, and network components such as routers and switches. Suppose the application server is the front end of the load balancer. When we access a Web application, we generate two types of network traffic.

• traffic between the client (browser on the side of the data center) and the load balancer (located in the data center).

• traffic between load balancers, application servers, databases, and so on, all located in data centers.

In this example, the first type of network traffic, the network traffic between the client and the load balancer, is called north–south traffic. In short, north–south traffic is Server-Client traffic. The second type of network traffic, which is traffic between different servers or between data centers and different data centers, is called east–west traffic. In short, east–west traffic is Server-Server traffic.

Today, east–west traffic far exceeds north–south traffic, especially in today's big data ecosystem. For example, the Hadoop ecosystem (where a large number of servers reside in data centers and are processed with Map/Reduce) has far more east–west traffic than north–south traffic.

The use of names such as north and south, east and west may stem from the habit of drawing typical network charts. In a chart, the core network components are usually drawn at the top (north), clients are drawn at the bottom (south), and different servers in the data center are drawn at the same horizontal location (east–west).

In practice, to judge whether a flow is north–south or east–west, a certain reference is needed. In general, north–south traffic and east–west traffic to the router as the demarcation point, through the router traffic for north-south traffic, not through the router traffic for east–west traffic. In the case of a physical router, as shown in Fig. 4.12, the router is deployed at the boundary of the Internet Data Center (IDC) room, connected up to the extranet (which can be the Internet, or the enterprise's own defined extranet) and down to the business network of the IDC

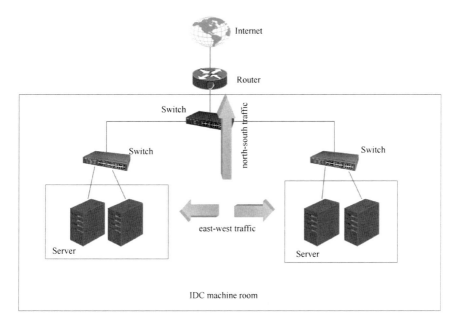

Fig. 4.12 Cloud computing traffic diagram

room (e.g., mail system, office system), when the computer in the IDC room accesses the Internet, the traffic is north–south traffic, when the computer in the IDC room accesses the business inside the computer room or communicates with other computers in the room, there is no need to go through the router, the traffic is east–west traffic.

With the development of cloud computing, more and more computing is concentrated in the IDC rooms cluster. Sometimes the customer sends only one instruction, and a lot of operations are performed between IDC's different businesses. If you use the desktop cloud, the client even runs in the IDC room. Simultaneously, the high availability of virtualization allows virtual machines to move freely across different physical servers in the data center, resulting in an increasing share of east–west traffic, from about 20 percent previously to about 70 percent today. This situation has also brought about changes in the network structure, the traditional three-tier network architecture has developed into the so-called second-tier architecture, the so-called second-tier architecture can better meet the requirements of large east–west traffic.

3. Two Types of Access to the Server

Virtual machines, which are the core components of a cloud computing environment, are also part of the network, which was previously almost always accessed over a bridge, but now use virtual switches extensively to network virtual machines for ease of management and configuration. A virtual machine can be connected to a virtual switch, multiple virtual network cards can be

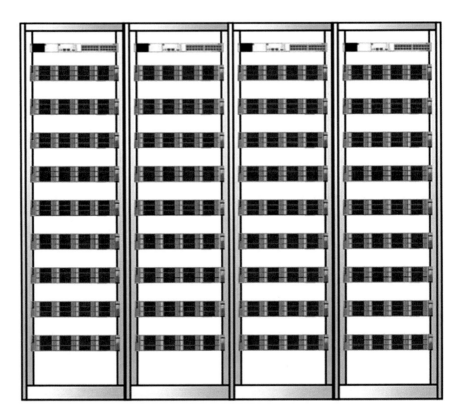

Fig. 4.13 ToR wiring method

connected, and other virtual machines can be connected through a virtual network card.

In a virtualized environment, the hosting business is a virtual machine, and the virtual machine is running inside the physical server, in order to make the virtual machine access to the network, we must first solve the network access problem of the physical server, which involves two types of access methods of the server.

In the data center room, servers are placed in separate cabinets, and for better cooling, cabinets are arranged in columns, so the two current mainstream server access networks are Top of Rack, ToR, and End of Row, EoR. As the name implies, ToR is the switch that connects the server to the network on top of the cabinet. ToR switches can be selected to consider the use of Gigabit or 10 Gigabit devices according to the actual situation. The ToR switch connects the physical server to the network by connecting the server network port, the federation aggregation, or the core switch. The way the ToR is routed is shown in Fig. 4.13.

EoR is a separate switch in a cabinet that connects the server to the network, also known as the EoR switch. EoR switches are typically placed in the middle of

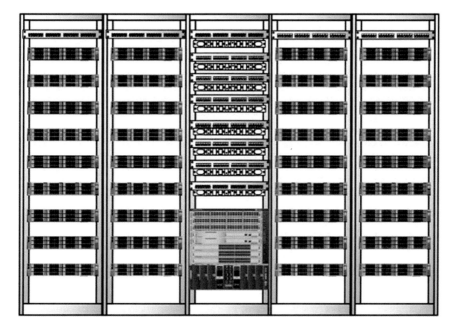

Fig. 4.14 EoR wiring method

a column of cabinets to reduce the length of server-to-switch wiring. EoR is routed as shown in Fig. 4.14.

Both ToR and EoR have their own usage scenarios and limitations. ToR is more scalable than EoR.

After the server is connected to the network, we can classify it according to network traffic, which is generally divided into business traffic, storage traffic, and management traffic. Users access the required business through business traffic, and if the business data is not placed locally on the server, but on a professional storage device, the server generates storage traffic when it accesses the storage device. Management traffic is primarily the amount of traffic that users generate when they manage servers, virtual machines, and storage devices. Each physical device now has a separate management port, called Out-of-Band if the management traffic is separated from the business traffic, using different physical lines and interfaces, and In-Band if the management traffic and business traffic use the same physical channel.

In a cloud computing data center, a network is designed with a high-end three-tier switch at the heart of the entire network, and the default gateway for all traffic segments is set on top, which means that all traffic that crosses the broadcast domain passes through the switch. There are several reasons for this.

- High-end three-tier switch has a good forwarding performance, can meet the full network traffic forwarding requirements.

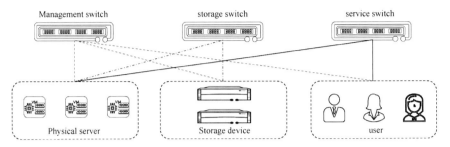

Fig. 4.15 The access layer uses different physical switches to carry different traffic

- High-end three-tier switches are modular in design to ensure their high fault tolerance and scalability. In addition to power supply, fans, and other necessary modules, high-end three-layer switch core components such as engine board using a 1-1 thermal backup method greatly improve the availability of equipment.
- High-end three-tier switches can support boards with different bandwidth interfaces, such as 10GB, 40GB, and 100GB, and can support high-capacity, high-tight server access, and ToR uplink aggregation to meet the requirements of high-performance, the ultra-large capacity of data center networks.
- High-end three-tier switches have basic routing switching capabilities, they also have features that meet cloud computing requirements, such as soda architecture, support stacking, and virtualization.

    Before accessing the core switch, all traffic generally access the second-tier switch, access in the way we talked about earlier—EoR or ToR. Depending on the type of access traffic, access switches can be divided into management switches, storage switches, and business switches. In the case of a data center with very large traffic, it is recommended that the access layer use different physical switches to host different traffic when designing the network fabric. That is, each traffic uses a separate switch, as shown in Fig. 4.15. In the case of a data center with general traffic, you can use the same physical switch and use VLAN to isolate different traffic logically.

4. Link Aggregation Technology

    The physical server connects to the network through its physical network card, and all virtual machine traffic enters the network through various types of network cards. Typically, a physical network card corresponds to a physical link, but a port (link) aggregation increases link bandwidth by bundling multiple Ethernet physical links together to become a logical link. At the same time, these bundled links can effectively improve the reliability of the links by dynamically backing them up with each other.

    Link aggregation technology can increase link bandwidth by bundling multiple physical interfaces into one logical interface without a hardware upgrade. Compared with increasing bandwidth by replacing high-speed devices, this

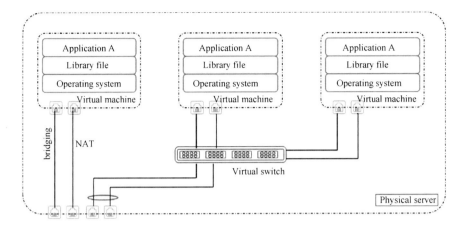

Fig. 4.16   The virtual switch in the virtual network architecture

method is flexible and more cost-effective, and at the same time, the link aggregation technology adopts the backup link mechanism, which can effectively improve the reliability of the inter-device link and meet the user's QoS requirements for the backbone link.

5. Normal Virtual Switches and Distributed Virtual Switches

   With the popularity of cloud computing and virtualization, virtual machines are replacing physical servers as the carriers of business. Originally the physical server will have at least one network cable connected to the switch, running on this server's business exclusive network cable, and now a physical server running multiple virtual machines, they will share this network cable, so that the network cable will carry a variety of traffic. How do I manage these traffics, and how do I see the status of these traffics? These have become new problems.

   Figure 4.16 shows a virtual network architecture in which multiple virtual machines running on the same physical server connect to the physical network through a virtual switch.

   In addition, according to the structure, the virtual switch can be divided into two types: a normal virtual switch and the other is a distributed virtual switch. A normal virtual switch runs on only one separate physical host, and all network-related configurations apply only to virtual machines on this physical server; one of the conditions for a virtual machine to be able to perform a thermal migration is to have a distributed virtual switch.

6. Examples of Common Virtual Switch Products

   Currently, virtualization vendors have their virtual switch products, such as VMware's vSwitch, Cisco's Nexus 1000V, Huawei's DVS, and open source products such as Open vSwitch (OVS). Here we take open source OVS as an example to introduce virtual switches.

   OVS is an open source, high-quality virtual switch that supports multi-layer protocols and is designed to support distribution across multiple physical servers (i.e., with distributed virtual switch capabilities), using an open source Apache

2.0 license agreement, developed by Nicira Networks, with the main implementation of portable C code. Its purpose is to support large-scale software-based network automation extensions, as well as standard management interfaces and protocols such as NetFlow. In addition, OVS supports a variety of Linux virtualization technologies, such as Xen and KVM.

OVS has the following characteristics:

(1) The status can be migrated

When a virtual machine runs on a different host, all network states associated with it should be easily identified and migrated. OVS supports cross-instance configuration and migration of network state, such as when a virtual machine is migrated, migrating the network configuration associated with it, and migrating the network state of the virtual machine at this time. In addition, the state of the OVS can be output and backed up using the developer's data model.

(2) Respond to dynamic networks

The dynamic and high-frequency change of network environment is one of the characteristics of virtualization. It is common for multiple virtual machines to migrate at the same time, and each migration changes the logical network environment. When the network changes, OVS supports the independent monitoring and management of the network through network management tools such as NetFlow, IPFIX, and SFlow and can respond promptly if there is a change. OVS also supports remote access to traffic control via the OpenFlow protocol.

(3) Support for logical label maintenance

Distributed virtual switches typically uniquely identify virtual machines by attaching appropriate labels to network packets. The main problem in building distributed virtual switches is how to manage these tags efficiently and correctly. OVS contains a variety of methods for specifying and maintaining label rules, all of which are accessible to remote processes of the business process.

(4) Support and hardware integration

Many vendors are currently working to port OVS to hardware chipsets. These include multiple commercial chipsets (Broadcom and Marvell) and platforms for many specific vendors. The advantage of hardware integration is speed, which improves performance in virtualized environments.

4.4.4   The Network Characteristics of Huawei's Virtualization Products

The virtual switch used by Huawei's virtualization products is a distributed virtual switch, and we use Huawei FusionCompute as an example to introduce Huawei DVS.

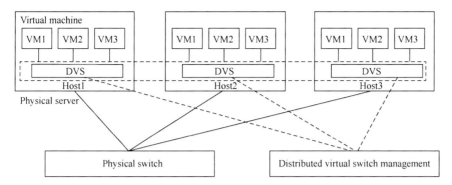

Fig. 4.17 Huawei DVS schematic

1. The Structure and Characteristics of Huawei DVS

Huawei DVS provides centralized virtual switching and management capabilities. Centralized management simplifies user management by providing a unified portal for configuration management.

Figure 4.17 shows Huawei DVS. Through virtual switches distributed across physical servers, Huawei DVS provides the ability to communicate, isolate, and guarantee QoS between virtual machines.

Huawei DVS supports software-only virtual switching based on open source OVS, which has the following basic features:

- Virtualization administrators can configure multiple distributed switches, each covering multiple physical server nodes in the cluster with FusionCompute installed, known as computing node agents (Computing Node Agent, CNA).
- Each distributed switch has multiple distributed virtual ports (Virtual Switch Port, VSP), each with its properties, and the same port group belongs to the same VLAN to manage a set of convenient ports for using port groups to manage the same attributes.
- Virtualization administrators or business systems can choose different physical interfaces for management/storage/business use, and each distributed switch can be configured with a cascading port (UpLink Port) or a cascading port aggregation group for external communication of virtual machines. Cascading port aggregation groups can contain multiple physical ports and can configure load balancing policies.
- Each virtual machine can have multiple virtual network card interfaces, which can be connected to the switch's distributed virtual ports.
- Virtualization administrator or business system can create a virtual two-tier network in a cluster that allows two-tier migration and set up the VLAN information used by that network, depending on business needs.

  Virtualization administrators can simplify the setting of virtual machine port properties by defining port group properties, such as security, QoS. The port group here is a collection of ports with the same set of network properties.

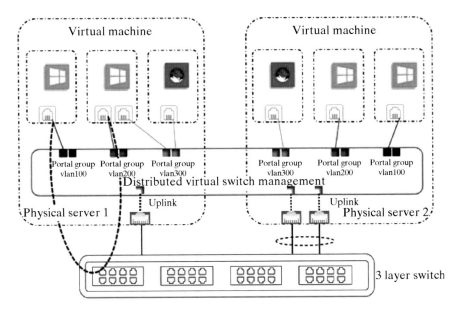

Fig. 4.18 Traffic trend of the same host and different port groups

Setting port group properties does not affect the normal operation of the virtual machine.

The characteristics of Huawei DVS can be summed up in the following points:

- centralized management: unified portal and centralized management, simplifying user management and configuration.
- open source OVS: integrate open source OVS to take advantage of and inherit open source community virtual switching capabilities.
- provides a wealth of virtual switching two-tier features, including switching, QoS, security isolation, and more.

2. How Huawei DVS Works

Let's look at how Huawei DVS works under different network architectures.

(1) Virtual machines run on the same host and have different port groups (see Fig. 4.18)

As we said earlier, virtual switches are essentially a two-tier switch, and a critical parameter in a port group is called VLAN ID, which, if two virtual machines are not in the same port group, represents that they are not in the same VLAN, so they cannot be found over the radio. In general, a virtual machine that belongs to a different VLAN, we will give it an IP address for a different segment. Therefore, if they need to communicate with each other, they need to use devices that work on the third layer of the network, such as a

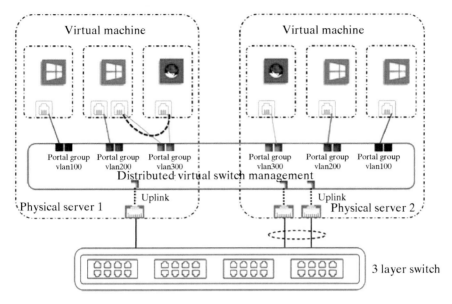

Fig. 4.19   Traffic trend of the same host and the same port group

three-tier switch or router. In Huawei's virtualization product FusionCompute architecture, three-tier functionality can only be provided by physical three-tier devices. Therefore, these two virtual machines' access traffic needs to be transmitted from inside the source host to the physical three-tier access switch, where it is forwarded and routed to the address before entering the destination host to complete communication.

(2) The virtual machine runs on the same host and the port group is the same (see Fig. 4.19)

If it belongs to the same port group, the virtual machine belongs to the same broadcast domain, and the virtual switch supports broadcasting. Therefore, if the same host, the same port group of virtual machines between the communication, can be done directly through the virtual switch, the traffic does not need to be passed to the physical network.

(3) Virtual machines run on different hosts but the port groups are the same (see Fig. 4.20)

Although virtual machines belong to the same port group and can be found on the broadcast, different physical servers require a physical switch to access the network (unless the two physical servers are directly interconnected, which is a special case, not considered). Therefore, if the virtual machine uses the same port group but runs on different physical servers, traffic needs to be passed through the physical server's network port to the physical switch before communication can be completed. But this physical switch does not have to be a three-tier switch.

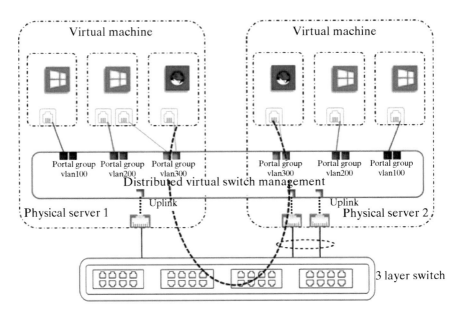

Fig. 4.20 The flow of different hosts and the same port group

3. Huawei DVS Security Group

In Chap. 2 of this book, we cover the security group. Users create security groups based on the security needs of virtual machines, each of which can set a set of access rules. When a virtual machine joins a security group, it is protected by the access rule group. Users securely isolate and access virtual machines by selecting the security groups to join when they are created. A security group is a logical grouping consisting of virtual machines within the same geography that have the same security requirements and trust each other. All virtual machine network cards located in the same security group will use this security group rule for network communication. Only one security group can be added to each virtual machine network card. Huawei DVS provides support for security groups. Figure 4.21 shows the security group for Huawei DVS.

Security groups function like firewalls, and they all use packet filtering mechanisms for security control.

4.5   Software-Defined Network

Relying on the data center network's cloud computing infrastructure, dynamic adjustments to the structure or behavior of the network are often required to provide efficient services to cloud users without interruption. Network management here should be automated because large data centers' workload would be unimaginable if they were manually managed.

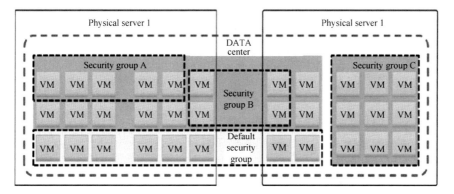

Fig. 4.21 Huawei DVS security group diagram

The core devices that make up the network include switches, routers, and many network products. Most of these equipment manufacturing practices come from Cisco, Broadcom, and other communication manufacturers and are not open and extensive. Therefore, for a long time, the hardware specification and software specification of network equipment are very closed. Especially for the support of standards such as routing protocols, users do not have the lead. Although the automated management of the network, there are simple network management protocols (SNMP) and other standardized protocols to define the management of IP network nodes, but these network management protocols cannot directly control the behavior of network devices, especially routing and forwarding policies. The idea of a software-defined network (SDN) was born to make it easier and more efficient to manage the network and use network resources.

4.5.1 Introduction to SDN

SDN is a new network innovation architecture that can define and control the network through software programming. Its characteristics of control plane and forwarding plane separation and open programmability are considered a revolution in the field of network, which provides a new experimental way for the research of new Internet architecture and greatly promotes the next generation of Internet.

After decades of rapid development, the Internet has evolved from a network that initially met the Best-Effort model of simple network services such as e-mail and file transfer to a converged network capable of providing multimedia data such as text, voice, and video. The expansion and complexity of network functions make the traditional SIMPLE IP-based network architecture increasingly bloated and unable to meet efficient and flexible business hosting needs.

From an abstract system structure, traditional networks are standard and open horizontally, and each network node, such as a computer, can be perfectly interconnected using standard protocols such as TCP/IP and surrounding network nodes. However, in the vertical direction, the network is "relatively closed" and "no architecture," in the vertical direction to create applications, deployment of business is relatively difficult. The vertical direction here refers to the level of computer applications, such as hardware, drivers, operating systems, programming platforms, applications, and other levels, the next layer is usually built on the basis of the next layer, using the services provided by the next layer. The innovation of SDN is to make the vertical orientation of the entire network system (not just network nodes) open, standardized, and programmable, making it easier and more efficient for people to use network resources. Specifically, SDN achieves flexible control of network equipment by separating data plane and control plane in the network and can effectively reduce equipment load, help network operators better control infrastructure, and reduce overall operating costs.

Compared with traditional networks, SDN has the following advantages: First, the decoupling of data and control makes application upgrades and device updates independent of each other, speeding up the rapid deployment of new applications. These advantages make SDN widely concerned in academia and industry.

4.5.2 Development of SDN

Speaking of SDN's birth and development, it is closely related to the emergence of virtualization and cloud computing technology. In the early days, storage, computing, and network resources were physically and operationally separate, and even the systems used to manage them were physically separate. Applications that interact with resources, such as operations monitoring systems, generally have complex access policies and rules to meet security and other requirements. But as the concept of cloud services becomes more and more popular, enterprises are increasingly inclined to migrate servers and storage devices that were previously dispersed across departments to a unified data center for management, both for administrative convenience and for resource sharing among enterprise users, while reducing the unit energy consumption of devices.

In data centers, a large number of IT devices come together, and how to operate and manage these resources effectively becomes a challenge. A prominent contribution to solving this problem is virtualization technology. VMware first introduced VMware Workstation in 1999, allowing one or more customer operating systems, such as Windows, to run on operating systems such as UNIX/Linux. This is the first commercial virtualization product for personal computers. Several server-based virtualization products followed this. VMware's virtualization software creates a virtual environment that integrates real computing environments, running isolated virtual machines, each running in its environment, with a separate customer operating system that can operate virtualized hardware and perform all kinds of computing and processing tasks that are performed by ordinary physical functions. In fact, a virtual machine is created by a virtual machine image stored on disk, and a virtual machine image is a normal file. So the migration and replication of virtual machines become very easy because they correspond to replicating files. The migration ability of virtual machines and computing tasks makes elastic computing a reality.

In an elastic computing environment, operations can migrate virtual machines to any physical location in the data center by simply pausing them and copying files. They can even create a new virtual machine by copying the same hypervisor image file and letting the hypervisor run it as a new instance. The flexibility of virtualization technology makes it easy for network administrators to configure and optimize data center resources. A network administrator might optimize the cooling load on the data center by consolidating all running virtual machines and hibernating or idling servers in other parts of the data center from an energy-saving perspective.

With the rise of cloud computing technology and the growing size of data centers that provide cloud services, computing, storage, and network resources within data centers often need to be serviced in separate or isolated pieces, which are needed to serve multiple tenants. In this environment, the migration of virtual machines often spans different segments and requires three layers of routing devices. Although virtual network technologies such as VPN or VLAN are supported, network configuration and management are still complex. This is because commercial network devices such as routers and switches are configured with management ports and support network administrators to configure and manage these devices using command-line interfaces, XML/Netconf, SNMP. But in general these devices typically hide the lowest details from network administrators, who can only take advantage of the interfaces and features already provided by the devices and cannot customize or develop the functionality they need.

Because of these aspects' needs, after many explorations, trial and error, network innovation has finally made a breakthrough, the representative of a new generation of information technology—SDN was born.

SDN originated in 2006 at Stanford University's Clean State research project. In 2009, Professor Nick McKeown formally introduced the concept of SDN. Early advocates of SDN found that network equipment vendors could not meet their needs, especially in the space for innovation in feature development and offer, but they also found a rapid decline in computing costs. This made them realize that they could use this computing power to run a centralized control plane that controls and manages existing network devices. Several engineers at Stanford University created the OpenFlow protocol, which uses a (logically) centralized controller to control and manage all network devices in the current network, all on a data plane. This centralized controller is responsible for maintaining all network paths and programming the network devices it controls. It also becomes the only control plane in the network. Figure 4.22 shows OpenFlow's architecture.

After the SDN concept was proposed, in addition to researchers from universities and research institutes, technicians from companies such as Cisco Juniper, Level3, and other manufacturers and operators contributed to network programmability. The Open Network Foundation (ONF) also provides commercial support for SDN and remains an authority on SDN standards and market promotion. In recent years, SDN research continues to be active, some advanced academic conferences include a large

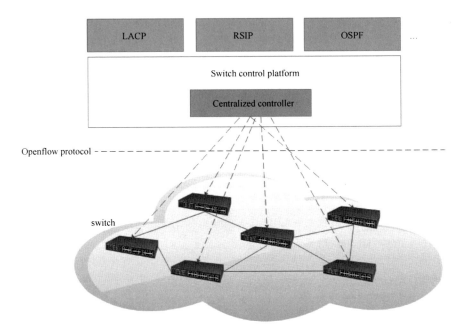

Fig. 4.22 OpenFlow architecture

number of SDN-related articles, and even SDN as a topic for discussion, so that SDN-related research into a new stage of development.

4.5.3 SDN Architecture

The SDN architecture proposed by the SDN Foundation for Open Networking consists of three levels: the infrastructure layer of the SDN (data plane), the controller layer of the SDN (control plane), the application layer of the SDN (application plane), the interface level of the south-way interface (the controller communicates with the network equipment at the infrastructure layer), and the north-bound interface (the NBI) (the controller communicates with the application services at the upper level) as shown in Fig. 4.23.

Since all the control logic of the network device has been concentrated in the central controller of the SDN, the flexibility and controllability of the network are significantly enhanced, the programmer can write policies on the controller, such as load balancing, firewall, network address conversion, VPN and other functions, and thus control the lower level devices. It can be said that SDN is essentially through virtualization technology and API to make direct control of the hardware possible, to achieve on-demand hardware management, so that network management programmable. The introduction of north-to-north interfaces in SDN architecture has brought

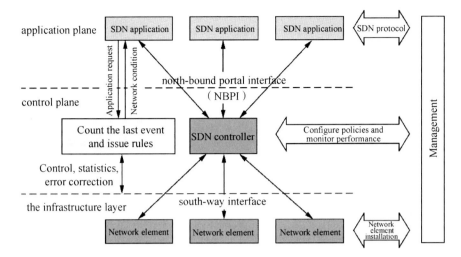

Fig. 4.23 SDN architecture

a wealth of applications to SDN. The north-speaking interface mainly refers to the interface between the controller and the network application in the SDN, which is generally represented as the controller's API for the application. North–south interfaces expose information within the controller to applications and management systems in the SDN to be used for various operations, such as requesting the status of devices in the network, requesting network views, and manipulating down-level network devices, and so on. Using the network resources provided by the north-to-north interface, programmers can customize their network strategy and interact with the network, taking full advantage of the network programmability benefits of SDN.

SDN's core idea is to break the shackles of the abstract layering of network system by the original network hardware system. From the perspective of system construction rather than data transmission, the network system is abstracted from the bottom up into three planes, i.e., the data plane, control plane, and application plan.

However, in the traditional network system design, the control plane is not very controllable. Because the network hardware determines the logic that determines network data forwarding control on its ASIC chip. Unless the device manufacturer updates the firmware or replaces the chip, these control logic can only be modified with a few configuration parameters. Even if network devices support modification of control logic, there is another challenge to implement fast and flexible control logic switching: the control plane located on a single network device cannot obtain information for the entire network, and information can only be exchanged through distributed protocols and adjacent network devices, making it difficult to make fast and accurate decisions.

Therefore, to overcome these shortcomings, SDN has made the following improvements to the existing architecture.

(1) The data plane is separated from the control plane

One of the key innovations of SDN is the separation of the control plane from the data plane. The data plane consists of packets in the control plane forwarding table. The control logic is separated and implemented in the controller that is ready for release. These mechanisms greatly simplify the data plane and reduce the cost of hardware implementation.

(2) Build a centralized control plane

As for network control, centralized control has always been regarded as unreasonable design, and distributed control mode is one of the pillars of Internet design. Now, however, there are good reasons to support centralized control of the network. Because centralized control enables network systems to perceive network state more quickly than distributed protocols and dynamically adjust the network based on state changes.

Of course, there is a problem with scale expansion in a centralized style compared to distributed design. In this case, one solution is to divide the network into subnets small enough to have a common control strategy for centralized control. With centralized control, network state changes or policy changes propagate much faster than fully distributed systems. In addition, if the primary controller fails, the standby controller can be used to take over. But the data plane is still completely distributed.

4.5.4 SDN Key Technology

1. Key Technologies for Data Planes

   In SDN, data forwarding is separated from rule control, and the switch places control of the forwarding rule with the controller, which forwards packets only according to the controller's rules. To avoid frequent interaction between the switch and the controller, the rules agreed upon by both parties are flow-based and not per-packet. SDN data plane key technologies are mainly reflected in switch and forwarding rules.

   The data forwarding method of SDN switch is two kinds of hardware and software. The hardware approach is faster than the software approach, but the flexibility is reduced. New research and improvement methods have been proposed to make the hardware more flexible in data forwarding.

   Unlike hardware, software processing is slower than hardware, but software can increase forwarding rule processing flexibility. Using the switch's CPU or Network Processor (NP) to execute software control logic to handle forwarding rules avoids poor hardware flexibility. Because NP is designed to handle network tasks, it is slightly stronger than CPU in network processing.

2. Control Plane Key Technology

   Controller is the key component of control plane, and it is also the logic center of SDN architecture. The SDN controller realizes the control function corresponding to the distributed control plane and can realize the management

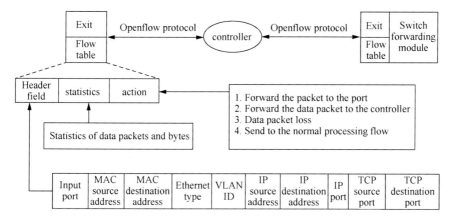

Fig. 4.24 Schematic diagram of the working architecture of the OpenFlow controller

of the network's instantaneous state. At present, SDN controllers are not standardized. Manufacturers such as VMware and Juniper have their commercial products, and the others are open source controllers. Most open source SDN controllers are based on the OpenFlow protocol. Figure 4.24 shows the working architecture of the OpenFlow controller.

With the expansion of the SDN network scale, the SDN network's processing capacity with a single-controller structure is limited, and performance bottlenecks are encountered, so the controller needs to be expanded. There are currently two-controller expansion methods: one is to improve its own controller's processing capability, and the other is to adopt a multi-controller method.

However, in most cases, it is far from enough for large-scale networks to rely on single-controller parallel processing to solve performance problems. It is more to use multi-controller expansion to optimize SDN. Controllers can generally be expanded in two ways: one is flat control; the other is hierarchical control.

In the flat control mode, the controllers are placed in different areas and are in charge of different network devices. The status of each controller is equal, and logically they have the information of the whole network. They rely on the east–west interface to communicate. When the network topology changes, all controllers will be updated synchronously, and the switch only needs to adjust the address mapping with the controller. Therefore, the flat control mode has little effect on the data plane. In the hierarchical control mode, the controller is divided into a local controller and a global controller. The local controllers manage the network devices in their respective regions and only control the network status of the region; while the global controller manages the local controllers and controls the entire network state, the interaction between local controllers is also done through the global controller.

4.5.5 The Advantage of SDN

The hierarchical network structure is one of the key factors for the great success of the Internet. However, after the network's traditional architecture is deployed on service requirements, since the equipment manufacturer controls the firmware of the network equipment, its parameters or configuration is locked. If the service requirements change, it is challenging to remodify the configuration on the corresponding network equipment. Simultaneously, with the continuous expansion of network scale, too many complex protocols are built into closed network equipment, which increases the difficulty for operators to customize and optimize the network. In the rapidly changing business environment of the Internet, compared to the network's high stability and high performance, sometimes flexibility and agility can become the key to meeting business needs. Therefore, SDN hopes to separate network control from the physical network to eliminate the limitations of hardware on the network architecture.

What SDN does is to separate the control rights on the network equipment and manage it by a centralized controller without relying on the underlying network equipment, thereby shielding the differences in the underlying network equipment. The control right is completely open, and the network routing and transmission strategy can be defined by the user, which makes the device more flexible and intelligent. After the SDN transformation, you only need to define simple network rules when you use it to complete the configuration of the configuration without configuring the routing nodes in the network one by one. Not only that, if the built-in protocol of the routing node does not meet the needs of users, it can also be modified programmatically to achieve better data exchange performance. In this way, network equipment can be upgraded or modified just like ordinary software to meet the needs of users for adjustment and expansion of the entire network architecture. The underlying switches, routers, and other hardware devices do not need to be replaced. While saving a lot of costs, the iterative cycle of the network architecture will also be significantly shortened.

As a new network paradigm, SDN adopts an architecture that separates the control plane and the data plane, which not only allows the control plane and the data plane to evolve independently, helps to solve the problem of network rigidity but also brings things that are not available in the traditional network architecture. Advantages: For example, programmability helps network innovation; centralized control facilitates and simplifies network management; global network view makes network fine-grained control possible; virtualization supports optimized scheduling and efficient use of network resources. All of this makes SDN one of the most popular network technologies at present. Its application frees manual operation, reduces network configuration errors, and makes the network easy to be deployed in a unified and rapid manner. It has been successfully applied to various fields such as enterprise networks and data centers. The Massachusetts Institute of Technology listed it as "one of the top ten innovative technologies that changed the world."

4.6 Exercise

(1) Multiple choices

  1. The topology of the Internet is.

    A. Bus type
    B. Star
    C. Ring
    D. Mesh

  2. The network devices that work at the network layer are ( ).

    A. Hub
    B. Router
    C. Bridge
    D. Switchboard

  3. The false saying about packet switching networks is ( ).

    A. Packet switching networks are segment-by-segment occupied by communication lines during data communication.
    B. Packet switching networks use storage and forwarding technology.
    C. Grouping selects routes independently in a packet switching network.
    D. The packet switching network needs to establish a source-to-destination communication line before transmitting the packet.

  4. The protocol that runs in the network layer in the TCP/IP model is ( ).

    A. TCP
    B. UDP
    C. IP
    D. HTTP

  5. The technique for logically dividing a physical LAN into broadcast domains is ( ).

    A. VPN
    B. VLAN
    C. Ipsec
    D. SNMP

  6. The effect that VLAN technology can't achieve is ( ).

    A. Restrict the broadcast domain
    B. Enhance the security of your local area network
    C. Improve the robustness of your network
    D. Flexible control of network equipment is achieved through software programming

7. The routing protocols commonly used on the Internet do not include ( ).

    A. CSMA/CD
    B. OSPF
    C. BGP
    D. RIP

8. The misconception about the virtual switch is ( ).

    A. Virtual switches leverage virtualization technology to logically integrate multiple physically connected switches.
    B. Using virtual switches can reduce the number of network devices and simplify the network fabric.
    C. The virtual switch can only run on a single physical host.
    D. One of the conditions for a virtual machine to be able to perform a thermal migration is to have a distributed virtual switch.

9. If multiple virtual machines on a physical server are connected via Huawei DVS, the correct statement is ( ) about the traffic direction of traffic between two virtual machines belonging to different port groups.

    A. Communication is done directly through DVS inside the source host, and traffic does not need to be passed to the external network.
    B. Access traffic needs to be passed from inside the source host to an external three-tier switch and forwarded to complete the communication.
    C. Access traffic needs to come out from inside the source host, but externally it can be forwarded using a two-tier switch.
    D. Different port groups cannot communicate.

10. The misconception about SDN is ( ).

    A. Distributed control mode is the core concept of SDN
    B. The SDN separates the data plane from the control plane in the network
    C. SDN provides flexible control over network devices and effectively reduces device load
    D. D.The SDN concentrates all the control logic of the network device in the central controller

(2) Fill in the blanks

1. The main purpose of the computer network is to provide _____ and implement data communication.
2. The network is divided by geographic coverage_____、 _____and_____.
3. Computer networks can be divided into three categories: _____, _____, and the Internet by application type.
4. Computer network is the product of the close combination of _____ and _____.

5. To communicate between computers and exchange information, you need certain conventions and rules, which are _____.
6. Mac frames for Ethernet, which typically contain fields such as destination address, _____, type field, frame data, and validation fields.
7. 7._____ is a network device that works at the data link layer and is characterized by an exclusive electrical signal path to any two network nodes connected to the device, which is also a significant difference from a hub.
8. If a host has an IP address of 192.168.1.11 and a subnet mask of 255.255.255.248, the network address of the subnet where the host is located is _____.
9. 9._____ are private networks that are secured by using public networks, and their functions include authentication, encryption, tunneling, and firewall functions.
10. 10._____ is a new network innovation architecture, which can define and control the network in the form of software programming.

(3) Answer the following questions

1. The main work of communication subnet and resource subnet is briefly described.
2. Briefly describe the advantages and disadvantages of bus, star, and ring topology.
3. Briefly describe the main functions of the data link layer.
4. Briefly describe the main principles of VLAN.
5. What is the difference between north–south traffic and east–west traffic?
6. What is a soda network?
7. What are the advantages of SDN over traditional networks?

Chapter 5
Storage Basics in Cloud Computing

In computer science, the storage uses different applications to save data to certain media in a reasonable, secure, and efficient manner and ensure effective access. In general, storage has two meanings. On the one hand, it is a physical medium in which data resides temporarily or permanently.

This chapter begins with an introduction to the basics of storage, followed by a complete introduction to the storage fundamentals involved in cloud computing in terms of basic storage units, networked storage, storage reliability technologies, storage virtualization, and distributed storage.

5.1 Basic Knowledge of Storage

5.1.1 Storage Development and Technological Evolution

As we all know, the development of civilization depends on the accumulation of knowledge, and the accumulation of knowledge cannot be separated from storage. Therefore, the ability to store information containing knowledge is an important part of the development of civilization. In a sense, it is one of the signs that human beings were entering civilized society. Historically, humans have created many ways to store information.

1. Perforated Paper Tape

    In 1725, Bouchon, a French textile mechanic, came up with a brilliant idea for a "perforated paper belt," as shown in Fig. 5.1. Bouchon first managed to control all movements with a row of knitted needles, then punched a row of holes in a roll of paper straps according to the woven pattern. After starting the machine, the woven needles lying against the small holes can pass through and hook up the thread, while the paper tape blocks the other needles. In this way, the braided needle automatically selects the thread according to the pre-designed pattern.

Huawei Technologies Co., Ltd., *Cloud Computing Technology*,
https://doi.org/10.1007/978-981-19-3026-3_5

Fig. 5.1 Perforated
paper tape

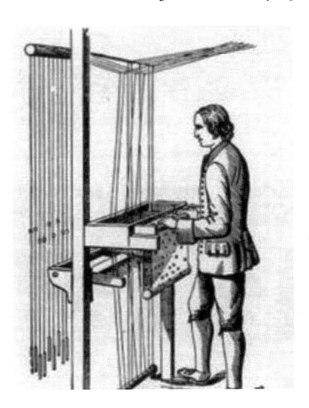

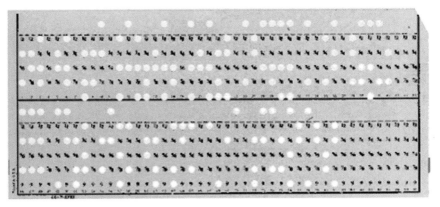

Fig. 5.2 Example of early perforated tape

Bjorn's "thoughts" were then "passed" to the knitting machine, and the "program" of the woven pattern was "stored" in small holes in the perforated tape.

Figure 5.2 shows an example of an early perforated tape with 90 column holes. As you can see, there is very little data that can be stored on this card, and

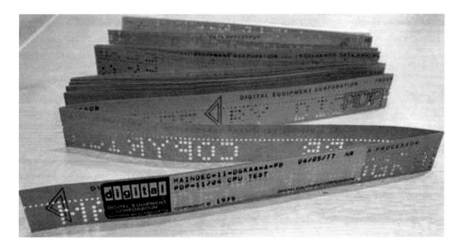

Fig. 5.3 Improved perforated paper

Fig. 5.4 Counting tube

virtually no one actually uses it to store data. Typically, it is used to hold settings parameters for different computers.

Alexander Bain, the inventor of the facsimile machine and the telegraph machine, first used the improved punched paper tape shown in Fig. 5.3 in 1846. Each line on the paper tape represents a character, and its capacity is larger than before and has increased significantly.

2. Electric tube counter

In 1946, RCA began researching counting tubes, storage devices used in early giant tube computers. A counting tube up to 10 in. (about 25 cm) can hold 4096 bits of data, as shown in Fig. 5.4. Unfortunately, it is extremely expensive. So it is a flash in the pan in the market and quickly disappears.

3. Disc tape

In the 1950s, IBM first used disk tapes for data storage, as shown in Fig. 5.5. Because a roll of tape could replace 10,000 punching paper cards, disc tape was a success, becoming one of the most popular computer storage devices until the 1980s.

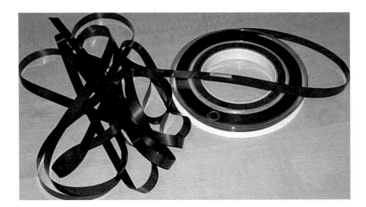

Fig. 5.5 Disc tape

Fig. 5.6 Floppy disk

4. Floppy disk

   The first floppy disk was invented in 1969 to hold 80KB of read-only data in an 8 in. (about 20 cm) piece of physical storage space. In 1973, a small but 256KB floppy disk was born, characterized by repeated reading/writing, as shown in Fig. 5.6. Then, there is the trend—disks are getting smaller and smaller in diameter, and the capacity is getting bigger and bigger. By the late 1990s, 3.5 in. (about 9 cm) floppy disks with a capacity of 250MB had emerged.

Fig. 5.7 Hard disk

5. Hard Disk

The hard drive is a storage device that is still in development, as shown in Fig. 5.7, the Hitachi Deskstar 7K500, which is the first hard drive to reach 500GB.

5.1.2   *Cutting-Edge Storage Technologies and Development Trends*

In the era of big data, it is important to store large-scale data securely, efficiently, and cost-effectively. Throughout the development of computer storage technology, from the first mechanical hard disk in 1956, to the emergence of SAN in the 1970s, to the invention of NAS in the 1980s and the emergence of object storage in 2006, computer storage has been developing rapidly. As can be seen from the development of storage technology, storage technology is constantly integrated with applications. However, these technologies are not completely replacing applications, but the application is expanding, so even now, hard disk, SAN, NAS technology is still widely used in related fields.

Virtual storage and network storage are two of the major themes of current storage technology development. The development of storage technology not only meets the basic user requirements for large capacity and high speed, but also places higher demands on cost-effectiveness and security, as well as the scalability of storage in time and spatial scalability, which will lead to the convergence of various storage devices and storage technologies, ultimately unified within a standard architecture.

1. Virtual Storage

   At present, the main direction of storage technology development is virtualization technology. As the amount of information increases exponentially, efficient use of existing storage architecture and storage technology to simplify storage management, thereby reducing the maintenance cost has become the focus of attention. Virtual storage refers to integrating many different types of physical storage entities that exist indepéndently into a logical virtual storage unit through software and hardware technology, which is managed and made available to users. The storage capacity of a logical virtual storage unit is the sum of the storage volumes of the physical storage bodies it centrally manages, while the read/write bandwidth it has is close to the sum of the read/write bandwidths of each physical storage. The development and application of virtual storage technology can help to more effectively develop current storage devices' storage capacity and improve storage efficiency. At the heart of storage, virtualization is how to map physical storage devices to a single pool of logical resources.

   In general, virtualization technology is achieved by establishing a virtual abstraction layer. This virtual abstraction layer provides the user with a unified interface that hides complex physical implementations. According to the region where the virtual abstraction layer is located in the storage system, the implementation of storage virtualization can be divided into three ways: virtual storage based on a storage device, virtual storage based on storage network, and virtual storage based on server-side.

2. Internet Storage

   With the increase of information demand, storage capacity is expanding at high speed, and the storage system network platform has become a core of development. Accordingly, applications are increasingly demanding these platforms, not just in demand for storage capacity but also in the areas of access performance, transport performance, control, compatibility, expansion capabilities, and more. It can be said that the comprehensive performance of the storage system network platform will directly affect the normal and efficient implementation of the whole system. Therefore, the development of an economical and manageable advanced storage technology will become an inevitable development trend.

   Network storage is one of many data storage technologies, it is a special kind of dedicated data storage server, including storage devices (such as disk arrays, tape drives, or removable storage media) and embedded system software, and can provide platform file-sharing capabilities. Typically, a network is stored on a local area network with its own nodes and does not require an application server's intervention, allowing users to access data on the network. In this mode, networked storage centrally manages and processes all data on the network, with the advantage of unloading the load from the application or enterprise server, reducing the total cost of ownership. There are three broad networked storage architectures: Direct Attached Storage (DAS); NAS; and SAN. They can all use RAID to provide efficient, secure storage space. Because NAS is the most common form of networked storage for consumers, so generally referred to as networked storage refers to NAS.

With the continuous development of storage technology and enterprises' changing needs, Server SAN is gradually becoming the mainstream storage form of enterprises. Whether it is a public or private cloud, there is much interest in distributed storage. With the continuous development of new business, the supply model of new resources has gradually changed from "chimney" to "cloud" mode. Because traditional storage is built to meet a single application and scenario and does not meet the needs of today's elastic scaling, cloud storage that can scale elastically on demand is bound to develop. A more advanced storage method is software-defined fully converged cloud storage, a system based on a common hardware platform that provides block, file, and object services on demand, and is suitable for cloud resource pools in industries such as financial development testing, government affairs, policing, and large enterprises, as well as scenarios such as carrier public cloud.

5.1.3 Common Storage Products and Solutions

To ensure high availability, high reliability and economy, cloud computing uses distributed storage to store data, and redundant storage to ensure the reliability of storage data, that is, multiple copies of the same data storage. In addition, cloud computing systems need to meet the needs of many users at the same time and serve a large number of users in parallel. Therefore, cloud computing data storage technology must be characterized by high throughput and transmission rates.

Distributed data storage technology typically includes Google's non-open source Google File System (GFS) and the open source HDFS for GFS developed by the Hadoop development team. Most IT vendors, including Yahoo! Intel's "cloud" program uses HDFS data storage technology. Future developments will focus on large-scale data storage, data encryption and security assurance, and continued improvements in I/O rates.

Huawei offers several widely used solutions in cloud storage.

1. Storage as a Service

   Storage as a Service (STaaS) is a storage resource implemented as an on-premises service that provides users with the same immediacy as public cloud storage, scalability, and pay-as-you-go flexibility without security and performance variability issues. In addition, when staffing becomes a problem, it can be used as a managed service. It also enables customers to access new technologies on-demand as needed, rather than investing capital resources in technologies that have become increasingly obsolete over time.

2. OceanStor DJ

   OceanStor DJ is Huawei's business-driven storage control software for cloud data center development, which manages data center storage resources in a unified way, provides business-driven, automated storage services, and improves the utilization of storage resources and efficiency of storage services in a cloud-driven environment. At its core is the enhancement of OpenStack-related services for unified storage resource management, on-demand allocation, and data protection services. OceanStor DJs decouple applications with underlying storage, breaking the monopoly of traditional devices and application vendors. In a clouded scenario, capabilities such as storage and data protection are provided as services, adapting to the transfer of storage value chains to software and services.

3. OceanStor Dorado V3

OceanStor Dorado V3 is an all-flash storage system for business-critical enterprises. It uses smart chips, NVMe architectures, and FlashLink intelligent algorithms with a latency of up to 0.3 ms for end-to-end acceleration and a three-fold increase in business performance. Supports smooth expansion to 16 controllers to meet unpredictable business growth in the future. A system that supports both SAN and NAS, with enterprise-class features, provides higher quality services for applications such as databases and file sharing. Supports gateway-free dual-life solutions, which can be smoothly upgraded to three-center schemes and converged data management schemes in both places, resulting in 99.9999% reliability assurance. Operating Expense (OPEX) saves 75% by providing data reduction ratios of up to 5:1 with online redeleting and online compression technology. At the same time, to meet the needs of databases, virtual desktops, virtual servers, file-sharing scenarios, to help finance, manufacturing, operators, and other industries to the flash era smooth evolution.

4. OceanStor

OceanStor is a next-generation enterprise storage solution that is cost-effective and sophisticated enough to meet application needs such as OLTP/OLAP, Exchange, server virtualization, and video surveillance for large, medium, and small business databases. The rich Hyper family of data protection software meets users' local, off-site, and multi-site data protection needs, ensuring user business continuity and data availability. The unique ease-of-use software SmartConfig dramatically simplifies the storage configuration process, solves the bottleneck of IT operations professional skills, and meets the critical needs of small- and medium-sized enterprises for IT simplicity and ease of use.

5. FusionStorage

FusionStorage is a distributed storage volume device that forms a virtualized pool of storage resources on the server's local hard disk that provides network RAID protection for virtual machines. FusionStorage enables on-demand data services in storage that genuinely help customers meet cloud challenges based on the performance and capacity of a fully distributed architecture, a flexible and optional infrastructure, and open compatibility for the cloud. FusionStorage starts with the convergence of "three-in-one" distributed block storage, distributed file storage, and distributed object storage. FusionStorage also has the excellent quality of a storage system: good elasticity. FusionStorage features a fully symmetrical distributed architecture based on standard hardware that can easily scale to 4096 nodes, EB-level capacity, and 10 million IOPS (Input/Output

Operations Per Second, read and write per second) to support enterprise-critical business clouding such as high-performance data queries. FusionStorage's last feature is openness, based on an open architecture design that supports mainstream virtualization software, provides an open API for standard interface protocols, and is naturally integrated into the OpenStack cloud infrastructure and Hadoop big data ecosystem.

Cloud storage has become a trend in the future of storage development. Today, cloud storage vendors combine search, application technologies, and cloud storage to deliver a range of data services to enterprises. The future of cloud storage is focused on providing better security and more convenient and efficient data access services.

5.1.4 Data Security Technology of Cloud Storage

Cloud storage enables data sharing stored in a network environment and efficient storage and access to user data, thus providing users with more efficient, convenient, and higher quality of service storage services. However, the security of the cloud storage system itself is often the focus of attention. Cloud storage service providers and related technical personnel must do an excellent job in the security of the stored data protection work to effectively protect the data's privacy and integrity as an entry point. The application of a variety of existing security technologies to improve the security of data in cloud storage.

The data security technologies commonly used in cloud storage are as follows:

1. Identity authentication technology

    Authentication is the first line of defense against data security in cloud storage. There are three standard authentication techniques. First, and easiest, is to use your account number and password to verify before logging into the system. During authentication, users only need to enter the account number and password corresponding to the system requirements to pass the authentication. Once the account number or password is incorrect, it cannot be verified. Second, Kerberos are used for certification. The essence of this authentication method belongs to third-party authentication, which owns the authorized server, and has clear criteria for applying the server to verify the user's password during the resource visit. If verified, the services provided in the system can be obtained. Third, the application of PKI certification. This authentication method is based on the non-symmetric key (public/private key) and is complex, a typical PKI system includes PKI policy, software/hardware system, certificate authority, certificate registrar, certificate issuing system and PKI application.

2. Data encryption technology

    Data encryption technology mainly includes symmetric encryption and asymmetric encryption. There are some differences between the two technologies. In symmetric encryption, encryption and decryption use the same key, the algorithm is simple, the encryption/decryption is easy, efficient, and the execution is fast.

However, the key transmission and management is inconvenient, easy to lose secret due to key leakage, cannot be digitally signed. Asymmetric encryption uses both public and private keys, and even if the redaction is intercepted and the public key is obtained, the private key cannot be obtained. It is not possible to decipher the text. So more security, but the encryption algorithm is complex, encryption and decryption efficiency is low. Symmetric encryption and non-symmetric encryption can be well combined, such as non-symmetric encryption technology to transfer a symmetric key between the two parties, the sending and receiving parties then use the symmetrical key to encrypt/decrypt subsequent transmission of data. This can not only guarantee the security of key transmission, but also improve the encryption/decryption efficiency of data.

3. Technology for data backup and integrity

Cloud computing data centers generally have backup and recovery capabilities for stored data, which largely avoids data loss and ensures data integrity. To call at any time, the system also applied snapshot technology, through the use of those storage devices that can be expanded into a larger capacity. This allows data in the physical space to be stored appropriately and allows the system's data management and control methods to be updated and improved in a timely and effective manner. After application, this technology can break through the space limitations existing in physical containers, and thus improve the stability and security of the system.

5.2 Basic Storage Unit

In modern computer systems, the common storage media are hard disk, optical disk, tape, etc. Hard disk capacity, low price, fast reading speed, high reliability, and other storage media cannot replace the advantages and are considered an important storage device. This section will provide a detailed description of the hard drive from both the mechanical drive and the SSD.

5.2.1 Hard Disk Drive

Mechanical hard drives started in 1956. The world's first disk storage system, IBM 305 RAMAC, was invented by IBM. It has 50 24 in. (about 61 cm) disks, weighs about 1 t, and has a capacity of 5MB. In 1973, IBM successfully developed a new type of hard disk IBM 3340. This hard drive has several coaxial metal discs coated with magnetic material. These disks are sealed in a box together with a movable magnetic head, which can read magnetic signals from the rotating disk surface. This is the closest "ancestor" to the hard drive we use today, and IBM calls it the Winchester hard drive. Because the IBM 3340 has two 30MB storage units, and there was a well-known "Winchester Rifle" caliber and the charge also contained

Fig. 5.8 Winchester hard drive

two numbers "30," so the internal code name of this hard drive was designated as "Winchester." In 1980, Seagate produced the first Winchester hard drive on a personal computer. This hard drive was similar in size to the floppy drive at that time, with a capacity of 5MB. Figure 5.8 shows the Winchester hard drive.

The hard disk's read speed was limited by the rotational speed of the hard disk at that time. Increasing the rotation speed can speed up accessing data, but the head and the platters of the hard disk are in contact with each other. The excessive rotation speed will cause the disk to be damaged, so technicians thought of letting the head "fly" above the platters. The platters' high-speed rotation will generate flowing wind, so as long as the shape of the magnetic head is appropriate, the platters can be rotated quickly without worrying about friction causing malfunctions. This is Winchester technology.

Winchester hard disk uses innovative technology. The magnetic head is fixed on an arm that can move in the disc's radial direction, and the magnetic head does not contact the disc. When the magnetic head moves relative to the disc, the magnetic head can sense the magnetic poles on the disc surface and record or change the magnetic poles' state to complete data reading/writing. Since the magnetic head moves at a high speed relative to the disk and the distance between the two is very close, even a little dust will cause damage to the disk at this time. Therefore, the hard disk needs to be packaged in a sealed box to ensure that the head and the disk are efficient and effective. Work reliably.

The hard disk we usually say mainly refers to the mechanical hard disk, which is mainly composed of the disc, the spindle and the spindle motor, the pre-signal amplifier, the head assembly, the voice coil motor and the interface, as shown in Fig. 5.9.

- Disc and spindle motors. The disc and spindle motor are two closely connected parts, the disc is a circular sheet coated with a layer of magnetic material to record the data, the spindle is driven by the spindle motor, driving the high-speed disc rotation.

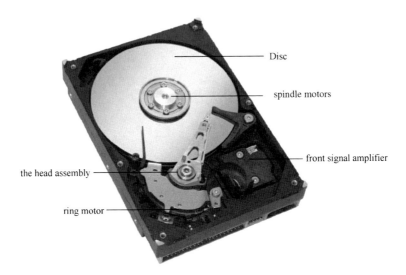

Fig. 5.9 Mechanical hard disk

- The head assembly. The head assembly consists of a read/write head, a drive arm, and a drive shaft. When the platter rotates at high speed, the drive arm drives the reading/writing head of the front end with the drive shaft as the center of the drive to move in the vertical direction of the platter rotation, and the head senses the magnetic signal on the platter to read or change the magnetism of the magnetic material in order to write information.
- Ring motor. It consists of a head-driven car, motor, and shock-proof mechanism, and its function is to drive and position the head with high precision, so that the head can read/write quickly and accurately on the specified track.
- Front signal amplifier. The front-facing signal amplifier is an amplification line sealed in the shielded cavity, which mainly controls the head's induction signal, spindle motor speed control, drive head and head positioning, etc.
- Interface. Interfaces typically contain power interfaces and data transfer interfaces. The current mainstream interface types are SATA and SAS.

A disc inside a hard drive used to store data is a metal disc coated with magnetic material. The platter surface is divided into a circle of tracks, and when the platter rotates at high speed under the drive of the motor, the head set on the platter surface reads and writes data along the track. When the system writes data to the hard disk, a current in the head changes with the contents of the data, which creates a magnetic field that changes the state of the magnetic material on the surface of the disc, and this state remains permanent after the current magnetic field disappears, which is equivalent to saving the data. When the system reads data from the hard disk, the head passes through the designated area of the platter, the magnetic field on the surface of the platter makes the head produce a change in induction current or coil impedance, which is arrested, after some processing, it can restore the original written data.

5.2.2 Solid-State Drive

The world's first SSD appeared in 1989. SSDs were costly at the time, but their performance was much lower than that of ordinary hard drives, so they were not widely used. SSDs have developed to some extent in these areas due to the unique seismic, mute, and low power consumption properties of SSDs in particular markets, such as medical work and military markets.

With the increasing maturity of SSD technology, the manufacturing process's improvement, and the reduction of production costs, SSDs gradually entered the consumer field. In 2006, Samsung released its first laptop with a 32GB SSD. In early 2007, SanDisk released two 32GB SSDs. In 2011, a major flood happened in Thailand. Many mechanical hard drive manufacturers such as Western Digital and Seagate in Thailand's factories were forced to close, resulting in a sharp decline in mechanical hard drive production that year, prices soared. This has largely stimulated demand for SSDs, resulting in a "golden age" for SSDs. Today, SSDs are significantly improved in capacity, cost, transfer rate, and service life compared to their original products. The current market capacity of common SSDs has reached hundreds of GIGb to a few TB, and the price per GB is only a fraction of what it was then, which many consumers can afford. SSDs are one of the essential storage devices in the field of ultra-thin laptops and tablets. In the next few years, it is foreseeable that SSDs will continue to receive great attention.

SSDs consist of master chips and memory chips, which are hard drives made up of SSD arrays. SSDs have the same interface specifications, definitions, functions, and usage methods as hard drives and are identical in form and size to a hard drive. SSDs consist of master chips and memory chips, which, in short, are hard drives made up of arrays of solid-state electronic chips. SSDs have the same interface specifications, definitions, functions, and usage methods as normal hard drives and are identical to normal hard drives in terms of product form factor and size. Because SSDs do not have the rotating structure of ordinary hard drives, they are extremely earthquake-resistant, and the operating temperature range is very large. The extended temperature of electronic hard drives can operate at –45 °C to 85 °C.

SSDs can be widely used in automotive, industrial control, video surveillance, network monitoring, network terminals, power, medical, aviation, navigation equipment, and other fields. Traditional mechanical hard drives are disk-type, with data stored in disk sectors, while the common SSD storage medium is flash or dynamic random access memory (Dynamic Random Access Memory, DRAM). SSDs are one of the trends in the development of hard drives in the future. The internal structure of the SSD is shown in Fig. 5.10.

SSD consists of a memory chip and a master chip. The memory chip is responsible for storing the data, while the master chip controls the read/write process of the

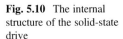

Fig. 5.10 The internal structure of the solid-state drive

data. Memory chips are divided into two types by storage medium, the most common being flash memory as storage media, and the other using DRAM as storage media.

1. Flash-based SSDs

   The most common SSDs use flash memory as storage media. Flash memory can be made into various electronic products, such as SSDs, memory cards, and USB drives, depending on how they are used, all of which are small in size and high in portability. The SSDs discussed in this chapter are flash-based SSDs.

2. DRAM-based SSDs

   This type of SSDs uses DRAM as storage media. This storage medium is currently widely used in memory, performs very well, and has a long service life. The downfall is that it can only store data when it is powered, and if it loses power, the information stored by DRAM is lost, so it needs additional power to protect it. At present, these SSDs are more expensive and have a narrow range of applications.

SSDs have many advantages over traditional hard drives, as follows:

(1) Read fast

Because SSDs use flash as storage media and do not have a disk-motor structure, they save seeking time when reading data, especially when reading randomly. At the same time, the performance of SSDs is not affected by disk fragmentation.

(2) Good earthquake resistance

There are no mechanical moving parts inside the SSD, no mechanical failure, and no fear of collisions, shocks, and vibrations. This does not affect normal use even at high speeds, even with flip tilts, and minimizes the possibility of data loss when a laptop accidentally drops or collides with a hard object.

(3) No noise

There is no mechanical motor inside the SSD, so it is a truly noise-free silent drive.

(4) Small size and lightweight

A small, lightweight circuit board can be integrated with an SSD.

(5) The operating temperature range is larger.

A typical hard drive can only operate in the range of 5–55 °C. Most SSDs can operate in the −10 to 70 °C range, and some industrial-grade SSDs can operate in temperatures ranging from −40 to 85 °C.

However, SSDs also have two big drawbacks, making them unable to substitute for system mechanical hard drives. One drawback is the high cost. At present, the price per unit capacity of SSDs is still significantly higher than traditional mechanical hard drives. High-capacity SSDs are still relatively rare in the market, so those applications that are not sensitive to data read/write speed and system mechanical hard drives are still the first choice. Another drawback is the limited life of SSDs. General high-performance flash memory can be erased 10,000 to 100,000 times, ordinary consumer-grade flash memory can only be erased 3,000 to 30,000 times. As the manufacturing process continues to improve and the size of the memory cell gets smaller, the maximum erase count of flash memory will be further reduced. Fortunately, SSD's master chips can balance chip losses, allowing memory chips to be consumed more evenly, extending service life.

SSDs, as storage devices with higher read/write speeds than traditional mechanical hard drives, are now receiving widespread attention. Because it works differently from traditional mechanical hard drives and does not have any mechanical components, SSDs improve performance quickly. Simultaneously, it also has earthquake-resistant, small size, noise-free, small heat dissipation, and other traditional mechanical hard drives do not have the advantages, so many people hope to replace the traditional mechanical hard drive and become a new generation of storage equipment. However, the cost of SSDs is still higher than that of traditional mechanical drives, and the performance of traditional mechanical drives has been able to meet most of the needs, so in the next few years, traditional mechanical drives and SSDs will coexist and develop together.

Fig. 5.11 DAS

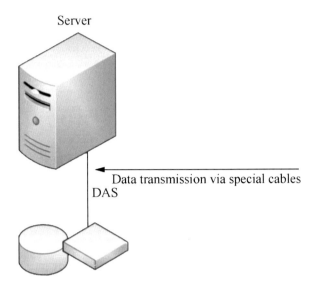

5.3 Network Storage

5.3.1 DAS

DAS refers to connecting an external storage device directly to a server via a connecting cable, as shown in Fig. 5.11. Server structure with a direct external storage scheme is like the personal computer structure, external data storage devices are connected directly to the internal bus using SCSI technology, or Fibre Channel (FC) technology, and data storage devices are part of the entire server structure. In this case, it is often the data and the operating system that are not separated. DAS is a direct connection that meets the storage expansion and high-performance transfer needs of a single server, and the capacity of a single external storage system has grown from a few hundred gigabytes to a few terabytes or more. With the introduction of high-capacity hard drives, the capacity of a single external storage system will increase. In addition, DAS can form a two-machine, highly available system based on disk arrays to meet data storage requirements for high availability. On a trend basis, DAS will continue to be used as a storage mode.

The open system's DAS technology is the first storage technology adopted and has been used for nearly 40 years. Like the structure of a personal computer, DAS hangs external data storage devices directly on the bus inside the server, which is part of the server structure. However, because this storage technology is to hang (storage) devices directly on the server, with the increasing demand, more and more (storage) devices added to the network environment, the server becomes a system bottleneck, resulting in low resource utilization, data sharing is severely restricted. As user data continues to grow, these systems are increasingly plaguing system administrators

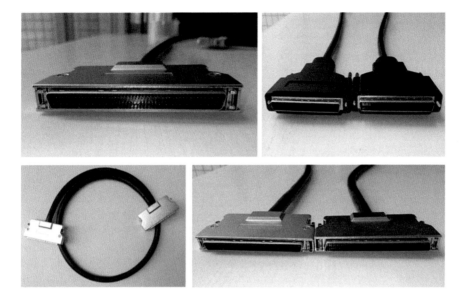

Fig. 5.12 Different types of SCSI cable interfaces

with backup, recovery, scaling, disaster preparedness, and more. Therefore, DAS is only available for small networks.

DAS relies on the server host operating system for data read/write and storage maintenance management. Data backup and recovery requirements consume server host resources (including CPUs, system I/O, etc.). The data flow requires a return host to the hard disk or tape drive connected to the server. Data backup typically consumes 20–30% of the server host resources. As a result, daily data backups for many enterprise users are often made late at night or when business systems are not busy to not interfere with the operation of normal business systems. The greater the amount of data in DAS, the longer it takes to back up and recover, and the greater the dependency and impact on server hardware.

The connection channel between the DAS and the server host is usually an SCSI connection. With the processing power of server CPU becoming more and more powerful, storage hard disk space is getting larger and larger, and the number of array hard disks is increasing, SCSI channel will become I/O bottleneck. The server host SCSI ID has limited resources and limited SCSI channel connectivity. Figure 5.12 shows some common disk interfaces.

Whether it is a DAS or a server host expansion, a cluster of multiple servers from one server, or an expansion of storage array capacity, it can cause downtime of business systems and economic loss to the enterprise. This is unacceptable for key business systems that provide $24\times$ services in the banking, telecommunications, media, and other industries. These reasons have also led to DAS being gradually replaced by more advanced storage technologies.

5.3.2 SAN

SAN is a high-speed storage private network independent of the business network system and uses block-level data as its basic access unit. The main implementations of this network are Fibre Channel Storage Area Network (FC-SAN) and IP storage area network (IP-SAN). Different forms of implementation use different communication protocols and connections to transfer data, commands, and states between servers and storage devices.

Before SAN, DAS was most used. Early data centers used disk arrays to scale storage capacity in the form of DAS, with storage devices per server serving only a single application, creating an isolated storage environment that was difficult to share and manage. With user data growth, the disadvantages of this expansion in terms of expansion and disaster preparedness are becoming evident. The emergence of SAN solves these problems. SAN connects these "storage silos" over a high-speed network shared by multiple servers, enabling offsite backup of data and excellent scalability. These factors have led to the rapid development of SAN.

As an emerging storage solution, SAN mitigates the impact of transmission bottlenecks on systems and greatly improves remote disaster backup's efficiency with its advantages of faster data transfer, greater flexibility, and reduced network complexity.

SAN is a network architecture consisting of storage devices and various system components, including servers that use storage device resources, host bus adapters (HBA) cards for connecting storage devices, and FC switches.

In SAN, all traffic-related to data storage is done on a separate network isolated from the application network, which means that when data is transferred in SAN, it does not impact the existing application system data network. As a result, SAN can improve the overall I/O capabilities of the network without reducing the original application system's efficiency network while increasing redundant links to storage systems and providing support for highly available cluster systems.

With the continuous development of SAN, three types of storage area network systems have been formed: FC-based FC-SAN, IP-based IP-SAN, and SAS-SAN-based saS bus. Here we learn about FC-SAN and IP-SAN.

In FC-SAN, two network interface adapters are typically configured on a storage server: a network interface adapter for a normal network card (Network Interface Card, NIC) that connects to a business IP network through which the server interacts with the client, and a network interface adapter that is an HBA connected to the FC-SAN through which the server communicates with the storage device in the FC-SAN. The FC-SAN architecture is shown in Fig. 5.13.

IP-SAN is a popular network storage technology in recent years. In the early SAN environment, data was propagated in Fibre Channel as a block-based access unit. For instance, the early SAN was FC-SAN. FC-SAN must be procured and deployed separately because FC protocols are not IP compatible, and its high price and complex configuration are a challenge for many small and medium-sized businesses. Therefore, FC-SAN is mainly used for high-end storage requirements with high

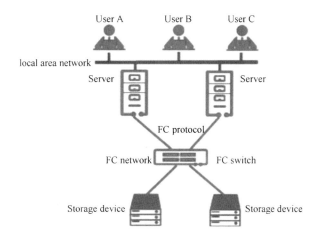

Fig. 5.13 FC-SAN architecture

performance, redundancy, availability, etc. In order to increase the popularity and scope of SAN and take full advantage of the architectural advantages of SAN itself, the direction of SAN began to consider integration with the already popular and relatively inexpensive IP network. Therefore, IP-SAN, which uses an existing IP network architecture, has emerged. IP-SAN combines standard TCP/IP and SCSI instruction sets based on IP networks to achieve block-level data transmission.

The difference between IP-SAN and FC-SAN is that the transport protocol and transport media are different. Common IP-SAN protocols are iSCSI, FCIP, iFCP, etc., where iSCSI protocol is the fastest-growing protocol standard. Usually, we refer to IP-SAN refers to the iSCSI protocol-based SAN.

The purpose of an iSCSI protocol-based SAN is to establish an SAN connection to iSCSI Target (target, usually a storage device) over an IP network using the local iSCSI Initiator (launcher, usually a server). The IP-SAN architecture is shown in Fig. 5.14.

Compared with FC-SAN, IP-SAN has the following advantages.

- Access standardization. There is no need for dedicated HBA cards and FC switches, just plain Ethernet cards and Ethernet switches for storage and server connectivity.
- Transmission distance is far. In theory, IP-SAN can be used as long as it is accessed by IP networks, which is one of the most widely used networks.
- It is maintainable. On the one hand, most network maintenance personnel have an IP network foundation, IP-SAN is naturally more acceptable than FC-SAN. On the other hand, IP network maintenance tools have been very developed, IP-SAN fully developed the "take it."
- It is easy to extend the bandwidth in the future. Because the iSCSI protocol is hosted by Ethernet, with the rapid development of Ethernet, IP-SAN single-port bandwidth expansion to more than 10GB is an inevitable result of development.

These benefits reduce the Total Cost of Ownership (TCO). For example, to build a storage system, the total cost of ownership includes the need to purchase disk

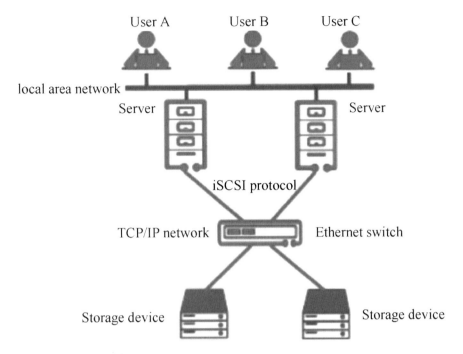

Fig. 5.14 IP-SAN architecture

arrays and access devices (HBA cards and switches), personnel training, routine maintenance, subsequent expansion, disaster tolerance expansion, etc. Because of the wide application advantages of IP network, Ip-SAN can significantly reduce the cost of purchasing access equipment for a single purchase, reduce maintenance costs, and subsequent expansion and network expansion costs are significantly reduced. Ip-SAN and other aspects of FC-SAN are shown in Table 5.1.

5.3.3   NAS

NAS is a technology that consolidates distributed, independent data into large, centrally managed data centers for access by different hosts and application servers. Typically, NAS is defined as a special dedicated file storage server that includes storage devices such as disk arrays, CD/DVD drives, tape drives, removable storage media, and embedded system software that provides cross-platform file-sharing capabilities.

The emergence of NAS is inextricable to the development of the network. After the emergence of THEPANET, modern network technology has been developed rapidly. People share more and more data in the network, but sharing files in the

Table 5.1 Comparison between IP-SAN and FC-SAN

Description	IP-SAN	FC-SAN
Network architecture	Use an existing IP network	Build FC networks and HBA cards separately
The transmission distance	Theoretically, there is no distance limit	Limited by FC transmission distance
Management, maintenance	It is as easy to operate as an IP device	Technology and management are complex.
Compatibility	Compatible with all IP network devices	Poor compatibility
Performance	At present, the mainstream 10GB, 100GB, higher latency	Mainly using 8GB and 16GB, low latency
Cost	Purchase and maintenance costs are low	Purchase (FC switches, HBA cards, FC disk arrays, etc.) and maintenance costs are high.
Disaster tolerance	It can be local and offsite disaster tolerance, and the cost is low	Disaster-tolerant hardware and software costs are high.
Security	Lower	Higher

network faces cross-platform access and data security and many other problems. Early network sharing was shown in Fig. 5.15.

To solve this problem, you can set up a dedicated computer to hold many shared files, connect to an existing network, and allow all users on the entire network to share their storage space. Through this approach, the early UNIX network environment evolved into a way of relying on "file servers" to share data.

Using specialized servers to provide shared data storage, with a large amount of storage disk space, is necessary to ensure data security and reliability. Simultaneously, a single server is responsible for many servers' access needs and needs to optimize the file-sharing server in terms of file I/O. Also, computers used in this manner should have an I/O-only operating system connected to an existing network, which is not required for such servers. Users on the network can access files on this particular server as if they were accessing files on their workstation, essentially fulfilling the need for file sharing for all users throughout the network. The TCP/IP network sharing indication in the early UNIX environment is shown in Fig. 5.16.

With the development of the network, there are more and more data sharing needs between different network computers. In most cases, systems and users on the network are expected to connect to specific file systems and access data, so that remote files from shared computers can be processed in the same way as local files in the local operating system, providing users with a virtual collection of files. The files in this collection do not exist on the local computer's storage device, and their location is virtual. One of this storage approach's evolutions is integration with traditional client/server environments that support Windows operating systems. This involves issues such as Windows network capabilities, private protocols, and UNIX/Linux-based database servers. In its early stages of development, a Windows network consisted of a network file server that is still in use today and uses a

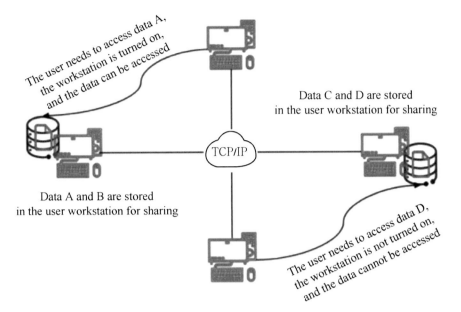

Fig. 5.15 Early network sharing

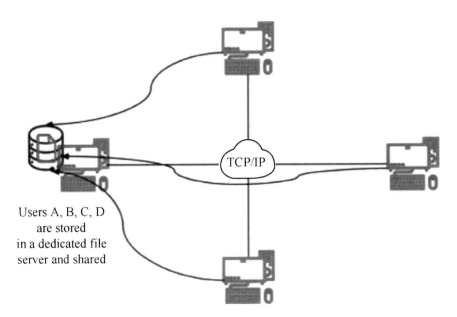

Fig. 5.16 TCP/IP network sharing in the early UNIX environment

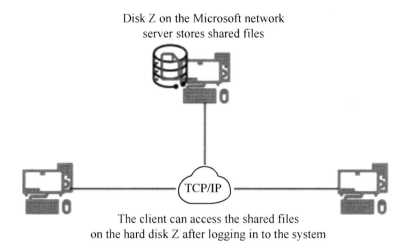

Disk Z on the Microsoft network
server stores shared files

TCP/IP

The client can access the shared files
on the hard disk Z after logging in to the system

Fig. 5.17   Early Windows file server diagram

dedicated network system protocol. Early Windows file servers were shown in Fig. 5.17.

The advent of file-sharing servers has led to the development of data storage toward centralized storage, which has led to rapid growth in centralized data and business volumes. As a result, NAS, which focuses on file-sharing services, has emerged.

NAS typically has its nodes on a local area network, allowing users to access file data directly over the network without an application server's intervention. In this configuration, NAS centrally manages and processes all shared files on the network, freeing the load from applications or enterprise servers, effectively reducing the total cost of ownership and protecting users' investments. Simply put, an NAS device is a device that is connected to a network and has file storage capabilities, hence the name "network file storage device." It is a kind of dedicated file data storage server, with the file as the core, realizes the storage and management of Chinese pieces, completely separates the server's storage device, thus freeing up bandwidth and improving performance.

Essentially, NAS is a storage device, not a server. NAS is not a Lite file server. It has features that some servers do not have. The role of the server is to process the business. The role of the storage device is to store data. In a complete application, the environment should be the two devices organically combined.

NAS's intrinsic value lies in its ability to leverage existing resources in the data center to deliver file storage services in a fast and low-cost manner. Today's solutions are compatible across UNIX, Linux, and Windows environments and easily provide the ability to connect to the user's TCP/IP network. The NAS indication is shown in Fig. 5.18.

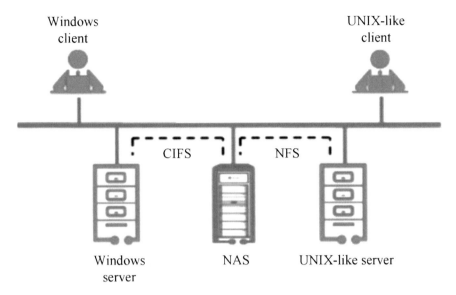

Fig. 5.18 NAS schematic

NAS requires storing and backing up large amounts of data, based on which a stable and efficient data transfer service is required. Such requirements cannot be accomplished by hardware alone, and NAS needs some software to do so.

NAS devices support reading/writing to CIFS or NFS, as well as both.

CIFS is a public, open file system developed by Microsoft's SMB. SMB is a set of file-sharing protocols set by Microsoft based on NetBIOS. CIFS allows users to access data on remote computers. In addition, CIFS provides a mechanism to avoid read and write conflicts and thus support multi-user access.

In order for Windows and UNIX computers to share resources, Windows customers can use the resources on their UNIX computers as if they were using a Windows NT server without changing settings, and the best way to do this is to install the software in UNIX that supports the SMB/CIFS protocol. When all major operating systems support CIFS, "communication" between computers is convenient. Samba software helps Windows and UNIX users achieve this. People set up a CIFS-based shared server, share resources to its target computer, the target computer in their system through a simple shared mapping, the CIFS server shared resources mounted to their systems, as their local file system resources to use. With a simple mapping, the computer customer gets all the shared resources they want from the CIFS server.

NFS was developed by Sun, which enables users to share files and is designed to be used between different systems, so its communication protocols are designed to be independent of hosts and operating systems. When users want to use remote files, only the use of mount commands, you can mount the remote file system under their file system. The use of remote files and native files is no different.

The NFS platform-independent file-sharing mechanism is based on the XDR/RPC protocol.

External Data Representation (XDR) can transform the data format. Typically, XDRs transform data into a uniform standard data format to ensure data consistency representing different platforms, operating systems, and programming languages.

Remote Procedure Call (RPC) requests service from the remote computer. The user transmits the request over the network to the remote computer, which processes the request.

Using the Virtual File System (VFS) mechanism, NFS sends user requests for remote data access to the server through a unified file inquiry protocol and remote procedure calls. NFS continues to evolve, and since its emergence in 1985, it has undergone four versions of the update and been ported to all major operating systems, becoming the de facto standard for distributed file systems. NFS appears in an era of unstable network conditions, initially based on UDP transmission, rather than highly reliable TCP. While UDP works well on higher reliability LANs, it is not up to the task when running on less reliable WAN networks such as the Internet. At present, with the improvement of TCP, NFS running on TCP has high reliability and good performance.

5.4 Storage Reliability Technology

5.4.1 Traditional RAID Technology

RAID technology has been continuously developed, now has RAID 0 to RAID 6, a total of 7 basic RAID levels. In addition, there are some basic RAID-level combinations, such as RAID 10 (a combination of RAID 1 and RAID 0) and RAID 50 (a combination of RAID 5 and RAID 0). Different RAID levels represent different storage performance, data security, and storage costs. Here we only cover RAID 0, RAID 1, RAID 5, and RAID 6.

1. RAID 0

   RAID 0, also known as Stripe, is based on combining multiple physical disks into a large logical disk. It represents the most efficient storage performance of all RAID levels, is not redundant, cannot be parallel I/O, but is the fastest. When data is stored, the data is segmented based on the number of disks that build RAID 0, and then written in parallel into the disk at the same time, so RAID 0 is the fastest of all levels. However, RAID 0 does not have redundancy, and if a physical disk is corrupted, all data is lost. Theoretically, the number of disks and total disk performance should be multiplied, and the full disk performance is equal to the "single disk performance × number of disks." However, due to bus I/O bottlenecks and other factors, RAID performance is no longer multiplied by the number of disks. Assuming that one disk's performance is 50MB/s, the RAID 0 performance of two disks is about 96MB/s, and the RAID 0 of 3 disks is

Logical Disk

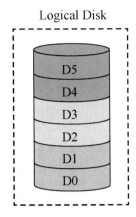

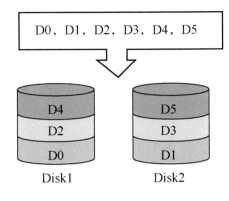

Fig. 5.19 RAID 0 schematic

probably 130MB/s instead of 150MB/s, so the RAID 0 of both disks is the most prominent performance improvement. Figure 5.19 shows the RAID 0 indication. There are two disks, Disk1 and Disk2, and RAID 0 does this by dividing the stored content into two parts based on the number of disks. D0 and D1 are stored in Disk1 and Disk2, respectively, and when D0 storage is complete, D2 is stored in Disk1, with the rest of the data block being the same. This allows you to think of two disks as a large disk with I/O on both sides. However, if a piece of data is corrupted, the entire data is lost.

RAID 0 has good read and write performance, but there is no data redundancy. Therefore, RAID 0 is suitable for applications that have fault tolerance for data access, and applications that can reform data through other means, such as Web applications and streaming media.

2. RAID 1

RAID 1 is also called Mirror or Mirroring. Its purpose is to maximize the availability and repairability of user data. The principle of RAID 1 is to automatically copy 100% of the user's data to the disk to another disk. While RAID 1 stores data on the primary disk, it also stores the same data on the mirror disk. When the primary disk is damaged, the mirror disk replaces the work of the primary hard disk. Because there are mirrored disks for data backup, the data security of RAID 1 is the best among all RAID levels. However, no matter how many disks are used for RAID 1, the effective data space is only a single-disk capacity, so RAID 1 has the lowest disk utilization among all RAID levels.

Figure 5.20 shows a schematic of RAID 1. There are two disks Disk1 and Disk2 in the picture. When storing data, store the content to be stored in Disk1, and store the data again in Disk2 to achieve data backup.

RAID 1 has the highest unit storage cost among all RAID levels. However, because it provides higher data security and availability, RAID 1 is suitable for read-intensive On-Line Transaction Processing (OLTP) and other applications

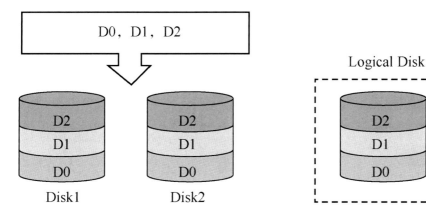

Fig. 5.20   RAID 1 schematic

that require high read/write performance and reliability of data, such as e-mail, operating systems, application files, and random access environments.

3. RAID 5

RAID 5, whose full name is "Independent Data Disk and Distributed Check Block," is one of the most common RAID levels in advanced RAID systems and is widely used due to its excellent performance and data redundancy balance design. RAID 5 uses parity for checking and error correction. RAID 5 is shown in Fig. 5.21. In the figure, for example, three disks, P is the check value of the data, and D is the real data. RAID 5 does not back up stored data, but instead stores the data and corresponding parity information on the disks that make up RAID 5, and the data and corresponding parity information are stored on different disks. When one of RAID 5's disk data is corrupted, the corrupted data can be recovered using the remaining data and the corresponding parity information. As a result, RAID 5 is a storage solution that combines storage performance, data security, and storage costs.

RAID 5, despite some capacity losses, provides better overall performance and is therefore a widely used data protection solution. It is suitable for I/O intensive, high read/write ratio applications, such as online transaction processing.

4. RAID 6

RAID 6 is a RAID level designed to enhance data protection further. RAID 6 adds a second independent parity block compared to RAID 5. As a result, each block of data's equivalent has two check protection barriers (one for hierarchical checks and the other for general checks), so RAID 6's data redundancy performance is excellent. However, with the addition of a check, write efficiency is lower than RAID 5, and the design of the control system is more complex, and the second verification area reduces effective storage space.

The common RAID 6 techniques are P-Q and DP, which have different methods of obtaining verification information, but both allow for the loss of data on two disks throughout the array. RAID 6 is shown in Fig. 5.22.

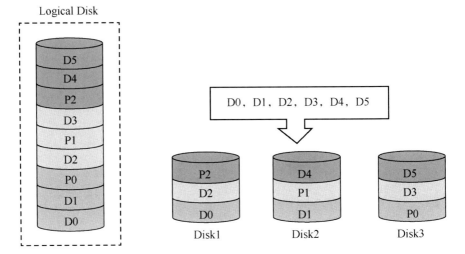

Fig. 5.21 RAID 5 schematic

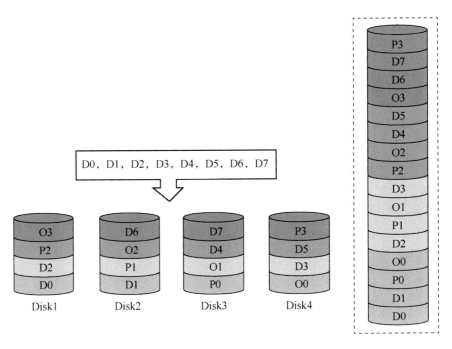

Fig. 5.22 RAID 6 schematic

RAID 6's data security is higher than RAID 5, even if two disks in the array fail. The array is still able to continue working and recover data from the failed disk. However, RAID 6 controller design is more complex, write speed is not very fast, and computational verification information and verification of data correctness takes more time. When writing for each block of data, two independent validation calculations are performed, and the system load is heavy. Disk utilization is lower than RAID 5, and the configuration is more complex, making it suitable for environments that require more data accuracy and completeness.

5.4.2   RAID 2.0 + technology

RAID technology is a technique for storing the same data in different places on multiple disks. By storing data on multiple disks, input/output operations can overlap in a balanced manner, improving performance, and increasing the average time between failures.

However, there is no reliability guarantee for the traditional RAID system during the refactoring process. If a lousy disk occurs before the refactoring is complete, the data will be lost and unrecoverable. Therefore, for a storage system, the most important sign of its reliability is that the shorter the RAID refactoring time, the better, thereby reducing the probability of another bad disk before the refactoring is complete. Early storage systems mostly used FC disks and had a capacity of only a few tens of gigabytes, so the refactoring time is short and the probability of another bad disk in refactoring is low. However, with the rapid growth of disk capacity, disk read/write speed is affected by disk speed and other aspects of slow growth, cannot meet the system's refactoring time requirements. Over the past few years, companies in many storage areas, such as Huawei and 3PAR, have evolved RAID technology columns from disk-based RAID to more flexible RAID 2.0 and RAID 2.0 plus technologies that integrate data protection and cross-disk planning for data distribution, while fully meeting storage applications in virtual machine environments.

RAID 2.0 is an enhanced RAID technology that effectively solves the problem that data is easily lost during reconstruction due to the increasing capacity of mechanical hard drives and the increasing time required to reconstruct a mechanical hard drive (i.e., the growing refactoring window of traditional RAID groups). The basic idea is to cut a large mechanical hard drive into smaller chunks (Chunk) at a fixed capacity, usually 64MB in length, and raid groups are built on these small chunks, called Chunk Groups. At this time, the hard disk no longer constitutes a traditional RAID relationship. However, it may have a larger number of hard disk groups (recommended maximum number of hard drives 96 to 120, not recommended more than 120 disks), each hard disk on different blocks can be with this hard disk group on different hard drives on the block to form different RAID type of blocking groups, such a hard disk block can belong to multiple RAID types of multiple chunk groups. In this form of organization, a storage system based on RAID 2.0 technology can be refactored concurrently on all hard drives on a hard drive group after a failure, rather than on a single hot backup disk of a traditional RAID. Thus, it greatly reduces the refactoring time, reduces the risk of data loss due to the expansion of the refactoring window, and ensures the performance and

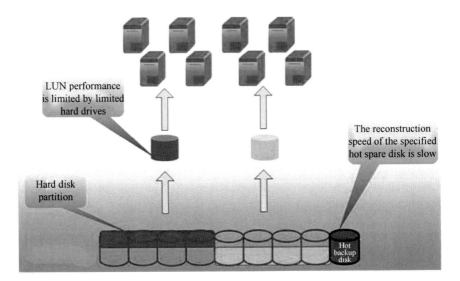

Fig. 5.23 Storage array failure recovery mechanism based on traditional RAID technology

reliability of the storage system while increasing the hard disk's capacity significantly. Figures 5.23 and 5.24 show the storage array failure recovery mechanism based on traditional RAID technology and the storage array failure recovery mechanism based on RAID 2.0 technology. RAID 2.0 does not change the traditional algorithms for various RAID types but narrows the RAID range to a block group. As a result, RAID 2.0 technology has the following technical characteristics:

- Several dozens or even hundreds of mechanical hard drives to form a hard disk group.
- The hard disk group of hard drives are divided into dozens or hundreds of gigabytes of chunks, different hard disk blocks form a block group.
- RAID calculations are performed within a chunk group, the system no longer has a hot backup disk, but is replaced by a hot backup block that is retained within the same chunk group.

Storage systems that use RAID 2.0 technology have the following advantages because refactoring can occur concurrently on hot backup space reserved for all other hard drives in the same hard drive group after a failure of a hard drive in a storage system using RAID 2.0 technology.

- Quick refactoring: All hard drives in the storage pool are involved in refactoring, significantly faster than traditional RAID refactoring.
- Automatic load balancing: RAID 2.0 allows hard drives to share the load evenly, no more hot backup disks, improving system performance and hard drive reliability.

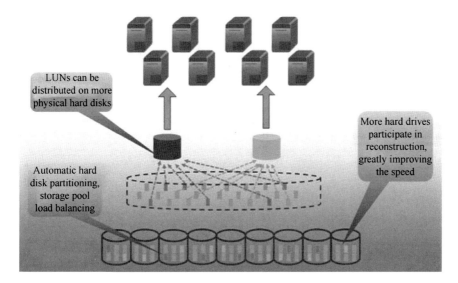

Fig. 5.24 Storage array failure recovery mechanism based on RAID 2.0 technology

- System performance improvement: LUNs are created based on chunk groups and can be distributed on more physical hard drives regardless of the number of traditional RAID drives, resulting in an effective increase in system performance as hard disk I/O bandwidth increases.
- Self-healing: When a hard drive alert occurs, there is no need for a hot backup disk, no need to replace the fault disk immediately, and the system can be quickly refactored for self-healing.

RAID 2.0 plus provides more granular resource particles (up to tens of kilobytes) on top of RAID 2.0, forming standard allocation and recycling units for storage resources, similar to virtual machines in computational virtualization, which we call virtual blocks. These consistent virtual blocks of capacity make up a unified pool of storage resources in which all applications, middleware, virtual machines, and operating systems can allocate and reclaim resources on demand. Compared to traditional RAID technology, RAID 2.0 plus technology virtualizes and pre-configures storage resources, and the application and release of storage resources is fully automated through storage pools, eliminating the need for time-consuming and error-prone manual configuration processes such as RAID group creation, LUN creation, and LUN formatting of traditional RAID arrays. As a result, RAID 2.0 plus technology addresses the need for dynamic on-demand allocation and release of storage resources in a virtual machine environment. Based on RAID 2.0, RAID 2.0 plus technology has the following technical characteristics:

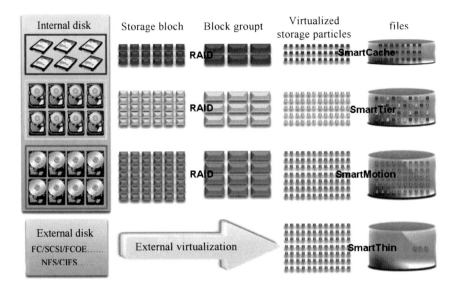

Fig. 5.25 Storage framework based on RAID 2.0+ technology

- On the basis of RAID 2.0, the chunk group is divided into virtualized storage particles with a capacity of 256KB to 64MB.
- Storage resources are automatically allocated and released in the particles mentioned above.
- The granularity mentioned above can be measured in storage pools or between different storage pools for fine-grained graded storage.
- After the system scales performance or capacity by extending the controller, these standard particles can be migrated automatically for load balancing purposes.

Figure 5.25 shows a storage array based on RAID 2.0 plus technology.

RAID 2.0 plus technology is primarily used to intelligently allocate system resources to meet the storage needs of virtual machine environments. The advantages are as follows:

- Storage resources are automatically allocated and released on demand to meet the most essential storage needs of virtual machines (see Fig. 5.26).
- Different data can be stored hierarchically based on real-time business conditions to meet high-performance business needs through flexible provisioning of high-performance storage resources such as SSDs (see Fig. 5.27).
- Automatic migration of data based on business characteristics to improve storage efficiency (see Fig. 5.28).

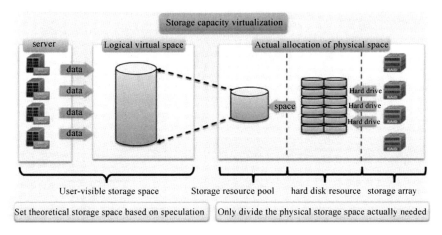

Fig. 5.26 Storage capacity virtualization based on RAID 2.0 + technology

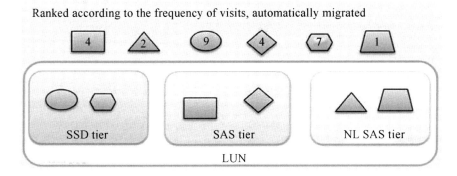

Fig. 5.27 Real-time resource allocation based on RAID 2.0 + technology

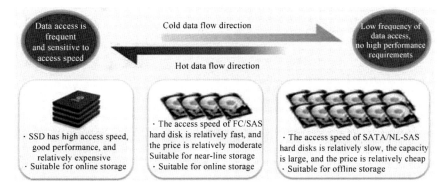

Fig. 5.28 Automatic data migration based on RAID 2.0 + technology

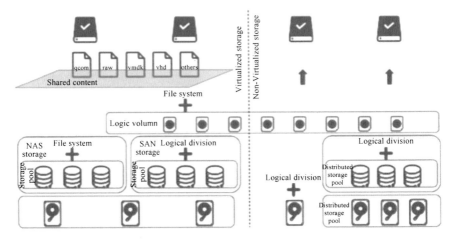

Fig. 5.29 Virtualized storage architecture

5.5   Storage Virtualization

Storage virtualization is the process of transforming traditional computer hardware data storage into virtual storage. Storage virtualization integrates a single function within the system, improving the comprehensiveness of the system. Storage virtualization technology is a means of storage virtualization, which virtualizes complex and diverse real-world technology devices abstractly and achieves reasonable control over real-world physical devices. From the consumer's point of view, storage virtualization is the original disk, hard disk storage data technology to virtualize, the application of all the data stored through virtualization, consumers no longer have to consider storage location and storage security. From enterprise managers' perspective, storage virtualization stores all enterprise data information in virtualized storage pools and integrates information management, enabling enterprise managers to use information more quickly and efficiently.

The virtualized storage architecture is shown in Fig. 5.29. In this architecture, the bottom layer is the physical disk. The top layer is the cloud hard disk. The middle through a series of logical division, file system formatting and other operations.

5.5.1   Virtualization of I/O Paths

I/O virtualization is a complex but essential part of virtualization technology. Overall, I/O virtualization includes software-assisted virtualization and hardware-assisted virtualization. Software-assisted virtualization can be divided into full virtualization and semi-virtualization. If broken down according to device type, it can also be divided into character device I/O virtualization (keyboard, mouse,

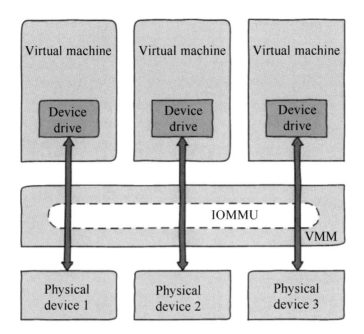

Fig. 5.30 IOMMU architecture

monitor), block device I/O virtualization (disk, CD), and network device I/O virtualization (network card).

Both full and semi-virtualization are implemented at the software level, and performance is naturally not too high. The best way to improve performance is through hardware. If you let a virtual machine dominate a physical device and use it as a host, performance is undoubtedly the best. A critical virtualization technology in I/O virtualization is called I/O pass-through technology, enabling virtual machines to access physical devices directly through hardware without having to pass through VMM or be intercepted by VMM. Because direct access to physical devices by multiple virtual machines involves memory access, which is shared, the appropriate technology (the IOMMU architecture shown in Fig. 5.30) is required to isolate memory access by individual virtual machines.

I/O pass-through technology requires appropriate hardware support to complete, typically VT-d technology, which is achieved through chip-level retrofits. This approach has a qualitative improvement in performance, does not require modification of the operating system, portability is also outstanding.

However, there are limitations to this approach, and if another virtual machine occupies the device, the current virtual machine can no longer use the device. To solve this problem so that more virtual machines can share a physical device, academics and industry have made many improvements. PCI-SIG released the SR-IOV specification (SR-IOV architecture shown in Fig. 5.31), which details how hardware vendors share single I/O device hardware across multiple virtual

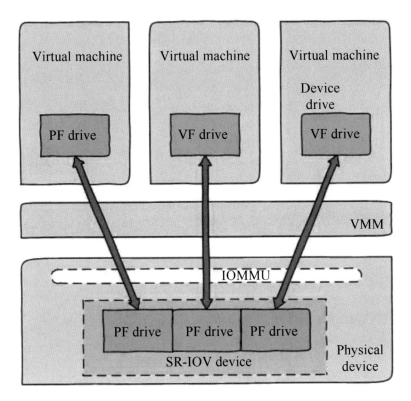

Fig. 5.31 SR-IOV architecture

machines. In general, clients drive the SR-IOV capabilities of discovery devices through Physical Functions (PF) and divide physical resources, including send and receive queues, into subsets based on the number of Virtual Functions (VF), and then PF drivers abstract those resource subsets into VF devices so that VF devices can be assigned to virtual machines through some communication mechanism.

Although virtualized I/O pass-through technology for hardware storage I/O paths eliminates the additional overhead associated with VMM intervention in virtual machine I/O, I/O devices can cause significant disruption in I/O operations. Virtual machines cannot handle outages directly for security reasons, so interrupt requests need to be routed securely and isolated from the VMM to the appropriate virtual machines. So in practice, it is generally a combination of software/hardware virtualization methods.

5.5.2 Block-Level and File-Level Storage Virtualization

1. Block-level storage virtualization

With the increase of single-disk capacity, the problems brought about by the traditional RAID method are becoming more and more apparent, especially after the appearance of lousy disk RAID reconstruction time is getting longer and longer, and the reliability of the system is greatly challenged. Block-level storage virtualization breaks the traditional RAID method, abstracts the real physical address of storage to the user, and provides a storage service for the user's program's logical storage. At the software level, it parses logical I/O requests and maps them to the correct physical address. As a result, storage virtualization allows administrators to provide freely scalable storage capacity without users being aware of the trivial details of storage extensions, data protection, and system maintenance behind their storage.

Because of the advanced nature of block-level storage virtualization technology, many storage vendors are starting to use it in their storage product lines through self-study or acquisition, such as:

- On January 2, 2008, IBM acquired XIV, an Israeli storage technology company whose technology and personnel were incorporated into the storage of the system business unit of IBM's Systems and Technology division.
- On January 29, 2008, Dell acquired Compellent for $1.4 billion.
- 2010, HP acquired 3PAR for $2.35 billion.

  The acquisition of new vendors by these traditional storage vendors values the new storage revolution brought about by their block-level storage virtualization technology, which enriches the product range of traditional storage vendors and is better suited to modern big data storage applications.

  The principle of block-level storage virtualization technology is to break a single disk into countless small chunks, each of which acts as the smallest cell for storing data, which is randomly and evenly distributed across all chunks. When you use a storage system, follow these steps.

- Step 1: For physical hard drives within the system, three types of storage pools are formed according to the media's performance and for external storage pools that are otherwise accessed to the system.
- Step 2: Cut each hard disk space inside the system into 64MB logical blocks.
- Step 3: Divide multiple logical blocks from different hard drives into logical block groups by RAID group.
- Step 4: Cut the logical block group into 512KB to 64MB, the default 4MB (size configurable) finer-grained logical block.
- Step 5: Make 1 to N fine-grained logical blocks into volumes/files on demand so that the configured storage space can be used the way it was.

  The logical structure of block-level storage virtualization is shown in Fig. 5.32.

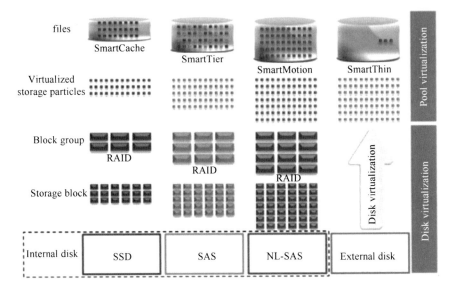

Fig. 5.32 Logical structure of block-level storage virtualization

2. File-level storage virtualization

The bottom-level physical disks and centralized and distributed storage consisting of physical disks are described earlier. Whether centralized or distributed storage, using RAID or replica mechanisms results in a physical volume, but in most cases the entire physical volume is not mounted to the upper-level applications (operating system or virtualization system, where we refer only to virtualized systems) for data security reasons. Physical volumes are typically grouped into volume groups, which are then divided into logical volumes, and the upper layer applies space that uses logical volumes.

In cloud computing, virtualization programs format logical volumes, and virtualized file systems vary from vendor to vendor. VMware uses Virtual Machine File System (VMFS) and Huawei use virtual mirror management systems, all of which are high-performance cluster file systems that allow virtualization to go beyond a single system and allow multiple compute nodes to access a consolidated clustered storage pool at the same time. A file system that computes a cluster ensures that a server or application does not fully control access to the file system.

In the virtual mirror management system, it is a clustered file system based on SAN storage, so when using FusionStorage to provide storage space, it can only be non-virtualized storage. FusionCompute manages virtual machine images and profiles as a file through a virtual image management system. The virtual image management system ensures the consistency of data reading/writing in the cluster through a distributed lock mechanism. The virtualization program's minimum storage unit is the LUN, which corresponds to the volume, which is the

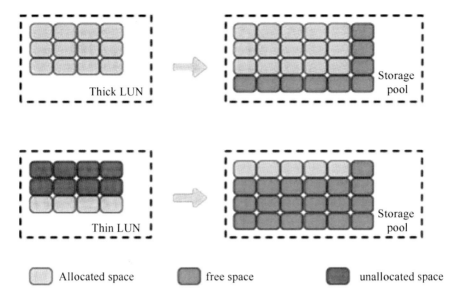

Fig. 5.33 Space allocation of Thick LUN and Thin LUN

management object inside the storage system, and the LUN is the external embodiment of the volume. LUNs and volumes are divided from a pool of resources.

With virtualization, LUNs can be divided into Tick LUNs and Sin LUNs.

The Chinese name of Thick LUN is Traditional Non-Thin LUN, a type of LUN that supports virtual resource allocation and enables easier creation, expansion, and compression operations. Once thick LUNs are created, a total amount of storage space is allocated from the storage pool, i.e., the LUN size is precisely equal to the allocated space. As a result, it has high, predictable performance.

Thin LUN, whose Chinese name is Thin LUN, is also a type of LUN that supports virtual resource allocation and enables easier creation, capacity expansion, and compression operations. When thin LUNs are created, you can set the initial allocated capacity. Once created, the storage pool allocates only the initial capacity size space, with the remaining space still in the storage pool. When the usage of the allocated storage space of the Sin LUN reaches the threshold, the storage system divides a certain amount of storage space from the storage pool to the Sin LUN until the Sin LUN is equal to the full capacity set. As a result, it has a higher utilization of storage space.

The main differences between Thick LUN and Sin LUN are as follows:

(1) Space allocation

Thick LUN allocates all the storage space needed when it is created, and Thin LUN is an on-demand spatial organization method that allocates all the storage space needed when it is created, but dynamically allocates it based on usage (see Fig. 5.33).

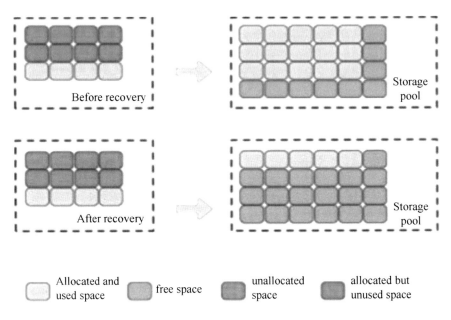

Fig. 5.34 Thin LUN space recovery

(2) Space recovery

Spatial reclaiming refers to freeing up resources in a storage pool that other LUNs can reuse. Thick LUN does not have the concept of space reclamation because it takes up all the storage space allocated to it by the storage pool at the time of creation, and even if the data in the Thick LUN is deleted, the storage space allocated to it by the storage pool is still occupied and cannot be used by other LUNs. If you manually delete an entire Thick LUN that is no longer in use, its corresponding storage space is also reclaimed.

Thin LUN can automatically allocate new storage space with the increase of space occupancy and realize the release of storage space when the files in Sin LUN are deleted, realize the reuse of storage space, and significantly improve storage utilization space. Thin LUN space reclamation is shown in Fig. 5.34.

(3) Performance difference

Because Thick LUNs have all the allocated space from the start, Thick LUNs have high performance when reading/writing sequentially but can waste some storage space.

Thin LUN is a real-time allocation of space, so each expansion needs to increase capacity, background reformatting, and performance. And each allocation of space can result in a discontinuity in the storage space on the hard disk, which can result in the hard disk spending more time looking for storage locations when reading/writing data and having an impact on performance when reading/writing in sequence.

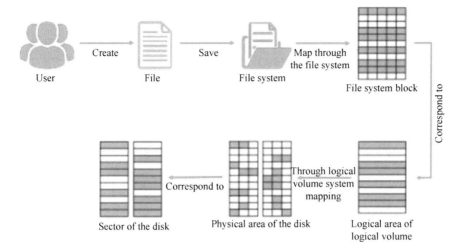

Fig. 5.35 Working process of the operating system file system

3. Application scenario

The use scenario for Thick LUN is as follows:

- Scenarios that require high performance.
- Scenarios that are less sensitive to storage utilization.
- Scenarios where the cost requirements are not too high.

The use scenario for Thin LUN is as follows:

- A scenario that requires general performance.
- Scenarios that are sensitive to storage utilization.
- Scenarios that are sensitive to cost requirements.
- It is hard to estimate storage space scenarios in real-world applications.

In addition to virtualized clustered file systems, common file systems include NAS Storage File Systems (NFS and CIFS, described above) and operating system file systems.

A file system is a hierarchical organizational structure of many files, and once the operating system has a file system, the data we see can be reflected as a file or folder before it can be copied, pasted, deleted, and recovered at any time. The file system uses how the directory organizes the data into layers, and the directory is where the file pointer is saved. All file systems maintain this directory, the operating system maintains only native directories, and clusters need to maintain NAS or shared directories formed by cluster file systems.

Common operating system file formats include FAT32 (Windows), NTFS (Windows), UFS (UNIX), EXT2/3/4 (Linux), and so on.

Figure 5.35 shows the working process of the operating system file system. These include:

- The user or application has created a file or folder.
- These files or folders are stored on the file system.
- The file system maps the data corresponding to these files to the file system block.
- The file system block corresponds to the logical region formed by the logical volume.
- Map the logical region to the physical area of the physical disk through the operating system or virtual machine, that is, the logical volume we mentioned earlier corresponds to the physical volume.
- The physical volume for the physical region may contain one or more physical disks.

5.5.3   Host-Based Storage Virtualization

Today, storage virtualization technology has become the main direction of the future development of information storage technology. There are many ways to implement it, and it is more mature, and it is widely used in practice. Virtual storage based on computer hosting is a vital storage virtualization technology based on volume management software. Today, most operating systems such as common host server systems, Windows or Linux, come with volume management software. If an enterprise wants to implement a host-based storage virtualization application, it does not need to purchase additional commercial software, which can be achieved with the operating system's software. So it is much cheaper to deploy than buying commercial storage virtualization products. At the same time, because the virtual layer and file system are on the same host server in host-based storage virtualization, the combination of the two can not only realize the flexible management of storage capacity, but also the logical volume and file system can dynamically adjust their capacity without downtime, have high stability, and support heterogeneous storage system.

But there are obvious drawbacks to this approach. Because virtual volume management software is deployed with the host, the volume management software running on the host consumes a portion of the host's running memory and processing time, resulting in reduced performance and relatively poor storage expansion performance, which is also a disadvantage of host-based storage virtualization. In addition, host upgrades, maintenance, and expansion are complex, and crossing multiple heterogeneous storage systems can require complex data migration processes that can affect business continuity. However, compared with other virtualization technology methods, host-based storage virtualization only needs to install virtual volume management software on the host. Many of them come with the operating system, which is relatively simple, convenient, suitable for storage requirements, and the number of users is small. Currently, Linux LVM is the most commonly used product in the host-based storage virtualization market.

5.5.4   Storage Virtualization Based on Storage Devices

Another approach to storage virtualization is storage virtualization based on storage devices. This approach to storage virtualization is virtualization capabilities to storage controllers, common in mid-to-high-end storage devices. Its purpose is to optimize user-oriented applications, integrate users' different storage systems into a single platform, solve data management challenges, and implement information life cycle management through tiered storage to optimize the application environment further. This technology is primarily used within the same storage device for data protection and data migration. Its advantages are not related to the host, do not occupy the host resources, data management functions are rich. However, it also has drawbacks: first, it is generally only possible to virtualize disks within the device. Second, data management functions from different vendors cannot be interoperable. Third, multiple sets of storage devices need to be configured with multiple sets of data management software. The cost is higher.

5.5.5   Network-Based Storage Virtualization

There is also a way to implement storage virtualization based on network-based storage virtualization. This approach is implemented by adding a virtualization engine to the SAN, such as a virtual gateway in SAN, to enable virtual network storage. With a virtual gateway, SANs can establish storage volumes with different storage capacities in the virtual storage pool, which can virtually manage the stored data. Network-based storage virtualization is primarily used for the consolidation of heterogeneous storage systems and unified data management. Its advantages are: first, it has nothing to do with the host, does not occupy the host resources. Second, it can support heterogeneous host, heterogeneous storage devices. Third, it can make the data management functions of different storage devices unified. Fourth, it can build a unified management platform, good scalability. But it also has disadvantages: first, some manufacturers' product data management function is weak, difficult to achieve the purpose of virtualization unified data management.

Network virtualization can be divided into Internet device virtualization and router device virtualization depending on the network virtualization devices.

1. Internet device virtualization

    In implementing Internet device virtualization, the consistency of the storage path through which information and data are controlled depends on the symmetry of the Internet device virtualization approach. Due to Internet devices' diversity and complexity, it is challenging to implement symmetrical storage virtualization, which can be used asymmetrically for Internet devices. Because its information control is not on the same path as data collection, asymmetric storage virtualization methods are easier to implement and store scalable performance than symmetrical storage virtualization methods.

2. Router device virtualization

Router device virtualization is a transformation of storage virtualization capabilities at the router level, which means that the vast majority of virtual enclosures are integrated into router software. This approach can also be combined with a host-based storage virtualization approach. In implementing router device virtualization, the router is placed in the host storage network channel, and the network storage command issued by the host can be acquired and processed to realize the function of storage virtualization. Therefore, in router device virtualization, the router becomes the host's service provider and the real data virtualization storage of the computer system. Router device virtualization is more independent, stable, and less impactful than host-based storage virtualization and Internet device virtualization. Although router device virtualization may also provide unfamiliar access to host-protected data, it is only for hosts connected to the router.

5.5.6   Storage Virtualization Products and Applications

This section focuses on the storage features of FusionCompute, Huawei's virtualization product.

FusionCompute uses storage resources that can come from local disks or dedicated storage devices. A dedicated storage device should be connected to the host via a network cable or fiber optic. Data storage is FusionCompute's unified encapsulation of storage units in storage resources. Once the storage resources are encapsulated as data stores and associated with the host, they can be further created into several virtual disks for use by virtual machines. Storage units that can be encapsulated as data storage include:

LUNs are divided as follows:

- SAN storage, including SAN storage for SCSI or Fibre Channel
- NAS storage file system divided
- storage pool on FusionStorage Block
- the host's local hard drive (virtualization)

These storage units are collectively referred to as "storage devices" in Huawei FusionCompute, while the physical storage media that provide storage space to virtualization is referred to as "storage resources," as shown in Fig. 5.36.

Before using data storage, you need to add storage resources manually. If the storage resource is IP-SAN, FusionStorage, or NAS storage, you need to add a storage interface to the hosts in the cluster and then communicate with the centralized storage controller's service interface or the management address of the FusionStorage Manager through this interface. If the storage resource is IP-SAN, there is no need to add a storage interface separately.

After adding storage resources, you need to scan for storage devices on the FusionCompute interface, and finally add them as data storage.

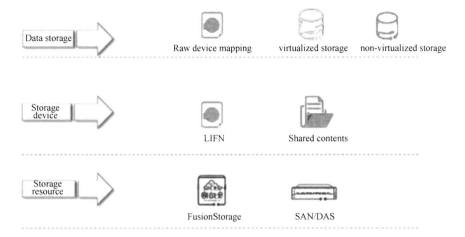

Fig. 5.36 Huawei storage model

Data storage can be virtualized or non-virtualized, and LUNs on SAN storage can also be used directly as data storage for virtual machines instead of creating virtual disks. This process is called raw device mapping. Raw device mapping currently only supports virtual machines of some operating systems, which is suitable for scenarios that require large disk space, such as building database servers.

5.6   Distributed Storage

The success of Internet companies such as amazon, Google, Alibaba, Baidu, and Tencent gave birth to technologies such as cloud computing, big data, and artificial intelligence. A key goal of the infrastructure behind the various applications provided by these Internet companies is to build a high-performance, low-cost, scalable, and easy-to-use distributed storage system.

Although the distributed storage system has a history of many years, it is only in recent years that it has been applied to engineering practice on a large scale due to the rise of big data and artificial intelligence applications. Compared with traditional storage systems, a new generation of distributed storage systems has two important characteristics: low cost and large scale. This is mainly based on the actual needs of the Internet industry. It can be said that Internet companies have redefined large-scale distributed storage systems.

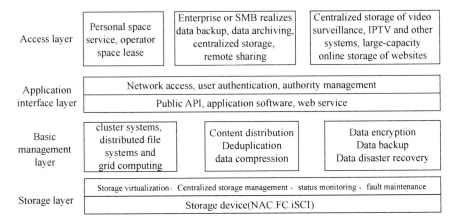

Fig. 5.37 Structure model of cloud storage system

5.6.1 Overview of Cloud Storage

Cloud storage is a new concept extended and developed from the concept of cloud computing. In fact, cloud storage is part of the cloud computing system, but it is different from the super processing power of cloud computing, emphasizing the "cloud." Cloud storage refers to a system that integrates many different types of storage devices in the network through application software through functions such as cluster applications, grid technology, or distributed file systems to work together to provide data storage and business access functions to the outside world.

Compared with traditional storage devices, cloud storage is a piece of hardware and a complex system that includes network devices, storage devices, servers, application software, public access interfaces, access networks, and client programs. Each part takes the storage device as the core and provides data storage and business access services to the outside through application software. The structural model of the cloud storage system is shown in Fig. 5.37.

The structural model of the cloud storage system consists of four layers.

(1) Storage layer

The storage layer is the most essential part of cloud storage. The storage device can be an FC storage device, an IP storage device such as NAS and iSCSI, or a DAS storage device such as SCSI or SAS. Storage devices in cloud storage are often large in number and distributed in different places and are connected through a wide area network, the Internet, or an FC network. Above the storage device is a unified storage device management system, which can realize logical virtualization management of storage devices, multi-link redundancy management, as well as status monitoring and fault maintenance of hardware devices.

(2) Basic management layer
      The basic management layer is the core part of cloud storage and the most
      challenging part to realize. The basic management layer uses cluster systems,
      distributed file systems and grid computing to realize the collaborative work
      between multiple storage devices in cloud storage. Multiple storage devices can
      provide the same service and provide better data access performance. Content
      distribution and data encryption technology ensure that unauthorized users will
      not access the data in cloud storage. Simultaneously, various data backup and
      data disaster recovery technologies and measures can ensure that cloud storage
      data will not be lost and ensure that the cloud store its security and stability.
(3) Application interface layer
      The application interface layer is the most flexible part of cloud storage.
      Different cloud storage operating units can develop different application service
      interfaces and provide different application services according to actual business
      types.
(4) Access layer
      Any authorized user can log in to the cloud storage system through a standard
      public application interface and enjoy cloud storage services. Different cloud
      storage operating units have different access types and access methods provided
      by cloud storage, such as video surveillance application platform, interactive
      Internet TV (IPTV) and video on demand application platform, network hard
      disk reference platform, and remote data backup application platform.

5.6.2   HDFS

HDFS is a core sub-project of the Hadoop project, the basis of data storage
management in distributed computing, developed to meet the needs of streaming
data patterns to access and process large files and run on inexpensive commercial
servers. Its high fault tolerance, high reliability, high scalability, high acquisition,
high-throughput rate, and other characteristics provide a high degree of fault-tolerant
storage solutions for massive data. For Large Data Sets, application processing has
brought a lot of conveniences. The overall structure of HDFS is shown in Fig. 5.38.
      HDFS consists of a named node (NameNode) and multiple data nodes
(DataNode). NameNode is the central server that manages the namespace of the
file system (NameSpace) and client access to files, while DataNode is usually a
common computer responsible for specific data storage. HDFS is very similar to a
familiar stand-alone file system in that it creates directories, creates, copies, deletes
files, or views file contents. However, its underlying implementation is to cut the file
into pieces, and then these blocks are scattered on different DataNode. Each block
can also be copied several copies stored on different DataNode to achieve fault
tolerance and disaster tolerance purposes. NameNode is at the heart of the entire
HDFS, which records how many blocks each file is cut into by maintaining some

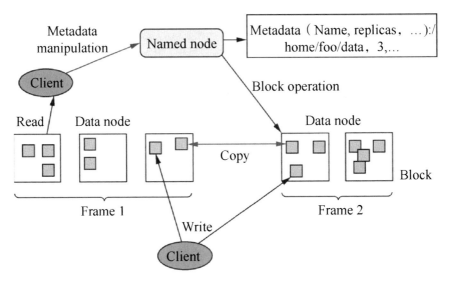

Fig. 5.38 Overall structure of HDFS

data structure, from which DataNode is available, and how important information such as the status of each DataNode is obtained.

The following will be from the point of view of the write and read process of HDFS, respectively, to introduce the implementation process of HDFS.

(1) The writing process of HDFS

NameNode is responsible for managing metadata stored on all files on HDFS, which confirms the client's request and records the file's name and the DataNode collection that stores the file. It stores this information in the file allocation table in memory.

For example, if the client sends a request to NameNode to write a .log file to HDFS, its execution process is shown in Fig. 5.39.

One of the challenges in the design of distributed file systems is how to ensure data consistency. For HDFS, the data is not considered written until DataNode, which wants to save the data, confirms that they have a copy of the file. Therefore, data consistency is done during the write phase. A client will get the same data no matter which DataNode it chooses to read from.

(2) The reading process of HDFS

To understand the read process of HDFS, it can be thought that a file is made up of blocks of data stored on DataNode. The execution process for the client to view what was previously written is shown in Fig. 5.40.

The client takes a block of files from different DataNodes in parallel, and then merges them into complete files.

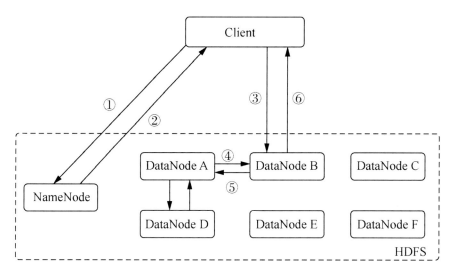

Fig. 5.39 HDFS writing process

- Step 1: The client sends a message to NameNode, ready to write the .log state file to HDFS (see Fig. (1))
- Step 2: NameNode sends a message to the client, commanding the client to write data nodes A, DataNode B and DataNode D and contact DataNode B directly (see Fig. (2))
- Step 3: The client sends a message to DataNode B, orders that a .log file be saved, and sends a copy to DataNode A and DataNode D (see Fig. (3))
- Step 4: DataNode A sends a message to DataNode B asking for a .log file (see Fig. (4))
- Step 5: DataNode B sends a message to DataNode A, transmits a .log file, and sends a copy to DataNode D (see Fig. (5))
- Step 6: DataNode D sends a confirmation message to DataNode A
- Step 7: DataNode A sends a confirmation message to DataNode B
- Step 8: DataNode B sends a confirmation message to the client indicating that the write is complete (see Fig. (6) in the figure)

5.6.3 Peer Storage System

Peer-to-peer storage technology refers to a technology that forms a storage network in a functionally reciprocal manner between storage nodes, which is a type of distributed storage.

Unlike the traditional centralized control mode, the peer-to-peer storage system's storage nodes are equal in status. Specifically, a peer-to-peer storage system can be composed entirely of server nodes in a peer-to-peer manner, can also be composed entirely of user desktops, or a mixture of servers and desktops in a peer-to-peer manner. As long as the storage system is organized in a functionally equivalent manner is a peer-to-peer storage system. Peer-to-Peer (P2P) technology is the foundation and physical support of peer-to-peer storage technology.

A peer-to-peer network is a complex overlay network with high dynamics, also known as an "overlay network" or "overlay network." Peer-to-peer network is a virtual layer built on several existing physical networks. By overlaying another layer

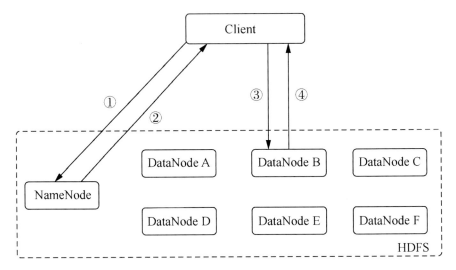

Fig. 5.40 HDFS read process
- Step 1: The client asks NameNode to read the file (see Fig. (1))
- Step 2: NameNode sends block information to the client (the block information contains the IP address of DataNode, which holds a copy of the file, and the block ID that DataNode needs to find the block on the local hard drive) (see Fig. (2))
- Step 3: The client checks the block information, contacts the relevant DataNode, and requests the block (see Fig. (3) in the figure)
- Step 4: DataNode returns the file contents to the client, then closes the connection and completes the read operation

of a more abstract network based on the original physical network, the interconnection of different networks can be realized without changing the existing network structure realize the sharing of resources.

A peer-to-peer system built on a peer-to-peer network is a distributed system built on the application layer. Each node communicates through a unified routing protocol, and messages are transmitted along with the peer-to-peer network's logical connection.

Compared with the traditional client/server model, the peer-to-peer storage system has the following advantages.

(1) High scalability

The most important feature of a peer-to-peer storage system is that each network node has two roles: client and server. In this mode, its capacity can be expanded arbitrarily. If its system structure is structured, the capacity can be expanded and contracted arbitrarily without disturbing the system's normal operation at all.

(2) Large system capacity

Since there is no direct mapping relationship between data and server, storage capacity is not limited by hardware. Today, the capacity of an IDE hard disk can exceed 1TB, and statistics show that the utilization rate of storage media is less than 50%. That is, a large amount of storage media is wasted. A peer-to-peer storage system can pool a large amount of free disk space on different computers and share it with users who need it.

(3) Good service performance

Severely unstable network conditions usually cause irreparable losses to traditional client/server storage systems. For a peer-to-peer storage system, because data is stored on each node of the system, and many nodes share the risk, the change in the number of nodes will not have a serious impact on system performance, and it can well adapt to the dynamic changes of the network. Moreover, its unique feature of keeping file copies at different locations in the network enables nodes to achieve nearby access, reducing access latency and improving data reading capabilities.

(4) High reliability

Peer-to-peer storage systems are usually self-organizing, which can better adapt to the dynamic joining and exiting of nodes. The peer-to-peer storage system also implements the file fault tolerance function. Even if some nodes fail, the target file can still be obtained. Besides, because the system's nodes are distributed in different geographical areas, local devastating disaster events such as earthquakes and partial power outages will not destroy the entire system. That is, the data has good disaster tolerance.

(5) Low system cost

Users do not need to spend large amounts of money to purchase file servers and various network equipment to build a large-capacity, high-performance file storage system. For a peer-to-peer storage system, it does not have high requirements on the performance of computing devices. As long as its storage resources can be interconnected with the network to achieve an effective organization, storage services can be provided. In addition, due to the principle of nearby access to different nodes, a large amount of network traffic is usually confined to a local area network, such as a campus network, so that most of the network traffic does not have to pass through the external network, which will significantly save the network costs based on traffic billing.

The peer-to-peer storage system is precise because of the above advantages, which has aroused researchers' general attention and in-depth research.

The software Napster launched in 1999 has gradually made the peer-to-peer model replace the client/server model as a research and application hotspot. With the widespread popularity of the Internet, the significant increase in network bandwidth, and the rapid increase in ordinary computers' computing power, end-user equipment has gradually become an available computing resource that breaks the storage bottleneck. Until now, the research of peer-to-peer networks has been pervasive, roughly including the following aspects: data storage, parallel computing, and instant messaging. Well-known peer-to-peer storage systems include Gnutella, Napster, Kazaa, Morpheus, Freenet, Chord, CAN, Pastry, BitTorrent, FreeHaven, etc. Each of these peer-to-peer storage systems has its characteristics and characteristics in network node concentration and network topology. An important feature of the classification of peer-to-peer storage systems is the Degree of Centralization, the

Table 5.2 Peer-to-peer storage system classification

Type	Structured	Non-structured
Completely decentralized	Chord, CAN, OceanStore, Pastry, CFS	Gnutella
Partially centralized		Kazaa, Morpheus
Mixed decentralized		Napster, BitTorrent

degree of reliance on the server, which specifically refers to whether the server's adjustment is required between the communicating nodes. The peer-to-peer storage systems can be divided into the following categories according to the degree of node organization concentration.

(1) Completely decentralized

There is no server at all, and the roles of all nodes in the network are the same. They are both a server and a client. The system does not intervene and regulate the communication of any node. Typical representatives of such peer-to-peer storage systems are Gnutella, Pastry, etc.

(2) Partially centralized

There is a SuperNode different from ordinary nodes in the system, and it plays a more critical role than ordinary nodes. The supernode contains the file directories of other nodes in the network area. However, the supernodes in the system are not "lifetime," but are dynamically designated by a fixed election algorithm. Typical representatives of such peer-to-peer storage systems are Kazaa and Morpheus.

(3) Mixed decentralized

There is a file server in the system, and the file index on all nodes in the system is recorded on the server. When the system is running, the server is responsible for querying the file's location required by the requesting node in the network, and then the requesting node is connected to the target node to achieve communication. Obviously, the mixed decentralized node and server are still in the client/server model. Typical representatives of such peer-to-peer storage systems are Napster and BitTorrent.

According to the degree of network node concentration and network topology, several existing peer-to-peer storage systems can be classified, as shown in Table 5.2.

5.7 Exercise

(1) Multiple choices

1. When you create a port group in Huawei FusionCompute, the following operation is incorrect ( ).

A. Set the VLAN ID to "5000".

B. Set the name of the port group to "ceshi".

C. Set the port type to Normal

D. Add "This is a test port" to the description.

2. In Huawei FusionCompute, the role of the uplink is ( ).

A. Assign IP address

B. To virtual machines connect virtual and physical networks

C. Manage virtual machine MAC address

D. Detect the status of the virtual network card

3. The following description of cloud computing is correct ( ).

A. Cloud computing is a technology that enables easy, on-demand access to IT resources anytime, anywhere.

B. Various IT resources in cloud computing are available for a fee.

C. IT resources acquired in cloud computing need to be used over the network.

D. In the process of acquiring IT resources, users need to negotiate repeatedly with cloud computing service providers.

4. In the development of the Internet, there are many milestone events, the following options for milestone events in a normal order is ( ).

A. TCP/IP Establishment—The Birth of ARPANET—The World Wide Web Is Officially Open to the Public—The Birth of DNS

B. The World Wide Web is officially open to the public—the birth of DNS—TCP / IP establishment—the birth of ARPANET

C. The birth of ARPANET—TCP/IP establishment—THE BIRTH OF DNS—The World Wide Web is officially open to the public

D. Dns Birth—TCP/IP Establishment—ARPANET Birth—The World Wide Web is officially open to the public

(2) Answer the following questions

1. Briefly summarize the benefits of virtualization technology in physical devices.

2. List common RAID technologies and compare the differences between different RAID technologies.

3. What improvements has RAID 2.0 made and what have been the improvements in storage performance?

4. Explain the principles of GFS and HDFS, and briefly explain their respective advantages.

Chapter 6
OpenStack

To meet user needs or availability requirements, cloud computing environments often require the flexibility to manage and use connected resources across multiple data centers and require robust cloud operating system architectures or software. Public or private organizations have developed many management frameworks within themselves to manage public resources. OpenStack is one of many commercial or open source cloud management software. OpenStack is the framework for building a cloud operating system, an open source project designed to provide software for the construction and management of public and private clouds, comprising a large number of peripheral components, integrating and managing a wide range of hardware devices, and hosting a variety of upper-level applications and services, resulting in a complete and robust cloud computing system.

By dissecting the components of OpenStack, explaining their relationship to the underlying resources (computing, storage, networking, etc.), focusing on the core components and Keystone, Nova, Glance, Cinder, Neutron, etc., this chapter explores how OpenStack works and helps readers understand how OpenStack components work through examples, procedures, pictures, logs, etc. It enables readers to acquire the skills to implement and manage OpenStack and configure and adapt to their needs.

6.1 Overview of OpenStack

OpenStack is the most popular open source cloud operating system framework. Since its first release in 2010, OpenStack has grown and matured through the joint efforts of thousands of developers and tens of thousands of users. At present, OpenStack is powerful and rich, has been in private cloud, public cloud, NFV, and other fields have been increasingly widely used.

© The Author(s) 2023

Huawei Technologies Co., Ltd., *Cloud Computing Technology*,

https://doi.org/10.1007/978-981-19-3026-3_6

6.1.1   OpenStack Architecture

Whether it is Linux on servers and personal computers, Windows, or Android and iOS on your phone, it is a common example of an operating system. Correspondingly, a complete cloud operating system is a distributed cloud computing system consisting of a large number of software/hardware. As with a normal operating system, a cloud operating system needs to be managed. OpenStack is a key component in implementing a cloud operating system, primarily deploying infrastructure as a service (IaaS), or building a complete framework for a cloud operating system. Figure 6.1 shows the cloud operating system in the cloud computing framework, and you can see OpenStack's position in the complete cloud computing framework.

The cloud operating system framework is not equal to the cloud operating system. Building a complete cloud operating system requires the organic integration of many software components that work together to provide the functionality and services that system administrators and tenants need. On the other hand, OpenStack does not have all the capabilities required for a complete cloud operating system on its own. For example, OpenStack cannot independently implement resource access and abstraction, but needs to work with the underlying virtualization software, software definition storage, software definition network, and other software. OpenStack

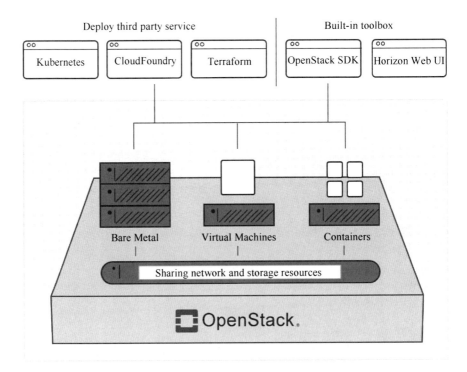

Fig. 6.1 Cloud operating system in the cloud computing framework

cannot independently provide comprehensive application life cycle management capabilities but needs to integrate various management software platforms at the upper level. OpenStack itself does not have complete system management and maintenance capabilities, and when put into use, it needs to integrate various management software and maintenance tools. OpenStack's human–machine interface is not rich, powerful, etc.

It is not hard to see how building a complete cloud operating system based on OpenStack requires integrating OpenStack with other software components to provide capabilities that OpenStack itself can't provide. As a result, OpenStack's precise positioning is a cloud operating system framework. Based on this framework, different components can be integrated to implement cloud operating systems that meet the needs of different scenarios, and on this basis, a complete cloud computing system can be built.

6.1.2 OpenStack Core Components

OpenStack contains many components, including Nova, Swift, Glance, Keystone, Neutron, Cinder, Horizon, MQ, Heat, Ceilometer, and seven core components.

1. Nova

    Nova is OpenStack's controller that supports all the activity processing required for the life cycle of instances within the OpenStack cloud. Nova manages computing resources and scaling requirements in the OpenStack cloud as a management platform. However, Nova cannot provide its virtualization capabilities, and it uses Libvirt's API to support interactions between hypervisors.

2. Swift

    Swift provides object storage services that allow files to be stored or retrieved, but not by mounting directories on the file server. Swift provides OpenStack with distributed, ultimately consistent virtual object storage. With distributed storage nodes, Swift can store billions of objects. Swift has built-in redundancy, fault management, archiving, streaming capabilities, and Swift is highly scalable.

3. Glance

    Glance provides a directory and storage repository for virtual disk images that can provide storage and retrieval of virtual machine images. These disk images are widely used in Nova components. Glance can perform mirror management and tenant private mirror management in multiple data centers. Although a mirror service is technically optional, a cloud of any size can demand that service.

4. Keystone

    Keystone provides authentication and authorization for all services on OpenStack. Authentication and authorization are complex in any system, especially projects as large as OpenStack, and each component requires unified authentication and authorization.

5. Neutron

   Neutron is the core component of providing network services in OpenStack, based on the idea of a software-defined network, software-based network resource management, and fully utilizes various network-related technologies in Linux operating system to support third-party plug-ins.

6. Cinder

   Cinder is an essential component of the virtual infrastructure and the basis for storing disk files and the data used by virtual machines. Cinder provides block storage services for instances. The allocation and consumption of storage are determined by block storage drives or multi-back-end configured drives.

7. Horizon

   Horizon provides a Web-based interface that enables cloud administrators and users to manage a variety of OpenStack resources and services.

6.1.3 Logical Relationship Between OpenStack Components

OpenStack's services are called through a unified REST-style API to achieve loose coupling of the system. The advantage of a loosely coupled architecture is that developers of individual components can focus only on their domains, and modifications to their domains will not affect other developers. On the other hand, however, this loosely coupled architecture also brings some difficulties to maintaining the whole system, and operations personnel need to master more system-related knowledge to debug the components that are in trouble. So both developers and maintenance personnel must understand the interchange relationships between components. Figure 6.2 shows the logical relationship between the various components of the virtual machine.

6.2 OpenStack Operating Interface Management

OpenStack needs to provide a simple, user-friendly interface for end-users and developers to browse and manipulate computing resources that belong to a subset, which is OpenStack's operator panel component Horizon.

6.2.1 Introduction to OpenStack Operation Interface

Horizon is the portal to the entire OpenStack application architecture. It provides a Web-based graphical interface service portal. Users can access and control their compute, storage, and network resources, such as launching virtual machine instances, assigning IP addresses, setting access control, and more, using the

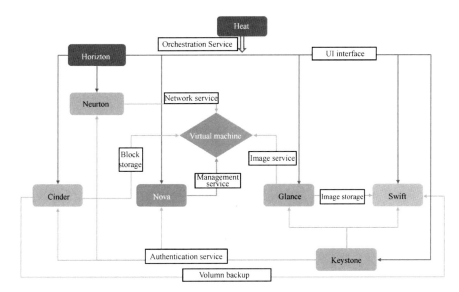

Fig. 6.2   The logical relationship between OpenStack components

graphical interface provided by Horizon through their browser. Horizon provides a different interface for users in both roles.

- Cloud administrator: Horizon provides a holistic view of cloud administrators, who can get an overview of the resource size and health of the entire cloud, create end-users and projects, assign projects to end-users, and manage resource quotas that projects can use.
- End-users: Horizon provides end-users with an autonomous service portal that allows end-users to use compute, storage, and network resources in projects assigned by cloud administrators that do not exceed quota limits.

6.2.2   The Architecture and Functions of the OpenStack Operation Interface

Horizon uses the Django framework, a popular Python-based open source Web application framework, and Horizon follows the pattern of the Django framework to generate several apps that combine to provide a complete implementation of the OpenStack interface. Figure 6.3 shows the interface in which Horizon created the instance.

Horizon consists of three Dashboards (Django called Apps): user Dashboard, System Dashboard, and Set Dashboard. These three Dashboards make up Horizon's core application. Figures 6.4–6.6 show the user Dashboard's functional architecture, the system Dashboard, and the Set Dashboard.

Fig. 6.3 Horizon interface

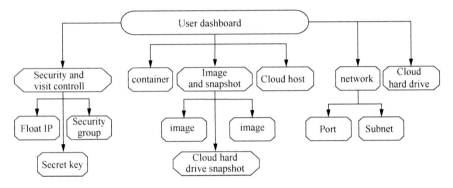

Fig. 6.4 Functional architecture of User Dashboard

User Dashboard is an autonomous service portal for end-users who can freely operate and use compute, storage, and network resources in projects assigned by cloud administrators that do not exceed quota limits. System Dashboard and Settings Dashboard is an interface for cloud administrators who can get an overview of the resource size and health of the entire cloud, create end-users and directories, and assign projects and resource quotas that can be used by projects to end-users.

In addition to providing these main Web interface features, Horizon controls other details of the page through various options for the profile, such as setting a Logo image on the OpenStack home page through the profile local.setting.py, or specifying the title of the page.

6.3   OpenStack Certification Management

Security is an unavoidable problem for every software, and no software can do without considering security considerations, and of course no software can solve all security problems. Even a small-cost software takes into account the security and

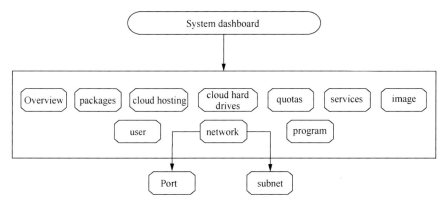

Fig. 6.5 The functional architecture of the System Dashboard

Fig. 6.6 Setting the functional architecture of Dashboard

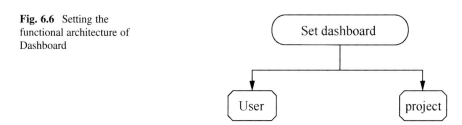

privacy of end-users, especially OpenStack, which provides cloud infrastructure services.

6.3.1   Introduction to OpenStack Authentication Service

Keystone is a component of the OpenStack framework that manages authentication, service access rules, and service token functionality. User access to resources requires verification of the user's identity and permissions, and service execution also requires permission detection, which needs to be handled through Keystone. Keystone is similar to a service bus or registry of the entire OpenStack framework. The OpenStack service registers its Endpoint (the URL of service access) through Keystone, and any calls between services need to be authenticated by Keystone, obtain the Endpoint of the target service, and then call.

Keystone's main features are as follows:

- manage users and their permissions
- maintain the OpenStack Service Endpoint
- certification and authorization

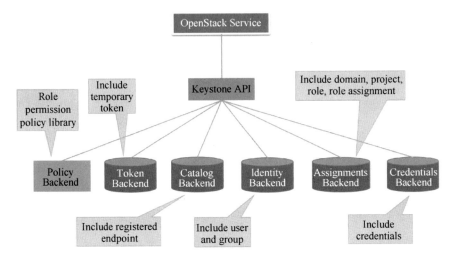

Fig. 6.7 Keystone architecture

Keystone's architecture is shown in Fig. 6.7.

Mastering Keystone requires understanding some basic concepts, such as User, Credentials, Vis Token, and more.

1. User

   User refers to any entity that uses OpenStack, which can be a real user or another system or service. When the User requests access to OpenStack, Keystone verifies it.

2. Credentials

   Credentials is the information that the User uses to prove his identity. This can be:

   - username and password
   - Token (a Keystone assigned identity token)
   - username and API Key (key)
   - other advanced ways

3. Authentication

   Authentication is Keystone's process of verifying User's identity. When User accesses OpenStack, it submits a username and password form to Keystone, which, upon verification, issues User with a Token as follow-up access.

4. Token

   Token is a string of numbers and letters that, after User is successfully certified, are assigned to User by Keystone. Token is used as a credit for accessing the service, which verifies Token's validity through Keystone. Token also has the concept of scope, indicating what the Token acts on, such as an engineering scope or a domain scope, and Token can only be used to certify User's operations on resources within a specified range. Token is valid by default at 24h.

5. Project

   Project is used to group and isolate OpenStack's resources (compute, storage, and network resources). Project can be a department or project team in a private enterprise cloud, similar to the VPN concept of a public cloud. Ownership of resources belongs to Project, not User. Each User (including an administrator) must hang in a Project to access the Project's resources, and a User can belong to more than one Project.

6. Service

   OpenStack's Services include Computing (Nova), Block Storage (Cinder), Image Services (Glance), Neutron, and more. Each service provides several Endpoints through which User accesses resources and performs operations.

7. Endpoint

   Endpoint is an accessible address on the network, usually a URL. Service exposes its OWN APIs through Endpoint. Keystone is responsible for managing and maintaining the Endpoint for each service.

8. Role

   Security consists of two parts: Authentication and Authorization. Keystone uses Role to realize authorization. Role is global, so its name must be unique within the jurisdiction of a keystone. Horizon manages Role in the Identity Management → Role: You can assign one or more Roles to User.

9. Group

   A Group is a collection of Domain partial Users designed to facilitate Role allocation. Assign a Role to a Group, and the result will be assigned to all Users within the Group.

10. Domain

    Domain represents a collection of Project, Group, and User, often representing a customer in a public or private cloud, similar to the concept of a virtual machine data center. Domain can be thought of as a namespace, like a domain name, globally unique. Within a Domain, the names of Project, Group, and User cannot be repeated, but within two different Domains, their names can be repeated. Therefore, when determining these elements, you need to use both their names and their Domain IDs or names.

6.3.2 Principles of OpenStack Authentication Service

As a stand-alone security authentication module in OpenStack, Keystone is responsible for OpenStack user authentication, token management, and service directories that provide access to resources, and access control based on user roles. User access to the system's username and password verification, Token issuance, service (Endpoint) registration, and determining whether the user has access to a particular resource are all dependent on the involvement of the Keystone service.

Based on the core concepts described earlier, Keystone provides services in four areas: Identity (Certification), Token, Catalog, and Polly (Security Policy, or Access Control).

(1) Identity

The user's Identity is verified, the user's credentials are typically presented as a username and password, and the Identity service provides the extraction of metadata related to that user.

(2) Token

After identity confirms the user's Identity, it is given a token to verify that Identity and can be used to request subsequent resources, and the Token service verifies and manages the token used to verify the Identity. Keystone issues two types of tokens to users through the Identity service. One is a token that is not related to Tenant, which allows you to look up the Tenant list from Keystone, where the user can select the Tenant to access, and then you can get another type of token bound to this Tenant that can access the resources in this Tenant only through a token bound to a particular Tenant. Tokens are only valid for a limited period of time and can be removed if you need to remove a specific user's access.

(3) Catalog

Catalog provides a service catalog query, or Endpoint list for each service. The service directory contains Endpoint information for all services, and resource access between services begins with the Endpoint information for that resource, usually a list of URLs, before resource access can be made based on that information. From the current version, Keystone provides a service directory that is returned to the user simultaneously as the token.

(4) Policy

A rule-based authentication engine that uses configuration files to define how actions match user roles. Strictly speaking, this part is no longer part of the Keystone project, since access control is involved in different projects, so this part is developed and maintained as part of online and offline interaction (Online, Service, Offline, OSO).

Keystone builds a bridge between the user and the service, the user obtains the token and the service list from Keystone, sends the user's token when the user visits the service, and the related service seeks the legitimacy of the token from Keystone. Figure 6.8 shows the service user interaction process based on the Keystone mechanism.

6.4 OpenStack Image Management

Mirroring is self-evident for cloud and virtualization. This section provides an overview of OpenStack mirror management by describing the Glance components. Glance provides a directory and storage repository for virtual disk images and can

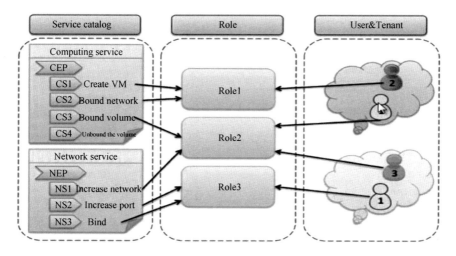

Fig. 6.8 Service user interaction process based on the Keystone mechanism

Fig. 6.9 The relationship between Glance, Nova, and Swift

provide storage and retrieval of virtual machine images. These disk images are often widely used in OpenStack's Nova-compute components.

6.4.1 Introduction to OpenStack Image Service

As a mirroring service for OpenStack's virtual machines, Glance provides a range of REST APIs to manage and query the image of virtual machines, supporting a variety of back-end storage media. For example, use the local file system as storage media and Swift as storage media. Figure 6.9 describes Glance's relationship with Nova and Swift.

As you can see, through Glance, the three components of OpenStack are connected as a whole, Glance provides mirror lookups for Nova, and Swift provides actual storage services for Glance, which Swift can see as a concrete implementation of the Glance storage interface.

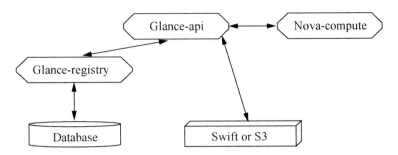

Fig. 6.10 The process of creating an instance

6.4.2   Principles of OpenStack Image Service

The OpenStack mirroring service consists of two main parts: API Server and Registry Server. Glance is designed to fit as many back-end storages and registration database scenarios as possible. API Server (running the "Glance-API" program) acts as a communication hub. For example, various client programs, the registration of mirror metadata, and storage systems that contain virtual machine mirror data all communicate through it. API Server forwards the client's request to the mirror metadata registry and its back-end storage. The Glance service uses these mechanisms to save virtual machine images.

Glance-API is primarily used to receive various API call requests and provide appropriate actions. Glance-registry is used to interact with mySQL databases, store or obtain mirrored metadata. Note that Swift does not save metadata in its storage service, where metadata refers to some information about mirroring stored in the MySQL database and belongs to Glance.

The operation of actually creating an instance is done by the Nova-compute component, which is inextricably linked to Glance. The process for creating an instance is shown in Fig. 6.10.

6.5   OpenStack Computing Management

Nova is the core component of OpenStack, responsible for maintaining and managing computing resources for cloud environments. OpenStack is the cloud operating system for IaaS, and virtual machine life cycle management is achieved through Nova.

6.5.1   Introduction to OpenStack Computing Service

At the heart of the OpenStack architecture is the computing organization controller in the OpenStack cloud, providing large-scale, scalable, on-demand self-service

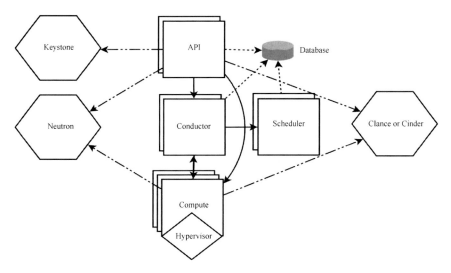

Fig. 6.11 Nova architecture

computing resources. All activities in the instance life cycle in the OpenStack cloud are handled by Nova, making Nova a scalable platform for managing computing resources.

In the first few versions of OpenStack, computing, storage, and networking were implemented by Nova, which gradually split the storage and networks. Currently, Nova specializes in computing services, relying on Keystone's authentication services, Neutron's web services, and Glance's mirror services. The Nova architecture is shown in Fig. 6.11.

6.5.2   Principles of OpenStack Computing Services

The Nova architecture is complex and contains many components that can be divided into the following categories. These components run as subservices (background Daemon processes), and their operating architecture is shown in Fig. 6.12.

1. Nova-API

   The Nova-API is the portal for the entire Nova component and is responsible for receiving and responding to customers' API calls. All requests to Nova are handled first by the Nova-API. Nova-API exposes several HTTP REST APIs to the outside world. In Keystone, we can query the Endpoint of the Nova-API. The client can send the request to the address specified by Endpoint and request action from the Nova-API. Of course, as an end-user, we do not send REST API requests directly. OpenStack CLI, Dashboard, and other components that need to be exchanged with Nova are used by these APIs.

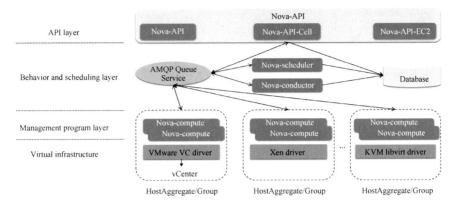

Fig. 6.12 Nova operating architecture

2. Nova-scheduler

Nova-scheduler is a virtual machine scheduling service that decides which compute node to run the virtual machine on. When an instance is created, the user raises resource requirements such as CPU, memory, and how much disk each requires. OpenStack defines these requirements in a type template (Flavor) where the user only needs to specify which Flavor to use.

Nova-scheduler implements scheduling by:in /etc/nova/nova.conf, Nova filter_

The scheduler parameter is configured with Nova-scheduler. Filter Scheduler is the default scheduler for Nova-scheduler, and the scheduling process is divided into two steps.

- Select the eligible compute node (run Nova-compute) through the Filter.
- Use Weighting to select to create instances on the optimal (most weighted) compute node.

    Nova allows the use of a third-party Scheduler and configures scheduler_driver. This once again reflects OpenStack's openness. The scheduler can filter multiple Fillers, and then the filtered nodes select the most suitable node by calculating the weights.

3. Nova-compute

Nova-compute is the core service for managing virtual machines running on compute nodes. The life cycle management of instances on the node is achieved by calling the Hypervisor API. OpenStack's operations on the instance are ultimately left to Nova-compute. Nova-compute works with Hypervisor to implement OpenStack's management of the instance life cycle.

Hypervisor is a virtualization manager running on a compute node, the lowest level program in virtual machine management. Different virtualization technologies offer their Hypervisor. Common Hypervisor is KVM, Xen, VMware, etc.

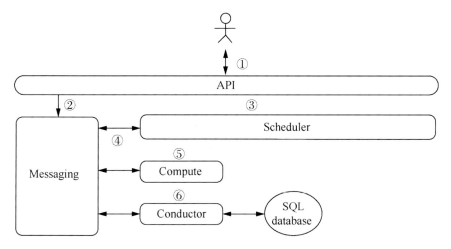

Fig. 6.13 Nova workflow

Nova-compute defines a unified interface for these Hypervisors, which Hypervisor only needs to implement to plug and play in the form of a Driver and use in OpenStack systems.

4. Nova-conductor

Nova-compute often needs to update databases, such as updating and getting the status of virtual machines. For security and scalability reasons, Nova-compute does not access the database directly, but delegates this task to Nova-conductor. There are two benefits to this: greater system security and better system scalability.

5. Messager Queue

We have learned that Nova contains several subservices that need to be coordinated and communicated with each other. To decouple each subservice, Nova uses Messenger Queue as an information transit point for the child service. So on the Nova operating architecture, we can see no direct connection between the subservices, which is contacted through Messenger Queue.

Finally, let us look at how Nova's subservices work together from the virtual machine creation process to understand Nova's specific workflow. Figure 6.13 shows the Nova service process.

(1) The customer (who can be an OpenStack end-user or some other program) sends a request to the API (Nova-API): "Help me create a virtual machine."
(2) After the API did some necessary processing of the request, it sent a message to Messaging (RabbitMQ): "Let Scheduler create a virtual machine."
(3) Scheduler gets the message sent to it by the API from Messaging and then executes a scheduling algorithm to select the compute node A from several compute nodes.

(4) Scheduler sent Messaging a message: "Create this virtual machine on compute node A."
(5) Nova-compute node A gets the message sent to it by Scheduler from Messaging and starts the virtual machine on a hypervisor of the node.
(6) During the creation of a virtual machine, Compute sends a message to Nova-conductor via Messaging if it needs to query or update database information, and Conductor is responsible for database access.

These are the core steps to create virtual machines, which show us how to collaborate between subservices in Nova and reflect OpenStack's distributed design philosophy across the system, which is very helpful for us to understand OpenStack in depth.

6.6   OpenStack Storage Management

OpenStack offers various types of storage services that users can choose freely based on their business needs. This section focuses on the block storage service Finder in OpenStack and briefly describes the object storage service Swift.

6.6.1   Introduction to OpenStack Storage Service

OpenStack's storage services are important because multiple service components use them. Storage is divided into Ephemeral Storage and Persister Storage, as shown in Fig. 6.14.

If a virtual machine uses temporary storage, all data information in the virtual machine instance is lost once it is shut down, restarted, or deleted. In the OpenStack project, after deploying the Nova-compute service component, users can use the

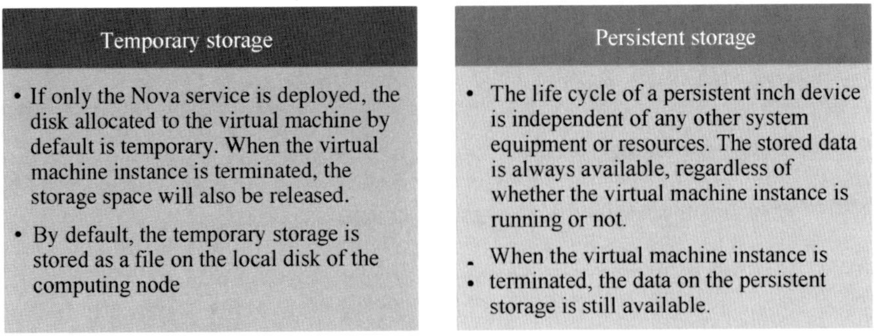

Temporary storage	Persistent storage
• If only the Nova service is deployed, the disk allocated to the virtual machine by default is temporary. When the virtual machine instance is terminated, the storage space will also be released.	• The life cycle of a persistent inch device is independent of any other system equipment or resources. The stored data is always available, regardless of whether the virtual machine instance is running or not.
• By default, the temporary storage is stored as a file on the local disk of the computing node	• When the virtual machine instance is terminated, the data on the persistent storage is still available.

Fig. 6.14 Storage classification in OpenStack

nova boot command to create virtual machine instances, which use temporary storage without any security guarantees.

Persistent storage includes block storage, file system storage, and object storage. Regardless of whether the virtual machine instance is terminated, their data is continuously available, and the security is relatively high. The three types of storage are in the order of block → file → objects. Files are usually implemented based on blocks, and the underlying or back-end storage of object storage is usually implemented based on the local file system.

Block storage "communicates" with the host, just like a hard disk directly attached to the host, generally used for the host's direct storage space and database applications (such as MySQL) storage, divided into the following two.

- DAS: One server has one storage, and multiple machines cannot be shared directly. It requires the use of operating system functions, such as shared folders.
- SAN: A high-cost storage method involving optical fiber and various high-end equipment, with high reliability and performance. The disadvantage is that the equipment is expensive and the operation and maintenance cost is high.

File system storage is different from lower level block storage. It has risen to the application layer, generally referring to NAS, which is a set of network storage devices, accessed through TCP/IP, and the typical protocol is NFS. Due to the network and the use of upper-layer protocols, the file system storage has a large overhead and the delay is higher than that of block storage. It is generally used for sharing data with multiple cloud servers, such as centralized server log management and office file sharing.

Object storage deals with self-developed applications (such as network disks). It has the characteristics of high-speed block storage and sharing of file system storage. It is more intelligent and has its CPU, memory, network, and disk, which is higher level than block storage and file system storage. Cloud service providers generally provide REST APIs for uploading, downloading, and reading user files to facilitate application integration of such services.

6.6.2 Principles of OpenStack Storage Service

1. Block storage

   Block storage, also known as volume storage, provides users with block-based storage device access, and user access and interaction to block storage devices are achieved by mapping block storage devices to running virtual machine instances that can be read/written, formatted, and so on. The block storage schema is shown in Fig. 6.15.

   Block storage is persistent and the data on the block store is unaffected when mapping between the block storage device and the virtual machine instance or when the entire block store is remapped to another virtual machine instance. Block storage is provided by Cinder components in the OpenStack project and

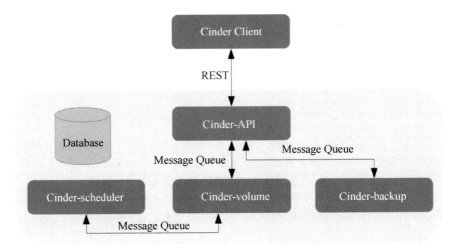

Fig. 6.15 Block storage architecture

currently supports several back-end storage types, depending on the storage already included.

The Finder component in the OpenStack project provides a block storage device for virtual machine instances and a comprehensive set of methods for managing storage devices, such as volume snapshots, volume types, and so on. Block storage types are determined by drivers or back-end device configurations such as NAS, NFS, SAN, iSCSI, and Ceph. The Cinder-API and Cinder-scheduler services of the Cinder component typically run on control nodes, and Cinder-volume services can run on control nodes, compute nodes, or stand-alone storage nodes.

Cinder-API provides the REST API externally, parses operational requirements, and calls processing methods such as create/Delete/List/Show. Cinder-scheduler is responsible for collecting capacity and capability information for back-end escalation, scheduling volumes to the specified Finder-volume according to the set algorithm, and then filtering out the appropriate back end through filtering and weighting. Cinder-volume multi-node deployment, using different configuration files, access to different back-end devices, by each storage vendor inserted Driver code to interact with the device, to complete the device capacity and capacity information collection, volume operations, and so on.

Figure 6.16 shows the process of creating a volume for Cinder, in which the Cinder components involved consist of the following service processes.

- Cinder-API: Receive API requests and forward them to Finder-volume.
- Cinder-volume: Interacts directly with block storage, handling tasks such as those assigned by Cine-scheduler, and interacting with those tasks through message queues. It also maintains the state of the block store by driving interactions with various types of storage.

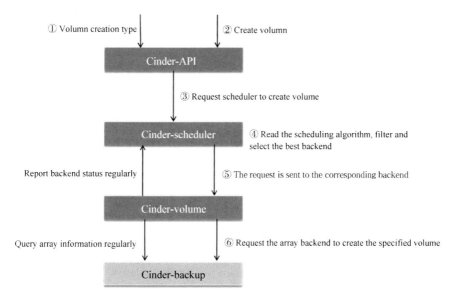

Fig. 6.16 Cinder-volume creation process

- Cinder-scheduler: Choose the best storage node to create a volume. (Nova-scheduler has similar functionality.)
- Cinder-backup: Provides backups of any type of volume.

   Many storage drivers support virtual machine instances that have direct access to the underlying storage without having to go through layer-by-layer transformations that result in performance consumption and improve overall I/O performance. Cinder components also support the use of common file systems as block devices. In the NFS and GlusterFS file systems, you can create a stand-alone file to map to the virtual machine instance as a block device. Similar to creating virtual machine instances in QEMU, which are files that are saved in the /var/lib/nova/instances directory.

2. Object storage

   The Swift component in the OpenStack project provides object data storage and retrieval through the REST API, and it must be used at least in conjunction with the Keystone component to make sure that Keystone is ready before deploying the Swift component. Swift components support multi-tenant use, low cost of investment, high scalability, and the ability to store large amounts of unstructured data.

   The Swift component includes the following sections.

- Proxy Server: A proxy server responsible for communication between the rest of the Swift architecture, receives API and HTTP requests stored by objects, modifies metadata, and creates containers. For each client's request, it queries the location of the account, container, or object in the ring and forwards the request accordingly. You can also use the public API to send requests to the proxy server. It also provides a list of files or containers on the graphical Web interface and uses MemCached to provide caching capabilities to improve performance.

- Account Server: Account server that manages accounts within object storage.
- Container Server: Container servers, whose first task is to process lists of objects and manage the mapping between object stores and folders. The container server does not know where objects are stored; it knows only which objects are stored in the specified container. This object information is stored as an SQLite database file and is backed up on a cluster like an object. Container servers also do some tracking statistics, such as the total number of objects, container usage.
- Object Server: An object server that manages real object data is a simple binary large object storage server that can store, retrieve, and delete objects on a local device. Each object is stored using a path consisting of hash values of the object name and action timestamps. The last write is sure to succeed, and the latest version of the object is processed. Deletion is also considered a version of the file (a file with an extension of ".ts" and ts represents a tombstone). This ensures that deleted files are copied correctly and do not result in earlier versions of "magical reproduction" due to a failure scenario.
- All Periodic Processes: Performs day-to-day transactions in which replication services guarantee continuity and effectiveness of data, including auditing services, update services, and deletion services.
- WSGI Middleware: Handle authentication-related issues and connect to Keystone components.
- Swift Client: Allows various users with permissions to submit commands and takes action on the client.
- Swift-Init: The script for initializing the Ring file requires the daemon name as an argument and provides an action command.
- Swift-Recon: Command-Line Interface, CLI tool for retrieving various performance metrics and status information for a cluster.
- Swift-Ring-Builder: A tool for creating and rebalancing ring.

     Swift object storage relies on software logic design to distribute the data evenly, typically by default saving three copies of the data. The location where the three pieces of data are stored has a significant impact on the cluster's overall performance, with the option of saving on different hard drives on the same server or different servers within the same rack. Figure 6.17 shows the Swift data model. Swift has three layers of logical structure: Account/Container/Object (i.e., account/container/object). There is no limit to the number of nodes per tier and can be extended at will.

     In Swift object storage clusters, when the host nodes that store data go down, the load of the entire cluster is very high (a copy problem, there will be several times the data needs to be transferred, rebalancing), in practice to use

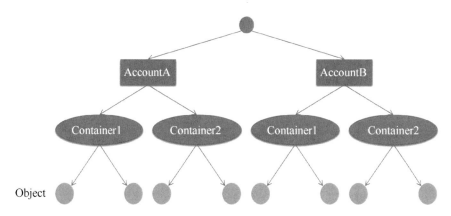

Fig. 6.17 Swift data model

as many technologies as possible network card aggregation and solid-state disk to improve overall performance.

3. File system storage

File system storage is a remote file system that can be mounted. It is shared and can be used by multiple users by mounting on a virtual machine instance. File system storage can be mounted and accessed by multiple users at the same time. A file storage system can perform a series of operations, such as creating a file and file system protocol of a specified capacity size, creating files that can be distributed across one or more servers, specifying access rules and security protocols, supporting snapshots, restoring a file system through snapshots, viewing usage, and so on. In an OpenStack project, the program code name for file system storage is Manila, which supports multiple back-end storage drivers and is shared through multiple storage protocols.

6.7   OpenStack Network Management

Like storage, the network is one of the most critical resources managed by OpenStack. Nova realizes the OpenStack virtual machine world's abstraction, and Swift and Cinder provide the virtual machine with a "safe haven," but without a network, any virtual machine will be just an "island" in the world, unaware of the value of their survival. Initially, network services in OpenStack were provided by a separate module in Nova, Nova-network, but in order to provide a richer topology, support more network types, and better scalability, a dedicated component, Netron, was created to replace the original Nova-network.

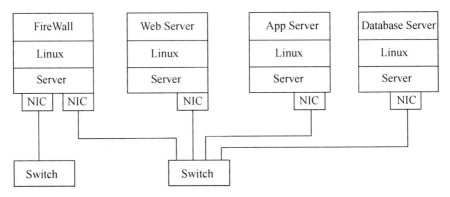

Fig. 6.18 Traditional two layer switch

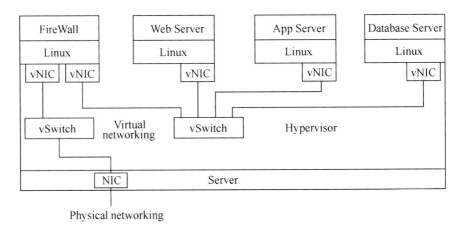

Fig. 6.19 Virtual machine structure

6.7.1 Basics of Linux Network Virtualization

Neutron's central task is to abstract and manage the two-tier physical network. In a traditional physical network, there may be a set of physical servers running a variety of applications, such as Web services, database services, and so on. In order to communicate with each other, each physical server has one or more physical network cards (NICs) that are connected to physical switching devices, such as switches, as shown in Fig. 6.18.

With the introduction of virtualization technology, multiple operating systems and applications shown in Fig. 6.18 can share the same physical server as virtual machines generated and managed by Hypervisor or VMM. The network structure shown in Fig. 6.18 has evolved into the virtual machine structure shown in Fig. 6.19.

A virtual machine's network capabilities are provided by a virtual network card (vNIC), and Hypervisor can create one or more vNICs for each virtual machine.

From the virtual machine's point of view, these vNICs are equivalent to NICs. In order to achieve the same network structure as traditional physical networks, virtual switches, like NICs, are virtualized as virtual switches, each vNIC is connected to the port of the virtual switch, and finally, these virtual switches access the external physical network through the NIC of the physical server.

Thus, it is mainly to complete the virtualization of two network devices for a virtual two-tier network structure: NIC hardware and switching devices. Virtualization of network devices in Linux environments takes several forms, and Neutron is based on these technologies to build user-private virtual networks.

1. TAP, TUN, and VETH

TAP and TUN are virtual network devices implemented by the Linux kernel, with TAP working on the second floor and TUN working on the third floor. The Linux kernel sends data through the TAP and TUN devices to the user space program that binds the device. Conversely, user space programs can send data through TAP/TUN devices just as they do with hardware network devices.

Based on tap drivers, vNIC functions can be implemented, and each vNIC of a virtual machine is connected to a TAP device in Hypervisor. When a TAP device is created, a corresponding character device file is generated in the Linux device file directory, and the user program can open the file to read/write as if it were a normal file.

When writing on this TAP device file, for the Linux network subsystem, it is equivalent to the TAP device received data, and requested the kernel to receive it, Linux kernel received this data will be based on the network configuration for subsequent processing, processing process similar to ordinary physical network card received data from the outside world. When the user program performs a read operation, it is equivalent to querying the kernel whether there is data on the TAP device that needs to be sent, and in other cases, taking it out of the user program to complete the function of sending data to the TAP device. In this process, the TAP device can be used as a native network card, and the application operating the TAP device is equivalent to another computer, which communicates with the native through a read/write system call. Subnet is a three-tier concept in a network that specifies an IPv4 or IPv6 address and describes its associated configuration information attached to a two-tier network and indicates the range of IP addresses that can be used by virtual machines that belong to the network.

VETH devices always appear in pairs, and data sent to one end of the request is always sent from the other in the form of a request to receive. Once created and configured correctly, the data is entered to one end, and VETH changes the direction of the data and feeds it into the kernel network subsystem to inject the data, which can be read at the other end.

2. Linux Bridge

The Linux Bridge (see Fig. 6.20) is a second-tier virtual network device that functions like a physical switch.

Fig. 6.20 Linux network
bridge

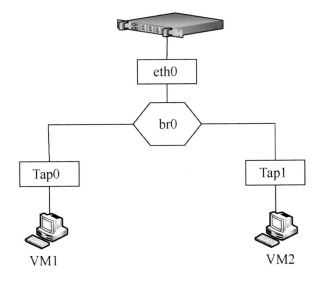

Bridges can bind other Linux network devices as slave devices and virtualize
those slaves as ports. When a slave device is bound to a bridge, it is equivalent to
a switch port in a real network plugged into a network cable connected to a
terminal. In Fig. 6.20, the bridge device br0 binds the actual device eth0 to the
virtual device Tap0/Tap1, at which point, for hypervisor's network protocol stack
upper layer, only br0 can be seen and does not care about the details of the bridge.
When these packets are received from the device, they are submitted to br0 to
determine where the packets are going, and br0 forwards them based on the
mapping relationship between the MAC address and the port.

Because the bridge works on the first and second floors, the slave devices eth0,
Tap0, and Tap1 bound to br0 need not set IP addresses. For the upper routers,
they are all on the same subnet, so set the IP address for br0 (the bridge device
works on the second layer, but it is only one abstraction of the Linux network
device and can be understood by setting the IP address), such as 10.0.1.0/24. At
this point, eth0, Tap0, and Tap1 are all in the 10.0.1.0/24 segment through br0.

Because it has its IP address, br0 can be added to the routing table and sent
data, whereas a device does the actual sending process. If eth0 had its IP address,
such as 192.168.1.1, its IP address would have expired after binding to br0, and
the user program would not have received the data sent to that IP address. Linux
receives only packets with a destination address of br0 IP.

3. OVS

OVS is a product-quality virtual switch developed in the C language, taking
into account portability between different virtualization platforms. At the same
time, it follows Apache 2.0 licenses and is therefore very commercially friendly.

As mentioned earlier, the virtualization of switching devices is a critical part of
virtual networks, and virtual switches are responsible for connecting physical and

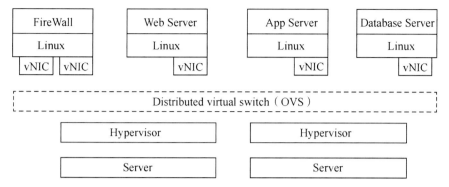

Fig. 6.21 OVS

virtual networks. Although Linux bridges are already well placed to perform this role, we also need OVS to do the extra functionality.

In the traditional data center, the network administrator can control the physical machine's network access by configuring the ports of the switch and completing a series of work such as network isolation, traffic monitoring, packet analysis, and QoS configuration traffic optimization. However, in a cloud environment, network administrators cannot distinguish which virtual machine, operating system, and user the "flowing" packets on the bridged physical network card belong to with the support of a physical switch alone. The introduction of OVS makes it easy to manage virtual networks in cloud environments and monitor network status and traffic.

For example, we can assign each virtual machine that accesses OVS (which also creates one or more virtual switches on the physical server for each virtual machine to access) to a different VLAN to isolate the network, just as we can configure a physical switch. We can also configure QoS for virtual machines on the OVS port. OVS also supports many standard management interfaces and protocols, including NetFlow and sFlow, through which we can perform traffic monitoring and other work

In addition, OVS provides support for OpenFlow, which Open Flow Controller can manage, as shown in Fig. 6.21. In summary, OVS implements distributed virtual switches on a variety of virtualization platforms in a cloud environment, such as Xen and KVM. Distributed virtual switches are virtual network management methods that manage virtual switches (software-based virtual switches or smart network card virtual switches) on multiple hosts, including hosts' physical and virtual port management.

To understand distributed virtual switches, let's take a look at box switches. Box switches have a master board, interface board. The main control board is responsible for managing the plane work, and the interface board is responsible for the data plane work. Interface boards can have multiple, distributed across multiple slots, and can even be stacked to expand the interface boards further. In OVS network, the control plane is the controller's responsibility, the interface board work is handed over to the virtual switches, these virtual switches are distributed in the network of multiple servers and pure software implementation, so there is the concept of a distributed virtual switch. Distributed virtual switches act as virtual devices between hosts, connecting hosts and virtual machines for sharing as if the entire network were using a single large virtual switch.

6.7.2   Introduction and Architecture of OpenStack Network Services

Unlike Nova and Swift, Neutron has only one major service process, Netron-server. Neutron-server runs on a network control node and provides the REST API as an entry point to access Neutron, and the user HTTP requests received by Neutron-server are ultimately made by various agents spread across the computing and network nodes.

Neutron offers several API resources that correspond to a variety of Neutron network abstractions, of which L2's abstract Network/Subnet/

Port can be considered a core resource, while other abstraction levels, including routers and numerous high-level services, are extended resources.

To make scaling easier, Neutron organizes code in a Plugin way, each of which supports a set of API resources and completes specific operations that are ultimately performed by Plugin calling the appropriate agent via RPC.

These Plugins are made with some distinctions. Some of the Plugins that provide support for the underlying two-tier virtual network are called Core Plugins, and they must implement at least three major abstractions of L2, and administrators need to choose one of these already-implemented Core Plugins. Plugin other than Core Plugin is referred to as a service plugin, such as a firewall plugin that provides firewall services.

As for L3 abstract Roler, many Core Plugins were not implemented, and version H was previously modeled with mim, incorporating standard router features to provide L3 services to tenants. In version H, Neutron implements L3 Router Service Plugin to provide router services.

Agents are typically part of a feature that uses physical network devices or some virtualization technology to do something practical—for example, L3 Agent, which implements routing-specific operations.

The Neutron architecture is shown in Fig. 6.22.

Because there is a lot of duplicate code between the various Core Plugin implementations, such as access operations to the database, Neutron in version H implements an ML2 Core Plugin. The ML2 Core Plugin is implemented with a more flexible structure that supports the various Core Plugins available in a Driver form. Therefore, it can be said that the emergence of ML2 Core Plugin is intended to replace all current Core Plugin.

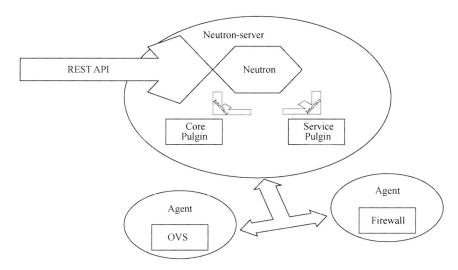

Fig. 6.22 Neutron architecture

For ML2 Core Plugin and the various Service Plugins, while it is possible to divest Neutron as a stand-alone project, the way they are implemented will not change much compared to what is covered in this chapter.

6.7.3   OpenStack Network Service Principle and Process

The Neutron network architecture consists of Neutron-API (running in Neutron-server) along with Neutron agents, including Linux Bridge Agent or Open vSwitch Agent, DHCP Agent, MetaData Agent, and L3 Agent.

To make Neutron easier for the reader to understand, use Linux Bridge Agent (in short for Neutron-LB Agent in the figure) as an example of the collaboration between the Neutron-API and the agents, as shown in Fig. 6.23.

Some of the main components and functions are described below.

(1) Neutron-API

Neutron-API is primarily used to receive instructions from cloud systems for network operations and then through Neutron-LB Agent to operate the Linux bridge plug-ins in network nodes and compute nodes to create specific interfaces, bridges, and VLANs. When creating a virtual machine, if you need to prepare the virtual machine's network operating environment, Neutron-API receives the network requirements for the Nova-API and further informs the Neutron-LB Agent in the compute node and network node of the network action request that will need to be created. Then the Agent operates the underlying Linux bridge plug-in to complete the specific network configuration.

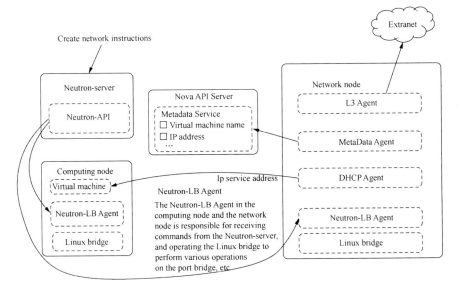

Fig. 6.23 Schematic diagram of the collaboration relationship between Neutron-API and each agent

(2) DHCP Agent

Simply put, the DHCP Agent component is used to complete the task of assigning IP addresses to virtual machines, setting up gateways, and also referring requests for metadata from virtual machines to MetaData Agent.

(3) MetaData Agent

The MetaData Agent component's primary purpose is to further forward a virtual machine's request for metadata (such as virtual machine name, ID, key, IP address) to the metadata service in the Nova-API server when the virtual machine is created or started, providing the required information.

(4) L3 Agent

The primary role of the L3 Agent component is to provide IP routing and NAT services to the cloud system user network. In the tenant's internal network, IP routing for different segments is done through the L3 Agent service, while external access to the tenant's internal network is done through the NAT service provided by L3 Agent.

6.7.4   Analysis of Typical Scenarios of OpenStack Network Services

1. Load Balance as a Service

Load Balance as a Service, LBaaS is a network premium service. As the name implies, users can dynamically create a load balancing device on their network.

Load balancing can be a relatively basic component of a distributed system that receives requests sent by the front end and then forwards requests to a processing unit in the back-end resource pool according to some balanced strategy for processing turn enables high availability and horizontal scalability.

OpenStack Neutron supports LBaaS in the form of advanced service extensions, which are currently implemented by default with HA Proxy software.

2. FireWall as a Service

Readers familiar with firewalls know that firewalls are typically placed on gateways to isolate access between subnets. Therefore, FireWall as a Service, FWaaS is also implemented on network nodes, specifically in the router namespace.

Currently, implementing a firewall in OpenStack is based on the iptables that come with the Linux operating system, so don't expect too much of its performance and functionality.

One concept that can be confusing is security groups. The object of the security group is a virtual network card, implemented by L2 Agent. For example, neutron_openvswitch_agent and neutron_linuxbridge_agent restrict access to virtual network cards by configuring iptables rules on compute nodes. Firewalls can isolate malicious traffic coming from outside before a security group, but communication between different virtual network cards within the same subnet cannot be filtered (unless it is to cross the subnet). You can deploy firewalls and security groups at the same time for dual protection.

3. Distributed Virtual Router

OpenStack users may find that, as Neutron was initially designed, all network services are performed on the network node, which means a lot of traffic and processing, putting much pressure on the network node. At the heart of this processing is the router service. Any access that requires cross-subnet access requires a router to route. Naturally, I wonder, can I also run router services on compute nodes? This design idea is undoubtedly more reasonable, but the implementation of many details of the technical considerations.

To reduce the load on network nodes while increasing scalability, OpenStack has officially introduced distributed routing (DVR) features (users can choose whether to use them or not) since the Juno release, allowing computing nodes to handle their large amounts of east-west traffic and non-source address translation (Source Address Network Translation, SNAT) north-south traffic.

In this way, the network node only needs to handle a portion of the SNAT traffic, greatly reducing the load and the system's dependence on the network node. Naturally, FWaaS can also be placed together on a compute node. DHCP services and VPN services still need to be centralized on network nodes.

6.8   OpenStack Orchestration Management

The growing popularity of cloud computing has led to the proliferation of various cloud computing platforms. Who will eventually be accepted by the industry and users depends on who can effectively support the orchestration of complex user applications. Heat's full support for orchestration will strongly support OpenStack's "leadership" in cloud computing, particularly in IaaS. This section describes OpenStack orchestration management, what is orchestration, Heat's location in orchestration, Heat templates, and how Heat templates and Heat are implemented and supported, from the perspectives of infrastructure, software configuration and deployment, automatic resource scaling, and load balancing, and finally, the integration of Heat and configuration management tools, and the integration of Heat and IBM UCDP/UCD.

6.8.1   Introduction to OpenStack Orchestration Service

Heat is a template-based service for orchestrating composite cloud applications. It currently supports Amazon's CloudFormation template format, as well as Heat's own HOT template format. The use of templates simplifies the definition and deployment of complex infrastructure, services, and applications. Templates support rich resource types. The relationship between Heat and other modules is shown in Fig. 6.24.

Heat currently supports templates in two formats, one is a JSON-based CFN template and the other is a YAML-based HOT template. CFN templates are primarily designed to maintain compatibility with AWS. HOT templates are Heat's own,

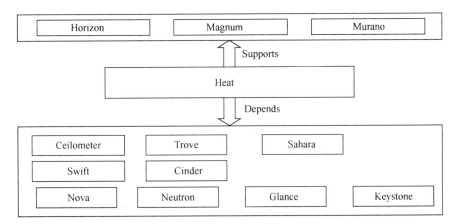

Fig. 6.24 The relationship between Heat and other modules

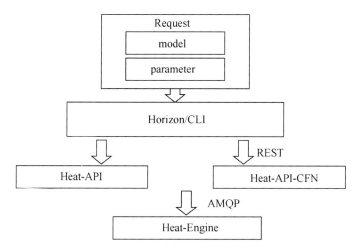

Fig. 6.25 Heat architecture

and the resource types are more prosperous and more reflective of Heat's characteristics.

A typical HOT template consists of the following elements.

- Template version: Required, specify the corresponding template version, Heat will be verified according to the version.
- List of parameters: Optional, refers to the list of input parameters.
- List of resources: Required, refers to the various resources contained in the resulting stack. You can define dependencies between resources, such as building Port, and then using Port to build virtual machines.
- Output list: Optional, refers to the information exposed by the resulting stack that can be used by the user or provided to other Stacks as input.

6.8.2   OpenStack Orchestration Service Architecture

Heat contains the following important components.

(1) Heat-API components implement the REST API that OpenStack naturally supports. The component processes API requests by transmitting them via AMQP to Heat-Engine.
(2) The Heat-API-CFN component provides an API that is compatible with AWS CloudFormation and forwards API requests to Heat-Engine via AMQP.
(3) Heat-Engine components provide Heat's most important collaboration capabilities.

The Heat architecture is shown in Fig. 6.25.

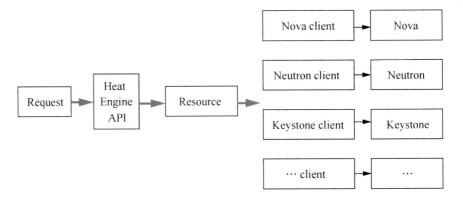

Fig. 6.26 Heat-Engine structure

The user submits a request containing templates and parameters in Horizon or CLI, which converts the request into an API call in REST format, and then calls the Heat-API or Heat-API-CFN. Heat-API and Heat-API-CFN verify the template's correctness and then pass the request asynchronously to Heat-Engine via AMQP.

When Heat-Engine receives a request, the request is resolved to various resources, each corresponding to an OpenStack another service client, and then to another service by sending a REST request. With such parsing and collaboration, the processing of requests is finalized.

The Heat-Engine structure (see Fig. 6.26) serves three layers: Layer 1 handles Heat-level requests to create Stack based on templates and parameters, where Stack consists of a variety of resources.

6.8.3 Principles of OpenStack Orchestration Service

OpenStack has from the very beginning provided CLI and Horizon to manage resources for users. However, typing a line of commands and clicking in the browser can be time-consuming and laborious. Even if you save the command line as a script, write additional scripts between input/output and interdependency for maintenance and are not easy to extend. Users writing programs directly through the REST API introduce additional complexity, which is also not easy to maintain and extend. This is not conducive to users using OpenStack for large-volume management, and even less conducive to the use of OpenStack to orchestrate resources to support IT applications.

Heat came into being in this case. Heat uses industry-popular templates to design or define orchestrations. Users open the text editor and write a template based on a key-value pair to get the orchestration they want easily. To make it easier for users to use, Heat provides several template examples. Most of the time, the user only needs to choose the desired arrangement, copy and paste the way to complete the template writing. Heat supports orchestration in four ways.

1. Heat's orchestration of the infrastructure

   OpenStack provides its infrastructure resources, including computing, networking, and storage. By orchestrating these resources, users can get the essential virtual machines. It is worth mentioning that users can provide some simple scripts to make some simple configurations for virtual machines during the orchestration of virtual machines.

2. Heat's orchestration of software configuration and deployment

   Users can configure virtual machines with complex configurations such as installing software and configuration software, such as Throughware Configuration and Software Deployment provided by Heat.

3. Heat's orchestration of automatic scaling of resources

   If users have some advanced functional requirements, such as a set of virtual machine groups that can be automatically scaled based on load, or a set of load-balanced virtual machines, Heat provides support such as AutoScaling and LoadBalance. Heat's support for complex applications such as AutoScaling and LoadBalance is well established and has a wide variety of templates for reference.

4. Heat's arrangement of load balancing

   If the user's application is complex, or if the user's application already has some deployment based on popular configuration management tools, such as a cookie book based on Chef, these cookies can be reused by integrating Chef, saving a lot of development time or migration time.

6.8.4   OpenStack Orchestration Service and Configuration Management Tool Integration

With the popularity of DevOps, many configuration management tools have emerged, such as Chef, Puppet, and Ansible. In addition to providing a platform framework, various tools also provide scripts that can be flexibly configured and referenced for a large number of middleware and software deployments. Take Chef as an example. It provides a large number of CookBooks for open source software. Major manufacturers have also written CookBook for their middleware. For example, IBM has provided CookBook for DB2. With these CookBooks, users can deploy complex middleware or software through simple configuration and application.

Heat supports these configuration management tools in the use of collaborative processes based on OS::Heat::SoftwareConfig and OS::Heat::SoftwareDeployment. First of all, for OS::Heat::SoftwareConfig, the group needs to be defined as the corresponding type, such as Ansible, Puppet, Docker-compose, and Salt. Then OS::Heat::SoftwareDeployment references OS::Heat::SoftwareConfig. In this way, when

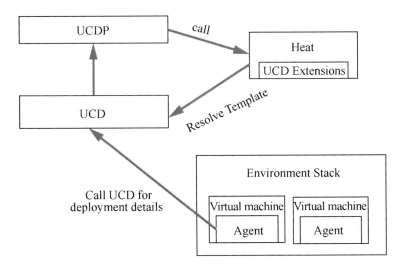

Fig. 6.27 Integration of Heat and IBM UCDP/UCD

the software is deployed, the corresponding script hook (Hook) Heat-config-ansible will be called to execute the corresponding software configuration.

The integration of Heat and IBM UCDP/UCD is shown in Fig. 6.27. With the gradual rise of cloud computing, various cloud computing-based orchestration tools have begun to appear. From the current point of view, these tools mainly have the characteristics of cross-platform, visualization, and powerful configuration management functions. Among them, IBM's UrbanCode Deploy with Patterns (UCDP) and UrbanCode Deploy (UCD) are powerful platforms with the features as mentioned above.

UCDP is full-stack environment management and deployment solution that supports users in designing, deploying, and updating full-stack environments for multiple clouds. The platform can integrate UCD, based on Heat, to realize automatic management of OpenStack infrastructure and optimize continuous delivery throughput. It has a visual operation interface, and you can create and edit cross-cloud platform templates by dragging icons.

UCD arranges application, middleware configuration, and database changes and automatically deploys them to development, test, and production environments. It allows users to deploy as needed or as planned through self-service. In UCD, it is possible to split complex application configuration according to configuration (Configuration-Only) or traditional code and configuration (Code-and-Configuration) and define step by step as shown in Fig. 6.27.

With the help of UCDP's powerful pattern design capabilities, we can make a complex template by dragging. Two types of resources are used: cloud computing resources, such as networks, security groups, and mirroring; the others are components defined in UCD, such as jke.db, MySQL Server, jke.war, and WebSphere Liberty Profile.

6.9 OpenStack Fault Management

OpenStack is a complex software suite, and there are quite a few problems to be solved for both beginners and experienced system administrators. Although there is no single troubleshooting method, understanding the important information in OpenStack logs and mastering the tools that can help track down errors will help solve the problems that may be encountered. However, it can be expected that without external support, it is impossible to solve all problems. Therefore, it is imperative to collect demand information to help the OpenStack community identify errors and propose corrections. It will help bugs or problems to be dealt with quickly and effectively.

6.9.1 OpenStack Troubleshooting

When OpenStack fails, the following methods can be used to diagnose and deal with the fault.

1. Check OpenStack service

OpenStack uses some basic commands to communicate with computing and other services, by viewing the running status of these services, and combining some general system commands to detect whether the environment is running as expected. To check whether the computing service is normal, execute the following command:

```
sudo nova-mange service list
```

2. Understand logs

Logs are critical to all computer systems. The more complex the system, the more it relies on logs to find problems, reducing troubleshooting time. Understanding the OpenStack system log is very important to ensure the health of the OpenStack environment. OpenStack generates a lot of log information to help troubleshoot OpenStack installation problems. The log locations of these services will be described in detail below.

(1) OpenStack computing service log

OpenStack computing service logs are located in /var/log/nova/, and the default permission holder is the Nova user. In order to read the information, log in as the root user. It should be noted that not all log files are included on every server. For example, in Nova-compute, the log is only generated on the compute node.

(2) OpenStack object storage log

OpenStack object storage logs are written to SysLog by default. In a Ubutun operating system, you can pass /var/log/syslog view. In other operating systems, the target may be located in /var/log/messages. The logs generated by the OpenStack block storage service are placed under /var/log/cinder by default.

(3) OpenStack network service log

The OpenStack network service Neutron, formerly known as Quantum, saves logs in /var/log/quantum/×.log, and each service has a separate log file.

3. Change log level

The default log level of each OpenStack service is WARNING. Logs of this level are sufficient for understanding the running system's status or basic error location, but sometimes it is necessary to increase the log level to help diagnose problems or lower the log level to reduce log noise.

Since each service's log setting methods are similar, here, we take the OpenStack computing service as an example to set the log level in the OpenStack computing service.

Log in to the machine running the OpenStack computing service and execute the following command:

```
sudo vim /etc/nova/logging.conf
```

Modify the log level of a listed service to DEBUG, INFO, or WARNING, as shown below:

```
[logger root]
Level= WARNING
handlers = null
[logger_nova]
Level = INFO
handlers = stderr
qualname = nova
```

6.9.2   OpenStack Troubleshooting Tools

OpenStack provides tools to detect different components of the service to detect whether they are operating normally. These basic level troubleshooting can ensure that the system is operating as expected. Commonly used troubleshooting tools are as follows:

1. Common network troubleshooting tools

- Use ip -a to check the status of the network interface: On a computing node or a node running Nova-Network, use the ip -a command to view the information of the network card, including the IP address, VLAN, and whether the network card is working.

- Find out the fault in the network path: Use the ping command to quickly find the network path's fault. In a virtual machine instance, first check whether the external host can be pinged successfully, which indicates that there is no network problem. If it does not work, try to ping the IP address of the computing node where the virtual machine instance is located. If it can be pinged, the problem may be between the computing nodes; if the ping fails, the problem is between the virtual machine instance and the computing node. Such as tcpdump and iptables are powerful network troubleshooting tools that can help quickly locate faults.
- Use Nova-Network to troubleshoot DHCP: A common network problem is that the virtual machine instance is successfully booted, but not connected. This is because it cannot obtain an IP address from dnsmasq. dnsmasq is also a DHCP service started by the Nova-Network service. The easiest way to check for this kind of problem is to look at the console output of the virtual machine instance. If DHCP fails, you can use the nova console-log <instance name or uuid> command to retrieve the console log.
- DNS troubleshooting: If you can use SSH to log in to a virtual machine instance, but it takes a long time to see the prompt, then there may be a problem with DNS. To quickly check whether DNS is working properly, one way is to use the host command to resolve the host name in the virtual machine instance.

2. Commonly used computing and storage troubleshooting tools

- Computing node failure and maintenance: Sometimes, a computing node will unexpectedly go down, or it needs to be restarted for maintenance purposes. Before restarting, you need to ensure that all virtual machine instances on this computing node are migrated, which can be achieved using the nova live-migration command. Other faults may also occur in the computing node, and users need to use the commands provided by the Nova service to locate the fault according to the specific situation gradually. Commonly used commands are lsb_release -a, uname -a, etc.
- Failure and maintenance of storage nodes: Because object storage is highly redundant, it is much simpler to deal with object storage node problems than computing node problems. If you encounter a storage node failure, you can try to restart it directly. Besides, shutting down the problematic storage node or replacing the Swift disk is also a way to solve the storage node problem. Commonly used storage fault handling commands are df -h, free -m, kpartx, etc.

3. View services and logs

- Reading logs: OpenStack service logs contain different levels, and log messages will only appear in the logs when they are more serious than a specific log level. The DEBUG level can record logs of various levels, and specific tracking of the system status can be achieved by adjusting the log level or adding a custom log statement.

- Tracking instance requests: When a virtual machine instance is abnormal and needs to be tracked from the logs of various Nova-× services, these logs are distributed in cloud controllers and computing nodes. The general method is to track the UUID of this virtual machine instance in these service logs.
- Centralized log management: The cloud system contains many servers, and sometimes it is necessary to check the logs of multiple servers to summarize an event. A better way is to send all service logs to a centralized place. Ubuntu uses rsyslog as the default log service. It can send logs remotely. By modifying the configuration file, log aggregation can be easily achieved.
- Monitoring: Monitoring ensures that all services are operational and monitors the use of resources over time to determine potential bottlenecks and upgrade requirements. Nagios is an open source monitoring service that can check the status of servers and network services by executing arbitrary commands.

6.9.3   OpenStack Troubleshooting Cases

This section will introduce troubleshooting from three cases of computing services, identity authentication, and networks.

1. Computing service failure

OpenStack computing services are very complex, and timely fault diagnosis can ensure these services' smooth operation. Fortunately, OpenStack provides some tools to help solve this problem, while Ubuntu also provides some tools to help solve the positioning problem.

Although OpenStack computing services' troubleshooting is a complex problem, solving the problem in an orderly manner can help users get a more satisfactory answer. When encountering corresponding problems, you can try the following solutions.

Case 1: Unable to ping or SSH to the instance

- When starting the instance, specify a security group. If not specified, the default security group is used by default. This mandatory security group ensures that the security policy is enabled in the cloud environment by default. For this reason, it must be clearly stated that the instance needs to be able to ping and SSH to the instance. For such a basic activity, these rules usually need to be added to the default security group.
- Network problems may also prevent users from accessing instances in the cloud. First, check whether the computing instance can forward packets from the public interface to the bridge interface. The command is as follows:

```
sysctl -A I grep ip_ forward
```

- net.ipv4.ip_forward should be set to 1. Otherwise, check/etc/sysctl.conf for comments on the following options:

```
net.ipv4.ip-forward=1。
```

- Run the following command to perform the update:

```
sudo sysctl -p
```

- Network issues may also involve routing issues. Check that the client communicates properly with the OpenStack compute node and that any routing records to these instances are correct.
- In addition, IPv6 conflicts may be encountered. If you don't need IPv6, you can add -use ipv6-false to/etc/nova/nova.conf file and restart the Nova-compute and Nova-Network services.
- If openStack Neutron is used, check the status of the Neutron service on the host and see if the correct IP namespace is used.
- Restart the host.

  Case 2:Error codes such as $40\times$, $50\times$ appear

  The main OpenStack services are essentially Web services, which means that service responses are clearly defined.

- $40\times$: Refers to a user-generated response event that has been started. For example, 401 is an authentication failure that requires a check of the certificate used to access the service.
- $50\times$:The error code means that a link service is not reachable, or an error causes the service to interrupt the response failure. Usually, this type of problem is that the service is not starting properly, so check the health of the service.

  If all the attempts don't solve the problem, you can turn to the community, where many enthusiastic friends can help.

2. Authentication failure

   OpenStack Authentication Services is a complex service that is responsible for authentication and authorization of the entire system. Common problems include endpoint misconfiguration, incorrect parameters, and general user authentication issues, such as resetting passwords or providing more detailed information to users. Because Keystone troubleshooting requires administrator privileges, the environment is first configured to facilitate Keystone-related commands' execution. When you encounter a problem, you can refer to and follow these steps.

   Case: Authentication issues

   Users have been experiencing a variety of authentication issues, including forgotten passwords or account expirations, as well as unpredictable

```
+-----------+------------------------------------------------+
| Property  |                    value                       |
+-----------+------------------------------------------------+
| email     | kevin@example.com                              |
| enablee   | Ture                                           |
| id        | 68ba544e500c40668435aa6201e557e4               |
| name      | kevinj                                         |
| tenantid  | 1a50d87215ba4444f8c62b42cb6b9de6f              |
+-----------+------------------------------------------------+
```

Fig. 6.28 Result information

authentication failures. Locating these issues allows the service to resume access or continue using the OpenStack environment.

The first thing to look at is the relevant logs, including /var/log/nova, /var/log/glance (if mirror-related) and /var/log/keystone logs.

Account-related issues may include account loss. Therefore, first use the following command to view the user: keystone user-list. If the user's account exists in the user list, further review the user's details. For example, after you get a user's ID, you can use the following command:

```
keystone user-get 68ba544e500c40668435aa6201e557e4
```

The result information returned is shown in Fig. 6.28.

This helps you understand if the user has a valid account. If you need to reset a user's password, you can reset the user's password (e.g., by setting it to openstack) using the following command:

```
keystone user-password-update  \
--pass openstack  \
68ba544e500c40668435aa6201e557e4
```

If your account is deactivated, you can simply re-enable it using the following command:

```
keystone user-update --enabled true
68ba544e500c40668435aa6201e557e4
```

Sometimes there is no problem with the account, the problem occurs on the client-side. Therefore, before looking for authentication issues, make sure that the user account is in the right environment.

3. Network failure

With the introduction of Neutron, OpenStack network services became a complex service because they allowed users to define and create their networks in a cloud environment. OpenStack network administrators' common problems include misconfiguration during Neutron installation, routing failures, and virtual

```
2018-08-23 21:09:30,162 - DataSourceEc2.py[WARNING]:'http:/169.254.169.254'failed:url error[(Error 111)Connection refused]
2018-08-23 21:09:35,174 - DataSourceEc2.py[CRITICAL]:Giving up on md after 120 seconds
```

Fig. 6.29 Console log

switch plug-in issues. Common problems for users include misunderstandings about Neutron functionality and restrictions set by administrators.

The next Neutron installation requires administrator privileges, so first, make sure that you log on to the control, compute, and network nodes as root, and configure your environment to run various commands. When you encounter a problem, you can follow these steps to correct the error.

Case: Cloud-init reports that the connection was denied when accessing metadata

In the instance's console log (viewed INSTANCE_ID the command nova console-log), you see two lines of errors as shown in Fig. 6.29.

There may be several reasons for the error, but the result is the same, i.e., the user cannot log on to the instance because it cannot be injected with a key.

First check that the physical network cards on the network nodes and compute nodes are configured for use by the operating system. You should also ensure that the following commands are run during installation and configuration:

```
ovs-vsctl add-port br-eth1 eth1
```

Where br-eth1 is a bridge created on the network card, eth1 is a physical network card.

Then check to see if the instance can be routed from the instance's gateway to the 169.254.169.254 metadata server, and if not, create a routing rule to the network. When creating a subnet and developing a gateway, the gateway's address should be routed to address 169.254.169.254. Otherwise, the error shown in Fig. 6.29 occurs. Use the following options to create a routing rule for instances to 169.254.169.254 at the same time when creating a subnet:

```
quantum subnet-create demoNet1 \
10.1.0.0/24 \
--name snet1 \
--no-gateway \
--host_ routes type=dict list=true \
destination=0.0.0.0/0, nexthop=10.1.0.1 \
--allocation-pool start=10.1.0.2, end=10.1.0.254
```

Neutron injects 169.254.169.254 routes into the instance using the no-gateway option and appears in the instance's routing table. However, in order to provide a default routing rule, the target address of 0.0.0.0/0 and the next address of the routing table are specified here so that the instance can access other locations.

6.9.4 OpenStack Troubleshooting-Related Items

1. Vitrage

Vitrage is a component of OpenStack that provides root analysis (Root Causes, RCA) services. The organization is used to organize, analyze, and extend OpenStack alerts and events, derive the root cause of the problem, generate derived alarms for the system, or set the derived state. Its main functions include physical-virtual entity mapping, deriving alarms and states, root cause analysis of alarms or events, and Horizon display.

2. Aodh

Aodh is a component separated by Ceilometer, and its main function is to provide resource alerting, support log, Webhook, and other alerts. It consists of four modules: alarm condition trigger calculation module, alarm notification module, listening module, Aodh start module.

3. Monasca

Monasca is a high-performance, scalable, highly available monitoring-as-a-service solution. It is an open source monitoring scheme based on open source technology. It uses the REST API to store and query historical data. Unlike other monitoring tools that use special protocols and transport methods, such as Nagios' NSAA, Monasca uses only HTTP. When multi-tenant authentication, metrics are submitted and certified using keystone components, and metrics are defined using key-value pairs. Real-time thresholds and alarms can be given to system indicators, and composite alarms can be set, which are simple to use and consist of sub-alarm expressions and logical operators. The monitoring agent supports the results of checks on built-in systems and services, as well as Nagios' Checks and Statsd.

4. Mistral

Mistral is a relatively new project in the OpenStack ecosystem, a workflow component contributed by Mirantis to the OpenStack community, providing Workflow As a Service, similar to AWS's SWS (Simple Workflow Service), and Oozie services in the Hadoop ecosystem.

5. Freezer

Freezer is an open source backup software that helps users automate data backup and data restoration. Freezer has now officially introduced OpenStack for data backup, an official project in the OpenStack community that aims to provide Solutions for OpenStack's data backup environment. Freezer introduced support from the OpenStack Liberty version, which required minor modifications.

6.10 Exercise

(1) Multiple choices

1. The OpenStack component does not include ( ).

   A. Nova
   B. Swift
   C. Keystone
   D. EC2

2. In the OpenStack platform, the following () components are responsible for supporting all activities of instances and managing the life cycle of all instances.

   A. Glance
   B. Neutron
   C. Swift
   D. Nova

3. In the OpenStack platform, ( ) is used to define a collection of resources that can be accessed.

   A. User
   B. Project
   C. Role
   D. Domain

4. In the OpenStack platform, network traffic packets can be filtered on the route to enhance network security.

   A. Securet Group
   B. ML2
   C. FWaaS
   D. LBaas

5. The basic features not provided by the Civic component in OpenStack are ( ).

   A. Provides basic block storage management capabilities
   B. Virtualize SAN management with iSCSI, FC, or NFS
   C. Provides long-lasting storage media and can be passed between virtual machines
   D. Provides high-performance file systems

6. ( ) is not Swift's design principle.

   A. Persistence of data
   B. Responsible algorithms to improve storage efficiency
   C. Symmetrical System Architecture
   D. No single point of failure

(2) Fill in the blanks.
1. OpenStack is the framework for building_____, managing all kinds of hardware devices through integration and hosting all kinds of upper-level applications and services, resulting in a complete system.
2. OpenStack is a free and open source platform that is primarily used to deploy _____.
3. OpenStack's key components are _____, _____, _____, _____, _____.
4. OpenStack's mirroring service supports a variety of virtual machine mirror formats, including _____, _____, _____, _____.
5. As a separate security authentication module in OpenStack, _____ is responsible for the authentication of OpenStack users, token management, the service directory that provides access to resources, and access control based on the user role.
6. Initially, network services in OpenStack were provided by a separate module _____in Nova.
(3) Answer the questions
1. What is OpenStack?
2. Summarize the main components of OpenStack and its features.
3. Summarize how OpenStack works together across service modules.
4. What services in OpenStack typically run on the control node?
5. What is a Neutron agent? How do I display all Neutron agents?

Chapter 7
Container Technology

As cloud computing technologies and applications mature, their range of applications continues to expand, leading to a huge transformation from client/server models to various forms of cloud services, driving a new era of cloud economy. Container technology is a mainstream technology in the cloud economy and IT ecosystem that effectively divides a single operating system's resources into isolated groups to better balance conflicting resource usage needs among isolated groups. Container technology, including core technology, platform technology, support technology, and a range of technologies, can significantly improve production efficiency and have attracted widespread attention in the industry.

With its agile features that integrate DevOps, container technology has brought new and transformative forces to the cloud computing market, especially the PaaS market, especially the container technology represented by Docker, which has developed rapidly and is now a well-established ecosystem. Kubernetes is a representative product of the new round of change. Based on the model of theory and practice, this chapter introduces the knowledge of container technology and container arrangement from the aspects of platform architecture, basic core function, network, security, and resource management, to make it easier for readers to have a more comprehensive understanding of the Docker and Kubernetes ecosystems.

7.1 Overview of Container Technology

7.1.1 Introduction to Container Technology

Cloud computing solves the problem of elasticity in computing, networking, and storage in computer infrastructure, but it leaves behind two problems: the scalability and migration of applications. In a cloud computing environment, two solutions have been come up. One is through automated scripting, but different environments vary widely, with one script often running correctly on one environment and the

Huawei Technologies Co., Ltd., *Cloud Computing Technology*,
https://doi.org/10.1007/978-981-19-3026-3_7

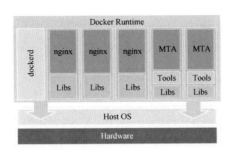 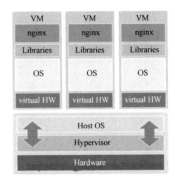

Fig. 7.1 The difference between a container (left) and a virtual machine (right)

other. The second is through the virtual machine image. However, the virtual machine image is too large, replication and download are too time-consuming.

In order to solve the above problems, container technology has been proposed. Drawing on traditional transportation solutions, it has been suggested that applications be packaged in a container-like manner (the dependencies required for an application to run), i.e., to package any application and its dependencies into a lightweight, portable, self-contained container. Isolate different processes running on the host with a kind of virtualization technology that isolates and does not affect each other between containers, containers, and host operating systems, enabling applications to run in the same way anywhere. Developers take notes on their own.

Containers created and tested on this computer can run on virtual machines, physical servers, or public cloud hosts of production systems without any modifications.

1. Container and virtual machine

When it comes to containers, you have to compare them to virtual machines because both provide encapsulation and isolation for your application.

Traditional virtualization technologies, such as VMware, KVM, and Xen, aim to create complete virtual machines. In order to run the app, install the entire operating system in addition to the app itself and its dependencies.

Containers consist of the app itself, and the IT resources on which the app depends, such as the libraries or other applications that the app requires. Containers run in the host operating system's user space and are isolated from other processes of the operating system, which is significantly different from virtual machines. Figure 7.1 shows the difference between a container and a virtual machine.

Figure 7.1 shows that because all containers share a host operating system, this makes the container much smaller in size than the virtual machine. In addition, boot containers do not need to start the entire operating system, so container deployment and startup are faster, less expensive, and easier to migrate.

2. The evolution of containers

Container technology dates back to the chroot command in the UNIX operating system in 1979, originally intended to facilitate switching root directories, providing isolation of file system resources for each process, which is also the origin of the idea of operating system virtualization.

FreeBSD Jails was issued in 2000 based on the chroot command, which was absorbed and improved by BSD. In addition to file system isolation, FreeBSD Jails adds isolation of user and network resources, and each Jail can assign a separate IP for some relatively separate software installation and configuration.

Linux VServer was released in 2001. Linux VServer continues the idea of FreeBSD Jails, isolating resources such as file system, CPU time, network address, and memory on an operating system, each partition is called a Security Context, and the internal virtualization system is called VPS.

In 2004, Sun released Solaris Containers. Solaris Containers is released as a feature in Solaris 10 and contains system resource control and binary isolation provided by Zones, where Zones exists as a fully isolated virtual server within the operating system instance.

In 2005, SWsoft released OpenVZ. OpenVZ is very similar to Solaris Containers in providing virtualization, isolation, resource management, and checkpoints through patched Linux cores. OpenVZ marks the true mainstream of kernel-level virtualization, followed by the addition of relevant technologies to the kernel.

In 2006, Google released Process Containers. Process Containers recorded and isolated each process's resources (including CPU, memory, hard disk I/O, network, etc.), changed its name to Control Groups, and was added to Linux Kernel 2.6.24 in 2007.

In 2008, the first more complete container technology, Linux Container (LXC), was available, based on Cgroups and Linux Namespaces implementations added to the kernel. LXC does not need to be patched to run on Linux on any vanilla kernel.

In 2011, CloudFoundry released Warden, and unlike LXC, Warden can work on any operating system, run as a daemon, and provide an API to manage containers.

In 2013, Google established an open source container technology stack. Google started this project to enable high-performance, high-resource utilization, and near-zero-cost virtualization technology through containers. Currently, the monitoring tool cAdvisor in Kubernetes originated from the lmctfy project. In 2015, Google donated the core technology of lmctfy to libcontainer.

Docker was born in 2013. Docker was originally an internal project of DotCloud, the predecessor of Docker, a PaaS company. Like Warden, Docker initially used LXC and later replaced LXC with libcontainer. Unlike other container technologies, Docker built a complete ecosystem around containers, including container imaging standards, container Registry, REST APIs, CLI, container cluster management tool Docker Swarm, and more.

In 2014, CoreOS created rkt to improve a container engine for Docker's security defect rewrites, including service discovery tools etcd and Web tool Frankel.

In 2016, Microsoft released Windows-based container technology Hyper-V Container. Hyper-V Container works like container technology under Linux to ensure that processes running in a container are isolated from the outside world, taking into account the security of virtual machines and the lightness of containers.

3. Container standardization

Today, Docker is almost synonymous with containers, and many people think Docker is a container. In fact, this is the wrong understanding. In addition to Docker, there are Coreos. So it is not just Docker in the container world. This makes it easy to disagree. Any technology requires a standard to regulate it. Otherwise, it can easily led to technology implementation fragmentation, a lot of conflict and redundancy. As a result, the Open Container Initiative (OCI) was established in 2015 by Google, Docker, CoreOS, IBM, Microsoft, Red Hat, and others, and the first open container standard was launched in April 2016. The standard consists primarily of the Easy Runtime Standard and the Image Spec. The introduction of standards helps to bring stability to the growing market. Therefore, enterprises can rest assured that the use of container technology, users in packaging, deployment of applications, can freely choose different containers runtime. Simultaneously, image packaging, establishment, certification, deployment, and naming can also be done according to the unified norms. These two standards mainly contain the following.

(1) Container running standard

    ① Creating:Use the create command to create a container, a process called creating.

    ② Created:The container has been created, but has not yet run, indicating that there are no errors in imaging and configuration, and that the container can run on the current platform.

    ③ Running:The container is running, the process inside is up, and the user-set tasks are being performed.

    ④ Stopped:The container is paused after the container runs completely, or if there is an error running, or after the stop command. In this state, the container also has a lot of information saved in the platform and has not been completely deleted.

(2) Container image standard

    (1) File system: A file system saved by layer, where each layer saves a portion of the change between the top layer, which files the layer should save, how to represent files that are added, modified, and deleted, and so on.

(2) Config files: The hierarchical information of the file system (hash values at each level, as well as historical information), as well as some information (such as environment variables, working directories, command parameters, mount lists) that is required for the container runtime, specifying the configuration of the image on a particular platform and system. This is closer to what we see <image_id> using docker inspect.

(3) Manifest file: Image's config file index, the manifest file holds a lot of information about the current platform.

(4) Index file: Optional file that points to manifest files from different platforms. This file guarantees that an image can be used across platforms, each with a different manifest file, indexed using index.

4. Container scenarios

The birth of container technology solves the technical implementation of the PaaS layer. Technologies such as OpenStack and CloudStack are primarily used to solve problems at the IaaS layer. So what are the main scenarios in which container technology is used? There are several mainstream applications at present.

(1) Containerized traditional applications

Containers not only improve the security and portability of existing applications, but also save money. Each enterprise environment has an older set of applications to serve customers or automate business processes. Even large-scale monomer applications benefit from container isolation by enhancing security and portability, reducing costs. Once containerized, these applications can scale additional services or transition to a microservices architecture.

(2) Continuous integration and continuous deployment

Accelerate application pipeline automation and application deployment with Docker. Data suggest that the use of Docker can increase delivery speeds by more than 13 times. Modern development processes are fast, continuous, and automated, with the ultimate goal of developing more reliable software. With Continuous Integration (CI) and CONTINUOUS Deployment(CD), IT teams can integrate new code every time a developer checks in and successfully tests it. As the basis for developing an operational approach, CI/CD creates a real-time feedback loop mechanism that continuously transmits small iterative changes, accelerating changes and improving quality. Ci environments are typically fully automated, triggering tests with git push commands, automatically building new images when successful, and then pushing them to the Docker image library. With subsequent automation and scripting, the new image's container can be deployed to the preview environment for further testing.

(3) Microservices

Use microservices to accelerate application architecture modernization. The application architecture moves from a monomer code base with waterfall model development to a loosely coupled service that is developed and deployed independently. Thousands of such services are connected to form applications. Docker allows developers to choose the tool or technology stack isolation service that best fits each service to eliminate any potential conflicts and avoid "hell-like matrix dependencies." These containers can be easily shared, deployed, updated, and instantly extended independently of the app's other service components. Docker's end-to-end security features enable teams to build and run the lowest privileged microservices model, where the resources required for the service (other applications, confidential information, computing resources, and so on) are created and accessed in real-time.

(4) IT infrastructure optimization

By making the most of your infrastructure, you can save money. Docker and containers help optimize the utilization and cost of your infrastructure. Optimization is not just about cutting costs. It is also about ensuring that the right resources are used effectively at the right time. Containers are a lightweight way to package and isolate application workloads, so Docker allows multiple workloads to run without conflict on the same physical or virtual server. Enterprises can consolidate data centers and consolidate acquired IT resources for mobility to the cloud while reducing maintenance of operating systems and servers.

7.1.2 Container Imaging

Imaging is the cornerstone of a container, a container is a running instance of an image, and an image is available to launch the container. This section describes container imaging in terms of the internal structure of the image, the construction of the image, image management, and distribution.

1. The internal structure of the image

If we want to build our images or understand why containers, such as Docker, are lightweight, we need to have an in-depth understanding of the image's internal structure. For ease of understanding, let's start with a minimal image hello-world.

Hello-world is an official image provided by Docker and is often used to verify that Docker was installed successfully. Let's first download the hello-world image from Docker's official repository via docker pull, as shown in Fig. 7.2.

Run hello-world through docker run, as shown in Fig. 7.3.

Dockerfile is a description of the image that defines how to build the Docker image. Dockerfile's syntax is simple and readable. Hello-world's Dockerfile is shown in Fig. 7.4.

As you can see, there are only three instructions in Dockerfile.

```
root@ubuntu: docker pull hello-world

Using default tag: latest
latest: Pulling from library/hello-world
m4b14d08d14: Pull compete
Digest: Sh0256 m256e8036e2070f7bf2d0b0763db0bdd6779851

Status: Downloaded newer image for hello-world: latest
```

Fig. 7.2 Download the hello-world image from the official Docker warehouse

```
root@ubuntu: docker run hello-world

Hello from Docker!
This message shows that you r installation appears to be working
```

Fig. 7.3 Run hello-world

Fig. 7.4 Contents of Dockerfile

```
FROM scratch

COPY hello /
CMD ["/hello"]
```

(1) FORM scratch: Images are built from scratch.
(2) COPY hello /: Copy the file "hello" to the image root.
(3) CMD ("/hello"): When the container starts, execute/hello.

There is only one executable "hello" in the image hello-world, which functions to output information such as "hello from Docker...". Hello-world is a complete image, but it has no practical use. In general, we want the image to provide a basic operating system environment where users can install and configure software as needed. Such an image is called a base image.

Base imaging has two meanings: it does not rely on other images, it is built from scratch, and other images can be extended on the basis of it. So what can be called base imaging is usually the Docker image of various Linux distributions, such as Ubuntu, CentOS, and so on.

The Linux operating system consists of kernel space and userspace. The kernel space is Kernel, and when Linux first starts, the bootfs file system is loaded, after which the bootfs are unloaded. The file system for user space is rootfs, including directories such as /dev, /bin, etc. that we are familiar with. For base imaging, the underlying uses the host's kernel space directly, just add rootfs yourself.

Docker supports extending existing images to build new ones. For example, we need to build a new image with Dockerfile as shown in Fig. 7.5.

Fig. 7.5 Dockerfile for
building a new image

```
FROM debian

RUN apt-get install emacs

RUN atp-get install apache2

CMD ["/bin/bash"]
```

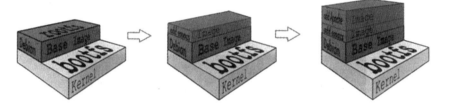

Fig. 7.6 The construction process of the new image

The new image does not need to start from scratch, but is directly built on the Debian base image, then install emacs and apache2, and finally set up the bash image to run when the container starts. The construction process of the new image is shown in Fig. 7.6.

As you can see, the new image is generated from a layer-by-layer overlay of the base image. For each software installed, a layer is added to the existing image. The most significant benefit of Docker's hierarchy is that resources can be shared.

At this point, someone might ask, if multiple containers share a base image, when one container modifies the contents of the base image, will the contents of the other containers be modified? If the answer is no, the modification is limited to a single container. This is known as the COW characteristics of containers. When the container starts, a new writeable layer is added to the top of the image, which is called the container layer, and the underside of the container layer is called the image layer. All changes to the container, whether added, deleted, or modified, occur only in the container layer, only the container layer is writeable, and all image layers below the container layer are read-only. It is visible that the container layer holds the part of the image that changes and does not make any modifications to the image itself.

2. Image construction

For Docker users, the best situation is that you do not need to create an image yourself. Commonly used databases, middleware, software, etc. have ready-made official Docker images or images created by other people and organizations, and we can use them directly with a little configuration. The benefits of using ready-made images are not only saving the workload of doing images yourself, but more

```
root@ubuntu: docker run -it ubuntu

root@ubuntu: vim

bash: vim :command not found

root@ubuntu: apt-get install -y vim

Reading package lists... Done

Building dependency tree

Reading state information. ...Done

The following additional packages will be installed :

file libexpat1 libgpm2 libmagic1 libmpdec2 ibpythor

libsqlite3-0 libssl1.0.0 mime-support
```

Fig. 7.7 Building a new image through the docker commit command

importantly, you can use the experience of predecessors, especially those official images, because Docker engineers know how to run software in containers better. Of course, in some cases we have to build the image ourselves, for example:

① Cannot find a ready-made image, such as software developed by oneself.

② Specific functions need to be added to the image. For example, the official image does not provide SSH.

Docker provides two ways to build images: docker commit command and Dockerfile build file.

The docker commit command is the most intuitive way to build a new image, and its process consists of three steps. The following is an example of installing Vim in the Ubuntu base image and saving it as a new image to illustrate how to build a new image through the docker commit command, as shown in Fig. 7.7.

① Run the container. The function of the -it parameter is to enter the container in interactive mode and open the terminal.

② Install Vim. First confirm that Vim is not installed, and then execute the installation command.

③ Save as a new image, you can use the docker ps command to view the containers running in the current environment in a new window. Silly-Goldberg is the name randomly assigned by Docker for our new container. Execute the docker commit command to save the container as a new image and rename it to ubuntu-with-vim.

```
root@ubuntu :pwd                                                    ①

/root

root@ubuntu: ls                                                     ②

Dockerfile

root@ubuntu : docker build -t ubuntu-with-vim-dockerfile .          ③

Sending build context to Docker daemon 32KB                        ④

Step 1: FROM ubuntu                                                ⑤

---> f753707788c5

Step 2 : RUN apt-get update & & apt-get install -y vim             ⑥

---> Running in 9f4d4166f7e3     :                                 ⑦

Setting up vim ( 2:7.4 1689-3ubuntu1.1)

---> 350a89798937                                                  ⑧

Removing intermediate container 9f4d4166f7e3                       ⑨

Successfully built 350a89798937                                    ⑩
```

Fig. 7.8 Contents of Dockerfile

The above steps demonstrate how to build a new image through the docker commit command. However, due to the considerations of error-prone manual creation, low efficiency, weak repeatability, and security, this method is not the preferred method officially recommended by Docker.

Dockerfile is another way to build an image. It is a text file that records all the steps of image building. Similarly, we take the ubuntu-with-vim image in the previous article to illustrate how to build a new image through this method.

To build a new image with Dockerfile, you first need to create a Dockerfile, whose content is shown in Fig. 7.8.

① The current directory is/root.

② Dockerfile is ready.

③ Run the Docker build command, it will name the new image ubuntu-with-vim-dockerfile, and the "." at the end of the command indicates that the build context is the current directory. Docker will find the Dockerfile from the build context by default, and we can also specify the location of the Dockerfile through the -f parameter.

④ Starting from this step is the real construction process of the image. First, Docker sends all the files in the build context to the Docker daemon, and the build context provides the files or directories needed for image building.

The ADD, COPY, and other commands in the Dockerfile can add files in the build context to the image. In this example, the build context is the current directory/root, and all files and subdirectories in this directory will be sent to the Docker daemon. Therefore, you have to be careful when using the build context, do not put extra files in the build context, and be careful not to use / and / usr as the build context; otherwise, the build process will be quite slow or even fail.

⑤ Step 1: Execute FROM and use Ubuntu as the base image. The Ubuntu image ID is f753707788c5.

⑥ Step 2: Execute RUN and install Vim, the specific steps are ⑦⑧⑨.

⑦ Start the temporary container with ID 9f4d4166f7e3 and install Vim in the container via apt-get.

⑧ After the installation is successful, save the container as an image with the ID 350a89798937. The bottom layer of this step uses commands similar to docker commit.

⑨ Delete the temporary container with ID 9f4d4166f7e3.

⑩ The image is successfully built.

In addition, it needs to be specially pointed out that Docker will cache the image layer of the existing image when building the image. When building a new image, if a certain image layer already exists, it will be used directly without re-creating it. This is called the caching feature of Docker images.

3. Image management and distribution

We have learned to build our image, and then we will talk about how to use the image on multiple Docker hosts. There are several methods you can use:

① Use the same Dockerfile to build images on other hosts.

② Upload the image to the registry, such as Docker Hub, and the host can be directly downloaded and used.

③ Build a private repository for the local host to use.

The first method is to rebuild an image through the Dockerfile described in the previous article. The following focuses on how to distribute images through a public/private registry.

Regardless of the method used to save and distribute the image, you must first name the image. When we execute the docker build command, we have given the image a name, such as docker build –t ubuntu-with-vim, where ubuntu-with-vim is the name of the image.

The most straightforward way to save and distribute images is to use Docker Hub. Docker Hub is a public registry maintained by Docker. Users can save their images in the free repository of Docker Hub. If you don't want others to access your image, you can also buy a private repository. In addition to Docker Hub, quay.io is another public registry that provides similar services to Docker Hub. The following describes how to use Docker Hub to access the image.

① First, you need to register an account on Docker Hub.

② Use the command docker login -u xx to log in on the Docker host. xx is the username, you can log in successfully after entering the password.

③ Modify the image repository to match the Docker Hub account. In order to distinguish images with the same name from different users, the Docker Hub must include the username in the registry of the image, and the complete format is [username/xxx]:[tag]. We rename the image through the docker tag command.

```
root@ubuntu: docker run -d -p 5000: 5000 -v /myregistry: /var/lib/registry registry:
2

Unable to find image 'registry: 2 locally

2: Pulling from library/registry

3690e4760f9: Pull complete

9305f1e8fue: Pull complete

feeaa9qcbdbc: Pull complete

61f85310d350: Pull complete

b6o82239858a: Pull complete

Digest: sha256: 11522917f9304e02d95ed14201e743b6dd70e10f9e6ebe530f78217

Status: Downloaded newer image for registry: 2

e12894887928ef732b349df6b1b890ffe696e6553e0751f90d62437
```

Fig. 7.9   Start the image registry:2

 注意 | Docker's official image maintained by itself does not have a username, such as httpd.

④ Upload the image to Docker Hub via docker push. Docker will upload each layer of the image. If this image is consistent with an official image, all the image layers are on the Docker Hub. Then there is very little data actually uploaded. Similarly, if our image is based on the base image, only the newly added image layer will be uploaded. If you want to upload all the images in the same repository, just omit the tag part, such as Docker push cloudman6/httpd.

Although Docker Hub is very convenient, it still has some limitations, such as an Internet connection and slow download and upload speeds. Anyone can access the images uploaded to Docker Hub. Although a private repository can be used, it is not free. For security reasons, many organizations do not allow images to be placed on the extranet.

The solution is to build a local registry. Docker has open sourced the registry, and there is also an official image registry on Docker Hub. Next, we will run our registry in Docker.

(1) Start the registry container

The image we started is registry: 2, as shown in Fig. 7.9.

-d:Start the container in the background.

```
root@ubuntu: docker tag cloud/httpd:v1 register.example.net:5000/cloud/httpd:v1
```

Fig. 7.10 Rename the mirror

```
root@ubuntu: docker push register.example.net:5000/cloud/httpd:v1

3690e4760f9: Pulled

9305f1e8fue: Pulled

feeaa9qcbdbc: Pulled

v1: digest: sha256: bf45daeba98eadeadffbeadec50accffeabbc193cd6555ddabdeedaa234ffb
size:1256
```

Fig. 7.11 Upload the image to the image warehouse

-p:Map port 5000 of the container to port 5000 of the host, where 5000 is the registry service port. Port mapping will be discussed in detail in Sect. 7.1.3.

-v:Map the container /var/lib/registry directory to the host's /myregistry to store image data. The use of -v will be discussed in detail in Sect. 7.1.4.

Use the docker tag command to rename the image to match the registry, as shown in Fig. 7.10.

We added the name and port of the host running the registry to the front of the image.

The complete format of the repository is [registry-host]:[port]/[username]/xxx.

Only the mirror on Docker Hub can omit [registry-host]:[port].

(2) Upload image via docker push

Upload the image to the mirror warehouse via docker push, as shown in Fig. 7.11.

Now the image can be downloaded from the local registry through docker pull, as shown in Fig. 7.12.

7.1.3 Container Network

In this section, Docker network is used as an example to discuss the container network. We first introduce several native networks provided by Docker and how to create a custom network. Then, we introduce how to communicate between containers and how to communicate with the outside world.

1. Docker network model

```
root@ubuntu: docker pull registry.example.net:5000/cloud/httpd:v1

v1: Pulling from cloudman6/httpd

3860066cd84a: Already exists

011d6b8e2f00: Pull complete

c107bee07eec: Pull complete

bd14067dec02: Pull complete

92b340d02810: Pull complete

Digest: sh0256: 5b40385b4b874e84174ee7e7B0599208180039903f6028047b9278f576b404d

Status: Downloaded newer image for registry.example.net: 5000/c10ud/httpd: v1

root@ubuntu : docker images registry.example.net: 5000/cloud/httpd
```

Fig. 7.12 Download the image from the local registry

```
root@ubuntu: docker network ls

NETWORK ID            NAME              DRIVER              SCOPE

cb325e4bbe5           bridge            bridge              local

f48f4d42ae8           host              host                local

252509338fd           none              null                local
```

Fig. 7.13 View network

Docker provides a variety of native networks such as None, Host, Bridge, Overlay, and Macvlan. The network coverage can be divided into a container network on a single host and a network across multiple hosts. We mainly discuss the former.

When Docker is installed, three networks will be automatically created on the host. We can view the networks through the docker network ls command, as shown in Fig. 7.13.

We discuss them separately below.

(1) None network

As the name implies, the None network is a network with nothing. The containers connected to this network do not have any other network cards except lo. When the container is created, you can specify to use the None network through—network-none, as shown in Fig. 7.14.

```
root@ubuntu: docker run -it --network-none busybox

/ #

/ # ifconfig

lo                    Link encap : local loopback

                      inet addr :   127.0.0.1 Mask: 255.0.0.0

                      inet6 addr: : : 1/128  Scope :  Host

                      UP LOOPBACK RUNNING MTU : 65536 Metric: 1

                      packets : 0 errors: 0 dropped: 0 overruns: 0 frame: 0

                      TX packets: 0 errors: 0 dropped:0 overruns : 0 carrier: 0

                      RX bytes:0 (0.0 B)   TX bytes : ( 0.0.B)

root@ubuntu:
```

Fig. 7.14 Start None network

This is a closed network. Some applications that require high security and do not require networking can use the None network.

(2) Host network

Containers connected to the Host network share the Docker Host network stack, and the network configuration of the container is the same as that of the host. You can specify the use of the Host network through -network-host, as shown in Fig. 7.15.

You can see all the host's network cards in the container, and even the hostname is also the host. The biggest advantage of using the Docker Host network directly is performance. If the container has higher requirements for network transmission efficiency, you can choose the Host network. Of course, the inconvenience is to sacrifice some flexibility. For example, to consider port conflicts, the ports already used on Docker Host can no longer be used.

(3) Bridge network

When Docker is installed, a Linux bridge named "docker0" is created. If you do not specify --network, the created container will be hung on docker0 by default, as shown in Fig. 7.16.

In addition to the three automatically created networks of None, Host, and Bridge, users can also create user-defined networks according to business needs. Docker provides three user-defined network drivers: Bridge, Overlay, and Macvlan. Overlay and Macvlan are used to create a cross-host network. We will not discuss it here.

```
root@ubuntu: # docker run -it --network-host busybox

/ #

/ #ip 1

1: lo: <LOOPBACK, UP, LOWER_UP> mtu 65536 qdisc noqueue qlen 1

   Link/loopback 00: 00: 00: 00: 00:  brd : 00: 00: 00: 00: 00

2 : enp0s3: <OROADCAST, MULTICAST, UP, LOWER-UP> mtu 1500 qdisc pfifo_fast
qlen 1000

   link/ether 08: 00: 27: 5f: 79: 3f brd ff: ff: ff: ff: ff: ff

3 : enp0s8: <OROADCAST, MULTICAST, UP, LOWER-UP> mtu 1500 qdisc pfifo_fast
qlen 1000

   link/ether08: 00: 27: 21: 9c: 3f brd ff: ff: ff: ff: ff: ff

8 : virbr0-nic:<QROADCAST, MULticast> mtu 1500 qdisc pfifo_fast master virbr0
qlen 1000

   link/ether08: 52: 54: 00: 96: f4 brd ff: ff: ff: ff: ff: ff

/ # hostname

Ubuntu

/ #
```

Fig. 7.15 Starting the Host network

```
root@ubuntu: brctl show

bridgeid name          bridge id           STP enable        interfaces

docker0                8000:0242360fc4     no

virbr0                 8000:524095f4fe     yes               virbr0-n
```

Fig. 7.16 Linux bridge information

2. Communication between containers

There are three ways to communicate between containers via IP address, Docker DNS service or Joined container.

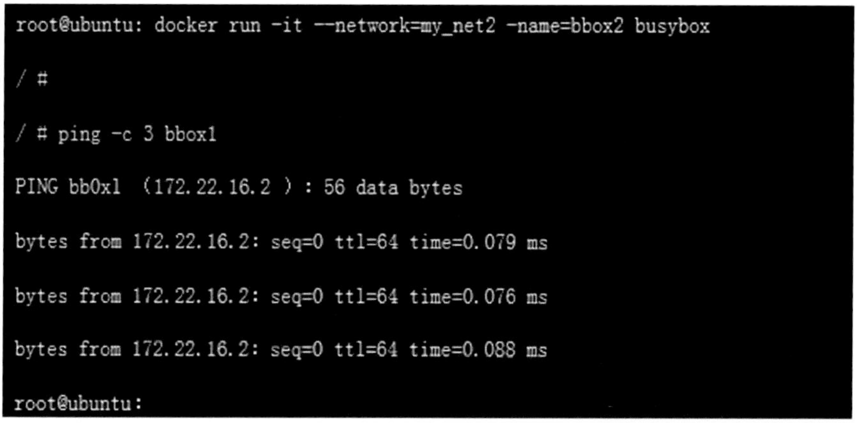

```
root@ubuntu: docker run -it --network=my_net2 -name=bbox2 busybox

/ #

/ # ping -c 3 bbox1

PING bb0x1 (172.22.16.2 ) : 56 data bytes

bytes from 172.22.16.2: seq=0 ttl=64 time=0.079 ms

bytes from 172.22.16.2: seq=0 ttl=64 time=0.076 ms

bytes from 172.22.16.2: seq=0 ttl=64 time=0.088 ms

root@ubuntu:
```

Fig. 7.17 Start a specific image

From the previous example, we can conclude that they must have network cards that belong to the same network for two containers to communicate. After this condition is met, the container can interact through the IP address. The specific method is to specify the corresponding network through --network when creating the container or add the existing container to the specified network through docker network connect.

Although accessing the container through the IP address satisfies the communication needs, it is still not flexible enough. Because it may not be determined before deploying the application, it will be troublesome to specify the IP address to be accessed after deployment. This problem can be solved through the DNS service that comes with Docker.

Starting from Docker 1.10, Docker Daemon has implemented an embedded Docker DNS service, allowing containers to communicate directly through the "container name." The method is straightforward, just use -name to name the container at startup. Start two containers bbox1 and bbox2 below:

```
docker run -it --network=my_net2 -name=bbox1 busybox
docker run -it --network=my_net2 -name=bbox2 busybox
```

Then, bbox2 can directly ping to bbox1 and start a specific image, as shown in Fig. 7.17.

There is a limitation when using Docker DNS Server: it can only be used in user-defined networks. In other words, the default Bridge network cannot use DNS.

Joined containers are another way to achieve communication between containers. Joined container is exceptional. It can make two or more containers share a network stack, network card, and configuration information. Joined containers can communicate directly through 127.0.0.1.

3. Container communicates with external world

```
root@ubuntu: docker run -it busybox

/#

/ # ping -c (www.bing.com)

PING www.bing.com  (202.89.233.104 ) : 56 data bytes

bytes from 202.89.233.104:  seq=Ø ttl=61 time=49.211 ms

bytes from 202.89.233.104:  seq=Ø ttl=61 time=50.986 ms

bytes from 202.89.233.104:  seq=Ø ttl=61 time=49.237 ms

root@ubuntu:
```

Fig. 7.18 Access to the external network of the container

We have solved the problem of communication between containers. Next, we will discuss how the container communicates with the external world, mainly involving the container's access to the external world and its access to the container.

In the current experimental environment, Docker Host can access the extranet. Let's see if the container can also access the extranet, as shown in Fig. 7.18.

It can be seen that the container can access the extranet by default. However, please note that the extranet here refers to the network environment outside the container network, not the Internet.

Next, we discuss another question, how does the extranet access the container? The answer is port mapping. Docker can map the port that the container provides external services to a certain port of the host, and the extranet accesses the container through this port. The port can be mapped through the -p parameter when the container is started.

After the container is started, you can view the host's port through the docker ps or docker port command. In addition to mapping dynamic ports, you can also specify the mapping to a specific host port in -p. For example, you can map port 80 to port 8080 of the host, as shown in Fig. 7.19.

7.1.4 Container Storage

Docker provides two kinds of data storage resources for containers—Storage Driver (management image layer and container layer) and data volume.

We have learned that the Docker image is a hierarchical structure. It consists of a writable container layer on the top and several read-only image layers. The data of

```
root@ubuntu: docker run -d -p 8080: 80  httpd

58401dd02d03950043f208dd28251413607280be579fd06b576

root@ubuntu: #

root@ubuntu: curl 10.0.2.15: 8080

<html><body><h1>It works! </h1></body> </html>
```

Fig. 7.19 Port mapping

the container is placed in these layers. The biggest characteristic of such layering is COW.

The hierarchical structure makes the creation, sharing, and distribution of images and containers very efficient, and these are all due to the Storage Driver. Storage Driver realizes the stacking of multiple layers of data and provides users with a single unified view after merging. Docker supports various Storage Drivers, including AUFS, Device, Mapper, Btrfs, VFS, and ZFS. They can all achieve a hierarchical structure, and at the same time, have their characteristics.

When Docker is installed, the default Storage Driver will be selected according to the current system configuration. The default Storage Driver has better stability because the default Storage Driver has been rigorously tested on the release version. Run the docker info command to view the default Storage Driver.

It is a good choice for some containers to put the data directly in the layer maintained by the Storage Driver, such as those stateless applications. Stateless means that the container has no data that needs to be persisted and can be built directly from the image at any time. However, this method is not suitable for another type of application. They need to persist data. When the container starts, it needs to load the existing data. When the container is destroyed, it hopes to retain the generated data. In other words, this type of container is stateful. This requires another data storage resource of Docker-data volume.

The data volume is essentially a directory or file in the Docker Host file system, which can be directly arranged in the container's file system. It has the following characteristics.

- Data volumes are directories or files, not unformatted disks or block devices.
- The container can read/write the data in it.
- The data in the data volume can be stored permanently, even if the container using it is destroyed.

In terms of specific use, Docker provides two types of Date Volume: Bind Mount and Docker Managed Volume.

1. Bind Mount

```
root@ubuntu:

root@ubuntu : cat htdocs/index.html

<html><body><h1>This is a file in host file system! </h1></body> </html>

root@ubuntu :
```

Fig. 7.20 File information

```
root@ubuntu:

root@ubuntu: docker run -d -p 80: 80 -v ~/htdocs: /usr/10cal/apache2/htdocs httpd
11911ef5f1bdd437801000260f6f36ed87bf824def500df7q3f854e67ddb28

root@ubuntu :
```

Fig. 7.21 Mount to httpd container

Bind Mount is to arrange the existing directories or files on the host into the container, as shown in Fig. 7.20.

Arrange it to the httpd container through -v, as shown in Fig. 7.21.

Bind Mount allows the host to share data with the container, which is very convenient in management. Even if the container is destroyed, Bind Mount is still there. In addition, when Bind Mount, you can also specify the data read/write permission, which is readable and writable by default.

Bind Mount has many application scenarios. For example, we can mount the source code directory into the container and modify the host's code to see the real-time effect of the application; or put the data of the MySQL container in Bind Mount, so that the host can be convenient back up and migrate data locally.

The use of Bind Mount is intuitive, efficient, and easy to understand, but it also has shortcomings: Bind Mount needs to specify the specific path of the host file system, limiting the portability of the container. When the container needs to be migrated to another host and that host does not have the data to be mounted or the data is not in the same path, the operation will fail. The more portable way is to use Docker Managed Volume.

2. Docker Managed Volume

The biggest difference between Docker Managed Volume and Bind Mount is that you do not need to specify the Mount source, just specify the Mount Point. Here, we will take the httpd container as an example, as shown in Fig. 7.22.

We use -v to tell Docker that a data volume is needed and mounted to /usr/local/apache2/htdocs.

Whenever a container applies for Mount Docker Managed Volume, Docker will generate a directory under /var/lib/docker/volumes. This directory is the Mount source.

Summarize the creation process of Docker Managed Volume.

```
root@ubuntu:

root@ubuntu :   docker run -d -P 80: 80 -v /usr/local/apache2/htdocs httpd

2102000729920082b729dd0425080b1f280603d08131e13030ed75

root@ubuntu :
```

Fig. 7.22 Specify Mount Point

① When the container starts, tell Docker that it needs a Data Volume to store data, and help us Mount to the specified directory.

② Docker generates a random directory in /var/lib/docker/volumes as the Mount source.

③ If the specified directory already exists, copy the data to the Mount source.

④ Move Docker Managed Volume to the specified directory.

In addition to using the Docker inspect command to view Volume, we can also use the docker volume command.

Then, we discuss sharing data. Sharing data is a key feature of Volume. We will discuss how to share data between containers and hosts and between containers through Volume.

(1) Sharing data between the container and the host

There are two types of data volumes for sharing data between the container and the host. Both of them can share data between the container and the host, but the methods are different. This is very clear for Bind Mount: Mount the shared directory directly to the container. Docker Managed Volume will be more troublesome. Since Volume is located in the directory on the host, it is generated when the container starts, so the shared data needs to be copied to the Volume. Use the docker cp command to copy data between the container and the host. Of course, we can also use the Linux cp command directly.

(2) Sharing data between containers

One method is to put the shared data in Bind Mount, and then mount it to multiple containers. Another method is to use Volume Container. Volume Container is to provide Volume specifically for other containers. The Volume it provides can be Bind Mount or Docker Managed Volume. Next we create a Volume Container, as shown in Fig. 7.23.

We named the container vc_data (vc is the abbreviation of Volume Container). Note that the docker create command is executed here because Volume Container's role is only to provide data, and it does not need to be running. The container is mounted with two Volumes:

① Bind Mount, used to store static files of the Web server.

② Docker Managed Volume, used to store some useful tools (of course it is empty now, here is just an example).

Other containers can use the vc_data Volume Container through volumes-from.

```
root@ubuntu:docker create —name vc_data \

>     —v ~/htdocs: /usr/local/apache2/htdocs \

>        —v /other/useful/tools \
>        busybox
2f459897d6dbd12d78fb41e6eb43e038f551ebdf3e47edkd0e083e709
```

Fig. 7.23 Create Volume Container

Finally, we discuss the characteristics of Volume Container.

① Compared with Bind Mount, Volume Container does not need to specify each container's host path. All paths are defined in the Volume Container. The container only needs to be associated with the Volume Container to realize the decoupling of the container and the host.

② The Mount Point of the container using Volume Container is consistent, which is conducive to the specification and standardization of the configuration, but it also brings certain limitations. It needs to be considered comprehensively when using it.

7.1.5   The Underlying Implementation Technology of the Container

In order to better understand the characteristics of containers, this section will introduce the underlying implementation technologies of containers, namely Cgroup and Namespace. Cgroup realizes resource quota, and Namespace realizes resource isolation.

1. Cgroup

    Linux operating system can set the limit of CPU, memory, and I/O resources used by the process through Cgroup.

    What does Cgroup look like? We can find it in /sys/fs/cgroup. To illustrate with an example, start a container, as shown in Fig. 7.24.

    In /sys/fs/cgroup/cpu/docker, Linux will create a Cgroup directory for each container (named after the container's long ID), which contains all CPU-related Cgroup configurations. What shares are saved is the configuration of cpu-shares, with a value of 512.

    Similarly, /sys/fs/cgroup/memory/docker   and   /sys/fs/cgroup/blkio/docker save the memory and the Cgroup configuration of Block 10.

2. Namespace

    In each container, we can see the file system, network card, and other resources. These resources look like the container itself. Take the network card

```
root@ubuntu:docker run -it --cpu-shares 512 progrium/stress -c 1

stress: info:  [ 1 ]dispatching hogs :  1 CPU,  0 io , 0 vm , 0 hdd

stress : dbug: [ 1 ] usi ng backoff sleep of 3000us

stress : dbug:  [1] --> hogcpu worker 1 [5]forked

root@ubuntu :
```

Fig. 7.24 Cgroup information

as an example. Each container will think that it has an independent network card, even if there is only one physical network card on the host. This approach is excellent. It makes the container more like an independent computer.

The technology that Linux implements this way is Namespace. Namespace manages the globally unique resource in the host and can make each container feel that only it is using it. In other words, Namespace realizes the isolation of resources between containers.

Linux uses the following Namespaces: Mount, UTS, IPC, PID, Network, and User. Mount Namespace makes the container appear to have the entire file system. UTS Namespace allows the container to have its hostname. IPC Namespace allows containers to have their shared content and semaphores to achieve inter-process communication. PID Namespace allows the container to have its own independent set of PID. Network Namespace allows the container to have its independent network card, IP, and routing resources. User Namespace allows the container to have the authority to manage its users.

7.2 Overview of Kubernetes

Kubernetes is the de facto standard for container orchestration engines. It is another popular technology after big data, cloud computing, and Docker, and it will be trendy for a long time in the future. For the IT industry, this is a valuable technology.

7.2.1 Introduction of Kubernetes

The popularity and standardization of Docker technology have activated the tepid PaaS market, followed by the emergence of various types of Micro-PaaS, and Kubernetes is one of the most representative ones. Kubernetes is Google's open source container cluster management system. It is built on Docker technology and provides a complete set of functions for containerized applications such as resource scheduling, deployment and operation, service discovery, capacity expansion and contraction, and can essentially be regarded as a Micro-Paas platform based on container technology.

Google started using container technology in 2004, released Cgroup in 2006, and internally developed powerful cluster resource management platforms Borg and Omega, which have been widely used in various infrastructures of Google products. Moreover, Kubernetes is inspired by Google's internal Borg system, and it has also absorbed the experience and lessons of container managers, including Omega.

Kubernetes means helmsman in ancient Greek and is also the etymology of Cyber. Kubernetes utilizes Google's practical experience and technical accumulation in container technology while absorbing the Docker community's best practices and has become the "helmsman" of cloud computing services.

1. Advantages of Kubernetes

   (1) Powerful container orchestration capabilities

   Kubernetes can be said to be developed together with Docker. It is deeply integrated with Docker and naturally adapts to the characteristics of containers. It has powerful container orchestration capabilities, such as container composition, label selection, and service discovery, to meet enterprise-level needs.

   (2) Lightweight

   Kubernetes follows the theory of microservice architecture. The entire system is divided into components with independent functions. The boundaries between the components are clear, the deployment is simple, and it can be easily run in various systems and environments. At the same time, many functions in Kubernetes are plug-in, which can be easily expanded and replaced.

   (3) Open and open source

   Kubernetes conforms to open and open source trends, attracting many developers and companies to participate in it and work together to build an ecosystem. At the same time, Kubernetes actively cooperates and develops together with open source communities such as OpenStack and Docker. Both enterprises and individuals can participate and benefit from it.

2. The evolution of Kubernetes

   Kubernetes has quickly gained attention since its launch. In July 2015, after more than 400 contributors' efforts for a year and as many as 14,000 code submissions, Google officially released Kubernetes 1.0, which means that this open source container orchestration system can be officially launched—used in a production environment. At the same time, Google and the Linux Foundation and other partners jointly established the Cloud Native Computing Foundation (CNCF). They used Kubernetes as the first open source project incorporated into the Cloud Native Computing Foundation's management system to help container technology. Ecological development. The development history of Kubernetes is shown below.

- June 2014: Google announced that Kubernetes is open source.
- July 2014: Microsoft, Red Hat, IBM, Docker, CoreOS, Mesosphere, and SaltStack joined Kubernetes.
- August 2014: Mesosphere announced the integration of Kubernetes into the Mesosphere ecosystem as a framework for the scheduling, deployment, and management of Docker container clusters.
- August 2014: VMware joined the Kubernetes community. Google's product manager Craig McLuckie publicly stated that VMware will help Kubernetes implement a functional model that uses virtualization to ensure physical host security.
- November 2014: HP joined the Kubernetes community.
- November 2014: Google's container engine Alpha was launched. Google announced that GCE supports containers and services and uses Kubernetes as the framework.
- January 2015: Google, Mirantis and other partners introduced Kubernetes into OpenStack, and developers can deploy and run Kubernetes applications on OpenStack.
- April 2015: Google and CoreOS jointly released Tectonic, which integrates Kubernetes and CoreOS software stacks.
- May 2015: Intel joined the Kubernetes community and announced that it would cooperate to accelerate the Tectonic software stack development.
- June 2015: Google's container engine entered the beta version.
- July 2015: Google officially joined the OpenStack Foundation, Google's product manager Craig McLuckie announced that Google will become one of the OpenStack Foundation initiators, and Google will bring its container computing expert technology Enter OpenStack to improve the interoperability of public and private clouds.
- July 2015: Kubernetes 1.0 was officially released.
- March 2016: Kubernetes 1.2 was released, and improvements include expansion, simplification of software deployment, and automated cluster management.
- December 2016: Kubernetes supports OpenAPI, allowing API providers to define their operations and models, and developers can automate their tools.
- March 2017: Kubernetes 1.6 was released. Specific updates include enabling etcd v3 by default, deleting the direct dependencies of a single container runtime, testing RBAC, and automatically configuring StorageClass objects.
- December 2017: Kubernetes 1.9 was released. New features include the general availability of apps/v1 Workloads API, Windows support (beta), storage enhancements, etc.
- March 2018: The first beta version of Kubernetes 1.10 was released. Users can test Kubelet TLS Bootstrapping, API aggregation, and more detailed storage metrics with the production-ready version.
- June 2018: Kubernetes 1.11 was released, and the cluster load balancing and CoreDNS plug-in reached universal availability. This version has key

functions in the network. It opens the two main SIG-API Machinery and SIG-Node functions for beta testing and continues to enhance storage functions.

7.2.2 Kubernetes Management Objects

Kubernetes follows the theory of microservice architecture. The entire system is divided into components with independent functions. The boundaries between the components are clear, the deployment is simple, and it can be easily run in various systems and environments.

1. Kubernetes architecture and components

Kubernetes belongs to a master-slave distributed architecture, and nodes are divided into Master and Node in terms of roles.

Kubernetes uses etcd as storage middleware. Etcd is a highly available key-value storage system, inspired by ZooKeeper and Doozer, and uses the Raft consensus algorithm to process log replication to ensure strong consistency. Kubernetes uses etcd as the configuration storage center of the system. Important data in Kubernetes is persisted in etcd, making the various components of the Kubernetes architecture stateless, making it easier to implement distributed cluster deployment.

The Master in Kubernetes refers to the cluster control node. Each Kubernetes cluster needs a Master node to be responsible for managing and controlling the entire cluster. All control commands of Kubernetes are sent to it, responsible for the specific execution process. All the commands we execute later are run on the Master node. The Master node usually occupies an independent server (three servers are recommended for high-availability deployment). The main reason is that it is too important. It is the "head" of the entire cluster. If it is down or unavailable, then apply it to the cluster content container. Management will be invalidated. The following key components are running on the Master node.

Kubernetes API Server: As the entrance to the Kubernetes system, it encapsulates the addition, deletion, modification, and query operations of core objects and provides external customers and internal component calls in the form of REST API. The REST objects it maintains will be persisted in etcd.

- Kubernetes Scheduler: Responsible for the cluster's resource scheduling and allocated machines for the new Pod. This part of the work is separated into a component, which means that it can be easily replaced with other schedulers.
- Kubernetes Controller Manager: Responsible for executing various controllers. Many controllers have been implemented to ensure the normal operation of Kubernetes.

In addition to the Master, the other machines in the Kubernetes cluster are called Node nodes, which are also called Minion nodes in earlier versions. Like the Master node, the Node node can be a physical host or a virtual machine. A Node node is a workload node in a Kubernetes cluster. The Master node will assign each Node node some workload (Docker container). When a Node node goes down, the workload will be automatically transferred to the other by the Master node.

The following key components are running on each Node node.

• kubelet: Responsible for tasks such as the creation and activation of the container corresponding to the Pod. At the same time, it works closely with the Master node to realize the basic functions of cluster management.

• kube-proxy: A vital component that realizes the communication and load balancing mechanism of Kubernetes Service.

• Docker Engine: Docker engine, responsible for the creation and management of local containers.

Node nodes can be dynamically added to the Kubernetes cluster during operation, provided that the above key components have been correctly installed, configured, and started on this node. By default, kubelet will register itself with the Master node, which is also the Node node management method recommended by Kubernetes. Once the Node node is included in the scope of cluster management, the kubelet process will regularly report its situation to the Master node, such as the operating system, Docker version, the CPU and memory of the machine, and which Pods are currently running. The Master node can therefore know the resource usage of each Node node and realize an efficient and balanced resource scheduling strategy. When a Node node does not report information for more than a specified time, it will be judged by the Master node as "lost connection," the status of the Node node is marked as not available (NotReady), and then the Master node will trigger the "work load transfer" Automatic process.

2. Basic object concept

Most of the concepts in Kubernetes, such as Node, Pod, Replication Controller and Service, can be regarded as "resource objects." Resource objects can be added, deleted, modified, and checked through the kubectl tool (or API programming call) provided by Kubernetes Operate and save it in persistent storage in etcd. From this perspective, Kubernetes is a highly automated resource control system. It achieves automatic control and automatic error correction by tracking and comparing the difference between the "resource expected state" saved in etcd and the "actual resource state" in the current environment.

(1) Pod

Pod is a combination of several related containers. The containers contained in the Pod run on the same host. These containers use the same network namespace, IP address and port, and can be discovered and communicated through the local host. In addition, these containers can also share a storage volume space. The smallest unit of creation, scheduling, and management in Kubernetes is a Pod, not a container. The Pod provides more flexible deployment and management model by providing a higher abstraction level.

(2) Replication Controller

Replication Controller is used to controlling and managing Pod replicas (Replica or instance). Replication Controller ensures that a specified number of Pod replicas are running in the Kubernetes cluster at any time. If there are less than the specified number of Pod replicas, the Replication Controller will start a new Pod replica. Otherwise, it will "kill" the excess replicas to ensure that the number remains unchanged. In addition, the Replication Controller is the core of the implementation of elastic scaling and rolling upgrades.

(3) Service

Service is an abstraction of real application services, which defines the Pod logical collection and the strategy for accessing this Pod logical collection. Service presents the proxy Pod as a single access interface to the outside, and the outside does not need to know how the back-end Pod operates, which brings many benefits to expansion and maintenance and provides a simplified service proxy and discovery mechanism.

(4) Label

Label is a key/value pair used to distinguish Pod, Service, and Replication Controller. In fact, any API object in Kubernetes can be identified by Label. Each API object can have multiple Labels, but each Label's key can only correspond to one value. Label is the basis for the operation of Service and Replication Controller. They all associate Pods through Label. Compared with the solid binding model, this is an excellent loose coupling relationship.

(5) Node

Kubernetes belongs to a master-slave distributed architecture, and Node nodes run and manage containers. As the operating unit of Kubernetes, the Node node is used to assign to the Pod (or container) for binding, and the Pod eventually runs on the Node node. The Node node can be considered as the host of the Pod.

(6) Deployment

Deployment is a higher level API object that manages ReplicaSet and Pod and provides functions such as declarative updates. The official recommendation is to use Deployment to manage ReplicaSet instead of directly using RelicaSet, which means you may never need to manipulate ReplicaSet objects directly.

(7) StatefulSet

StatefulSet is suitable for permanent software, has a unique network identifier (IP), can be stored persistently, and can be deployed, expanded, deleted, and updated appropriately.

(8) DaemonSet

DaemonSet ensures that all (or some) nodes are running on the same Pod. When a node joins the Kubernetes cluster, the Pod will be scheduled to run on the node; when the node is removed from the Kubernetes cluster, the Pod of the DaemonSet will be deleted. When the DaemonSet is deleted, all Pods created by it will be cleaned up.

(9) Job

A one-time task, the Pod will be destroyed after the operation is completed, and the container will not be restarted. Tasks can also be run regularly.

(10) Namespace

Namespace is a fundamental concept in the Kubernetes system. Namespace is used to implement resource isolation for multi-tenancy in many cases. Namespace "distributes" resource objects within the cluster to different Namespaces to form logically grouped different projects, groups, or user groups, so that different groups can be managed separately while sharing the resources of the entire cluster. After the Kubernetes cluster is started, a Namespace named "default"| will be created, which can be viewed through kubectl.

The object mentioned above components are the core components of the Kubernetes system, and together they constitute the framework and computing model of the Kubernetes system. By flexibly combining them, users can quickly and easily configure, create, and manage container clusters. In addition, many resource objects assist configuration in the Kubernetes system, such as LimitRange and ResourccQuota. In addition, for objects used in the system such as Binding, Event, etc., please refer to the Kubernetes API documentation.

7.2.3 Kubernetes Service

In order to adapt to rapid business needs, microservice architecture has gradually become the mainstream, and the application of microservice architecture needs outstanding service orchestration support. The core element Service in Kubernetes provides a simplified service proxy and discovery mechanism, which naturally adapts to the microservice architecture. Any application can easily run in Kubernetes without changing the architecture.

1. Service proxy and virtual IP address

In Kubernetes, when dominated by the Replication Controller, the Pod replica changes, such as when migration (to be precise, reconstructing the Pod) or scaling occurs. This is a burden for Pod visitors. Visitors need to discover these Pod copies and sense the changes of Pod copies to update them in time.

Service in Kubernetes is an abstract concept that defines Pod's logical collection and the strategy for accessing them. The association between Service and Pod is also done based on Label. The goal of Service is to provide a "bridge." It will provide visitors with a fixed access address, redirecting to the corresponding backend when accessing, which makes non-Kubernetes native applications without writing specific code for Kubernetes. Under the premise, the backend can be easily accessed.

Kubernetes assigns a fixed IP address to the Service. This is a virtual IP address (also known as ClusterIP), not a real IP address, but virtualized by

Kubernetes. The virtual IP address belongs to the virtual network inside Kubernetes, and the external network cannot be found. In the Kubernetes system, the Kubernetes Proxy component is responsible for implementing virtual IP routing and forwarding, so Kubernetes Proxy is running in the Kubernetes Node, thereby implementing a Kubernetes-level virtual forwarding network on top of the container overlay network.

2. Service discovery

Microservice architecture is a new and popular architecture model. Compared with the traditional monolithic architecture model, microservice architecture advocates dividing applications into a set of small services. However, the application of microservices will also bring new challenges. One of the challenges is to divide the application into multiple distributed components to run, and each component will be clustered and expanded. The mutual discovery and communication between components and components will become complicated, and a set of service orchestration mechanisms is essential.

Kubernetes provides powerful service orchestration capabilities. Service abstracts each component of a microservice-oriented application. Components and components only need to access the Service to communicate without being aware of component cluster changes. At the same time, Kubernetes provides service discovery capabilities for Service, and components and components can quickly discover each other.

In Kubernetes, two modes of service discovery are supported: environment variables and DNS.

(1) Environmental variables

When a Pod runs on a Node node, kubelet will add environment variables for each active Service. There are two types of environment variables.

- Docker Link environment variable: It is equivalent to the environment variable set when the container is connected by the -link parameter of Docker.
- Kubernetes Service environment variables: the form of environment variables set by Kubernetes for the Service, including {SVCNAME} _SERVICE_HOST and {SVCNAME}_SERVICE_PORT variables. The name of the environment variable is composed of capital letters and underlined.

    For example, there is a server named "redis-master" (its IP address is 10.0.0.11, port number is 6379, protocol is TCP), and its environment variables are shown in Fig. 7.25.

    Here, you can see that the IP address, port number, and protocol information of the "redis-master" Service are recorded in the environment variables. Therefore, applications in Pod can discover this service through environment variables. However, the environment variable method has the following limitations:

    ① Environment variables can only be used in the same namespace.

```
#Kubernetes Service环境变量:
REDIS_MASTER_SERVICE_HOST=10.0.0.11
REDIS_MASTER_SERVICE_PORT=6379
#Docker Link环境变量:
REDIS_MASTER_PORT=tcp://10.0.0.11:6379
REDIS_MASTER_PORT_6379_TCP=tcp://10.0.0.11:6379
REDIS_MASTER_PORT_6379_TCP_PROTO=tcp
REDIS_MASTER_PORT_6379_TCP_PORT=6379
REDIS_MASTER_PORT_6379_TCP_ADDR=10.0.0.11
```

Fig. 7.25 Environment variables

② The Service must be created before the Pod is created. Otherwise, the Service variable will not be set to the Pod.

③ DNS service discovery mechanism does not have these restrictions.

(2) DNS

DNS service discovery is based on Cluster DNS. The DNS server monitors new services and creates DNS records for each service for domain name resolution. In a cluster, if DNS is enabled, all Pods can automatically pass the name resolution service.

For example, if you have a service named "my-service" under the "my-ns" namespace, a DNS record named "my-service.my-ns" will be created.

- Under the "my-ns" namespace, Pod will be able to discover this service by the name "my-service".
- In other namespaces, Pod must use the name "my-service.my-ns" to discover this service. The result of this name is the Cluster IP.

Kubernetes also supports DNS SRV (Service) records for ports. If the "my-service.my-ns" service has a TCP port named "http", the value of the "http" port can be found by the name "_http._tcp.my-service.my-ns". Kubernetes DNS server is the only way to discover ExternalName type services.

3. Service release

The Service's virtual IP address belongs to the internal network virtualized by Kubernetes, and the external network cannot be found, but some services need to be exposed externally, such as the Web front end. At this time, it is necessary to add a layer of network forwarding, that is, the forwarding from the extranet to the intranet. Kubernetes provides NodePort Service, LoadBalancer Service, and Ingress to publish Service.

(1) NodePort Service

NodePort Service is a Service of type NodePort. In addition to assigning an internal virtual IP address to the NodePort Service, Kubernetes also exposes the port NodePort on each Node node. The extranet can access the Service through [NodeIP]:[NodePort].

(2) LoadBalancer Service

LoadBalancer Service is a Service of type LoadBalancer. LoadBalancer Service is built on the NodePort Service cluster. Kubernetes will assign an internal virtual IP address to LoadBalancer Service and expose the NodePort. In addition, Kubernetes requests the underlying cloud platform to create a load balancer with each Node node as the backend, and the load balancer will forward the request to [NodeIP]:[NodePort].

(3) Ingress

Kubernetes provides an HTTP routing and forwarding mechanism called Ingress. The implementation of Ingress requires the support of two components, namely HTTP proxy server and Ingress Controller. The HTTP proxy server will forward external HTTP requests to the Service, and the Ingress Controller needs to monitor the Kubernetes API and update the forwarding rules of the HTTP proxy server in real-time.

7.2.4 Kubernetes Network

Kubernetes is independent from Docker's default network model to form its own network model, which is more suitable for traditional network models, and applications can smoothly migrate from non-container environments to Kubernetes.

1. Communication between containers

In this case, the container communication is relatively simple because the container inside the Pod shares the network space, so the container can directly use the local host to access other containers. In this way, all containers in the Pod are interoperable, and the Pod can be regarded as a complete network unit externally, as shown in Fig. 7.26.

When Kubernetes starts a container, it starts a Pause container, which implements the communication function between containers. Each Pod runs a

Fig. 7.26 Pod network structure

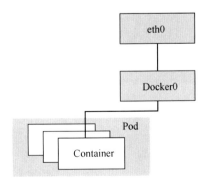

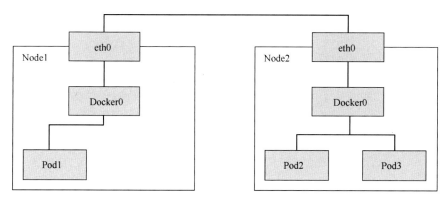

Fig. 7.27   The smallest Kubernetes network topology

special container called Pause, and other containers are business containers. These business containers share the Pause container's network stack and Volume mount volume, so the communication and data exchange between them is more Efficient. In design, we can make full use of this feature to put a group of closely related service processes into the same Pod.

2. Communication between Pod

The Kubernetes network model is a flat network plane. Pod as a network unit is at the same level as the Kubernetes Node network in this network plane. We consider a minimal Kubernetes network topology, as shown in Fig. 7.27. The following conditions are met in this network topology.

① Inter-Pod communication: Pod2 and Pod3 (same host), Pod1 and Pod3 (cross-host) can communicate.

② Communication between Node node and Pod: Node1 and Pod2/Pod3 (same host), Pod/1 (cross-host) can communicate.

So the first question is how to ensure that the IP address of the Pod is globally unique? In fact, the method is straightforward because the Docker bridge assigns the Pod's IP address. Therefore, you can configure the Docker bridges of different Kubernetes Nodes to different IP network segments.

In addition, Pods/containers on the same Kubernetes Node can communicate natively, but how do Pods/containers between Kubernetes Nodes communicate? This requires enhancements to Docker. Create an overlay network in the container cluster to connect all nodes. Currently, overlay networks can be created through third-party network plug-ins, such as Flannel and OVS.

(1) Use Flannel to create a Kubernetes overlay network

Flannel is an overlay network tool designed and developed by the CoreOS team. It creates an overlay network in the cluster, sets a subnet for the host, and encapsulates the communication messages between containers through a tunnel protocol to achieve cross-host communication between containers. Now we use Flannel to connect two Kubernetes Nodes, as shown in Fig. 7.28.

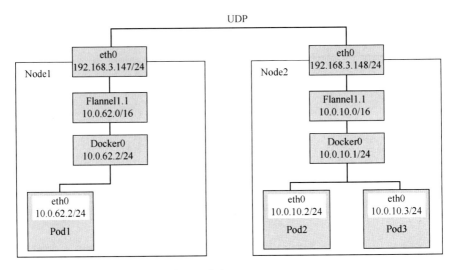

Fig. 7.28 Kubernetes Node connection mode 1

(2) Use OVS to create a Kubernetes overlay network

OVS is a high-quality, multi-layer virtual switch using the open source Apache 2.0 license agreement developed by Nicira Networks. Its purpose is to allow large-scale network automation to be extended through programming while still supporting standard management interfaces and protocols.

OVS also provides support for the OpenFlow protocol. Users can use any controller that supports the OpenFlow protocol to manage and control OVS

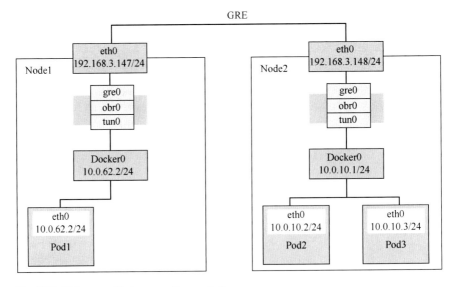

Fig. 7.29 Kubernetes Node connection mode 2

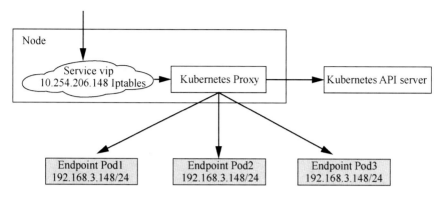

Fig. 7.30 Monitoring function of Kubernetes Proxy

remotely. OVS is a critical SDN technology that can flexibly create virtual networks that meet various needs, including overlay networks.

Next, we use OVS to connect two Kubernetes Nodes. In order to ensure that the container IP does not conflict, the network segment of the Docker bridge on the Kubernetes Node must be planned.

3. Communication between service and pod

Service acts as a service agent between Pods and acts as a single access interface externally, forwarding Pods' requests. Service network forwarding is a key part of Kubernetes' realization of service orchestration. Among them, Kubernetes Proxy, as a key component, is responsible for implementing virtual IP routing and forwarding, and a Kubernetes-level virtual forwarding network is implemented on top of the container overlay network. Kubernetes Proxy has two implementation modes, namely Userspace mode and Iptables mode, which can be specified by the startup parameter of Kubernetes Proxy—proxy-mode.

(1) Userspace mode

In Userspace mode, Kubernetes Proxy will enable a random port for each Service to monitor on the host and create an Iptables rule to redirect requests to the Service virtual IP address to this port, and Kubernetes Proxy will forward the request to Endpoint. In this mode, Kubernetes Proxy functions as a reverse proxy, and Kubernetes Proxy completes the forwarding of requests in user space. Kubernetes Proxy needs to monitor Endpoint changes and refresh forwarding rules in real time, as shown in Fig. 7.30.

(2) Iptables mode

In the Iptables mode, Kubernetes Proxy directly redirects requests for access to Endpoint's Service virtual IP address by creating Iptables rules. When the Endpoint changes, Kubernetes Proxy will refresh the relevant Iptables rules. In this mode, Kubernetes Proxy is only responsible for monitoring Service and Endpoint, updating Iptables rules, packet forwarding depends on the Linux kernel, and the default load balancing strategy is random, as shown in Fig. 7.31.

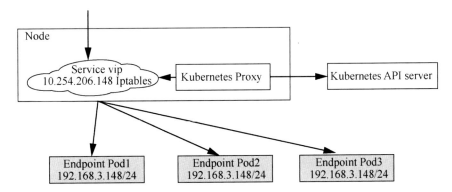

Fig. 7.31 Random load balancing strategy

7.2.5 *Kubernetes Storage*

1. Storage application scenario

   Services running in Kubernetes can be divided into three categories from simple to complex: stateless services, ordinary stateful services, and stateful cluster services.

   (1) Stateless service: Kubernetes uses ReplicaSet to guarantee the number of instances of a service. If a Pod instance "hangs" or crashes for some reason, ReplicaSet will immediately use this Pod template to create a Pod to replace it. Because it is a stateless service, the new Pod is the same as the old Pod. In addition, Kubernetes provides a stable access interface through service (multiple Pods can be linked behind a Service) to achieve high service availability.

   (2) Ordinary stateful services: Compared with stateless services, it has more state preservation requirements. Kubernetes provides a storage system based on Volume and Persistent Volume, which can realize service state preservation.

   (3) Stateful cluster service: Compared with ordinary stateful services, it has more cluster management requirements. There are two problems to be solved to run stateful cluster services: state preservation and cluster management. Kubernetes has developed StatefulSet (previously called PetSet) for this purpose to facilitate the deployment and management of stateful cluster services on Kubernetes.

   Analyzing the above service types, the use of storage in Kubernetes mainly focuses on the following two aspects:

   • Reading the basic configuration files of the service, password key management, etc.
   • Service storage status, data access, etc.

2. Storage system

In the design and implementation of Docker, the container's data is temporary. That is, when the container is destroyed, the data in it will be lost. If you need to persist data, you need to use the Docker data volume to mount files or directories on the host to the container.

In the Kubernetes system, when the Pod is rebuilt, the data will be lost. Kubernetes also provides the persistence of the Pod data through the data volume. The Kubernetes data volume is an extension of the Docker data volume. The Kubernetes data volume is at the Pod level and can be used to implement file-sharing of containers in the Pod.

Kubernetes data volume adapts to various storage systems, providing rich and powerful functions. Kubernetes provides multiple types of data volumes, which are divided into three categories: local data volumes, network data volumes, and information data volumes according to their functions.

(1) Local data volume

There are two types of data volumes in Kubernetes. They can only act on the local file system. We call them local data volumes. The data in the local data volume will only exist on one machine, so when the Pod is migrated, the data will be lost, which cannot meet the real data persistence requirements. However, local data volumes provide other uses, such as file-sharing of containers in Pod, or sharing the host's file system.

① EmptyDir

EmptyDir is an empty directory, which is a new directory created when the Pod is created. If the Pod is configured with an EmptyDir data volume, the EmptyDir data volume will exist during the life of the Pod. When the Pod is allocated to the Node node, the EmptyDir data volume will be created on the Node node and mounted to the Pod container. As long as the Pod exists, the EmptyDir data volume will exist (container deletion will not cause the EmptyDir data volume to lose data). However, if the Pod's life cycle ends (Pod is deleted), the EmptyDir data volume will be deleted and lost forever.

The EmptyDir data volume is very suitable for file-sharing of containers in Pod. Pod's design provides a good container combination model, each of which performs its duties and completes the interaction through shared file directories. For example, a full-time log collection container can be combined in each Pod and business container to complete the logs' collection and summary.

② HostPath

The HostPath data volume allows the file system on the container host to be mounted to the Pod. If the Pod needs to use some files on the host, you can use the HostPath data volume.

(2) Network data volume

Kubernetes provides many types of data volumes to integrate third-party storage systems, including some prevalent distributed file systems and storage support provided on the LaaS platform. These storage systems are distributed and share file systems through the network, so we call it network data volume.

Network data volumes can meet the persistence requirements of data. Pod is configured to use network data volume. Each time a Pod is created, the remote file directory of the storage system will be mounted to the container, and the data in the data volume will be permanently stored. Even if the Pod is deleted, it will only delete the mounted data volume. The data in the data volume is still stored in the storage system, and when a new Pod is created, the same data volume is still mounted.

① NFS

NFS is a file system supported by FreeBSD, which allows computers on the network to share resources via TCP/IP. In NFS applications, the local NFS client application can transparently read/write files located on the remote NFS server, just like accessing local files.

② iSCSI

iSCSI is researched and developed by IBM. It is an SCSI instruction set for hardware devices that can run on the IP address's upper layer. This instruction set can be implemented to run the SCSI protocol on the IP network, enabling it to perform routing selection on, for example, high-speed Gigabit Ethernet. iSCSI technology is a new storage technology that combines the existing SCSI interface with Ethernet technology to enable servers to exchange data with storage devices using IP networks.

③ GlusterFS

GlusterFS is the core of the horizontal expansion storage solution. It is an open source distributed file system with powerful horizontal expansion capabilities. Through expansion, it can support PB-level storage capacity and handle thousands of clients. GlusterFS uses TCP/IP or InfiniBand RDMA network to aggregate physically distributed storage resources and uses a single global namespace to manage data. GlusterFs is based on a stackable userspace design, which can provide excellent performance for various data loads.

④ RBD

Ceph is an open source, distributed network storage, and at the same time, a file system. Ceph's design goals are excellent performance, reliability, and scalability. Ceph is based on reliable, scalable, and distributed object storage, manages metadata through a distributed cluster, and supports POSIX interfaces. RBD (Rados Block Device) is a Linux block device driver that provides a shared network block device to interact with Ceph. RBD strips and replicates on the cluster of Ceph object storage to provide reliability, scalability, and access to block devices.

(3) Information data volume

There are some data volumes in Kubernetes, mainly used to pass configuration information to containers, which we call information data volumes. For example, Secret and Downward API both save Pod information in the form of a file and then mount it to the container in the form of a data volume, and the container obtains the corresponding information by reading the file. In terms of functional design, this is a bit deviating from the original intention of the data volume because it is used to persist data or file-sharing. Future versions may restructure this part, placing the functions provided by the information data volume in a more appropriate place.

① Secret

Kubernetes provides Secret to handle sensitive data, such as passwords, tokens, and secret keys. Compared to directly configuring sensitive data in the Pod definition or mirror, Secret provides a more secure mechanism to prevent data leakage.

The creation of the Secret is independent of the Pod, and it is mounted to the Pod in the form of a data volume. The Secret's data will be saved in the form of a file, and the container can obtain the required data by reading the file.

② Downward API

The Downward API can tell the container Pod information through environment variables. In addition, it can also pass values through data volumes. Pod information will be mounted in the container through the data volume in the form of a file. The information can be obtained by reading the file in the container. Currently, the Pod name, Pod Namespace, Pod Label, and Pod Annotation are supported.

③ Git Repo

Kubernetes supports downloading the Git warehouse to the Pod. It is currently implemented through the Git Repo data volume. That is, when the Pod configures the Git Repo data volume, it downloads and configures the Git warehouse to the Pod data volume, and then mounts it to the container.

(4) Storage resource management

Understanding each storage system is a complicated matter, especially for ordinary users, who sometimes do not care about various storage implementations, but only hope to store data safely and reliably. Kubernetes provides Persistent Volume and Persistent Volume Claim mechanisms, which are storage consumption models. Persistent Volume is a data volume configured and created by the system administrator. It represents a specific type of storage plug-in implementation, which can be NFS, iSCSI, etc.: For ordinary users, through Persistent Volume Claim, you can request and obtain a suitable Persistent Volume without the need to perceive the back-end storage implementation.

The relationship between Persistent Volume Claim and Persistent Volume is similar to Pod and Node node. Pod consumes the resources of Node node, and Persistent Volume Claim consumes the resources of Persistent Volume. Persistent Volume and Persistent Volume Claim are related to each other and have complete life cycle management.

(1) Preparation

The system administrator plans and creates a series of Persistent Volumes. After the Persistent Volume is successfully created, it is available.

(2) Binding

The user creates a Persistent Volume Claim to declare the storage request, including storage size and access mode. After the Persistent Volume Claim is successfully created, it is in a waiting state. When Kubernetes finds that a new Persistent Volume Claim is created, it will look for the Persistent Volume according to the conditions. When Persistent Volume matches, Persistent Volume Claim and Persistent Volume will be bound, and Persistent Volume and Persistent Volume Claim are both in a bound state.

Kubernetes will only select the Persistent Volume in the available state and adopt the minimum satisfaction strategy. When there is no Persistent Volume to meet the demand, the Persistent Volume Claim will be in a waiting state. For example, there are now two Persistent Volumes available, one Persistent Volume with a capacity of 50GB and one Persistent Volume with a capacity of 60GB, then the Persistent Volume Claim for 40GB will be bound to the Persistent Volume for 50GB, and the Persistent Volume Claim for 100Gi is requested. It is in a waiting state until a Persistent Volume larger than 100GB appears (Persistent Volume may be created or recycled).

(3) Use

When creating a Pod using Persistent Volume Claim, Kubernetes will query its bound Persistent Volume, call the real storage implementation, and then mount the Pod's data volume.

(4) Release

When the user deletes the Persistent Volume Claim bound to the Persistent Volume, the Persistent Volume is in the released state. At this time, the Persistent Volume may retain the Persistent Volume Claim data, so the Persistent Volume is not available, and the Persistent Volume needs to be recycled.

(5) Recycling

The released Persistent Volume needs to be recycled before it can be used again. The recycling strategy can be manual processing or automatic cleaning by Kubernetes. If the cleaning fails, the Persistent Volume will be in a failed state.

7.2.6   Kubernetes Service Quality

In order to realize the effective scheduling and allocation of resources while improving resource utilization, Kubernetes uses QoS to manage the quality of service on Pod according to the expectations of different service quality. For a Pod, the quality of service is reflected in two specific indicators: CPU and memory. When the memory resources on the node are tight, Kubernetes will deal with it according to the different QoS categories set in advance.

```
containers:
name: foo
resources:
   limits:
      cpu: 10m
      memory: 1GB
   requests:
      cpu: 10m
      memory: 1GB

name: bar
resources:
   limits:
      cpu: 100m
      memory: 100MB
   requests:
      cpu: 100m
      memory: 100MB
```

Fig. 7.32 Example of guaranteed configuration file

1. QoS Classification

QoS is mainly divided into three categories: Guaranteed, Burstable and Best-Effort, with priority from high to low.

(1) Guaranteed

All containers in the Pod must set limits uniformly, and the set parameters are consistent. If there is a container to set requests, then all containers must be set and the set parameters are consistent with the limits. The QoS of this Pod is the Guaranteed level.

Note: If a container only sets limits but not requests, the value of requests is equal to the value of limits.

Guaranteed example: Both requests and limits are set and the values are equal, as shown in Fig. 7.32.

(2) Burstable

As long as the requests and limits of a container in the Pod are not the same, the QoS of the Pod is the Burstable level.

Burstable example: set limits for the different resources of the container foo and bar (foo is memory, and bar is cpu), as shown in Fig. 7.33.

(3) Best-Effort

```
containers:
name: foo
resources:
  limits:
     memory: 1GiB


name: bar
resources:
  limits:
     cpu: 100m
```

Fig. 7.33 Burstable configuration file

```
containers:
name: foo
resources:
name: bar
resources:
```

Fig. 7.34 Best-Effort configuration file

If requests and limits are not set for all resources, the QoS of the Pod is the Best-Effort level.

Best-Effort example: neither container foo nor container bar has requests and limits set, as shown in Fig. 7.34.

2. Resource recovery strategy

When the available resources on a node in a Kubernetes cluster are relatively small, Kubernetes provides a resource recovery strategy to ensure the Pod service's normal operation on the node. When the memory or CPU resources on a node are exhausted, the Pod service scheduled to run on the node may become unstable. Kubernetes uses kubelet to control the resource recovery strategy to ensure that the Pod on the node can run stably when the node resources are relatively small.

According to the scalability of resources, Kubernetes divides resources into compressible resources and incompressible resources. CPU resources are currently supported compressible resources, while incompressible resources currently support memory resources and disk resources.

Compressible resources: The CPU is a compressible resource mentioned in the Compressed Resources section. When the Pod usage exceeds the set limits, the CPU usage of the Pod process will be restricted, but it will not be Killed ("killed").

Incompressible resources: When the Node node's memory resources are insufficient, a process will be killed by the kernel.

The sequence and scenarios of the three QoS Pods being Killed are as follows.

- Best-Effort type Pod: When the system runs out of all memory, this type of Pod will be killed first.

- Burstable type Pod: When the system runs out of all memory and no Best-Effort container can be killed, this type of Pod will be killed.

- Guaranteed type Pod: The system has used up all the memory, and there is no Burstable and Best-Effort container that can be killed, this type of Pod will be killed.

Note: If the Pod process uses more than the preset limits instead of the Node node's resource shortage, the system tends to restart the container on the machine where it was initially located or recreate a Pod.

3. QoS implementation recommendations

If the resources are sufficient, you can set the QoS Pod type to Guaranteed. Use computing resources for business performance and stability, reducing the time and cost of troubleshooting.

If you want to improve resource utilization better, business services can be set to Guaranteed, and other services can be set to Burstable or Best-Effort according to their importance.

7.2.7   Kubernetes Resource Management

Resource management is a key capability of Kubernetes. Kubernetes not only allocates sufficient resources to applications, but also prevents applications from using resources without restrictions. As the scale of applications increases by orders of magnitude, these issues become critical.

1. Kubernetes resource model

Virtualization technology is the foundation of cloud platforms. Its goal is to integrate or divide computing resources. This is a key technology in cloud platforms. Virtualization technology provides flexibility in resource allocation for cloud platform resource management, so that the cloud platform can integrate or divide computing resources through the virtualization layer.

Compared with virtual machines, the emerging container technology uses a series of system-level mechanisms, such as the use of Linux Namespace for space isolation, the mount point of the file system to determine which files the container can access, and the Cgroup to determine which container can use how many resources. In addition, the containers share the same system kernel, so that when multiple containers use the same kernel, the efficiency of memory usage will be improved.

Although the two virtualization technologies, containers and virtual machines, are entirely different, their resource requirements and models are similar. Containers like virtual machines require memory, CPU, hard disk space, and network bandwidth. The host system can treat the virtual machine and the container as a whole, allocate and manage the resources it needs for this whole. Of course, the virtual machine provides the security of a dedicated operating system and a firmer logical boundary, while the container is relatively loose on the resource boundary, which brings flexibility and uncertainty.

Kubernetes is a container cluster management platform. Kubernetes needs to count the overall platform's resource usage, allocate resources to the container reasonably, and ensure that there are enough resources in the container life cycle to ensure its operation. Furthermore, if the resource issuance is exclusive, the resource has been distributed to one container, the same resource will not be distributed to another container. For idle containers, it is very wasteful to occupy resources (such as CPU) that they do not use. Kubernetes needs to consider how to improve resource utilization under the premise of priority and fairness.

2. Resource requests and resource limits

Computing resources are required for Pod or container operation, mainly including the following two.

- CPU: The unit is Core.
- Memory: The unit is Byte.

    When creating a Pod, you can specify the resource request and resource limit of each container. The resource request is the minimum resource requirement required by the container, and the resource limit is the upper limit of the resource that the container cannot exceed. Their size relationship must be:

```
0<=request<=limit<=infinity
```

    In the definition of the container, resource requests are set through resources.requests, and resource limits are set through resources.limits. Currently, the only resource types that can be specified are CPU and memory. Resource request and resource limit are optional configurations, and the default value depends on whether LimitRange is set. If the resource request is not specified and there is no default value, then the resource request is equal to the resource limit.

    The Pod defined below contains two containers (see Fig. 7.35): the resource request for the first container is 0.5 core CPU and 255MB memory, and the resource limit is 1 core CPU and 512MB memory; the resource request for the second container is 0.25 core CPU and 128MB memory, the resource limit is 1 core CPU and 512MB memory.

```
apiVersion: v1
kind: Pod
metadata:
  name: frontend
spec:
  containers:
  - name: db
    image: mysql
    resources:
      requests:
        memory : "255MB"

        cpu :  " 500m "
      limits:
        memory:"512MB"
        cpu:"1000m "
  - name: wp
    image: wordpress
    resources:
      requests:
        memory: "128MB"

        cpu :  "250m"
```

Fig. 7.35 Setting resource request and resource limit

The resource request/limit of a Pod is the sum of all container resource requests/limits in the Pod. For example, the Pod's resource request is 0.75 core CPU and 383MB memory, and the resource limit is 2 core CPU and 1024MB memory.

When the Kubernetes Scheduler schedules a Pod, the Pod's resource request is a key indicator of scheduling. Kubernetes will obtain the maximum resource capacity of the Kubernetes Node (via the cAdvisor interface) and calculate the used resources. For example, the Node node can accommodate 2 core CPUs and 2GB memory, and 4 Pods have been running on the Node node, requesting a total of 1.5 core CPU and 1GB memory, and the remaining 0.5 core CPU and 1GB memory. When Kubernetes Scheduler schedules a

Pod, it checks whether there are enough resources on the Node node to satisfy the Pod's resource request. If it is not satisfied, the Node node will be excluded.

Resource requests can ensure that the Pod has enough resources to run, and resource restrictions prevent a Pod from using resources unrestrictedly, causing other Pods to crash. Especially in the public cloud scenario, malicious software often preempts the attack platform.

Docker containers use Linux Cgroups to implement resource limits, and the docker run command provides parameters to limit CPU and memory.

(1) --memory

The docker run command sets the memory quota available to a container through the --memory parameter. Cgroup will limit the memory usage of the container. Once the quota is exceeded, the container will be terminated. The value of --memory of the Docker container in Kubernetes is the value of resources.limits.memory, for example, resources.limits.memory=512MB, then the value of --memory is $512 \times 1024 \times 1024 \times 1024$.

(2) --cpu-shares

The docker run command sets the available CPU quota for a container through the --cpu-shares parameter. It is important to note that this is a relative weight and has nothing to do with the actual processing speed. Each new container will have 1024 CPU quota by default. When we talk about it alone, this value does not mean anything. However, if you start two containers and both will use 100% of the CPU, the CPU time will be evenly distributed between the two containers because they both have the same CPU quota. If we set the container's CPU quota to 512, compared to another 1024CPU quota container, it will use 1/3 of the CPU time, but this does not mean that it can only use 1/3 of the CPU time. If another container (1024CPU quota is easy) is idle, the other container will be allowed to use 100% of the CPU. For CPUs, it is difficult to clearly state how many CPUs are allocated to which container, depending on the actual operating conditions.

The value of --cpu-shares of the Docker container in Kubernetes is through resources.requests.cpu or resources.

The value of requests.cpu is multiplied by 1024. If resources.requests.cpu is specified, --cpu-shares is equal to resources.

requests.cpu multiplied by 1024; if resources.requests.cpu is not specified, but resources.limits.cpu is specified, --cpu-shares is equal to resources.limits. cpu multiplied by 1024; if resources.limits.cpu and resources. If limits.cpu is not specified, --cpu-shares takes the minimum value.

LimitRange includes two types of configurations, Container and Pod. The configurations, including constraints and default values, are shown in Tables 7.1 and 7.2.

Kubernetes is a multi-tenant architecture. When multiple tenants or teams share a Kubernetes system, the system administrator needs to prevent the tenants from occupying resources and define resource allocation strategies. Kubernetes provides the API object ResourceQuota to implement resource quotas. ResourceQuota can

Table 7.1 LimitRange container configuration

Type	Container
Resource Type	Memory CPU
Limit	Min:min $<=$ Request(required) $<=$ Limit(optional) Max: Limit(Required) $<=$ max
	续表
Limit	maxLimitRequestRatio:maxLimitRequestRatio$<=$ (Limit(required, non-zero)/ Request(required, non-zero))
Default value	Default:Limit Default value DefaultRequest:Request Default value

Table 7.2 LimitRange Pod configuration

Type	Pod
Resource type	Memory CPU
Limit	Min:min $<=$ Request(required) $<=$ Limit(optional) Max: Limit(Required) $<=$ max maxLimitRequestRatio:(Limit(required, non-zero)/Request(required, non-zero)) maxLimitRequestRatio
Default value	The default value of the Pod need to be configured directly, it is derived from the default value of the container

Table 7.3 Computing resource quota

Name of resource	Explanation
cpu	CPU quota
Memory	Memory quota

Table 7.4 Kubernetes API对象资源

Name of resource	Explanation
Pods	Total amount of Pod
Services	Total amount of Service
replicationcontrollers	Total amount of Replication Controller
Resourcequotas	Total amount of Resource Quota
Secrets	Total amount of Secret
persistentvolumeclaims	Total amount of Persistent Volume Claim

not only act on CPU and memory, but also limit the number of Pods created. The computing resource quotas and resources supported by ResourceQuota are shown in Tables 7.3 and 7.4.

7.3   Exercise

1. Fill in the blanks

    1. The emergence of container technology actually mainly solves the technical realization of the _____layer.
    2. Docker provides two ways to build images:_____and_____.
    3. Kubernetes uses etcd as storage middleware, etcd is a highly available key-value storage system, inspired by ZooKeeper and Doozer, processing log replication through_____to ensure strong consistency.
    4. Kubernetes provides powerful _____ capabilities. Each component of a microservice application is abstracted by Service. Components only need to access the Service to communicate with each other without being aware of component cluster changes.
    5. Kubernetesd's QoS is mainly divided into three categories: _____, _____, and _____.

2. Answer the following questions

    1. What is a container? What is the difference between container virtualization and traditional virtualization?
    2. How many components does Kubernetes contain? What is the function of each component? How do the components interact?
    3. What is the relationship between Kubernetes and Docker?

3. Practice
   Write a Dockerfile to achieve the following functions: open the container to view the "/" directory, and rewrite to view the "/mnt" directory, the image can be selected dependently.

Chapter 8
Cloud Computing Development Trends

Kubernetes is a multi-tenant architecture. When multiple tenants or teams share a Kubernetes system, the system administrator needs to prevent the tenants from occupying resources and define resource allocation strategies. Kubernetes provides the API object ResourceQuota to implement resource quotas. ResourceQuota can not only act on CPU and memory, but also limit the number of Pods created. The computing resource quotas and resources supported by ResourceQuota are shown in Tables 7.4 and 7.5.

8.1 Cloud Computing Development Trend

In the course of social change, the speed of technological evolution and break-throughs is often beyond people's imagination. Thirty years ago, I could not dream of the changes and convenience of people's lives by various new technologies represented by information technology. It is difficult to predict the future of a specific technology, especially the rapid development of information technology, there have been too many false predictions, and some have even become jokes. However, one thing is certain. Cloud computing will increasingly become an indispensable part of our daily lives. Like air, food, and sunlight, it will contribute to the improvement of human life and the improvement of social efficiency.

8.1.1 *The Development and Trend of Cloud Computing in China*

We will examine the development and trend of cloud computing in China from technology and industry levels.

© The Author(s) 2023
Huawei Technologies Co., Ltd., *Cloud Computing Technology*,
https://doi.org/10.1007/978-981-19-3026-3_8

1. Technology level

In recent years, in the process of industrial transformation, companies in various industries in China have used emerging technologies such as cloud computing and artificial intelligence to improve their production efficiency, innovation capabilities, resource utilization, drive changes in development models, and lay a solid foundation for the ultimate realization of digital transformation. Cloud computing has become the core infrastructure supporting the digital transformation of enterprises.

At present, the new generation of information technology is developing in the direction of deep integration. The development and popularization of one technology may promote the breakthrough of another technology. The superposition or combination of these new technologies will produce noticeable spillover effects. Among them, the combination of "5G+cloud computing+artificial intelligence" is the most representative, and the three are closely integrated, producing huge social effects. In the past, due to bandwidth, latency, connection density, and cost constraints, cloud computing, which can significantly improve computing efficiency, has not been widely extended to all walks of life. However, with the application and popularization of 5G technology, its high speed, low power consumption, and low-latency will be effective to solve this complex problem. "5G + cloud computing" can greatly increase the inclusiveness of computing resources. The development and popularization of artificial intelligence technology, which is considered to have disruptive potential, also requires 5G and cloud computing to pave the way.

Besides, although China's cloud computing industry is of vital importance as the core infrastructure for the digital transformation of enterprises, since most of the industry's core technologies are not in the hands of Chinese companies, once the international situation changes, the development of cloud computing industry may be constrained by others. From the perspective of national security and the healthy and sustainable development of the industry, independent and controllable core technology research and development have become a problem that must be solved in developing China's cloud computing industry.

2. Industry level

From the perspective of industrial structure, the cloud computing industry chain can be divided into upstream core hardware (CPU, flash memory, memory), midstream IT infrastructure (servers, storage devices, network equipment), and downstream cloud ecosystems (basic platforms, cloud-native applications).

The chip industry has always been the weak underbelly of China's technology industry, especially the ICT industry, and has long been subject to others. In cloud computing, the chip industry is still the top priority and is in the upstream position of the cloud computing industry. The independent controllability of chips directly affects the independent controllability of the cloud computing industry. Given the relatively weak overall development of the chip industry, the independent research and development capabilities of upstream chips in the cloud computing industry still have a certain gap compared with developed countries. The situation in the field of IT infrastructure equipment in the middle reaches is better. As a major manufacturing country, China has a number of powerful domestic IT manufacturers such as Huawei, Lenovo, and Inspur that can provide corresponding competitive hardware equipment or products. Regarding the downstream cloud ecology field, domestic companies are also catching up. Several major domestic IT companies such as Alibaba, Tencent, Huawei, and Baidu have all launched their cloud services, and their market share is also expanding.

In recent years, under the government and industry's dual promotion, cloud computing technology has been rapidly promoted in China, and the cloud computing industry has grown rapidly. Data show that by 2019, China's cloud computing industry's scale has exceeded 100 billion yuan, and the annual growth rate has exceeded 30% in recent years. However, compared with developed countries, China's cloud computing industry still has a big gap. For example, compared with the United States, the size of China's cloud computing market in 2018 was only about 8% of the US cloud computing market. China's cloud computing development level and economic development level show a severe mismatch.

From an industry perspective, currently, the primary users of cloud computing in China are concentrated on the Internet, transportation, logistics, finance, telecommunications, government, and other fields. In recent years, the amount of data in various industries has increased sharply, and more fields have begun to use cloud computing technology to tap the value of data. Although the Internet industry is still dominant, the scale of cloud computing in transportation, logistics, finance, and other industries also occupies an important position. However, in general, compared with developed countries, Chinese enterprises' cloud access rate is still lower, and there is huge potential for development. According to McKinsey research data, in 2018, the cloud access rate of US companies has reached over 85%, the cloud access rate of EU companies is also around 70%, while the cloud access rate of enterprises in various industries in China is only about 40%, which is in the core infrastructure of the digital economy. There is still a long way to go in construction.

In the future, the digital economy will lead to China's cloud computing industry's rapid development. New technologies and applications will bring new vitality to the cloud computing market. Edge computing, artificial intelligence, and machine learning-oriented parallel computing are expected to continue to drive the market to maintain growth; 5G will also drive new infrastructure growth and promote new application innovation. Promote the integration of new applications such as autonomous driving and intelligent networked vehicles with cloud computing, opening up new room for growth. The new crown epidemic in 2020 has promoted the large-scale popularization and application of cloud computing to a certain extent. China's cloud computing industry is expected to usher in a "golden development period" in the next few years.

8.1.2   The Development and Trend of Cloud Computing Abroad

Compared with China, developed countries led by the United States started earlier in developing cloud computing, with more advanced technologies, more complete industrial chains, and larger industrial scales. According to the "Global Public Cloud Market Share Report (2017)," global public cloud service revenue reached US$260.2 billion in 2017, an increase of approximately 18.5% over the previous year, and the report predicts that this number will grow to 411.4 billion US dollars. Furthermore, this data does not include a large number of private cloud and hybrid cloud revenue. Although the "cake" of cloud services is large and growing rapidly, it is extremely unevenly distributed among different countries. According to statistics, in the global cloud computing market, the United States has the largest share, accounting for about 60%, followed by Europe, accounting for about 25%, while emerging developing countries (including China) account for a small proportion. However, the good news is that these countries are to catch up with an astonishing rate of development.

The foreign cloud service market is divided by some "giant companies" in cloud computing. At present, the leading cloud computing vendors mainly include Amazon, Google, and Microsoft. These cloud computing giants have occupied a large share in the global cloud market by their leading technology and industry position, have a strong influence in the industry, and their cloud service revenue has also maintained a high growth rate. Take Amazon as an example. Its revenue has maintained a double-digit growth trend for more than 20 years. Even in the second quarter of 2020, when various industries are severely affected by the new crown epidemic, it still recorded 88.9 billion US dollars. An increase of 40% in the same period last year. Among them, e-commerce revenue was US$78.1 billion, an increase of 42%. At the same time, AWS revenue was US$10.8 billion, an increase of 29%. Amazon's profit in this quarter reached 5.24 billion US dollars, an increase of 99.7% over the same period last year, setting Amazon's highest profit record. This is in sharp contrast to other traditional industries' poor performance and even serious losses during the same period.

It can be predicted that the global cloud computing industry will still maintain a relatively high development speed, at least in the next few decades. New technologies will continue to emerge and new applications will continue to expand. Unless there are unpredictable changes, the "big bosses" in the industry will still maintain their monopoly and dominance for a long time. The rise and rapid development of developing countries, especially China, are worth looking forward to.

8.1.3 Problems to be Solved and Prospects for the Future Development of Cloud Computing

1. Problems to be solved in the future development of cloud computing

  (1) Data security issues

   Data security is one of the most concerning issues for enterprises. Data security includes two aspects: ensuring that data will not be lost, and the other is to ensure that data will not be leaked or accessed illegally. Data loss or sensitive data leakage will bring immeasurable losses to enterprises and customers no matter which scenario occurs. Although cloud computing has unparalleled advantages in many aspects, it saves users from building their own IT platform. It can provide almost unlimited data storage space and almost unlimited computing and processing capabilities, but users will not be willing to host their data on the cloud platform if user data security cannot be guaranteed. When using cloud services, users save data to the cloud platform, which means they lose control of the data. Users neither know where their data is stored nor can they determine whether the data has been peeped or tampered with. There are doubts about whether the cloud service provider hosting the data can ensure the security of the data. Therefore, to effectively solve the data security problem, in the future, cloud computing technology must consider more comprehensive and complete data security solutions, provide appropriate management mechanisms, and ensure that cloud service providers provide services based on honesty and credibility. In this way, users who are more sensitive to data security can use cloud services with confidence.

  (2) Network performance issues

   Improving network performance is also one of the challenges facing cloud computing. Users can use cloud computing services without the network, but low or unstable access to the network bandwidth will greatly reduce cloud computing performance. Therefore, we must vigorously develop access network technology. The development and landing of 5G technology also provide an opportunity to use mobile Internet to access cloud computing. In addition, in the cloud computing network, in order to complete the efficient processing of information, not only the cluster servers in the network need to have high computing and processing capabilities, but the communication facilities in the network must also have high performance, to ensure the high quality of cloud services and provide low-latency to cloud users.

  (3) Standardization of cloud computing

   There is no open public standard for cloud computing, which has caused much inconvenience to users. It is difficult for users to migrate a certain company's cloud computing applications to another company's cloud platform. In this way, the user is bound to a fixed cloud service provider, limiting the user's right to choose. Therefore, if cloud computing wants to develop better, it is necessary to formulate a unified cloud computing public standard.

In addition, the interoperability issues between different cloud systems need to be considered. Corresponding standards need to be formulated for the interface of cloud computing to facilitate access to the resources of another cloud system through one cloud system and cooperation between different cloud service providers.

2. Outlook

Due to the uncertainty of technology and social development, it is difficult to predict the future of cloud computing technology, but we can see the following trends.

(1) Cloud standardization and cross-cloud migration

Currently, there is no unified standard for cloud services, and different cloud service providers adopt different systems and solutions. Once an enterprise uses a certain cloud service provider's service, it is bound to the service provider, and the cost of migrating to other cloud services is very high. Just as computer networks' development has evolved from non-standardized proprietary networks to networks that adopt unified, standardized protocols, standardization in the field of cloud computing is also worth looking forward to. Once cloud computing is standardized, users do not have to worry about cloud service providers' lock-in. They can freely switch between multiple cloud services, and they can also migrate across clouds, which meets the needs of users for a more unified view across multiple cloud accounts. For example, users can respectively correspond development and production to different cloud service providers' cloud platforms. At the same time, standardization can also greatly reduce the cost of cloud infrastructure and provide services for cloud users with a higher price-performance ratio.

(2) A higher level of abstraction

A future development trend is that information technology and services will continue to become more abstract (close to the user, far away from the hardware). The development of new technologies such as serverless, containers, and application-defined hardware means that engineers/developers can pay less and less attention to infrastructure. Staying away from hardware details and focusing on business logic is an obvious trend, and it may continue for some time.

(3) Containers become mainstream

Application containerization is a new trend in cloud computing, and it is changing the way resources are deployed to the cloud. Containers use a sandbox mechanism, and there will be no interfaces between them, and an isolated and standardized operating environment can be built. At the same time, the container has the advantages of fast startup and small resource usage. In 2019, more and more companies used containers. According to ESG Research's forecast, one-third of hybrid cloud workloads will use containers in 2020. In the past few years, Kubernetes has become the preferred container orchestration platform. In the future, more companies will regard containers as an essential part of their IT strategy.

8.2   Other Fields Related to Cloud Computing

Cloud computing has a wide range of applications in many fields, especially in the application fields that require massive data processing, and it plays an important role. The following technologies are closely related to cloud computing and even use cloud computing technology as its support.

8.2.1   The Internet of Things

The Internet of Things (IoT) is an important part of a new generation of information technology and is called the "Internet of Things Connected." This has two meanings: first, the core and foundation of the Internet of Things is still the Internet, which is an extension and expansion of the Internet; second, the edge of the network extends and extends to ordinary non-intelligent items, and items can also be connected to the network and realized the interconnection between items.

Specifically, the Internet of Things uses radio frequency identification (RFID), infrared sensors, global positioning systems, laser scanners, and other information sensing equipment to connect items to the Internet according to an agreed protocol for information exchange and communication to realize the intelligent identification, positioning, tracking, monitoring, and management of items.

The main technologies used on the Internet of Things are as follows:

1. RFID

   RFID is a kind of automatic identification technology that uses radiofrequency to read/write the recording medium (electronic tag or radio frequency card) (usually a non-contact method) to identify the target and data exchange. RFID technology enables non-intelligent ordinary items to have the ability to interact, and ordinary items can be connected to the Internet of Things by attaching electronic tags to them.

2. Transducer

   A transducer is a detection device that can sense the measured information and transform the sensed information into electrical signals or other required forms of information output according to a certain rule to satisfy the requirements of transmission, processing, storage, display, record, and control of information. There are many types of sensors. Their basic sensing functions are divided into thermal, photosensitive, air-sensitive, force-sensitive, magnetic-sensitive, moisture-sensitive, and sound-sensitive. Connect all kinds of sensors through the network to realize data collection, processing and information sharing, forming a sensor network, which is an important type of the Internet of Things.

3. IPv6

IPv6 is the next-generation IP protocol designed by the Internet Engineering Task Force (IETF) to replace IPv4. Currently, the mainstream IPv4 only uses 4 bytes to represent the Internet's IP address, and the address space is seriously insufficient and has been exhausted. However, a large number of ordinary items need to be connected to the Internet. If these items need to be connected to the Internet, they usually need to be assigned IP addresses. This requires a huge number of IP addresses far beyond the past. IPv6 uses 16 bytes to represent IP addresses, and its address space is much larger than IPv4, and its number of addresses claims to be able to allocate an IP address to every grain of sand in the world. IPv6 effectively solves the problem of a serious shortage of network address resources on the Internet of Things and removes the barriers for multiple access devices to connect to the Internet, so it has also become one of the supporting technologies of the Internet of Things.

4. Cloud computing technology

The application of cloud computing, cloud storage, cloud services, cloud terminals, and other cloud computing technologies to the perception layer, application layer, and network layer of the Internet of Things can solve the problem of managing massive amounts of information and data on the Internet of Things. Specifically include the following questions.

(1) It can effectively solve the unreliability problem of server nodes on the Internet of Things and reduce the probability of server failure

With the rapid development of the Internet of Things, its scale is getting larger and larger, and it can even reach the scale of a metropolitan area network. The number of servers in the network is also increasing, leading to a sharp increase in server failure probability. If combined with cloud computing technology, through virtualization, clustering, and virtual machine migration technologies, it can effectively solve server nodes' unreliability problem on the Internet of Things and ensure the realization of uninterrupted security services for the Internet of Things.

(2) Flexible expansion can be achieved, ensuring low input and high output of the Internet of Things

The hardware resources of the server on the Internet of Things are limited. When the load is too large, the server may be paralyzed. The hardware resources of the server on the Internet of Things are limited. When the load is too large, the server may be paralyzed. Combined with cloud computing technology, through load balancing, elastic expansion, optimized load distribution strategy, or elastic expansion of the number of virtual machines, server overload can be effectively avoided.

(3) Sharing of information resources can be realized

Collecting data collected by sensors on the IoT to a cloud computing center through the Internet will facilitate the sharing and centralized processing of these information resources.

Cloud computing and the Internet of Things complement each other. Among them, cloud computing is the cornerstone of the development of the Internet of Things. At the same time, as one of the largest users of cloud computing, the Internet of Things continues to promote the rapid development of cloud computing. With the support of cloud computing technology, the Internet of Things can further improve data processing and analysis capabilities and is endowed with more robust work performance, which improves its work efficiency and makes its application fields more and more extensive. If there is no cloud computing as the basic support, the massive data information generated by the Internet of Things will not be smoothly transmitted, processed, and applied. The work efficiency of the Internet of Things will be greatly reduced, and its advantages over traditional technologies will no longer exist. Therefore, with the support of cloud computing technology, the development space of the Internet of Things has become broader.

Generally speaking, cloud computing can provide powerful processing capabilities for the massive data of the Internet of Things; cloud storage can provide enough storage space for the collected data; cloud services can use virtualization technology, cluster technology, and distributed technology. Integrate different types of IT resources to provide various functions such as data collection, storage, analysis, and processing for the Internet of Things.

In addition to the several technologies mentioned above, technologies such as QR code and short-range wireless communication are also core technologies of the IoT. Figure 8.1 shows the main supporting technologies of the Internet of Things.

8.2.2   Big Data

1. The concept of big data

   For any industry, enterprise, or organization, managing and analyzing data can usually bring great benefits. However, at the same time, it is arduous and challenging work. The data we need to process is often complex and diverse. Some data is structured and stored in relational databases, while some data is unstructured, such as documents, pictures, audio, and video. The source of the data is also different. Sensors or applications collect some data, and some data is manually entered or edited. Mobile devices with increasingly powerful functions, coupled with the Internet that can be accessed at any time, have also become a new data generation source. How to deal with these massive amounts of data from

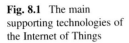
Fig. 8.1 The main
supporting technologies of
the Internet of Things

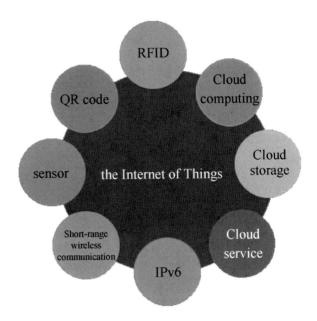

different sources and different data formats is no longer feasible with traditional
data management thinking. It is necessary to look at data management differently.
Big data refers to a collection of data that cannot be captured, managed, and
processed with conventional tools within a certain time frame. Big data is a
massive, high growth rate, and diversified information asset that requires new
processing models to have more substantial decision-making power, insight and
discovery, and process optimization capabilities.

With the rapid development of information technology, hardware, storage,
network upgrades, and computing models, such as virtualization and cloud
computing, traditional data management, and utilization methods have changed.
The integration of emerging technologies and reducing cycle costs from storage
to computing have changed the landscape of data and gave birth to big data. The
sources of big data are diversified. Computers or sensors can automatically
generate it, or it can be generated artificially through human–computer interaction. Big data usually has five characteristics (5 "Vs"): Volume (large), Velocity
(high speed), Variety (diversity), Value (low-value density), Veracity (authenticity). Among them, diversity is a distinctive feature of big data. Data can generally
be divided into three categories: structured data, unstructured data, and semi-
structured data. Structured data generally refers to data that has a certain length
and format. Typical structured data includes numbers, dates, and strings
representing specific meanings (such as names and addresses). Structured data
can be stored in a relational database, and structured query language can be used
to perform data operations such as query, insert, change, and delete. Unstructured
data refers to data without a fixed format, and most of the actual data is of this
type. For example, pictures, audios, videos, files, emails, logs, and webpages are

all unstructured data. The unstructured data mentioned here is not that the data itself is messy. Taking files as an example. Each file has its unique structure or format, but as a whole, the information inside the file does not have a unified format specification and is unstructured. Another type of data is semi-structured data, which lies between structured data and unstructured data. Although it does not have a fixed schema like structured data, it may have some formatting of its own, or contain something like "key-value". For example, XML, JSON, EDI, SWIFT, etc. are all semi-structured data.

2. Big data processing technology

Usually, big data includes not only the data but also the technology to process the data. Big data is important because it allows data processors to collect, store, manage, and manipulate these massive amounts of data at the right speed and at the right time to get a correct understanding of the data or extract valuable information from the data. Big data processing technology is not an isolated technology. On the contrary, it integrates technological changes in recent decades and embodies the latest technological achievements in the IT field. The core technologies of big data processing, such as virtualization, parallel processing, distributed file system, and memory database, have a history of decades of development. Moreover, like Hadoop and MapReduce, the development history is much shorter. When these technologies are combined, they can meet some important business needs.

Big data is an entirely new concept. Nevertheless, it is an evolution in the development of data. It is based on data management practice in the past few decades and has benefited from the development of software/hardware technologies in recent years and the rise of emerging technologies such as cloud computing. For example, because of the high cost of computing and storage, companies can only compromise on storing data snapshots or a subset of important information and cannot save all the data they need to analyze. With virtualization and cloud computing technology, data can be virtualized, storage efficiency is greatly improved, and cloud-based storage can also be used, improving efficiency and reducing costs. In addition, the increase in network bandwidth and reliability has greatly improved the efficiency of data transmission. These technologies provide the possibility for people to process massive amounts of data at an acceptable speed.

3. Big data and cloud computing

In the world of big data, cloud computing plays a crucial role. Big data and cloud computing are like a coin's pros and cons from a technical point of view. Big data requires the computing function of distributed clusters, and this happens to be the cloud architecture. Relying on the distributed processing, distributed database, cloud storage, and virtualization technology of cloud computing, it is possible to process and mine massive amounts of data. For example, real-time analysis of large data sets may require cloud computing frameworks such as MapReduce, with thousands of virtual machines located on distributed computers to complete the work.

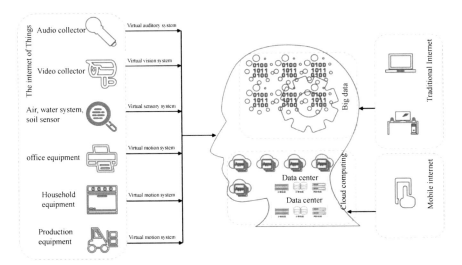

Fig. 8.2   The relationship between cloud computing, Internet of Things, and big data

The previous article introduced the inseparable relationship between the Internet of Things, big data, and cloud computing. The Internet of Things is an important source of big data. The Internet of Things corresponds to the perception layer of the Internet. Big data represents the information layer of the Internet. To dig out useful information from big data, the massive information processing capabilities of cloud computing are needed, as shown in Fig. 8.2. Therefore, cloud computing and the Internet of Things have promoted big data development, and big data has also promoted the progress of cloud computing and the Internet of Things.

8.2.3   Artificial Intelligence

1. The concept of artificial intelligence
   Artificial intelligence is a new technological science that studies and develops theories, methods, technologies, and application systems to simulate, extend, and expand human intelligence. Artificial intelligence covers a wide range of fields, including machine learning (deep learning), intelligent robots, image recognition, expert systems, natural language processing, computer vision, etc. Its goal is to make machines competent for complex tasks that usually require human intelligence to complete. Since the birth of artificial intelligence, theory and technology have become increasingly mature. The application field has been expanding, especially the breakthroughs in machine learning, making artificial intelligence a frontier technology currently focused on. A large number of artificial

intelligence applications and results have also become an important force that changes lives and changes the world.

2. Development of artificial intelligence

Artificial intelligence technology can be described as ups and downs. Artificial intelligence began in the 1950s and can be roughly divided into three stages of development. Stage 1 (the 50s to 1980s): At this stage, artificial intelligence was just born, and programmable digital computers based on abstract mathematical reasoning have beem emerged. Symbolism has developed rapidly, but because many things cannot be formalized, the established model has certain limitations. In addition, with the increasing complexity of computing tasks, the development of artificial intelligence once encountered a bottleneck. Stage 2 (the 1980s to the end of the 1990s): In this stage, the expert system has developed rapidly and the mathematical model has made breakthroughs. However, due to the lack of knowledge acquisition and reasoning ability of the expert system and the high development cost. The development of artificial intelligence has once again entered a low period. Phase 3 (from the beginning of the twenty-first century to the present): With the accumulation of big data, the innovation of theoretical algorithms, and the improvement of computing power, artificial intelligence has made breakthroughs in many application fields, ushering in another "prosperous period." After a long silence, artificial intelligence's resurgence is primarily due to breakthroughs in machine learning, intense learning technology. In fact, some deep learning algorithms (such as backpropagation algorithms) have been around for a long time. But at that time, they were limited to the computer's hardware level, and the processing power of the machine was very limited. At the same time, deep learning requires a lot of data for training. Generally, the larger the amount of data and the more accurate the data, the better the training effect. Unfortunately, there was also a lack of big data for training. In the past 10 years, the advancement of hardware technology (such as the emergence of GPU), the rapid development of cloud computing, and big data technology have created material conditions for deep learning technology development.

3. Artificial intelligence and cloud computing

Artificial intelligence is produced by inductive learning of massive data, and the processing of massive data cannot do without cloud computing. The von Neumann system's serial structure in the early years made computers unable to meet the hardware requirements of artificial intelligence. In recent years, the massive parallel and distributed computing capabilities of cloud computing have partially solved this problem, making artificial intelligence going forward. A big step forward.

In the cloud computing environment, all computing resources can be dynamically increased or decreased from the hardware infrastructure and can be flexibly expanded and contracted to meet work tasks' needs. The essence of cloud computing infrastructure is to maximize the utilization of IT investment by integrating and sharing dynamic hardware equipment supply, which significantly reduces the unit cost of using cloud computing and is also very conducive to artificial intelligence's commercial operation.

Fig. 8.3 The key between
artificial intelligence, big
data, and cloud computing

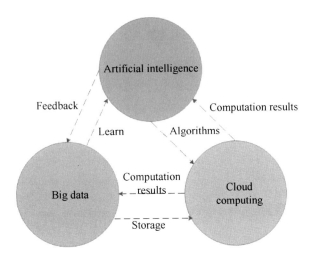

In addition, it is particularly worth pointing out that in recent years, GPU-based parallel computing has sprung up, and its parallel computing power far surpasses that of CPUs. A single GPU chip integrates many processing cores with weak processing capabilities and single functions. Compared with a small number of complex cores with more powerful functions in a CPU chip, it is more suitable for running distributed artificial intelligence algorithms. Now not only companies such as Google and Netflix use GPUs to build artificial neural networks, but companies such as Facebook, Amazon, and Salesforce also have GPU-based cloud computing capabilities. The domestic iFlytek also uses GPU clusters to support voice recognition technology.

In addition, because artificial intelligence algorithms mostly rely on a large amount of data, these data often need to be accumulated for a specific field (such as e-commerce) for a long time. Without data, artificial intelligence algorithms are useless. Cloud computing service providers often accumulate large amounts of data, and artificial intelligence algorithms can run on these data and provide the results as services. This is equivalent to SaaS in cloud computing. At the same time, running deep learning artificial intelligence algorithms requires compelling computing capabilities. The instant-available, robust, and elastically scalable computing capabilities provided by cloud platforms can ensure that artificial intelligence algorithms run successfully within an acceptable time. Figure 8.3 describes the relationship between artificial intelligence, big data, and cloud computing.

The rise of artificial intelligence is the inevitable result of cloud computing and big data evolution and maturity. The core of artificial intelligence is not only algorithms but also learning. Through the learning of data, value can be obtained from data. If cloud computing is the soil of big data, then big data is the water and fertilizer needed to grow artificial intelligence, and artificial intelligence is the final blooming flower. It is based on cloud computing and big data that artificial intelligence has made a qualitative leap. It is foreseeable that under the strong support of cloud computing and big data, the future of artificial intelligence is bound to be a glorious drama, worthy of people's expectation, while cloud computing and big data will continue to be unique in the era of the Internet of Everything.

8.2.4   5G

1. Concept of 5G

   5G is a new generation of cellular mobile communication technology and an extension after 4G (LTE-A, WiMax), 3G (UMTS, LTE), and 2G (GSM) systems. The performance goals of 5G are high data rates, reduced latency, energy savings, cost reduction, increased system capacity, and large-scale device connections. At present, 5G has entered the commercial stage. On October 31, 2019, the three major operators announced the 5G commercial package and officially launched the 5G commercial package on November 1st.

2. Development of 5G

   The development of 5G also comes from the increasing demand for mobile data. With the development of the mobile Internet, more and more devices are connected to the mobile network, the demand for mobile data "explosively" grows, and new services and applications emerge endlessly. The report of the Swedish telecommunications equipment company Ericsson shows that by 2022, the number of global mobile broadband users will reach 8.3 billion, an annual growth rate of more than 20%. The skyrocketing mobile data traffic will bring severe challenges to the communication network, and the existing mobile communication system cannot meet future demands. In order to solve the above challenges and meet the increasing demand for mobile traffic, it is urgent to develop a new generation of 5G network.

3. 5G and Cloud Computing

   5G is a complex new technology. Huawei is an international leader in 5G standard formulation and product development. Huawei puts forward that "5G technology will empower information and communication technology and trigger many changes in technology and business." It also pointed out five revolutionary changes that 5G technology may bring: platform connection, always-on, full cloud, and redefining the terminal and continuity. Here, we focus on the relationship between 5G technology and cloud computing.

   The landing application of 5G will play a comprehensive role in promoting the popularization of cloud computing. Traditional cloud computing mainly relies on fixed-line broadband to provide access services. With 5G technology, since 5G technology has significantly improved the response efficiency, reliability, and unit capacity of mobile networks, the mobile Internet carried by 5G technology can provide cloud computing with anytime, anywhere, high-bandwidth, low-latency, reliable performance, and low price. This will greatly promote cloud computing development, enabling cloud computing users to expand from central cities and towns that initially had to rely on fixed broadband lines to rural or various mobile scenarios, enabling cloud access anytime, anywhere. A large number of local computing services can also be more easily migrated to the cloud so that cloud computing can give full play to its advantages.

In the 5G era, the development trend of cloud computing will have the following characteristics.

(1) Terminal computing in the consumer Internet field will migrate to the cloud

In the consumer Internet field, including the entertainment field, the terminal's computing tasks will be migrated to the cloud, which can greatly reduce the cost of terminal hardware, thereby laying a foundation for the popularization of terminal products. On the Internet of Vehicles and wearable devices, because 5G technology will greatly improve response efficiency, cloud computing technology will be widely adopted in these two areas in the 5G era.

(2) Cloud computing will be combined with edge computing in the field of industrial Internet

The biggest difference between the industrial Internet field and the consumer Internet field lies in data's boundary requirements. The industrial Internet field usually has strict requirements on the boundaries of data. At the same time, the amount of data on the Internet of Things itself is huge. It is not realistic if all data processing tasks are sent to the cloud platform, so edge computing completes terminal data processing, and cloud computing completes. The final data processing cooperation method will be widely used.

(3) Cloud computing will stimulate innovation from the perspective of the industry

5G technology has significantly improved the basic communication capabilities, making it easy for many industry applications to use cloud computing as an important resource acquisition method, which will fundamentally affect product design ideas. It can be said that cloud computing will fully empower enterprise innovation in the 5G era. The continuous deepening of industry applications will further promote the improvement and development of cloud computing. Cloud computing can provide computing resource services and gradually develop other value-added services such as product research and development services.

8.3 Introduction to Other Emerging Technologies

8.3.1 Edge Computing and Fog Computing

1. Edge computing

   (1) The concept of edge computing

In the past few years, the diversification trend of computing platforms, equipment, and services has been eye-catching. For example, desktop computers used to be the mainstream computing platform for desktop offices. However, after entering the twenty-first century, handheld devices such as notebook computers and later tablets have gradually become the mainstream of office equipment, while wearable devices and the Internet of Things have become new popular trends. In the face of diversified terminal devices, "cloud" as a unified platform that can provide applications and service support for various terminal devices has been increasingly used.

There are a large number of cloud platforms that provide a wide range of services for different devices. As the platform is stable and reliable, third-party developers rely increasingly on cloud computing to provide end-users with high-quality services. Generally speaking, cloud services require developers to host services, applications, and data in off-site data centers. However, limited to specific applications, more and more services with high QoS requirements require computing tasks to be completed by end-users. For example, delay-sensitive real-time applications need to complete back-end services at the user's current location. Research in recent years has shown that performing computing tasks close to the end-user helps improve the end-user's service experience. This approach is usually called edge computing.

(2) Features of edge computing

Contrary to transferring data to a remote cloud for processing, edge computing provides computing and storage resources at the edge of the network close to the data source. In layman's terms, edge computing is decentralized or distributed cloud computing. The original data is not transmitted back to the cloud but is analyzed and processed locally. Because edge computing supports actual needs, especially on the Internet of Things, it is widely used so that edge computing may become the next successful technological breakthrough like cloud computing.

Figure 8.4 shows an example of an edge computing solution based on the Internet of Vehicles. In traditional solutions, the user needs to be processed layer by layer to the cloud computing center for calculation, and the calculation result is returned layer by layer, and the processing wait time is long. In the edge computing solution, the user's data is required to be directly sent to the edge device (such as the roadside device RSU) for processing, and the processing result can be returned immediately, and the waiting time is short. At the same time, it can also directly interact with neighboring users, which is more suitable for the Internet of Vehicles where the network topology changes at any time due to the rapid movement of vehicles and the response time is very demanding.

2. Fog computing

(1) The concept of fog computing

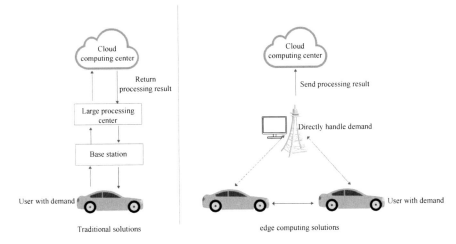

Fig. 8.4 Examples of edge computing solutions based on the Internet of Vehicles

There are several different forms of edge computing, and fog computing is an important one.

Fog computing refers to a computing model in which data processing and applications are concentrated in devices at the edge of the network, rather than all stored in the cloud. We can regard fog computing as an extended concept of cloud computing. The reason why it is named "fog computing" is because "fog" is closer to the ground (user terminal) than "cloud."

The rise of fog computing is closely related to the continuous enhancement of edge devices' processing capabilities. Due to the continuous enhancement of the latest chips, wireless devices and sensors, current edge devices can perform complex functions such as computing, storage, sensing, and network management. This provides hardware support for the sinking of processing power.

(2) Fog architecture and characteristics

The architecture corresponding to fog computing is called fog architecture, including networking, computing, and storage. The fog architecture uses one or a large number of collaborative end-user clients or edge devices close to the end-user to perform a series of operations such as storage, communication, control, configuration, measurement, and management. Fog architecture will be used in technical applications such as 5G, home/personal networking, embedded artificial intelligence systems, and the Internet of Things. Figure 8.5 shows several common types of fog architecture.

The fog architecture is different from the existing cloud, mainly reflected in the following three places.

- The fog architecture performs a large number of storage operations at or near the end-user. The cloud puts storage in large-scale data centers.

Fig. 8.5 Several common types of fog architecture

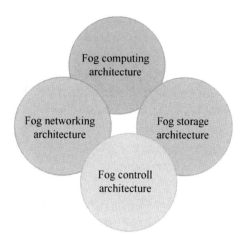

- The fog architecture performs a large number of communication operations at or near the end-user. The cloud is routed through the backbone network to centralized nodes for operation.
- The fog architecture performs a large number of calculation and management operations at or near the end-user, including network measurement, control, and configuration. The cloud is mainly controlled through the gateway.

(3) Advantages of fog computing

As a distributed computing infrastructure for the Internet of Things, fog computing can extend computing power and data analysis applications to the "edge" of the network, enabling users to analyze and manage data locally, with perception, efficiency, sensitivity, and low-latency.

- Perception: Perception that takes the client as the central goal. When the cloud cannot guarantee privacy and reliability or enhance security by shortening the communication distance, client-centric perception is particularly important.
- Efficient: Integrate local resources. There are a large number of idle processing capabilities on edge devices. The integration of these idle processing capabilities, perception capabilities, and wireless connection capabilities can make more efficient use of local resources.
- Sensitive: Rapid innovation and achievable scaling. Innovation led by cloud service providers is often slow and untimely. Applying the fog architecture, small companies can quickly use the programming interfaces provided by edge devices for business innovation.
- Low-latency: Reduce latency and realize real-time processing. Some applications, such as real-time applications on the Industrial Internet, have strict requirements on time delay. Using the fog architecture to

perform data analysis locally on the edge device and perform various operations through the control loop can provide milliseconds or less response time to meet real-time processing requirements.

Fog computing and cloud computing have their strengths, and they are aimed at different application scenarios. The two cooperate to meet a broader range of user needs.

8.3.2   Microservices

1. The concept of microservices

Microservices is another hot topic in application architecture, and it is considered the final product under SOA. As an architectural model, microservices advocate dividing a single application into a group of small services, each service can run independently, and the services coordinate and cooperate in providing users with ultimate value.

Microservices decompose the original business functions into multiple small services. Each service runs in its process. A lightweight communication mechanism is used between services to communicate (usually HTTP-based REST API). Each service is built around a specific business and can be independently deployed to a production environment, a production-like environment, etc. Microservice design principles have two points: First, each service is independent, and a unified and centralized service management mechanism should be avoided as much as possible. For specific services, appropriate languages and tools should be selected according to the business context to build them; The second is to ensure high availability and scalability of services.

The microservice architecture model has become a popular architecture model for application cloudification. Its core is to divide complex applications into small-grained, lightweight autonomous services and develop service development and service governance around microservices.

2. The characteristics of microservices

In practice, the microservices in the microservice architecture pattern have the following main characteristics.

(1) Small

The microservice architecture separates complex business logic into a set of small, specific, low-coupling, and highly autonomous services by analyzing and modeling specific business areas, each of which is a small application. The sparrow is small, but it has all five internal organs. Although each microservice is small, the service itself is still a complete application, which is different from the components, plug-ins, and shared libraries we usually say. As for how small microservices should be, there are no strict standards, and they are usually divided based on business logic.

(2) Independence

Independence refers to the independence of microservices. The independence here is mainly for the delivery process of a microservice application: the independence of development, testing, and deployment upgrades. In the microservice architecture, each service is an independent business unit. This business unit is an independent business process in terms of deployment form. Changes to a microservice will not affect other services. There is an independent code base for each microservice, and the code modification of the microservice will not affect other microservices. In addition, for each microservice, there is an independent test and verification mechanism, and there is no need to carry out a large-scale regression test for worrying about damaging the complete function (the existing research and development model of large integration and complete coverage testing is expensive, but the test results. But it is not reassuring).

(3) Light

Microservices emphasize service autonomy, so the interaction between services must be carried out in message communication. From the perspective of efficiency, a lightweight communication mechanism should be selected. In the practice of application implementation, the REST API method is widely adopted. The advantage of this communication mechanism is that it is language-independent and platform-independent, and it is effortless to develop communication protocols to ensure the forward compatibility of the interface.

In evolving from the traditional application architecture to the microservice architecture, the industry has partially retained the RPC communication mechanism in practice to ensure the forward compatibility of the interface. The purpose is to support the independence of services and the loosely coupled state of services.

(4) Looseness

Looseness refers to loose coupling between microservices. Each microservice can be deployed independently, and there is no dependency on the order of deployment. The interfaces of microservices are forward compatible, and the launch of individual microservices will not be related to other services and can be independently released and upgraded in grayscale. The grayscale release mentioned here refers to a release method that can smoothly transition between black and white. A/B test can be performed on it. That is, some users continue to use product feature A, and another part of users start to use product feature B. If users have no objections to B, then gradually expand the scope and migrate all users to B. Gray release to ensure the overall system's stability.

One more thing to note when implementing loose coupling between microservices is that a microservice should only accomplish one thing. The independence of business logic is the key to decoupling between microservices.

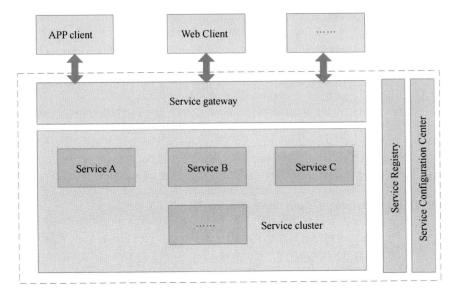

Fig. 8.6 Typical microservice architecture

3. The typical architectures of microservices

After splitting a sizeable single application and service into several or even dozens of microservices, to facilitate the search and configuration of microservices and the communication between services, it is usually necessary to configure a unified service registry and service configuration center. In addition, after splitting into microservices, a large number of services and a large number of interfaces will appear, making the entire call relationship chaotic. In order to solve this problem, the invocation of microservices is generally unified through the gateway. Usually, a layer of the gateway is added between the caller and the callee, and permissions are checked each time it is called. In addition, the gateway can also be used as a platform for providing service interface documents. Figure 8.6 shows a typical microservice architecture.

4. The advantages of microservices

The first advantage of microservice applications is that they often use computing resources more efficiently than traditional applications. This is because they deal with functional bottlenecks by extending components. In this way, developers only need to deploy computing resources for additional components instead of deploying a new iteration of a complete application. The result is that there are more resources available for other tasks.

The second advantage of microservice applications is that they are faster and easier to update. When developers make changes to a traditional integrated application, they must do detailed Quality Assurance (QA) testing to ensure that the changes will not affect other features or functions. However, with microservices, developers can update individual components of the application without affecting other parts. Testing microservice applications is still necessary, but it is easier to identify and isolate problems, thereby speeding up development and supporting DevOps (operations and maintenance) and continuous application development.

The third advantage of microservice applications is that the microservice architecture helps emerging cloud services, such as event-driven computing. Functions like AWS Lambda (AWS Lambda are Amazon's AWS serverless computing service, a fine-grained method for deploying code, managing services, and monitoring the running status of lightweight services) allows developers to write this type of code. It stays in the dormant state when idle, until the application event is triggered. Computing resources are only needed for event processing, and companies only need to pay for each event instead of a fixed number of computing instances.

8.3.3 Serverless Computing

1. The concept of serverless computing
   Suppose the microservice architecture is based on small functional modules that focus on a single responsibility and function, using modular methods to assemble complex large-scale applications. In that case, serverless architecture can provide a more "code fragmentation" application architecture Mode, that is, Functions as a Service (FaaS). The function as a service here is a smaller service entity than microservices.

   Serverless computing is a new way of hosting applications on an infrastructure that does not require end-user management. It is the next stage of IaaS evolution. It separates the developers' underlying infrastructure and virtualizes the runtime (a type of virtual machine, generally refers to the process-level virtual machine) and operation management. This is commonly referred to as FaaS. Serverless architecture allows users (generally developers) to perform given tasks without worrying about servers, virtual machines, or underlying computing resources. At present, serverless and FaaS have also become new hot trends in cloud computing.

   Like many new concepts, the concept of serverless currently does not have a universally accepted definition. Amazon gave this definition: "Serverless architecture is an Internet-based system in which application development does not use conventional service processes. Instead, they only rely on a combination of third-party services (such as AWS Lambda services), client-side logic, and service managed remote procedure calls."

2. Serverless computing architecture
   Serverless computing is a cloud service whose architecture tries to help users get rid of the setup and management of server equipment required to run back-end applications. When users use this service, the hosting service provider will

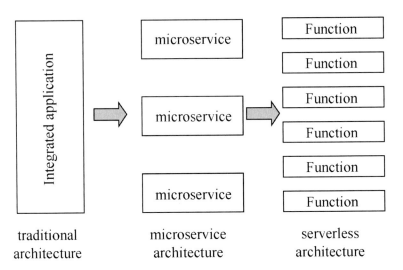

Fig. 8.7 Comparison of traditional architecture, microservice architecture, and serverless architecture

allocate sufficient resources to users in real time, instead of letting users pay in advance for dedicated servers or capacity. Serverless computing is not no-server computing (it means that you do not need to manage the server). However, the hosting service provider is responsible for maintaining the back-end infrastructure and provides developers with the required functions in a service manner, such as databases, messages, and authentication. In a word, this architecture allows users to focus only on the operation of the code without the need to manage any infrastructure. The program code is deployed on platforms such as AWS Lambda to trigger function calls through event-driven methods. When a predefined event that triggers the code occurs, the serverless platform executes a function call to complete the task. Obviously, this is an architecture technique ultimately aimed at developers. Its technical characteristics include event-driven invocation methods, as well as certain limited program operation methods. For example, the running time of AWS Lambda functions is 3s to 5min by default.

Serverless computing can be seen as a new abstraction layer built on the cloud infrastructure, using only the exact computing resources required to complete the task to execute the code (i.e., the function) written by the developer, neither more nor less. Every time the function is executed, the client pays some money. So some people think that the name FaaS is appropriate. It has different abstraction layers from an infrastructure perspective, and developers can interact with these abstraction layers. By stripping management of the workload, you only need to execute the code without worrying about the server infrastructure or management.

Figure 8.7 shows the comparison of traditional architecture, microserver architecture, and no-service architecture.

3. Advantages of Serverless Computing

Using serverless computing technology has the following advantages.

(1) Agility

Since developers do not need to deploy, manage, or expand the server when using the server, the operational overhead is significantly reduced. Serverless and microservice architecture are highly compatible, which also brings significant agility.

(2) Scalability

Serverless upgrades and adding computing resources no longer depend on the DevOps team. Serverless applications can automatically scale quickly and seamlessly to accommodate peak traffic; conversely, these applications will automatically scale down when the number of concurrent users decreases.

(3) Pay-per-use billing model

When using a serverless platform, you only need to pay for the computing resources you need. The serverless architecture introduces an accurate pay-per-use billing model. That is, users pay only when they perform a specific function. The serverless billing model makes it ideal for microservers with smaller load requirements and applications with high fluctuating traffic patterns. Unlike the traditional environment, there is no need to pay for virtual machines or containers often idle.

(4) Security

The serverless architecture provides security. Since users no longer need to manage servers, there are far fewer threats like Distributed Denial of Service (DDoS) attacks, and the automatic expansion function provided by the serverless architecture helps reduce the risk of such attacks.

Although the emergence of serverless architecture is not long, it has been widely used, such as back-end mobile applications and Internet of Things applications. The serverless architecture starts from a highly flexible usage model and event-driven features, which can help users reduce deployment, improve scalability, and reduce the maintenance burden of the infrastructure hidden behind the code.

8.4 Exercise

(1) Multiple Choices

1. IoT is an abbreviation for ().

    A. Internet
    B. Internet of Things
    C. Internet of Vehicles
    D. Enterprise Intranet

2. () Does not belong to the core technology of the Internet of Things.

   A. Sensor
   B. RFID
   C. Grid computing
   D. Cloud computing E. IPv6

3. The wrong statement about big data is ().

   A. Big data processing technology is a brand-new technology just born.
   B. Big data cannot be captured, managed, and processed with conventional software tools within a certain time frame.
   C. Data diversity is a distinctive feature of big data.
   D. Big data can be divided into three categories: structured data, unstructured data, and semi-structured data.
   E. Big data and cloud computing are like the pros and cons of a coin, inseparable.

4. () Is not the main research field of artificial intelligence.

   A. Intelligent robot
   B. Machine learning
   C. Expert system
   D. Parallel computing
   E. Computer vision

5. () Is not the main driving force behind the breakthrough development of deep learning technology.

   A. The emergence of GPU
   B. The development of big data technology
   C. 5G applications
   D. The development of cloud computing technology

6. The main promotion effect of the application of 5G to the further popularization of cloud computing is reflected in ().

   A. 5G can provide cloud computing with anytime, anywhere, high-bandwidth, low-latency, reliable performance, and cheap access services.
   B. 5G can increase the computing speed of cloud computing.
   C. 5G can bring rich application scenarios to cloud computing.
   D. 5G makes cloud computing services cheaper.

7. The wrong statement about the main difference between fog computing and cloud computing is ().

   A. Data and data processing in fog computing are concentrated in devices at the edge of the network, not in the cloud.
   B. The data in fog computing is concentrated on a central server, but it does not use cloud storage like cloud computing.

C. Fog computing performs a large number of storage operations at network edge devices, while cloud computing places storage in large-scale data centers.

D. Fog computing performs a large number of communication operations at network edge devices, while cloud computing is routed to centralized nodes through the backbone network for operations.

8. () Is not the advantage of fog computing.

A. Low cost
B. Efficient
C. Sensitive
D. Low-latency

9. () Is not a feature of microservices.

A. Little
B. Independence
C. Cheap
D. Loose (loosely coupled)

10. () Not the advantage of serverless computing.

A. Agility
B. Scalability
C. Pay-per-use
D. Strong processing power

(2) Answer the Questions

1. Talk about your views on the development trend of cloud computing.
2. Briefly describe the relationship between the Internet of Things, big data, and cloud computing.
3. Briefly describe the relationship between artificial intelligence and cloud computing.
4. Briefly describe the impact of 5G technology on the development of cloud computing.
5. What is the difference between fog computing and cloud computing? What are its advantages?
6. What are the main characteristics of microservices?
7. Briefly describe the concepts and advantages of serverless computing.

Bibliography

1. Yu F.Network functions virtualization based fault processing method and apparatus: U.S. Patent 10, 608, 871[P].2020-3-31.

2. Potdar A M, Narayan D G, Kengond S, et al. Performance Evaluation of Docker Container and Virtual Machine [J]. Procedia Computer Science, 2020, 171:1419-1428.
3. Hu H, Wen Y, Chua T S, et al. Toward scalable systems for big data analytics: A technology tutorial [J]. IEEE access, 2014, 2:652-687.
4. Zaharia M, Xin R S, Wendell P, et al. Apache spark: a unified engine for big data processing [J]. Communications of the ACM, 2016, 59(11), 56-65.
5. Erl T, Puttini R, Mahmood Z. Cloud computing: concepts, technology & architecture [M]. London: Pearson Education, 2013.
6. Arpaci-Dusseau R H, Arpaci-Dusseau AC. Operating systems: Three easy pieces [M]. Madison: Arpaci-Dusseau Books, 2018.
7. Valadarsky A, Shahaf G, Dinitz M, et al. Xpander: Towards optimal-performance datacenters [C]. Proceedings of the 12th International on Conference on emerging Networking EXperiments and Technologies. 2016:205-219.
8. Silva Y N, Almeida I, Queiroz M. SQL: From traditional databases to big data [C]. Proceedings of the 47th ACM Technical Symposium on Computing Science Education. 2016:413–418.
9. Zhang Y, Guo K, Ren J, et al. Transparent computing: A promising network computing paradigm [J]. Computing in Science & Engineering, 2017, 19(1):7-20.
10. Guo D, Wang W, Zhang J, et al. Cloudware: an emerging software paradigm for cloud computing [C]. Proceedings of the 8th Asia-Pacific Symposium on Internetware.2016:1–10.
11. Huai Y, Chauhan A, Gates A, et al. Major technical advancements in apache hive [C]. Proceedings of the 2014 ACM SIGMOD international conference on Management of data.2014:1235-z1246.
12. Jain R, Paul S. Network virtualization and software defined networking for cloud computing: a survey [J]. IEEE Communications Magazine, 2013, 51(11):24-31.
13. Buyya R, Vecchiola C, Selvi S T. Mastering cloud computing: foundations and applications programming [M]. Oxford: Newnes, 2013.
14. Barroso L A, Clidaras J, Hölzle U. The datacenter as a computer: An introduction to the design of warehouse-scale machines [J]. Synthesis Lectures on Computer Architecture, 2013, 8(3): 1-154.
15. Nunes B A A, Mendonca M, Nguyen X N, et al. A survey of software-defined networking: Past, present, and future of programmable networks [J]. IEEE Communications surveys & tutorials, 2014, 16(3):1617-1634.
16. Coulouris G F, Dollimore J, Kindberg T. Distributed systems: concepts and design [M]. London: Pearson Education, 2005.
17. Guo C, Wu H, Tan K, et al. Dcell: a scalable and fault-tolerant network structure for data centers [C]. Proceedings of the ACM SIGCOMM 2008 conference on Data communication.2008: 75-86.
18. McKeown N, Anderson T, Balakrishnan H, et al. OpenFlow: enabling innovation in campus networks [J]. ACM SIGCOMM Computer Communication Review, 2008, 38(2):69-74.
19. Karpoff W, Lake B. Storage virtualization system and methods: U.S. Patent 7, 577, 817 [P].2009-8-18.
20. Chisnall D. The definitive guide to the xen hypervisor [M]. London: Pearson Education, 2008.
21. Russel R.lguest: Implementing the little Linux hypervisor [J]. OLS, 2007, 7(1):173-178.
22. Cherkasova L, Gardner R. Measuring CPU Overhead for I/O Processing in the Xen Virtual Machine Monitor [C]. USENIX Annual Technical Conference, General Track. 2005, 50.
23. Amsden Z, Arai D, Hecht D, et al. VMI: An interface for paravirtualization [C]. Proc. of the Linux Symposium. 2006:363-378.
24. Buyya R, Venugopal S. A gentle introduction to grid computing and technologies [J]. Database, 2005, 2: R3.
25. Barham P, Dragovic B, Fraser K, et al. Xen and the art of virtualization [J]. ACM SIGOPS Operating Systems Review, 2003, 37(5):164-177.
26. Du Yahong, Zhang Dong, Huang Xin. Research on virtualization performance loss [J]. Railway Computer Application, 2020, 29 (05): 67-71.

27. Tian Xiujuan. Discussion on storage virtualization technology [J]. Information and Computer (Theoretical Edition), 2020, 32 (02): 15-17.
28. Hideto S. DevOps actual combat based on Kubernetes [M]. Beijing: Publishing House of Electronics Industry, 2019.
29. Wang Wei. Principles and Practice of Cloud Computing [M]. Beijing: People's Posts and Telecommunications Press, 2018.
30. Wang Wei, Liu Wei, Cui Haibo. A new generation of big data engineering training platform based on cloudware services [J]. Computer Education, 2018 (04): 162-166.
31. Li Wei, Guo Xue. Open source governance white paper [M]. Beijing: China Academy of Information and Communications Technology, 2018.
32. Shi Weisong. Edge Computing [M]. Beijing: Science Press, 2018.
33. Yang Baohua. Introduction to Docker technology and actual combat [M]. Beijing: Mechanical Industry Press, 2018.
34. CloudMan. Play Kubernetes in 5 minutes a day [M]. Beijing: Tsinghua University Press, 2018.
35. CloudMan. Play with Docker container technology in 5 minutes a day [M]. Beijing: Tsinghua University Press, 2017.
36. Hao Weidong. Cloud computing and its practical tutorial [M]. Xi'an: Xidian University Press, 2017.
37. Leader-us. Architecture decryption: from distributed to microservices. Beijing: Publishing House of Electronics Industry, 2017.
38. Chen Xianlu. Do your own handwriting Docker [M]. Beijing: Publishing House of Electronics Industry, 2017.
39. Rady B. Serverless architecture: serverless single page application development [M]. Zheng Meizan, Jian Chuanting, translated. Beijing: Publishing House of Electronics Industry, 2017.
40. Gong Zheng. The definitive guide to Kubernetes [M]. Beijing: Publishing House of Electronics Industry, 2017.
41. Bumgardner V K. OpenStack combat [M]. Beijing: People's Posts and Telecommunications Press, 2017.
42. Chiang M. Fog computing: technology, architecture and application [M]. Yan Shi, Peng Mugen, translated. Beijing: Mechanical Industry Press, 2017.
43. Liu Weiwei. Common technologies and case analysis of distributed systems [M]. Beijing: Publishing House of Electronics Industry, 2017.
44. Qi Zhengwei, Chen Rong, Zhang Xiantao. New hardware virtualization [J]. Communications of China Computer Society, 2017, 13(6): 11-17.
45. Wang Wei, Hu Changwu. A cloud operating system oriented to cloud software [J]. Computer Science, 2017, 44(11):33-40.
46. Yan Haifeng. OpenStack combat [M]. Beijing: People's Posts and Telecommunications Press, 2017.
47. Shen Jianguo, Chen Yong. OpenStack cloud computing infrastructure platform technology and application [M]. Beijing: People's Posts and Telecommunications Press, 2017.
48. Erl T, Mahmood Z, Puttini R. Cloud Computing: Concept, Technology and Architecture (Chinese Version) [M]. Gong Yili, He Lian, Hu Chuang, Trans. Beijing: Machinery Industry Press, 2016.
49. Ceph China Community. Ceph distributed storage combat [M]. Beijing: Machinery Industry Press, 2016.
50. Newman S. Microservice design [M]. Beijing: People's Posts and Telecommunications Press, 2016.
51. Wang Peng. Cloud computing and big data technology: concept, application and actual combat [M]. Beijing: People's Posts and Telecommunications Press, 2016.
52. Gu Jiongjiong. Cloud computing architecture technology and practice [M]. Version 2. Beijing: Tsinghua University Press, 2016.
53. SEL Laboratory of Zhejiang University. Docker container and container cloud [M]. Beijing: People's Posts and Telecommunications Press, 2016.

54. Liao Yu. Docker container combat [M]. Beijing: Publishing House of Electronics Industry, 2016.
55. Wu Longhui. Kubernetes combat [M]. Beijing: Publishing House of Electronics Industry, 2016.
56. Ye Yurui, Lei Yingchun, Li Xuanhui, etc. Software-defined storage: principle, practice and ecology [M]. Beijing: Machinery Industry Press, 2016.
57. SEL Laboratory of Zhejiang University. Docker: Containers and Container Cloud [M]. Version 2. Beijing: People's Posts and Telecommunications Press, 2016.
58. Desktop Cloud Working Group of China Open Source Cloud Alliance. China Desktop Cloud Standardization White Paper (V1.0) [R]. Beijing: China Open Source Cloud Alliance, 2016.
59. Cui Yong, Ren Kui, Tang Jun. Data security challenges and research progress in cloud computing [J]. Communications of the Chinese Computer Society, 2016, 5.
60. Lu Yusheng. Distributed real-time processing system: principle, architecture and implementation [M]. Beijing: Machinery Industry Press, 2016.
61. Zhang Zifan. OpenStack deployment practice (2nd edition) [M]. Beijing: People's Posts and Telecommunications Press, 2016.
62. Gregg B. Peak performance: Insight into systems, enterprises and cloud computing [M]. Xu Zhangning, Wu Hansi, Chen Lei, translated. Beijing: Publishing House of Electronics Industry, 2015.
63. Qian Yongchao. OpenStack Operation and Maintenance Guide [M]. Beijing: People's Posts and Telecommunications Press, 2015.
64. Zhang Xiaobin. OpenStack enterprise cloud platform architecture and practice [M]. Beijing: Publishing House of Electronics Industry, 2015.
65. Feng Chaosheng, Qin Zhiguang, Yuan Ding. Cloud data security storage technology [J]. Chinese Journal of Computers, 2015, 38(1): 150-163.
66. Chen Xi. Software Defined Data Center: Technology and Practice [M]. Beijing: Machinery Industry Press, 2015.
67. Nadeau T D, Gray K. Software-defined network SDN and OpenFlow analysis [M]. Bi Jun, Shan Ye, Zhang Shaoyu, et al. Beijing: People's Posts and Telecommunications Press, 2014.
68. Lin Y D, Hwang R H, Baker F. Computer network: an open source design and implementation method [M]. Chen Xiangyang, Wu Yuntao, Xu Ying, translated. Beijing: Mechanical Industry Press, 2014.
69. Hurwitz J, Nugent A, Halper F, et al. Big data written for everyone[M]. Wheat stalks create wisdom, translation. Beijing: People's Posts and Telecommunications Press, 2014.
70. Nadeau T D, Gray K. Software-defined network SDN and OpenFlow analysis [M]. Bi Jun, Shan Ye, Zhang Shaoyu, et al. Beijing: People's Posts and Telecommunications Press, 2014.
71. Jiang Kai. Desktop Virtualization Practical Collection [M]. Beijing: Publishing House of Electronics Industry, 2014.
72. Xu Baomin. Cloud Computing Decryption: Technical Principles and Application Practice [M]. Beijing: Publishing House of Electronics Industry, 2014.
73. Huang Kai. OpenStack cloud computing practice manual [M]. Version 2. Beijing: People's Posts and Telecommunications Press, 2014.
74. Hwang K, Fox G C, Dongarra J J. Cloud Computing and Distributed System: From Parallel Processing to Internet of Things [M]. Translated by Wu Yongwei, Tai Zhongyuan, Li Zhenyu, et al. Beijing: Mechanical Industry Press, 2013.
75. Chen Bolong. Cloud computing and OpenStack[M]. Beijing: Publishing House of Electronics Industry, 2013.
76. Xu Shoudong. Cloud computing technology application and practice [M]. Beijing: China Railway Press, 2013.
77. Chu Ya, Ma Tinghuai, Zhao Licheng. Cloud computing resource scheduling: strategies and algorithms [J]. Computer Science, 2013, 40(11): 8-13.
78. Fu Yingxun, Luo Shengmei, Shu Jiwu. An overview of secure cloud storage systems and key technologies [J]. Computer Research and Development, 2013, 50(1): 136-145.

79. Mei Hong, Guo Yao. Network-oriented operating system: status quo and challenges [J]. Science in China: Information Science, 2013, 43(3): 303-321.
80. Ren Yongjie, Shan Haitao. KVM virtualization technology: actual combat and principle analysis [M]. Beijing: Mechanical Industry Press, 2013.
81. Yang Chuanhui. Large-scale Distributed Storage System: Principle Analysis and Architecture Actual Combat [M]. Beijing: Mechanical Industry Press, 2013.
82. Zou Hengming. The Way of Cloud Computing [M]. Beijing: Tsinghua University Press, 2013.
83. Han Dezhi, Li Nannan, Bi Kun. Analysis of Virtualization Technology in Cloud Environment [J]. Journal of Huazhong University of Science and Technology (Natural Science Edition), 2012, 40 (S1): 262-265.
84. Yi Tao. Research on Cloud Computing Virtualization Security Technology [J]. Information Security and Communication Confidentiality, 2012 (05): 63-65.
85. Yang Zhenghong, Zhou Fawu. Cloud computing and Internet of Things [M]. Beijing: Tsinghua University Press, 2011.
86. Feng Dengguo, Zhang Min. Research on cloud computing security [J]. Journal of Software, 2011, 22(1): 71-83.
87. Virtualization and Cloud Computing Group. The practice of cloud computing: strategic blueprint and technical architecture [M]. Beijing: Publishing House of Electronics Industry, 2011.
88. Zhu Jinzhi. Smart cloud computing: a platform for the Internet of Things [M]. Version 2. Beijing: Publishing House of Electronics Industry, 2011.
89. Liu Peng. Cloud computing [M]. Beijing: Publishing House of Electronics Industry, 2010.
90. Lu Shiwen. Storage network technology and application [M]. Beijing: Tsinghua University Press, 2010.
91. Miller M. Cloud computing [M]. Translated by Jiang Jinlei, Sun Ruizhi, Xiang Yong, et al. Beijing: Machinery Industry Press, 2009.
92. Intel Open Source Technology Center. OpenStack design and implementation [M]. Beijing: Publishing House of Electronics Industry, 2003.
93. konglingbin. Comprehensive understanding of OpenStack: Detailed OpenStack architecture [EB/OL]. [2018-03-27]. https://www.cnblogs.com/klb561/p/8660264.html.
94. Resines. The basic concepts and architecture diagram of OpenStack [EB/OL]. [2018-10-16]. https://blog.csdn.net/genglei1022/article/details/83090500.
95. Tu Lanjing. IT basics: Uncover the mystery of OpenStack [EB/OL]. [2013-03-11]. http://cloud.zol.com.cn/363/3637543.html.
96. OpenStack Inc. OpenStack Docs[EB/OL]. [2020-05-01]. https://docs.openstack.org/ussuri.
97. weixin_30488313.OCI(Open Container Initiative)& OCF(Open Container Format)[EB/OL]. [2017-02-27]. https://blog.csdn.net/weixin_30488313/article/details/95342284.
98. blogzlh.Docker The difference between a container and a virtual machine [EB/OL]. [2018-04-23]. https://blog.csdn.net/blogzlh/article/details/80050094.
99. Docker Inc. Docker Docs[EB/OL]. [2020-05-01]. https://docs.docker.com/get-docker

Index

A

Access link, 172
Application layer, 40, 41, 158, 162, 188, 246, 267, 350
Application server, 41, 174, 202, 216, 219
Application Specific Integrated Circuit (ASIC), 166, 167, 189
Artificial intelligence (AI), 3, 52, 241, 344, 345, 354–357, 360, 368, 369
Asymmetric Digital Subscriber Line (ADSL), 23
Asymmetric encryption, 75, 76, 78, 79, 205, 206
Authentication, 80, 81, 95, 119, 139, 140, 169, 195, 205, 253, 257–260, 263, 288–290, 292, 294, 366

B

Binary translation, 107
Border Gateway Protocol (BGP), 165, 194
Browser/Server (B/S), 19
Business Process as a Service, 47

C

Carrier Sense Multiple Access with Collision Detection (CSMA/CD), 160, 170, 194
Catalog, 42, 260
Certificate authority (CA), 79, 94, 205
Chunk groups, 225–228
Cipher, 75
Client/server (C/S), 11, 12, 15, 17–19, 149, 217, 246–248, 295
Cloud applications, 46, 141, 280

Cloud-based security group, 82–83
Cloud Bursting Architecture, 90
Cloud computing, 1–95, 129, 139, 141, 143, 145–195, 197–249, 251–253, 280, 284, 295, 317, 318, 343–369
Cloud runtime environment, 46
Cluster computing, 18
Command-line interface (CLI), 263, 270, 282, 297
Common Internet File System (CIFS), 64, 128, 220, 237
Communications, 2, 9, 12, 13, 16, 35, 37, 39, 46, 48, 49, 60, 65, 67, 82, 115, 117, 138, 145–151, 153–157, 161, 162, 166, 167, 169, 170, 172–174, 181, 183–185, 193–195, 214, 220, 232, 248, 262, 269, 279, 310–312, 317, 321, 324, 326–329, 347, 349, 351, 357, 358, 360–364, 369
Computing node agent (CAN), 181, 247, 248
Core Plugins, 276, 277

D

Database as a Service, 47
Database server, 40, 217, 241
Data layer, 40, 48
Data storage server, 40, 202, 219
Default gateway, 166, 177
Desktop as a Service (DaaS), 118
Digital data network (DDN), 152
Digital signatures, 78–80, 94
Distributed computing, 9, 12, 16, 18, 19, 34, 38, 45, 168, 243, 355, 361
Distributed systems, 18, 19, 34, 45, 190, 246, 279

Printed in the United States
by Baker & Taylor Publisher Services